kimi ni todoke
From Me to You

Vol. 4

Story & Art by
Karuho Shiina

Volume 4

Contents

Story Thus Far

Sawako Kuronuma has always been a loner. Though not by choice, this optimistic 15-year-old can't seem to make any friends. Stuck with the unfortunate nickname "Sadako" after the haunting movie character, rumors about her summoning spirits have been greatly exaggerated. With her shy personality and scary looks, most of her classmates would barely talk to her, much less look into her eyes for more than three seconds lest they be cursed. Except for Shota Kazehaya. Kazehaya's the most popular boy in class, and his friendly attitude toward Sawako bewildered their classmates. But this unlikely friendship has changed Sawako's life. Drawn out of her shell by Kazehaya, Sawako is no longer an outcast in class. And with her new friends Yano and Yoshida, she's finally leading a more normal teenage life. As the day for the Sports Festival approaches, Kazehaya helps Sawako practice soccer, but the attention she's receiving from him hasn't gone unnoticed. Kurumi, one of the cutest girls in school, has suddenly become her BFF. But Sawako's willingness to do anything for a friend is put to the test when Kurumi wants her help in confessing her love... to Kazehaya!

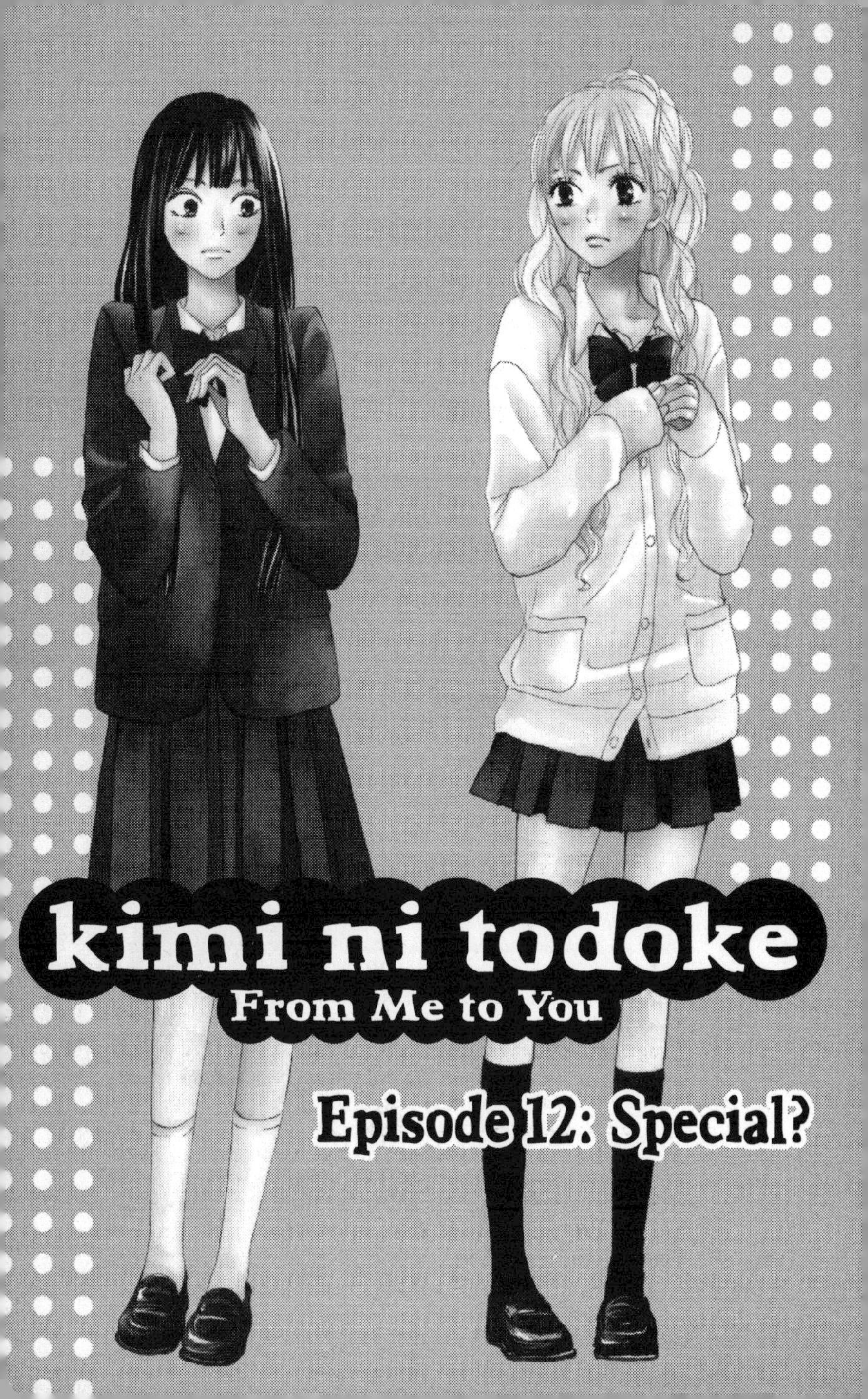
kimi ni todoke
From Me to You
Episode 12: Special?

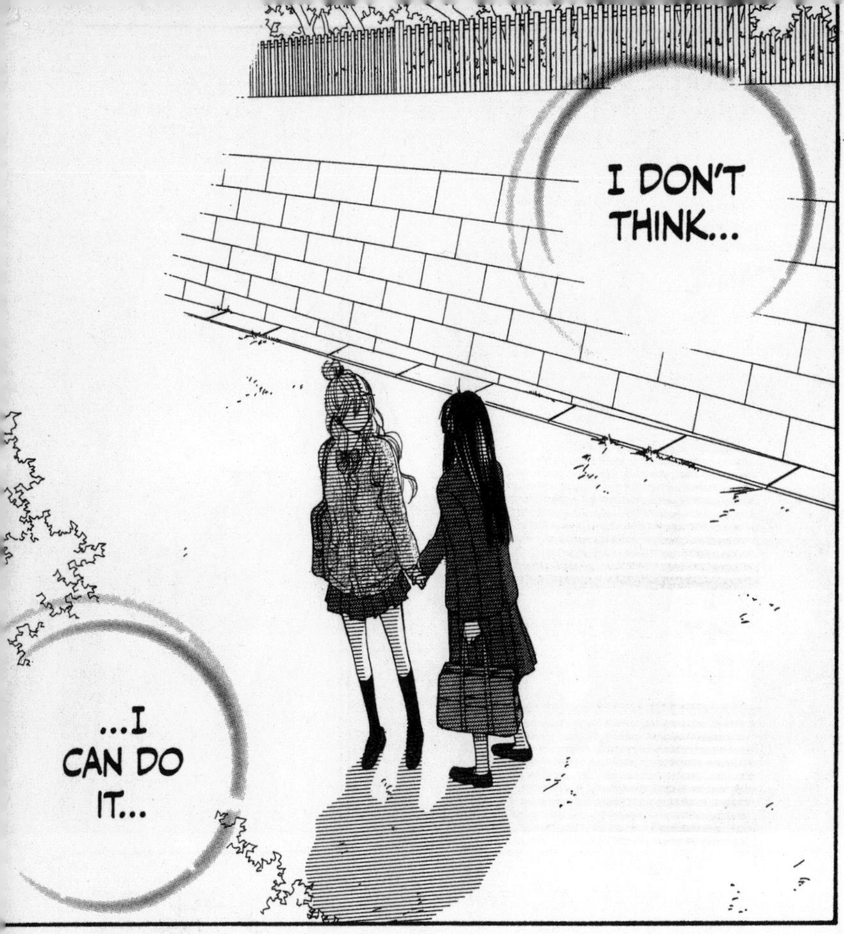
I DON'T THINK...
...I CAN DO IT...

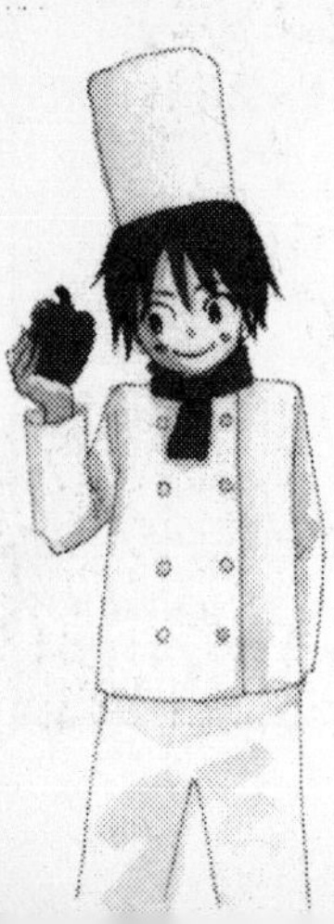

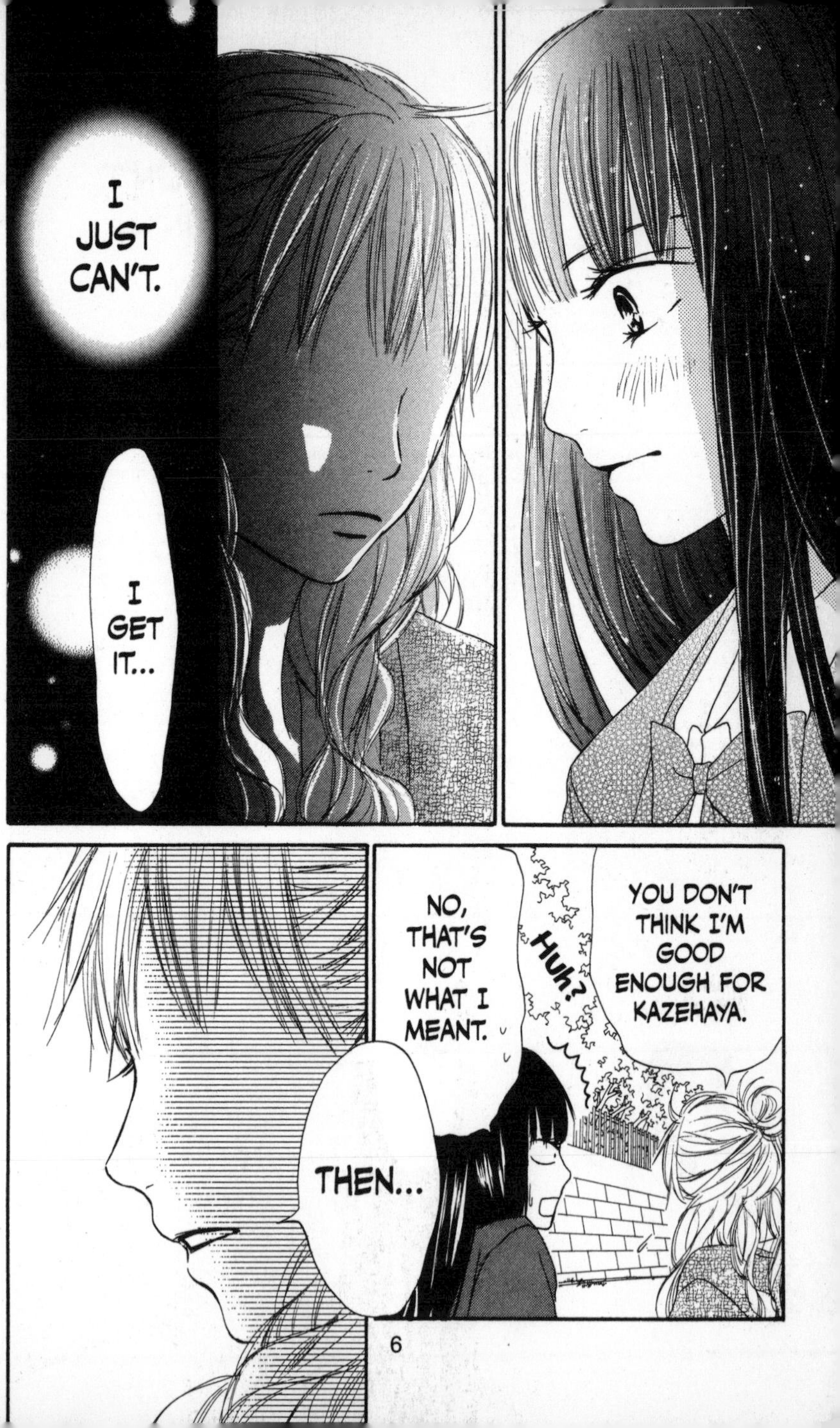
I JUST CAN'T.
I GET IT...
YOU DON'T THINK I'M GOOD ENOUGH FOR KAZEHAYA.
Huh?
NO, THAT'S NOT WHAT I MEANT.
THEN...

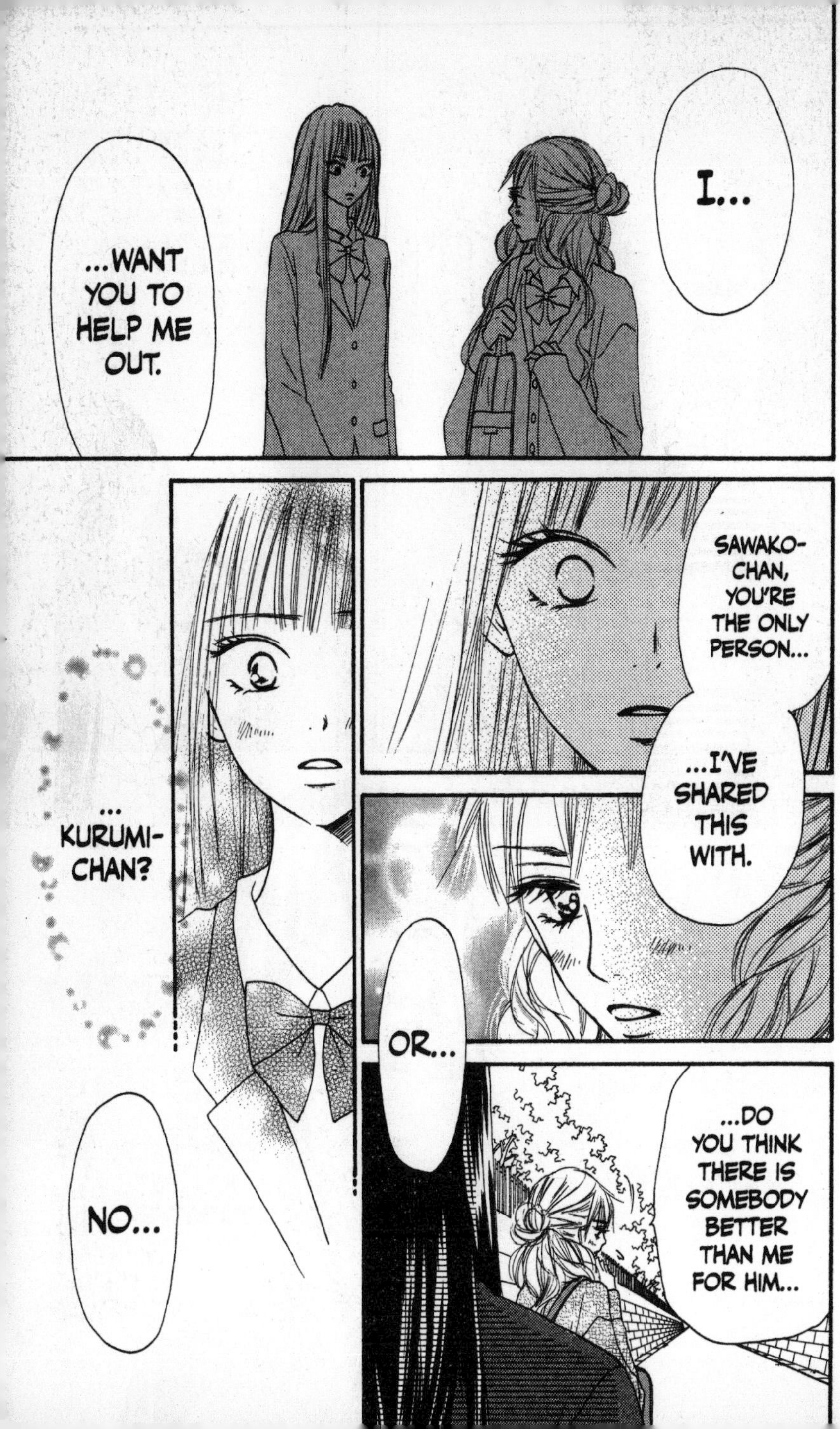
I...
...WANT YOU TO HELP ME OUT.
SAWAKO-CHAN, YOU'RE THE ONLY PERSON...
...I'VE SHARED THIS WITH.
OR...
...DO YOU THINK THERE IS SOMEBODY BETTER THAN ME FOR HIM...
...KURUMI-CHAN?
NO...

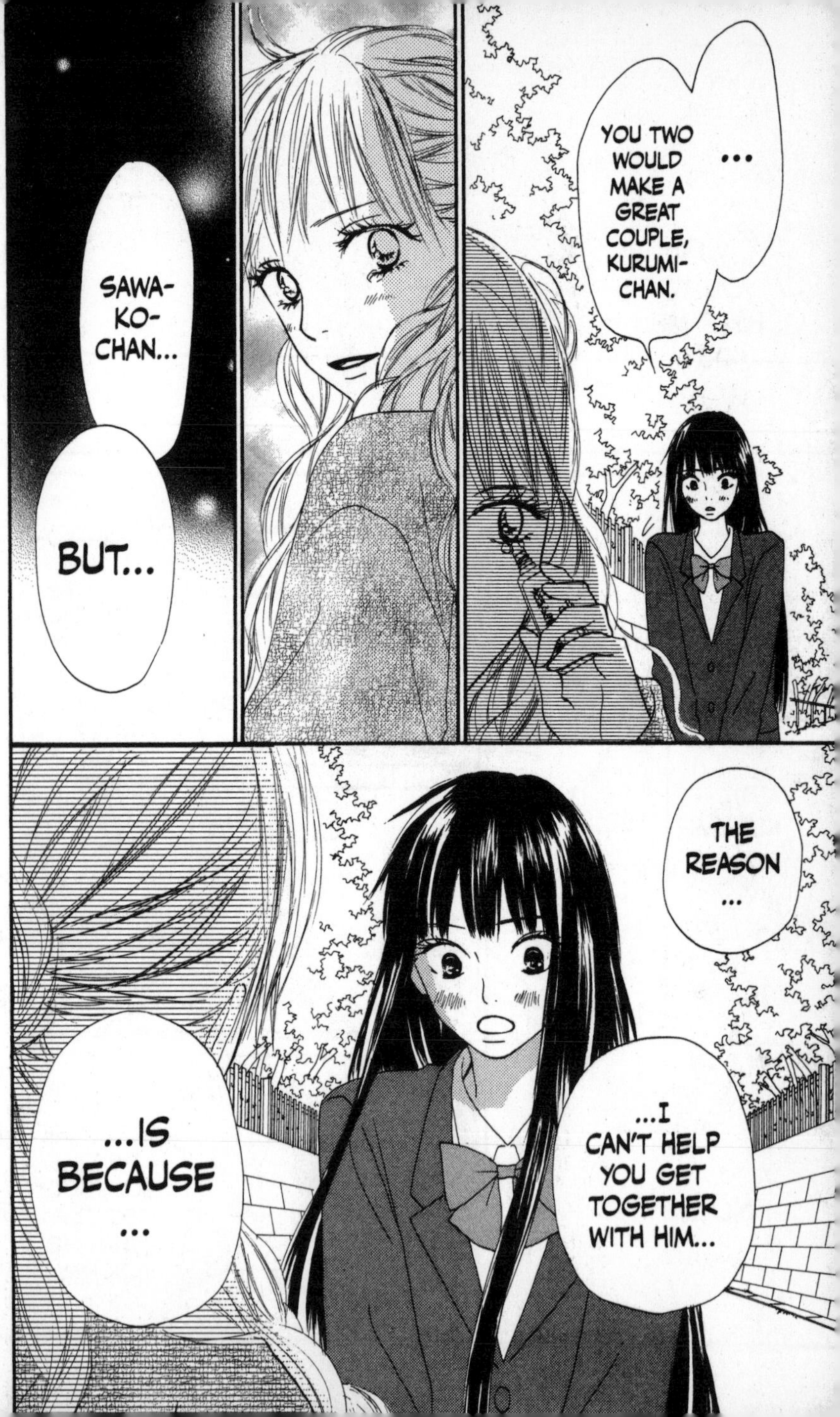
...
YOU TWO WOULD MAKE A GREAT COUPLE, KURUMI-CHAN.
SAWA-KO-CHAN...
BUT...
THE REASON ...
...I CAN'T HELP YOU GET TOGETHER WITH HIM...
...IS BECAUSE ...

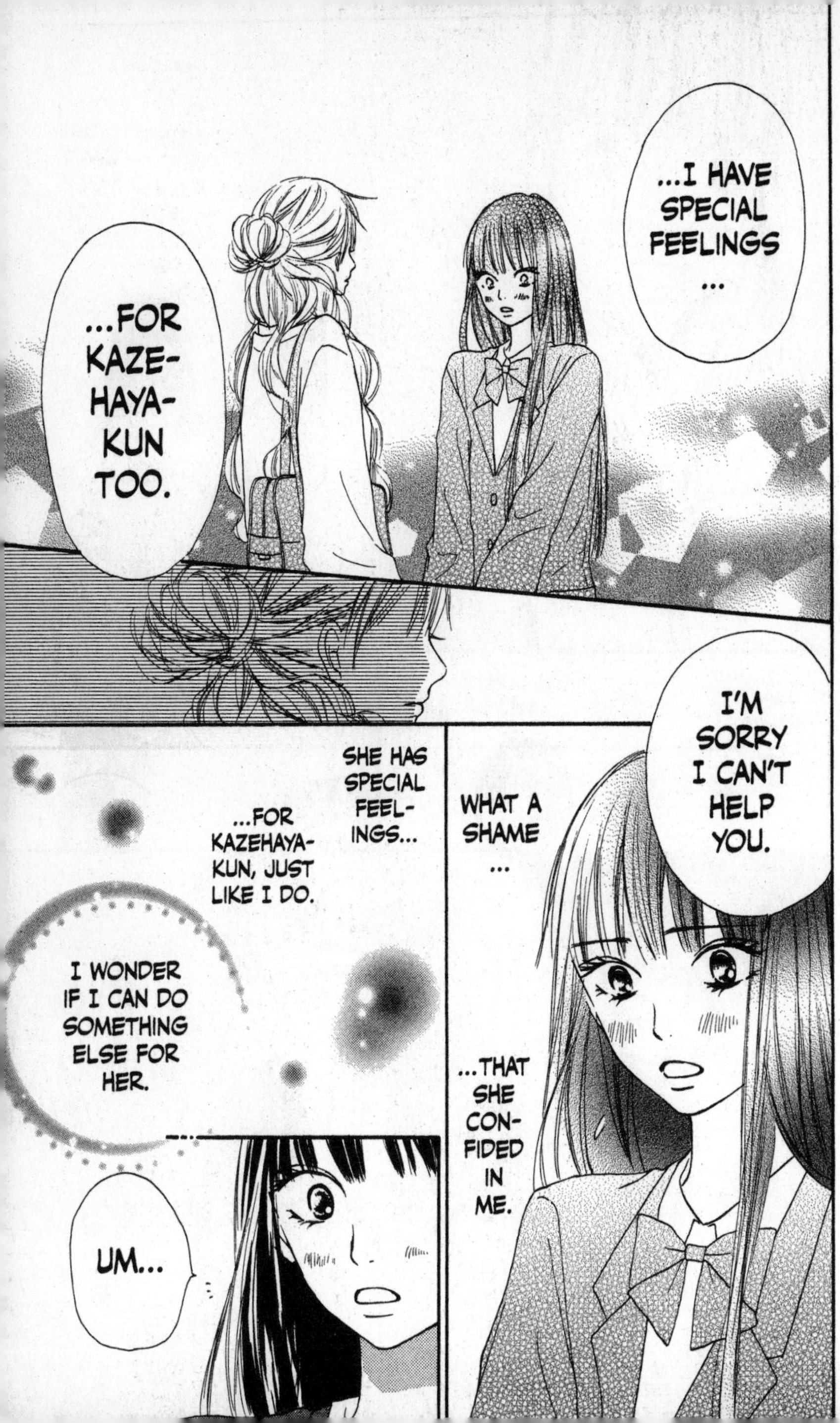
...I HAVE SPECIAL FEELINGS...
...FOR KAZE-HAYA-KUN TOO.
I'M SORRY I CAN'T HELP YOU.
WHAT A SHAME...
...THAT SHE CON-FIDED IN ME.
SHE HAS SPECIAL FEEL-INGS...
...FOR KAZEHAYA-KUN, JUST LIKE I DO.
I WONDER IF I CAN DO SOMETHING ELSE FOR HER.
UM...

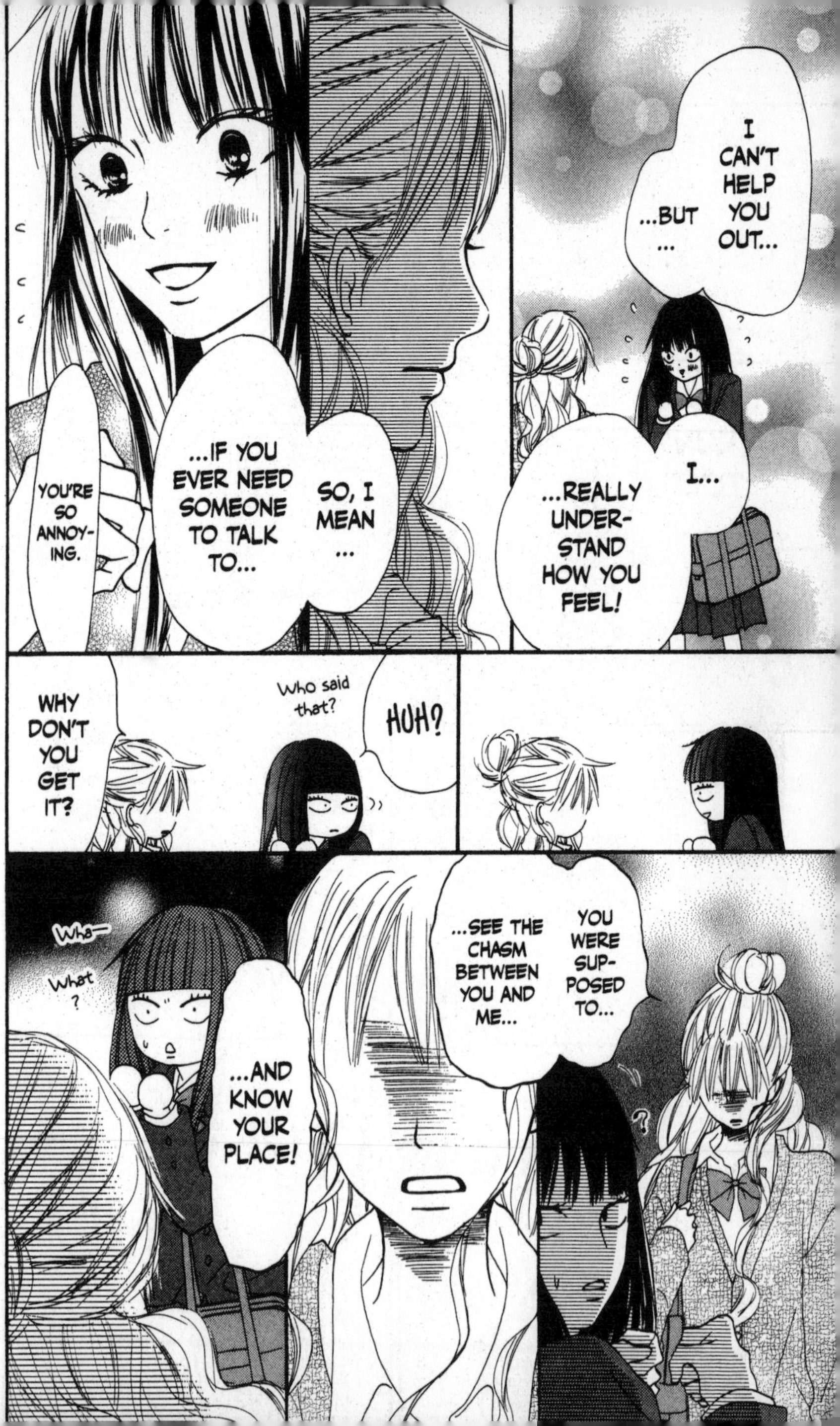
I CAN'T HELP YOU OUT...
...BUT ...
I...
...REALLY UNDERSTAND HOW YOU FEEL!
SO, I MEAN ...
...IF YOU EVER NEED SOMEONE TO TALK TO...
YOU'RE SO ANNOYING.
HUH?
Who said that?
WHY DON'T YOU GET IT?
YOU WERE SUPPOSED TO...
...SEE THE CHASM BETWEEN YOU AND ME...
...AND KNOW YOUR PLACE!
Wha—
What?

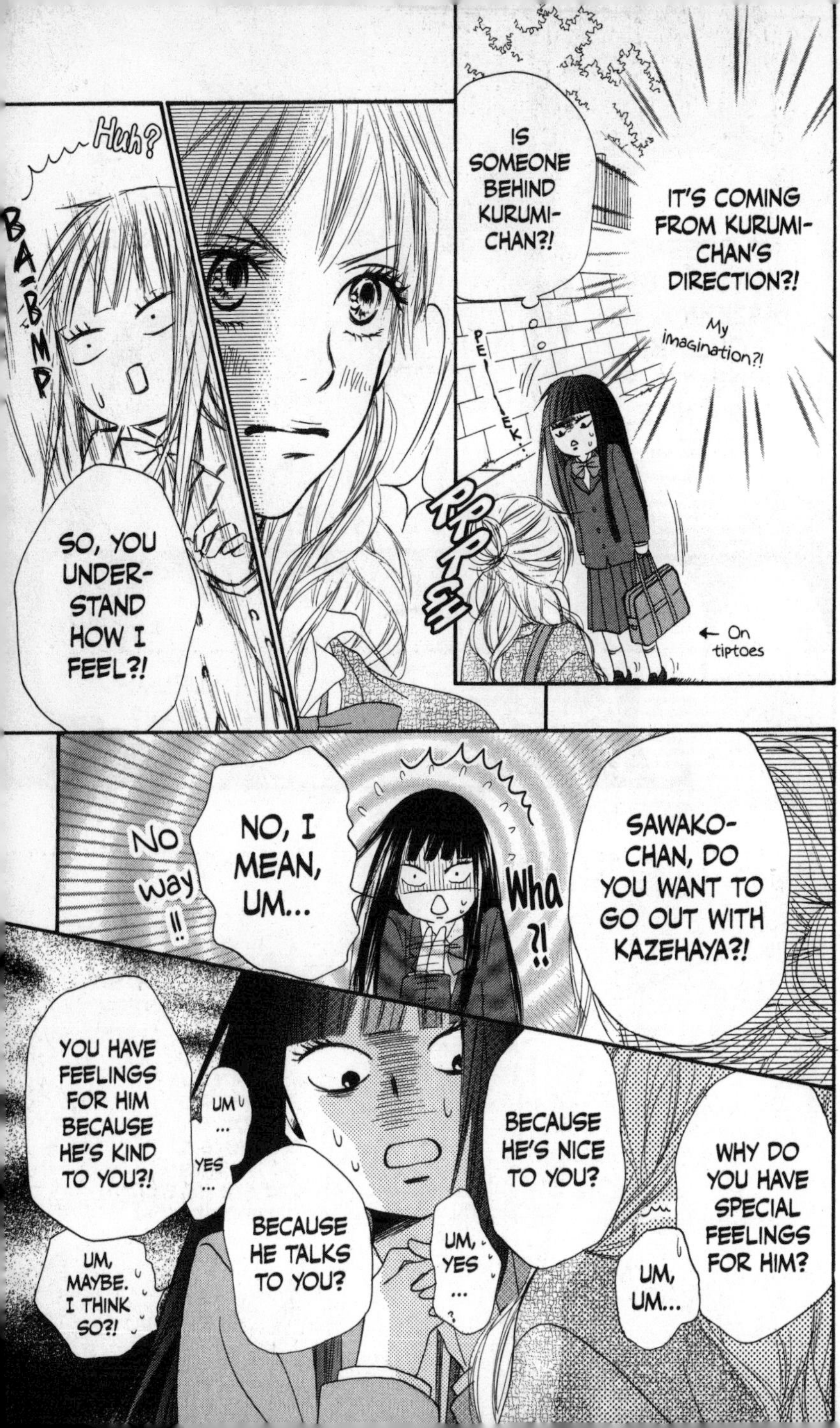
IT'S COMING FROM KURUMI-CHAN'S DIRECTION?!
IS SOMEONE BEHIND KURUMI-CHAN?!
My imagination?!
PE...EK...
← On tiptoes
Huh?
BA-BMP
SO, YOU UNDERSTAND HOW I FEEL?!
SAWAKO-CHAN, DO YOU WANT TO GO OUT WITH KAZEHAYA?!
Wha?!!
NO, I MEAN, UM...
No way!!
WHY DO YOU HAVE SPECIAL FEELINGS FOR HIM?
UM, UM...
BECAUSE HE'S NICE TO YOU?
UM, YES...?
BECAUSE HE TALKS TO YOU?
YOU HAVE FEELINGS FOR HIM BECAUSE HE'S KIND TO YOU?!
UM... YES...
UM, MAYBE. I THINK SO?!

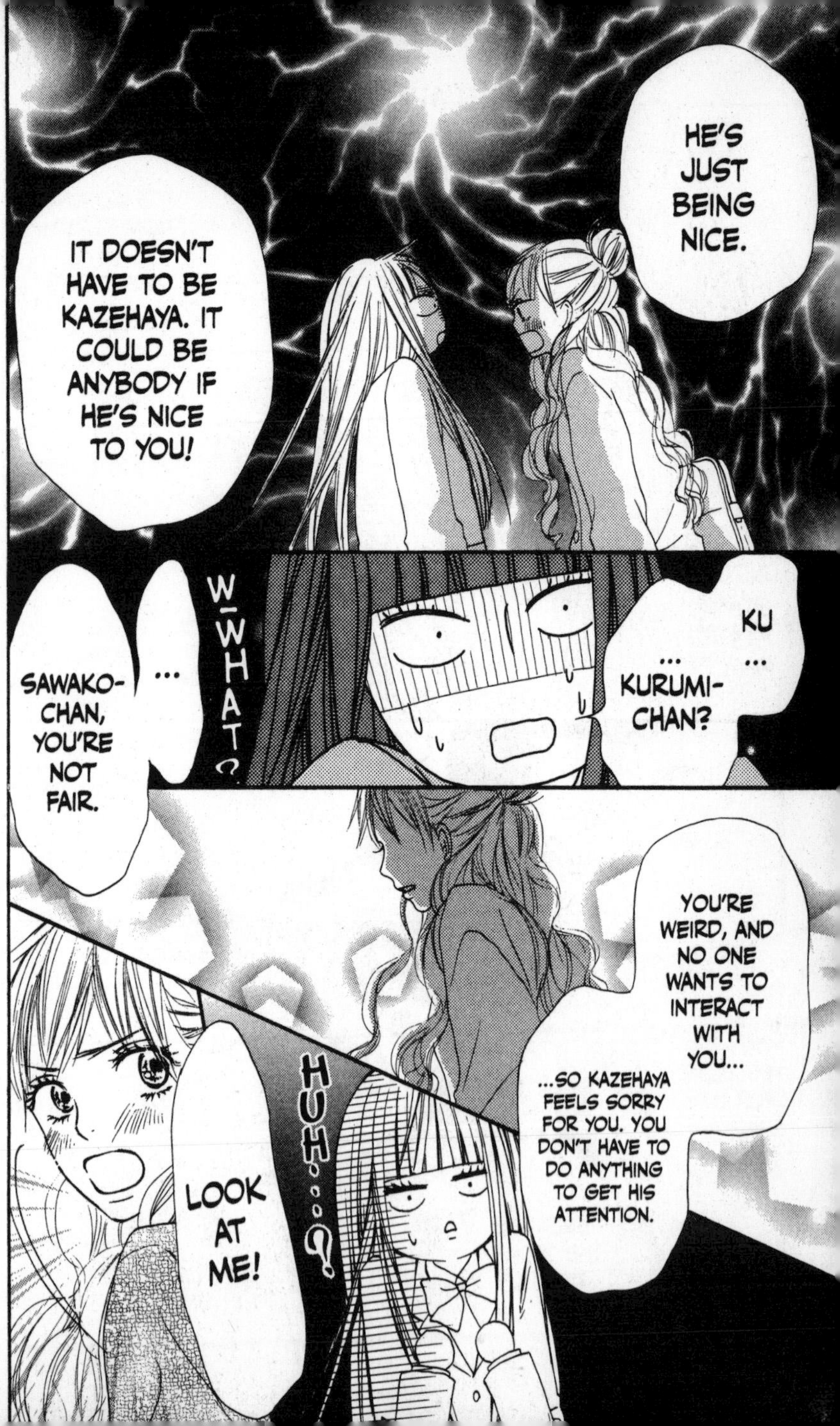
HE'S JUST BEING NICE.
IT DOESN'T HAVE TO BE KAZEHAYA. IT COULD BE ANYBODY IF HE'S NICE TO YOU!
KU... KURUMI-CHAN?
W-WHAT?
...
SAWAKO-CHAN, YOU'RE NOT FAIR.
YOU'RE WEIRD, AND NO ONE WANTS TO INTERACT WITH YOU...
...SO KAZEHAYA FEELS SORRY FOR YOU. YOU DON'T HAVE TO DO ANYTHING TO GET HIS ATTENTION.
HUH...?
LOOK AT ME!

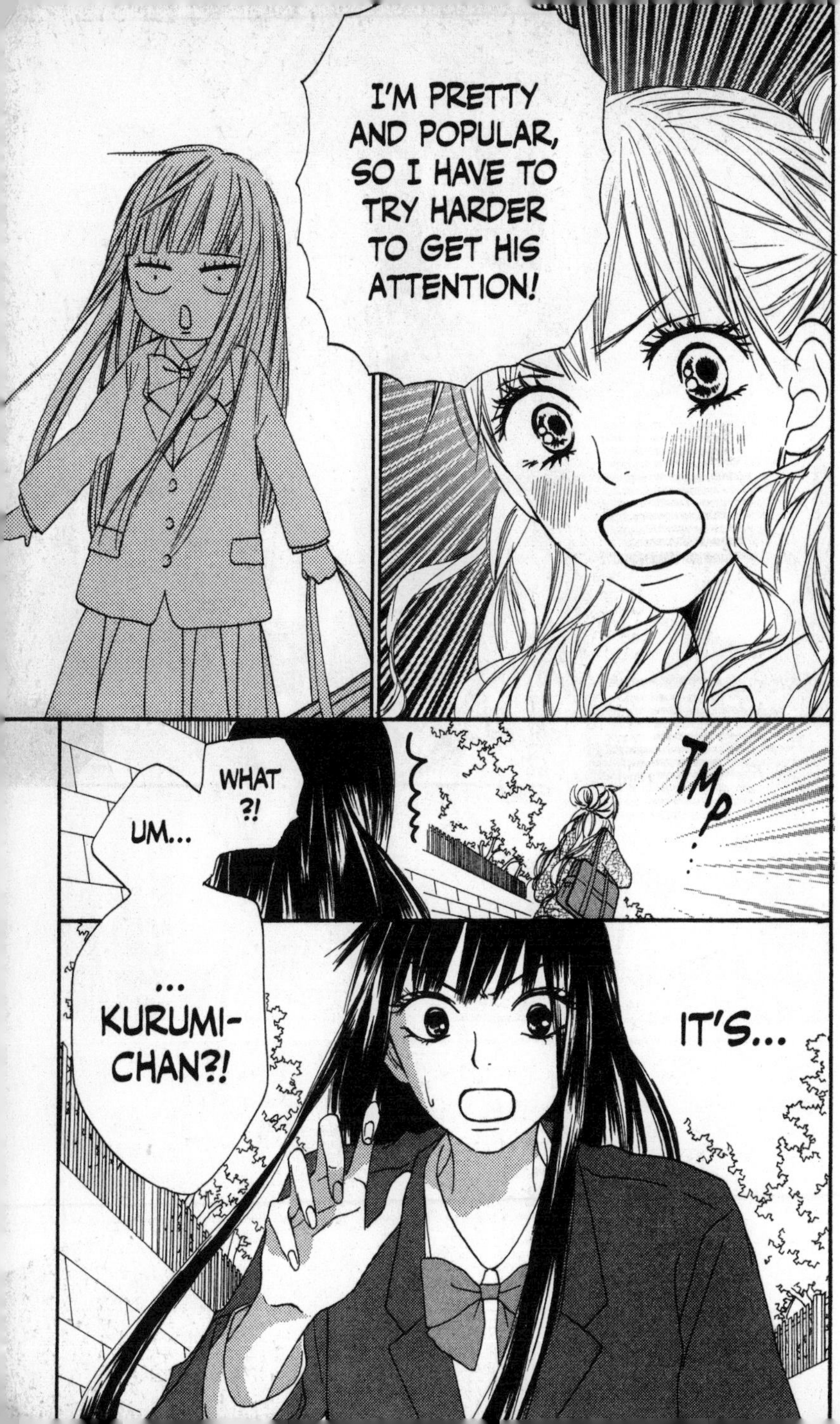
I'M PRETTY AND POPULAR, SO I HAVE TO TRY HARDER TO GET HIS ATTENTION!
TMP...
WHAT ?!
UM...
IT'S...
... KURUMI-CHAN?!

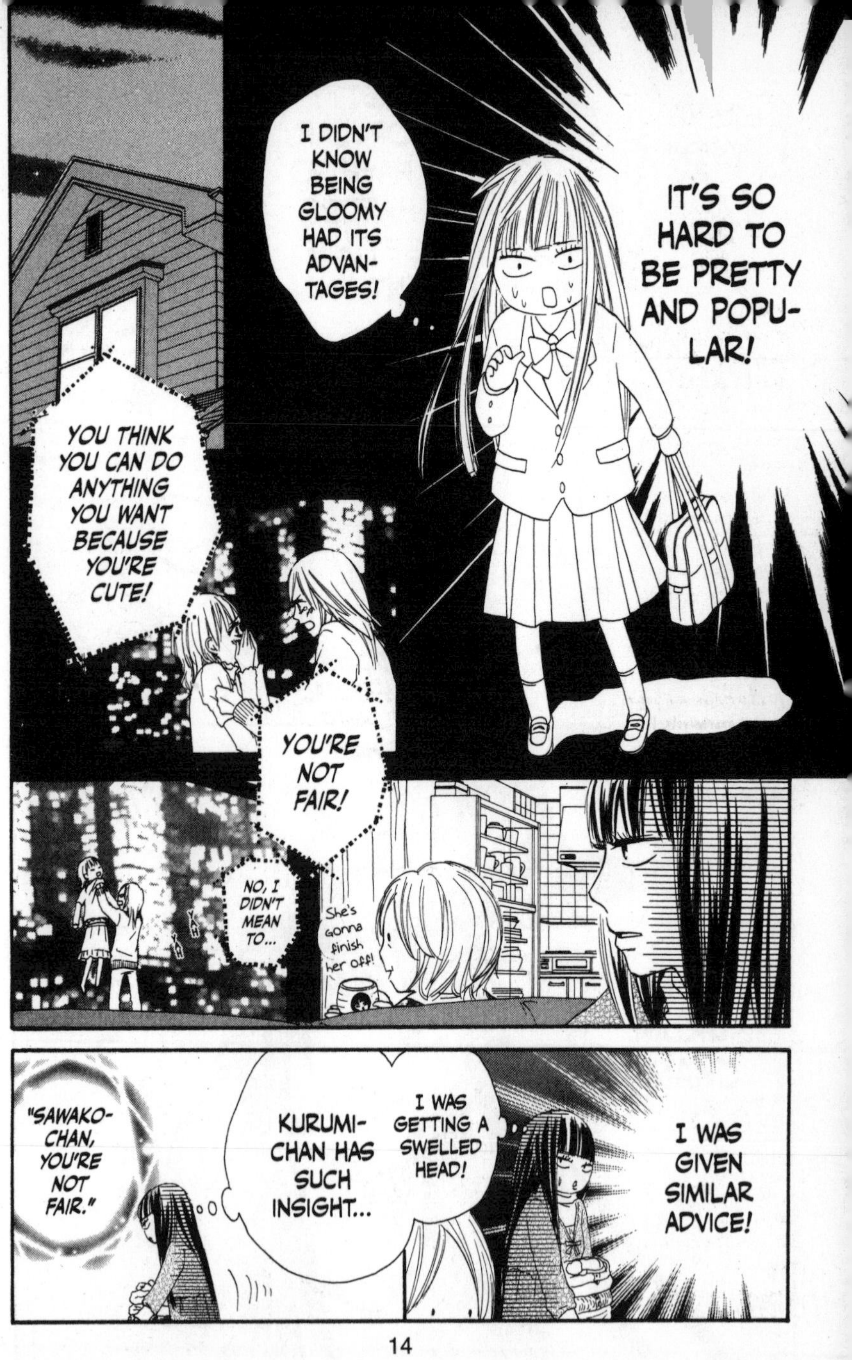
IT'S SO HARD TO BE PRETTY AND POPULAR!
I DIDN'T KNOW BEING GLOOMY HAD ITS ADVANTAGES!
YOU THINK YOU CAN DO ANYTHING YOU WANT BECAUSE YOU'RE CUTE!
YOU'RE NOT FAIR!
NO, I DIDN'T MEAN TO...
She's gonna finish her off!
I WAS GIVEN SIMILAR ADVICE!
I WAS GETTING A SWELLED HEAD!
KURUMI-CHAN HAS SUCH INSIGHT...
"SAWAKO-CHAN, YOU'RE NOT FAIR."

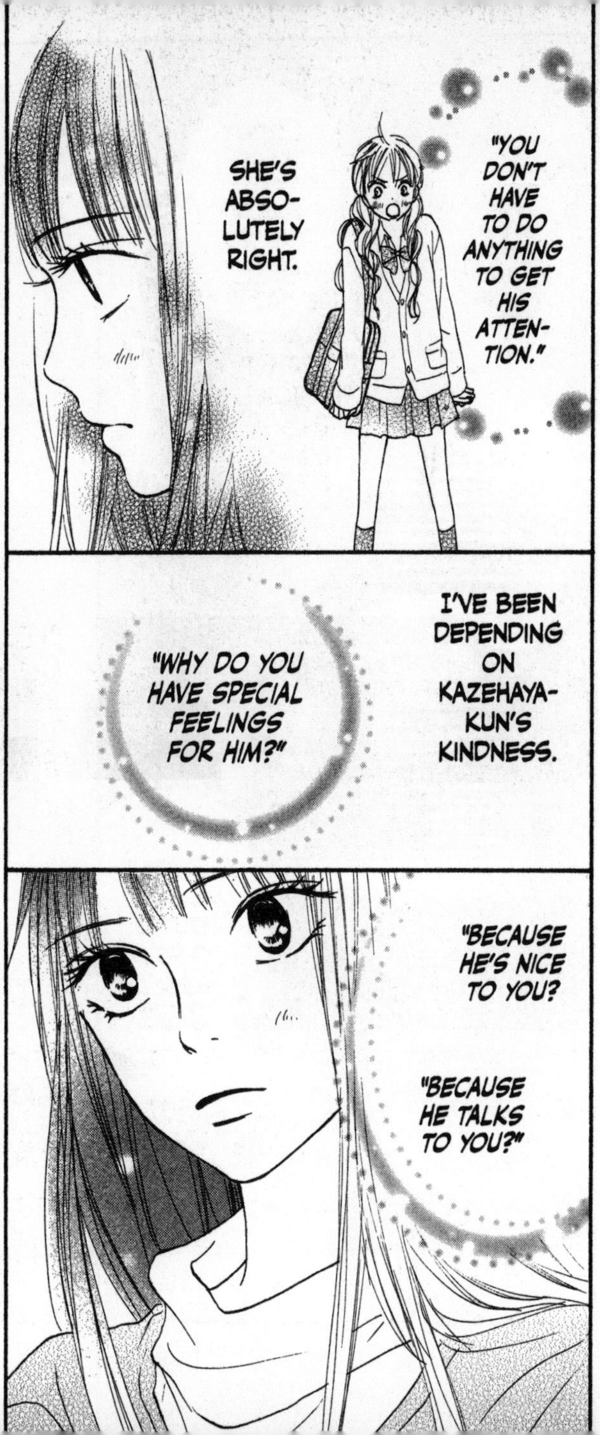
"YOU DON'T HAVE TO DO ANYTHING TO GET HIS ATTENTION."
SHE'S ABSOLUTELY RIGHT.
I'VE BEEN DEPENDING ON KAZEHAYA-KUN'S KINDNESS.
"WHY DO YOU HAVE SPECIAL FEELINGS FOR HIM?"
"BECAUSE HE'S NICE TO YOU?
"BECAUSE HE TALKS TO YOU?"

KARUPIN on JAPAN

1

Hello!
How are you doing?
My name is Shiina.
Nice to meet you.

Recently, I was reminded that I am actually a shy person.

I have been spending time only with people I know these last several years, and I had forgotten about my own shyness!

I'm meeting a lot of new people nowadays, and I get all nervous and begin to sweat excessively. It really surprises me how much people actually sweat when they're nervous. People who've met me for the first time must think I'm a person who sweats a lot. This bothers me a little bit. However, I dislike being unable to speak comfortably with people more than I dislike sweating.

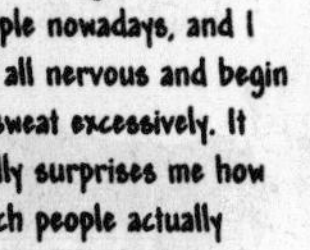
I didn't do well again today...
Talking to myself

Well, I'm used to not being able to speak comfortably with people.

Sorry for such a gloomy topic!

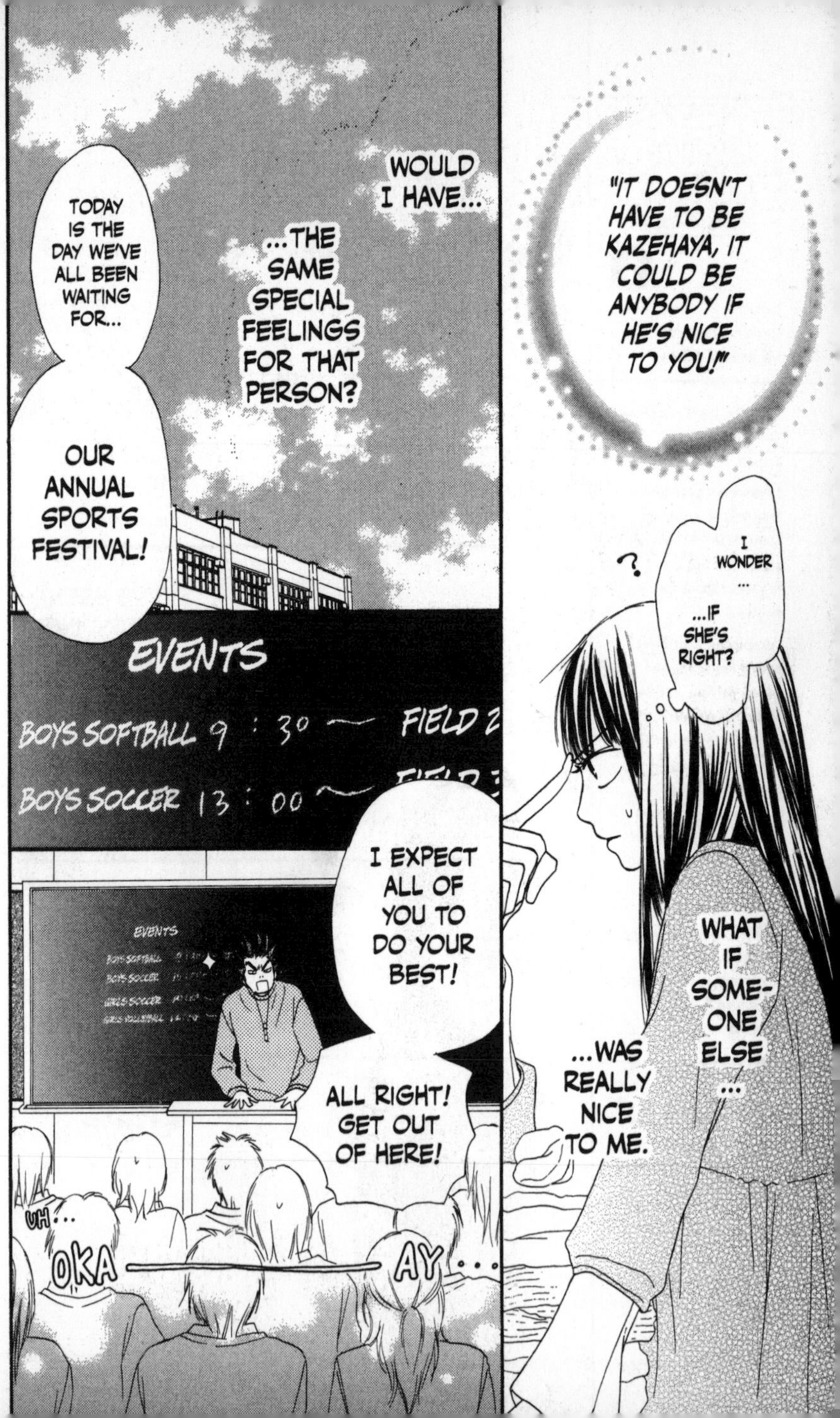
"IT DOESN'T HAVE TO BE KAZEHAYA, IT COULD BE ANYBODY IF HE'S NICE TO YOU!"
I WONDER...
...IF SHE'S RIGHT?
WHAT IF SOMEONE ELSE...
...WAS REALLY NICE TO ME.
WOULD I HAVE...
...THE SAME SPECIAL FEELINGS FOR THAT PERSON?
TODAY IS THE DAY WE'VE ALL BEEN WAITING FOR...
OUR ANNUAL SPORTS FESTIVAL!
EVENTS
BOYS SOFTBALL 9 : 30 ~ FIELD 2
BOYS SOCCER 13 : 00 ~
I EXPECT ALL OF YOU TO DO YOUR BEST!
ALL RIGHT! GET OUT OF HERE!
UH...
OKA——AY...

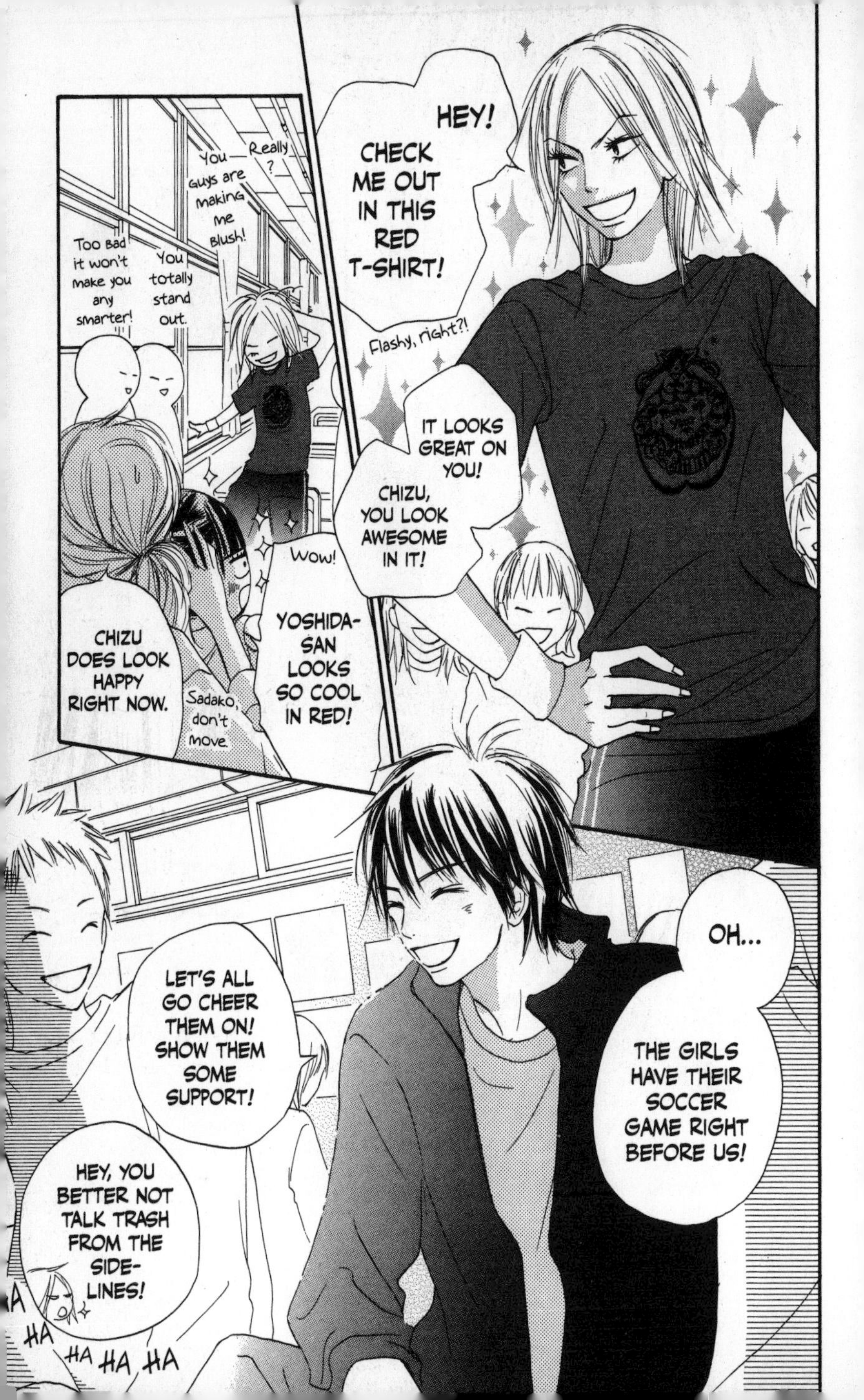
HEY!
CHECK ME OUT IN THIS RED T-SHIRT!
Flashy, right?!
IT LOOKS GREAT ON YOU!
CHIZU, YOU LOOK AWESOME IN IT!
Really?
You— Guys are making me blush!
You totally stand out.
Too bad it won't make you any smarter!
Wow!
YOSHIDA-SAN LOOKS SO COOL IN RED!
Sadako, don't move.
CHIZU DOES LOOK HAPPY RIGHT NOW.
OH...
THE GIRLS HAVE THEIR SOCCER GAME RIGHT BEFORE US!
LET'S ALL GO CHEER THEM ON! SHOW THEM SOME SUPPORT!
HEY, YOU BETTER NOT TALK TRASH FROM THE SIDE-LINES!
HA HA HA HA HA

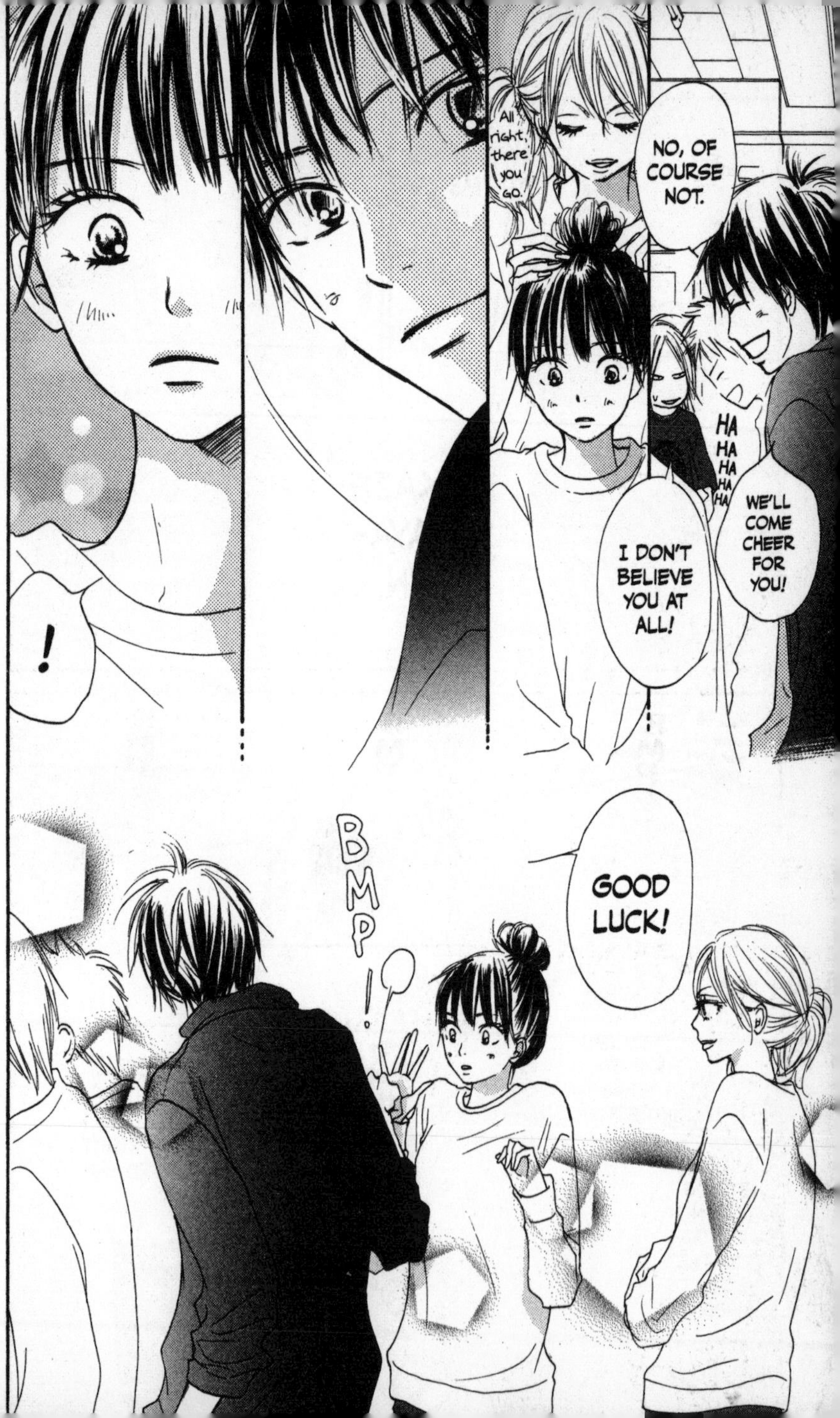
NO, OF COURSE NOT.
HA HA HA HA HA
WE'LL COME CHEER FOR YOU!
All right, there you go.
I DON'T BELIEVE YOU AT ALL!
!
GOOD LUCK!
BMP
!

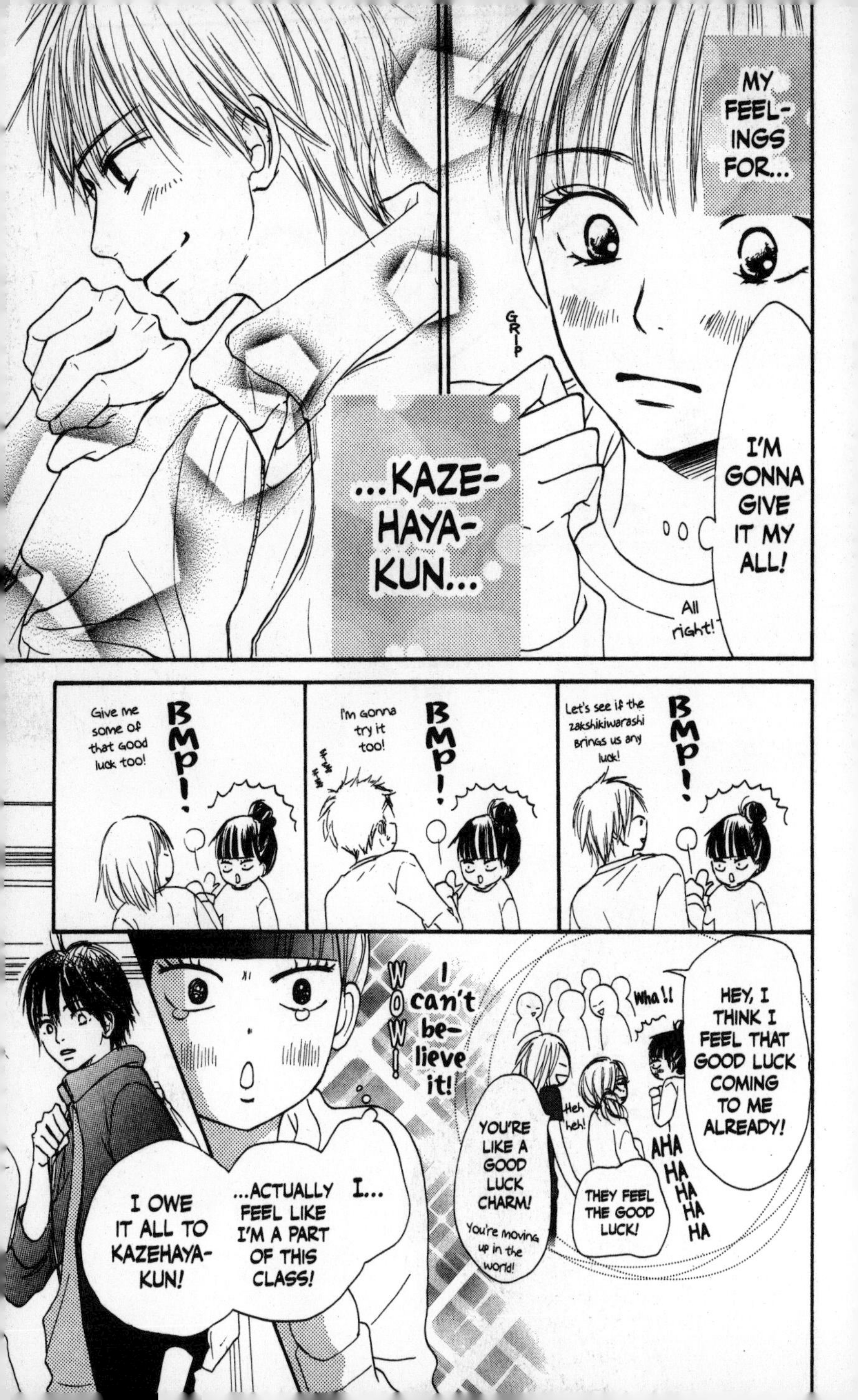
MY FEELINGS FOR...
...KAZEHAYA-KUN...
GRIP
I'M GONNA GIVE IT MY ALL!
All right!
Let's see if the zakshikiwarashi brings us any luck!
BMP!
I'm gonna try it too!
BMP!
Give me some of that Good luck too!
BMP!
HEY, I THINK I FEEL THAT GOOD LUCK COMING TO ME ALREADY!
Wha!!
AHA HA HA HA HA
THEY FEEL THE GOOD LUCK!
Heh heh!
YOU'RE LIKE A GOOD LUCK CHARM!
You're moving up in the world!
I can't be-lieve it!
WOW!
I...
...ACTUALLY FEEL LIKE I'M A PART OF THIS CLASS!
I OWE IT ALL TO KAZEHAYA-KUN!

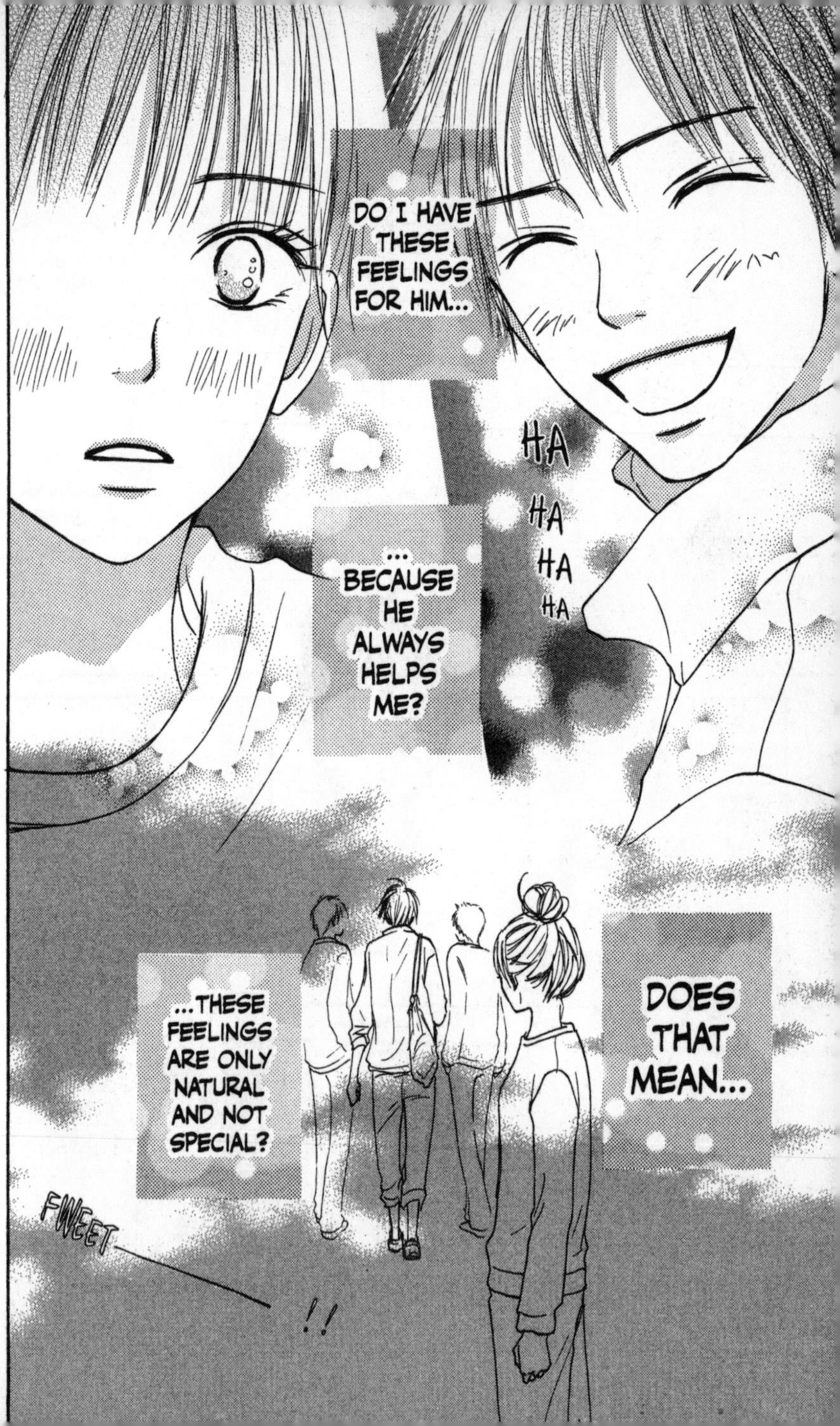
DO I HAVE THESE FEELINGS FOR HIM...
HA HA HA HA
...BECAUSE HE ALWAYS HELPS ME?
DOES THAT MEAN...
...THESE FEELINGS ARE ONLY NATURAL AND NOT SPECIAL?
FWEET
!!

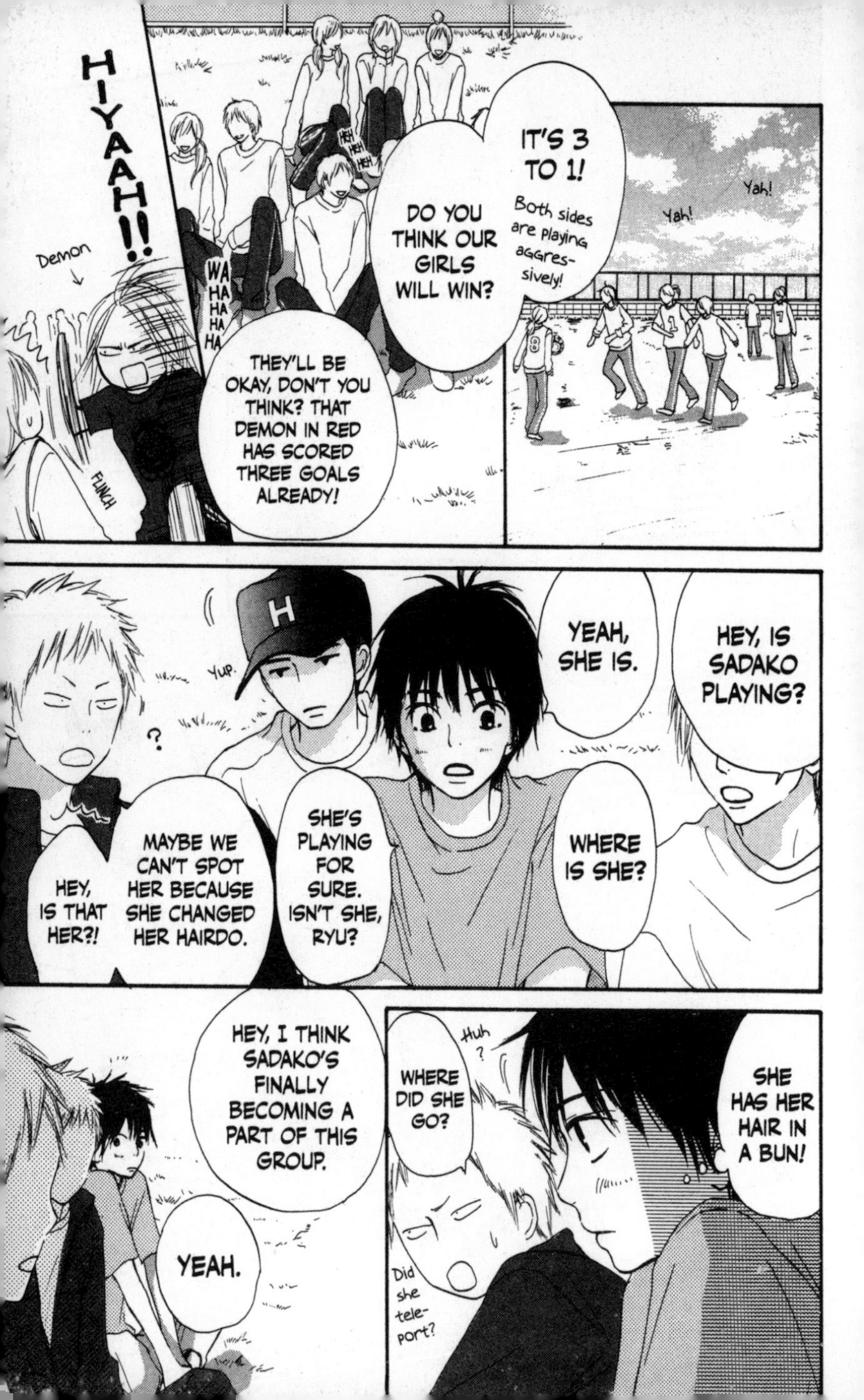
IT'S 3 TO 1!
Both sides are playing aggres-sively!
Yah!
Yah!
DO YOU THINK OUR GIRLS WILL WIN?
HEH HEH HEH
THEY'LL BE OKAY, DON'T YOU THINK? THAT DEMON IN RED HAS SCORED THREE GOALS ALREADY!
WA HA HA HA HA
HIYAAH!!
Demon
FLINCH
HEY, IS SADAKO PLAYING?
YEAH, SHE IS.
WHERE IS SHE?
SHE'S PLAYING FOR SURE. ISN'T SHE, RYU?
Yup.
MAYBE WE CAN'T SPOT HER BECAUSE SHE CHANGED HER HAIRDO.
?
HEY, IS THAT HER?!
SHE HAS HER HAIR IN A BUN!
Huh?
WHERE DID SHE GO?
Did she tele-port?
HEY, I THINK SADAKO'S FINALLY BECOMING A PART OF THIS GROUP.
YEAH.

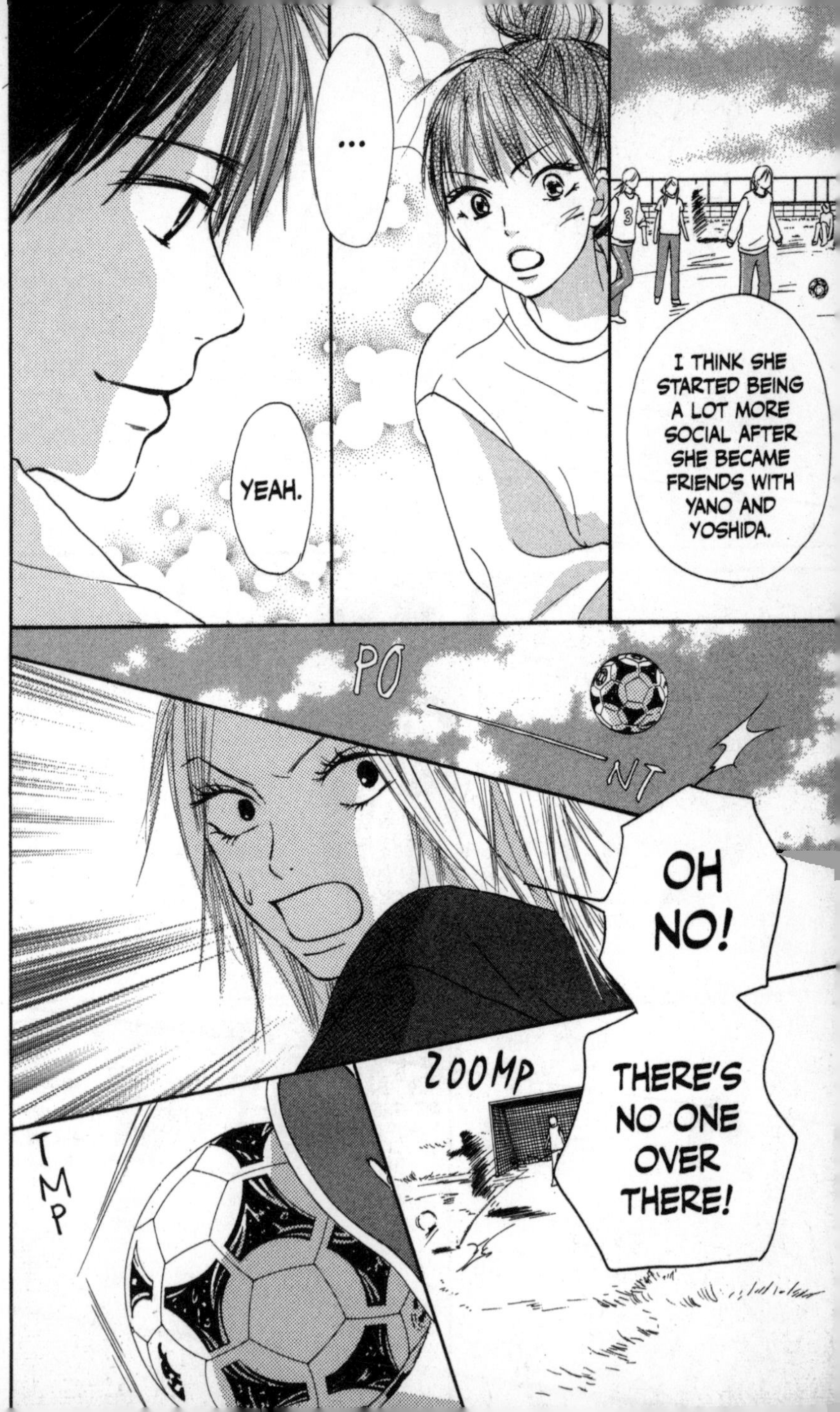
I THINK SHE STARTED BEING A LOT MORE SOCIAL AFTER SHE BECAME FRIENDS WITH YANO AND YOSHIDA.
...
YEAH.
PO
NT
OH NO!
THERE'S NO ONE OVER THERE!
ZOOMP
TMP

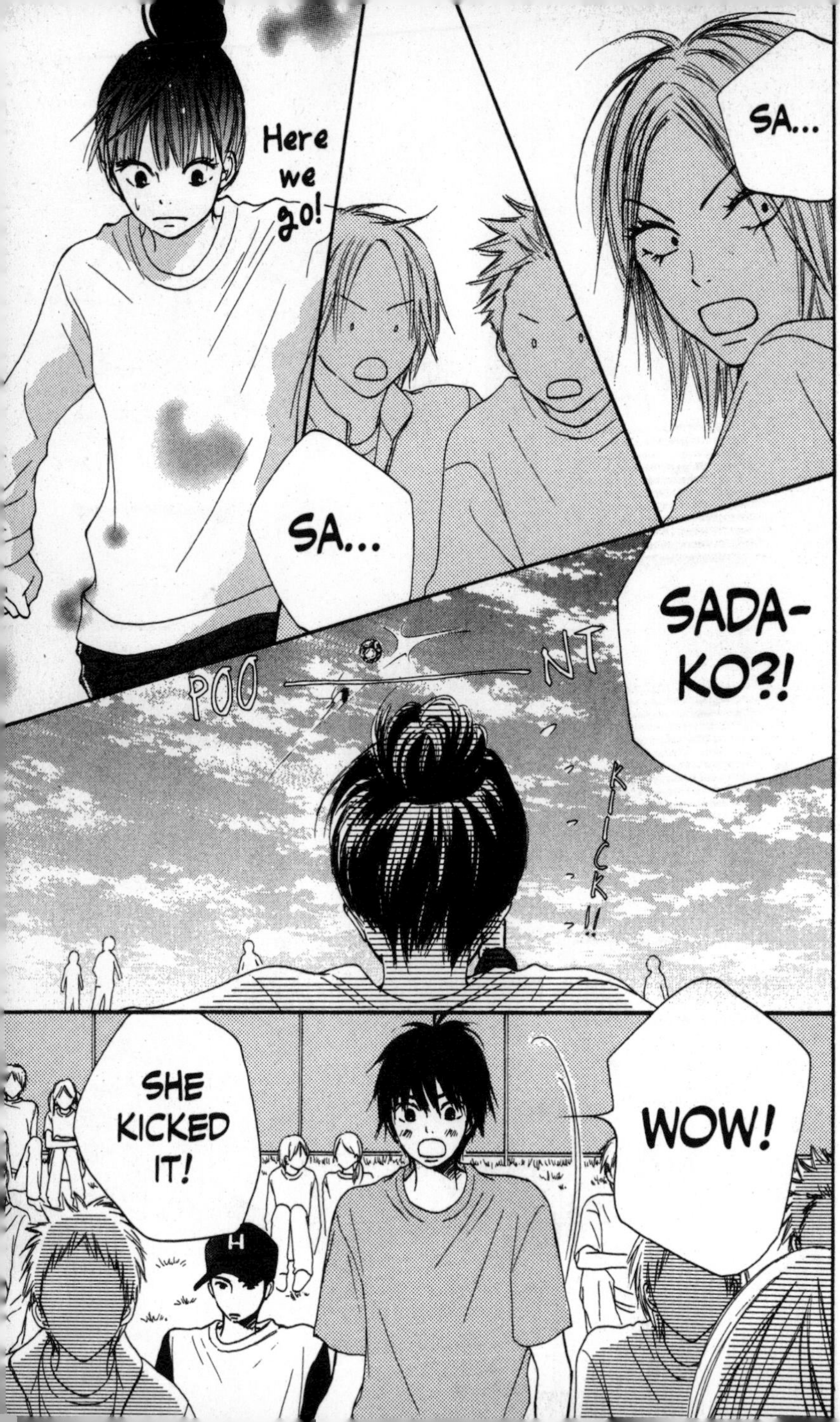
SA...
SA...
Here we go!
SADA-KO?!
POO——NT
KICK!!
WOW!
SHE KICKED IT!

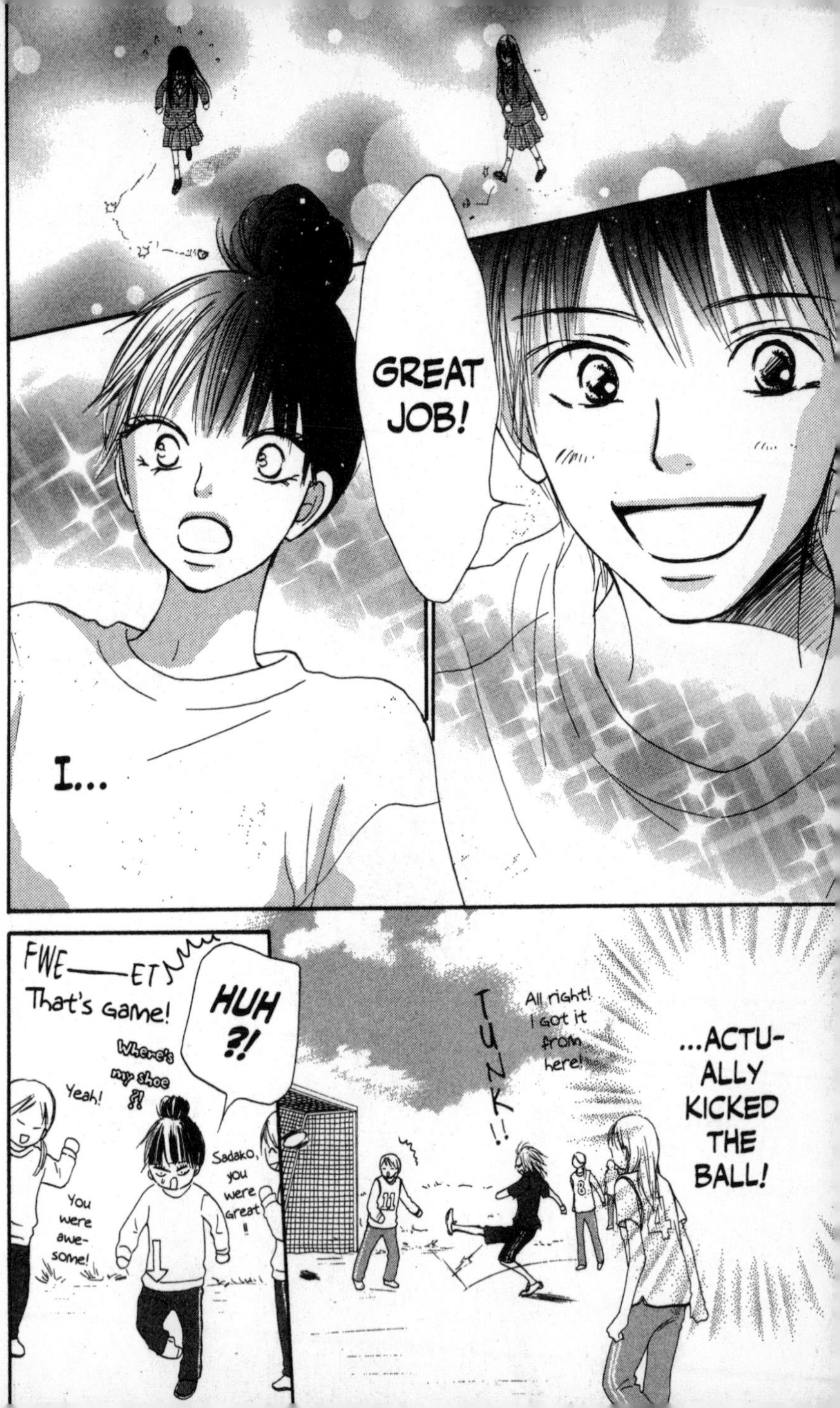
GREAT JOB!
I...
...ACTUALLY KICKED THE BALL!
All right! I got it from here!
TUNK!!
FWE——ET
That's game!
HUH?!
Where's my shoe?!
Sadako, you were great!!
Yeah!
You were awesome!

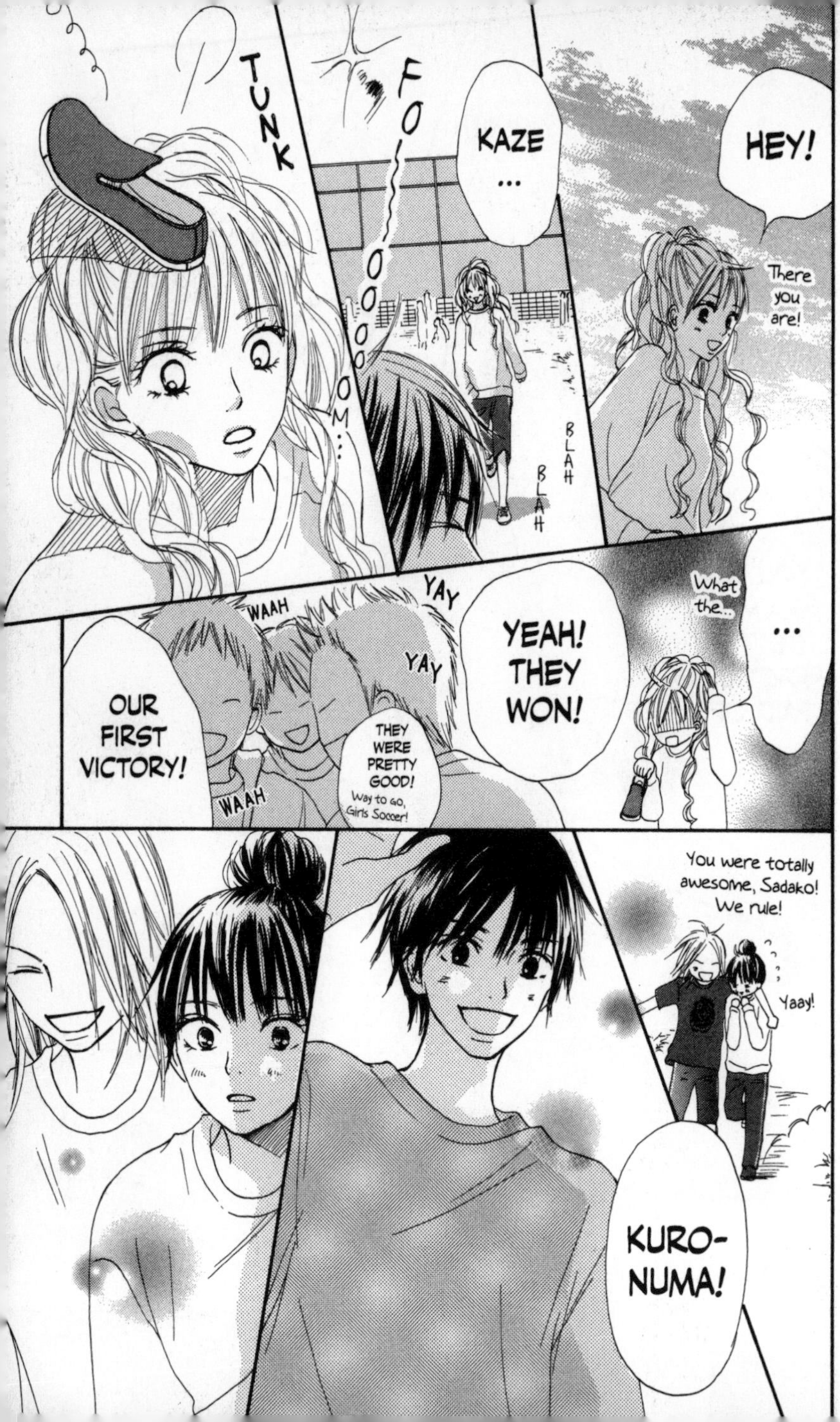
HEY!
There you are!
KAZE ...
BLAH BLAH
FO-OOOOOOM...
TUNK
What the...
...
YEAH! THEY WON!
YAY
YAY
THEY WERE PRETTY GOOD!
Way to go, Girls Soccer!
WAAH
OUR FIRST VICTORY!
WAAH
You were totally awesome, Sadako! We rule!
Yaay!
KURO-NUMA!

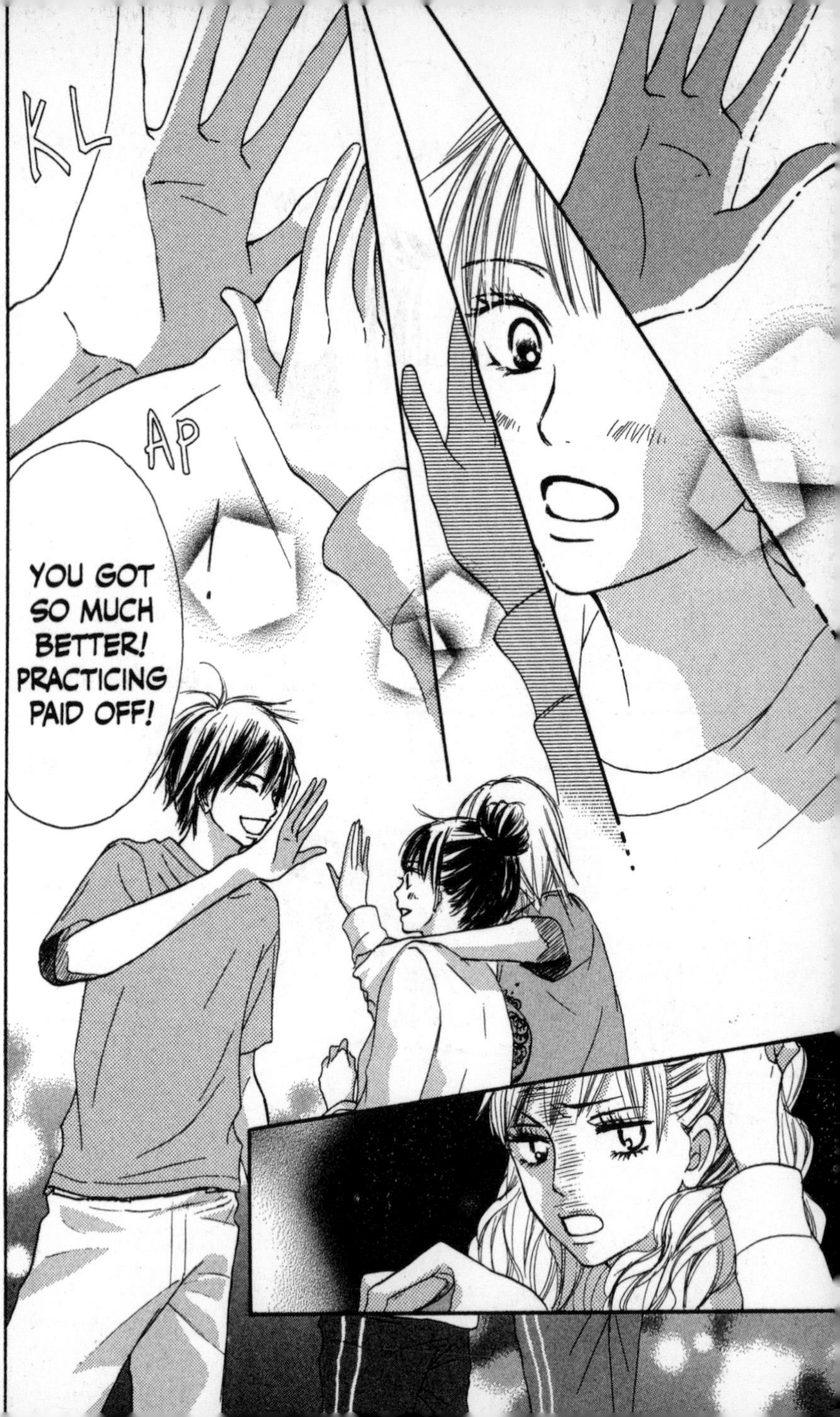
KL
AP
YOU GOT SO MUCH BETTER! PRACTICING PAID OFF!

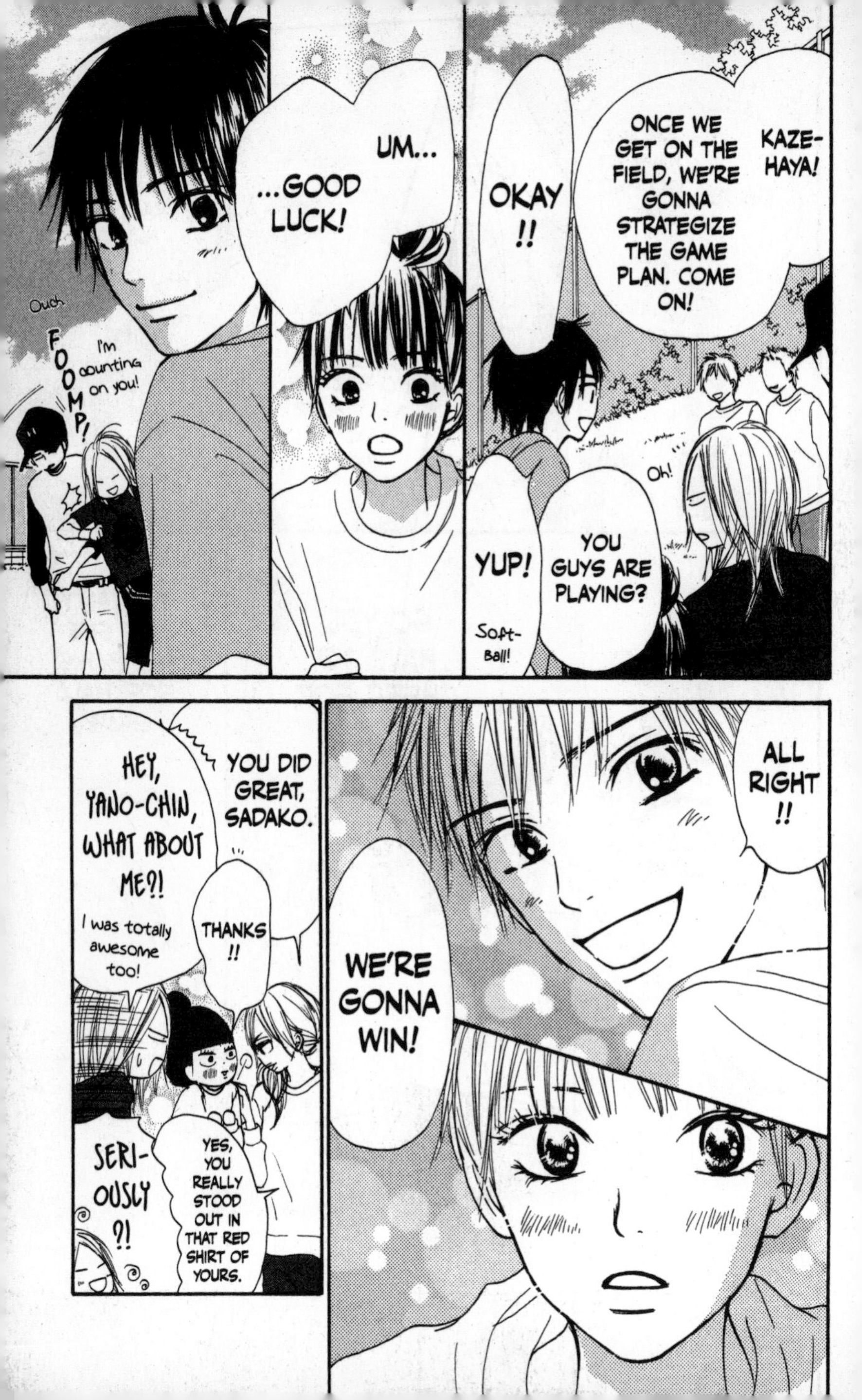
KAZE-HAYA!
ONCE WE GET ON THE FIELD, WE'RE GONNA STRATEGIZE THE GAME PLAN. COME ON!
OKAY !!
Oh!
YOU GUYS ARE PLAYING?
YUP!
Soft-Ball!
UM...
...GOOD LUCK!
I'm counting on you!
FOOMP!
Ouch
ALL RIGHT !!
WE'RE GONNA WIN!
YOU DID GREAT, SADAKO.
HEY, YANO-CHIN, WHAT ABOUT ME?!
I was totally awesome too!
THANKS !!
YES, YOU REALLY STOOD OUT IN THAT RED SHIRT OF YOURS.
SERI-OUSLY ?!

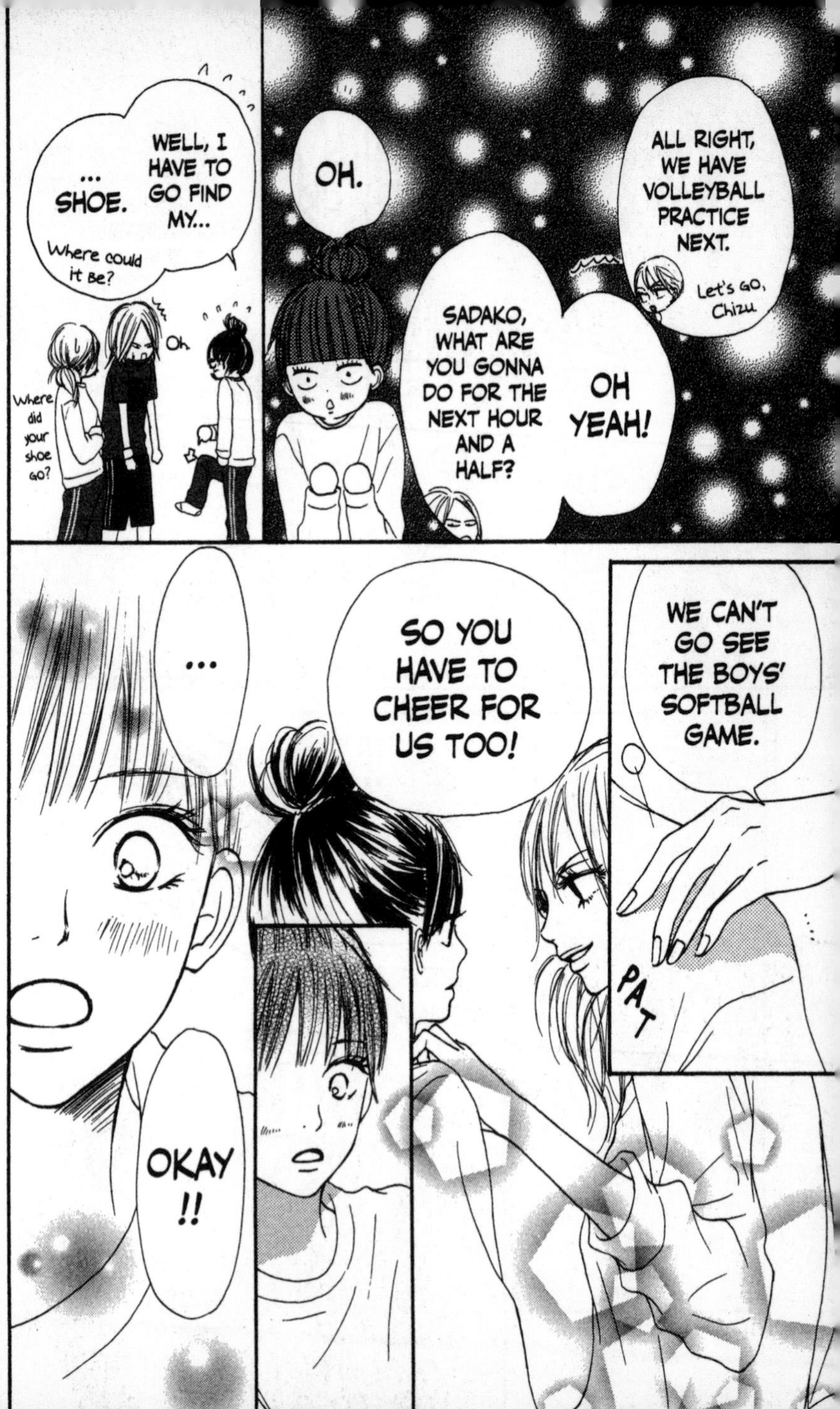
ALL RIGHT, WE HAVE VOLLEYBALL PRACTICE NEXT.
Let's go, Chizu.
OH.
OH YEAH!
SADAKO, WHAT ARE YOU GONNA DO FOR THE NEXT HOUR AND A HALF?
WELL, I HAVE TO GO FIND MY...
... SHOE.
Where could it be?
Oh.
Where did your shoe go?
WE CAN'T GO SEE THE BOYS' SOFTBALL GAME.
PAT
SO YOU HAVE TO CHEER FOR US TOO!
...
OKAY !!

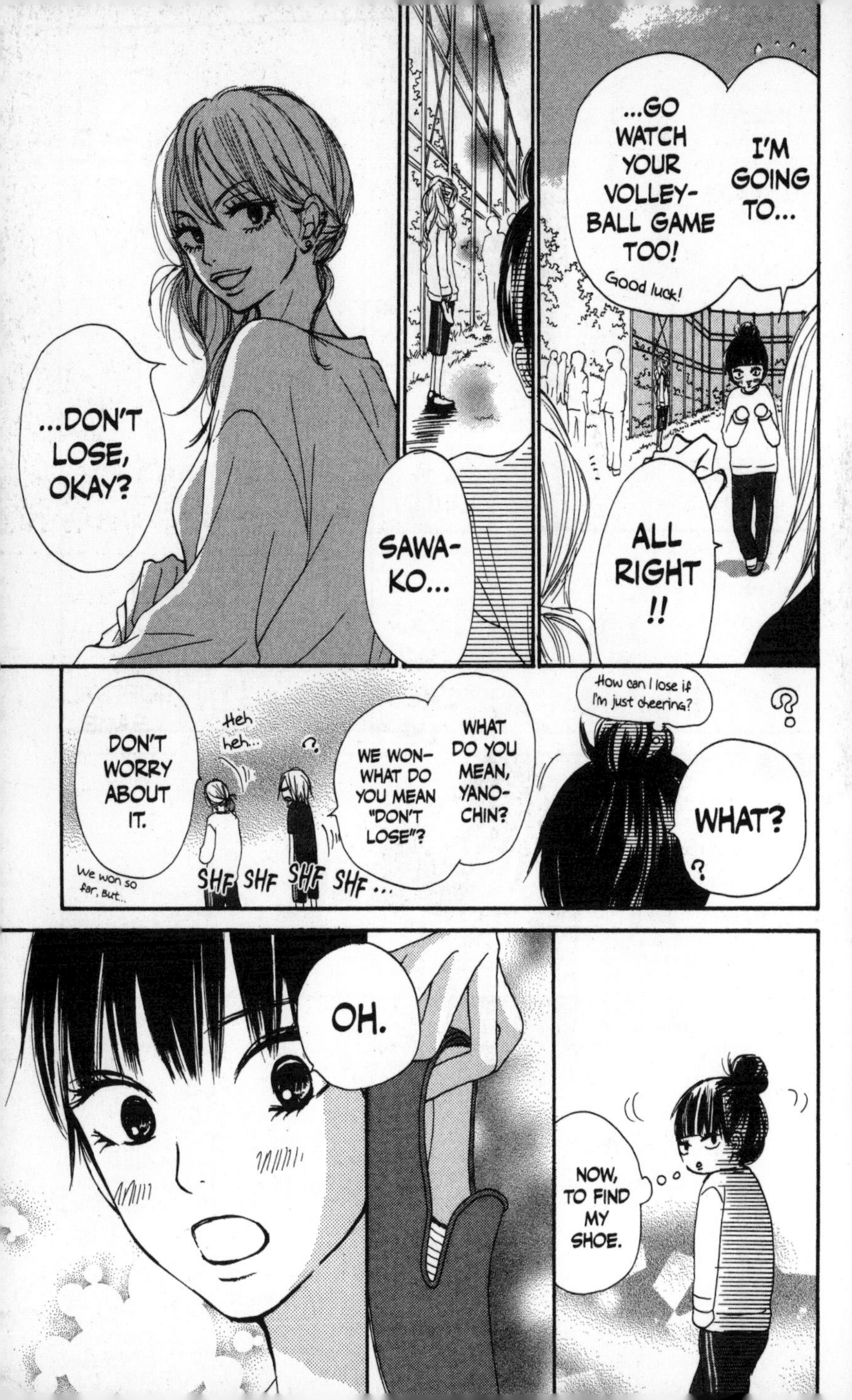
I'M GOING TO...
...GO WATCH YOUR VOLLEY-BALL GAME TOO!
Good luck!
ALL RIGHT !!
SAWA-KO...
...DON'T LOSE, OKAY?
How can I lose if I'm just cheering?
WHAT?
WHAT DO YOU MEAN, YANO-CHIN?
WE WON—WHAT DO YOU MEAN "DON'T LOSE"?
Heh heh...
DON'T WORRY ABOUT IT.
We won so far, but...
SHF SHF SHF SHF...
NOW, TO FIND MY SHOE.
OH.

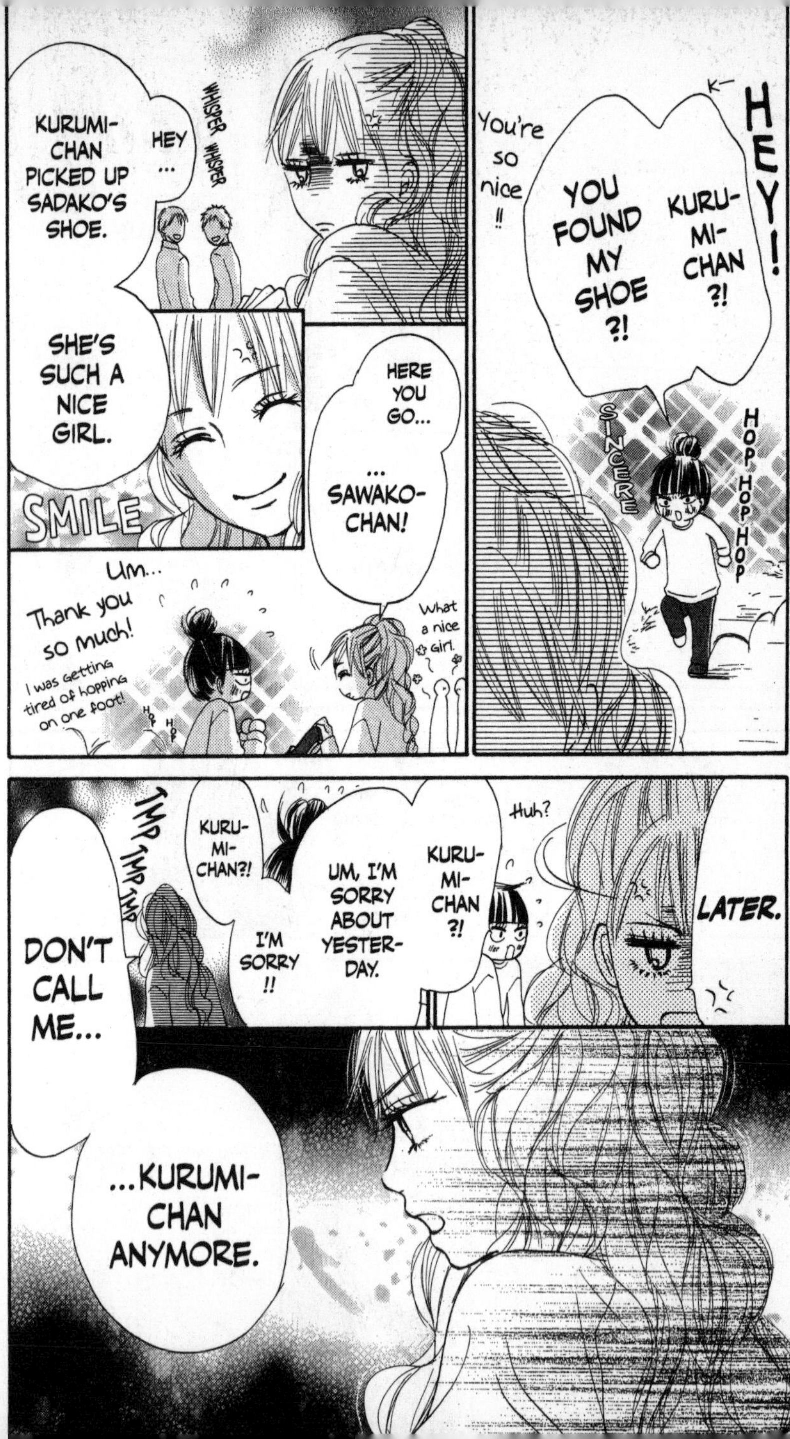
HEY!
KURU-MI-CHAN?!
YOU FOUND MY SHOE?!
You're so nice!!
SINCERE
HOP HOP HOP
WHISPER WHISPER
HEY...
KURUMI-CHAN PICKED UP SADAKO'S SHOE.
HERE YOU GO...
...SAWAKO-CHAN!
SHE'S SUCH A NICE GIRL.
SMILE
What a nice girl.
Um... Thank you so much!
I was getting tired of hopping on one foot!
HOP HOP
LATER.
Huh?
KURU-MI-CHAN?!
UM, I'M SORRY ABOUT YESTER-DAY.
I'M SORRY!!
KURU-MI-CHAN?!
TMP TMP TMP
DON'T CALL ME...
...KURUMI-CHAN ANYMORE.

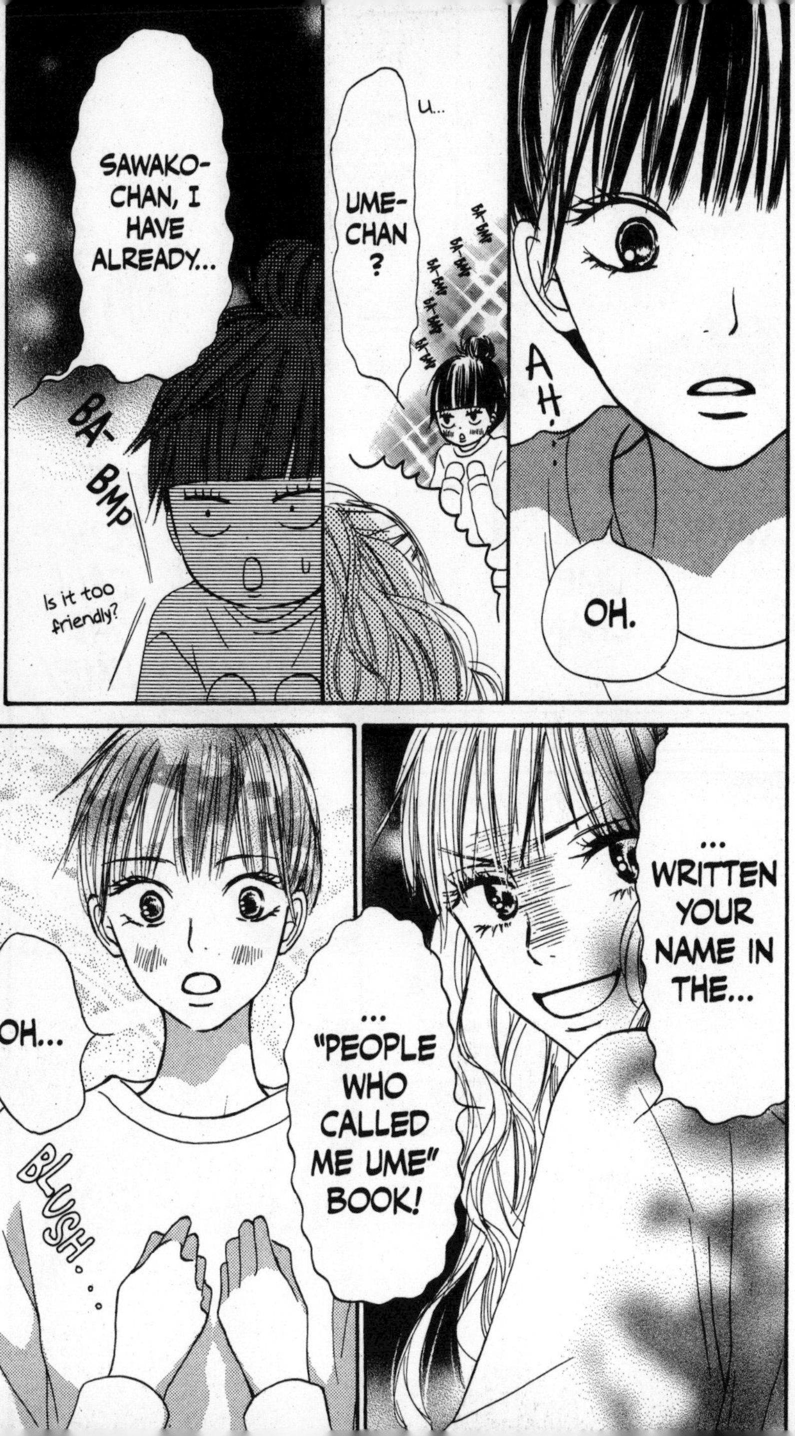
AH!
OH.
U...
UME-CHAN?
SAWAKO-CHAN, I HAVE ALREADY...
BA-BMP
Is it too friendly?
...WRITTEN YOUR NAME IN THE...
..."PEOPLE WHO CALLED ME UME" BOOK!
OH...
BLUSH...

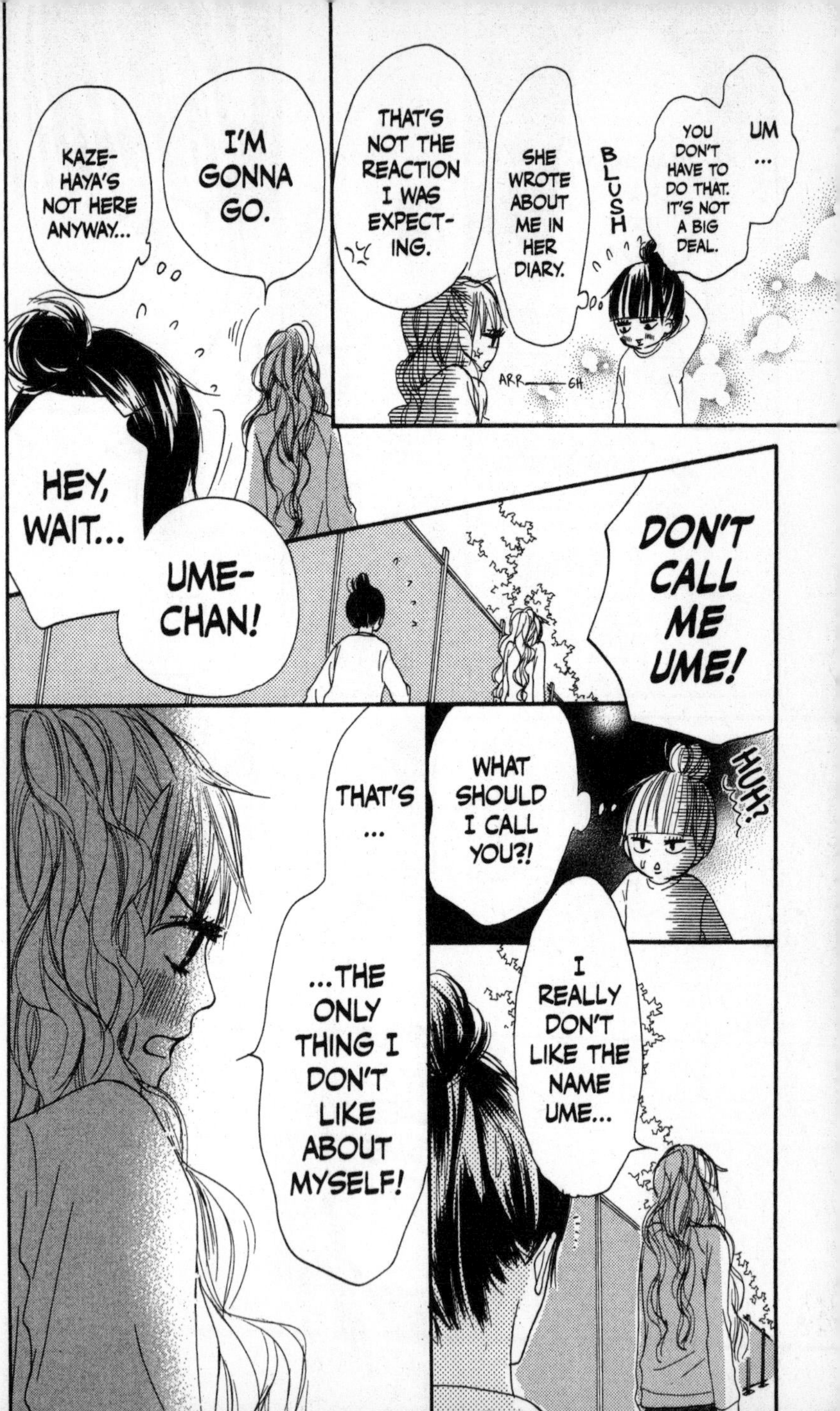
UM ...
YOU DON'T HAVE TO DO THAT. IT'S NOT A BIG DEAL.
BLUSH
SHE WROTE ABOUT ME IN HER DIARY.
THAT'S NOT THE REACTION I WAS EXPECTING.
ARR——GH
I'M GONNA GO.
KAZE-HAYA'S NOT HERE ANYWAY...
HEY, WAIT...
UME-CHAN!
DON'T CALL ME UME!
HUH?
WHAT SHOULD I CALL YOU?!
I REALLY DON'T LIKE THE NAME UME...
THAT'S ...
...THE ONLY THING I DON'T LIKE ABOUT MYSELF!

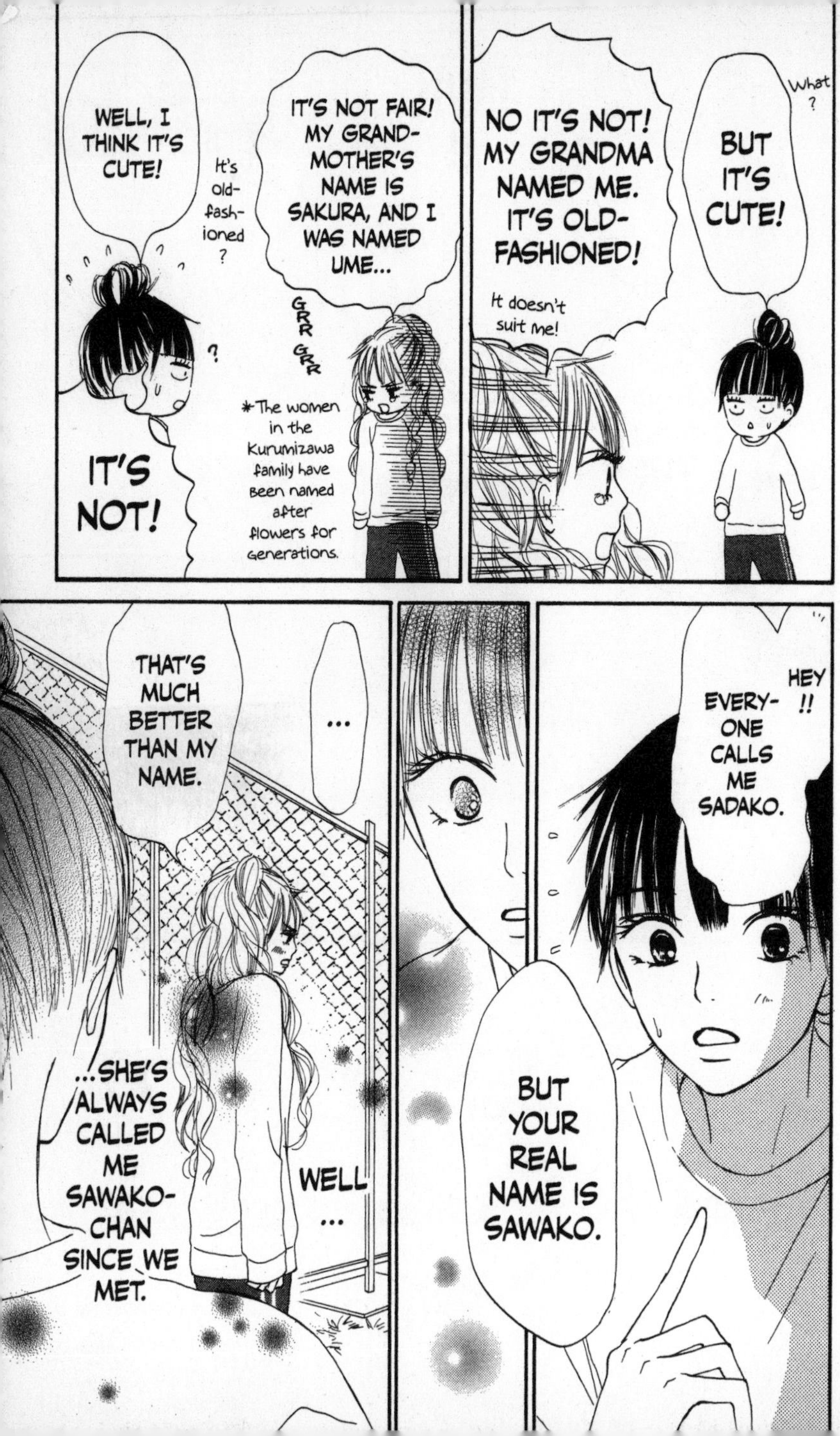

What?
BUT IT'S CUTE!
NO IT'S NOT! MY GRANDMA NAMED ME. IT'S OLD-FASHIONED!
It doesn't suit me!
IT'S NOT FAIR! MY GRANDMOTHER'S NAME IS SAKURA, AND I WAS NAMED UME...
GRR GRR
*The women in the Kurumizawa family have been named after flowers for generations.
It's old-fashioned?
WELL, I THINK IT'S CUTE!
IT'S NOT!
HEY!!
EVERYONE CALLS ME SADAKO.
BUT YOUR REAL NAME IS SAWAKO.
...
THAT'S MUCH BETTER THAN MY NAME.
WELL...
...SHE'S ALWAYS CALLED ME SAWAKO-CHAN SINCE WE MET.

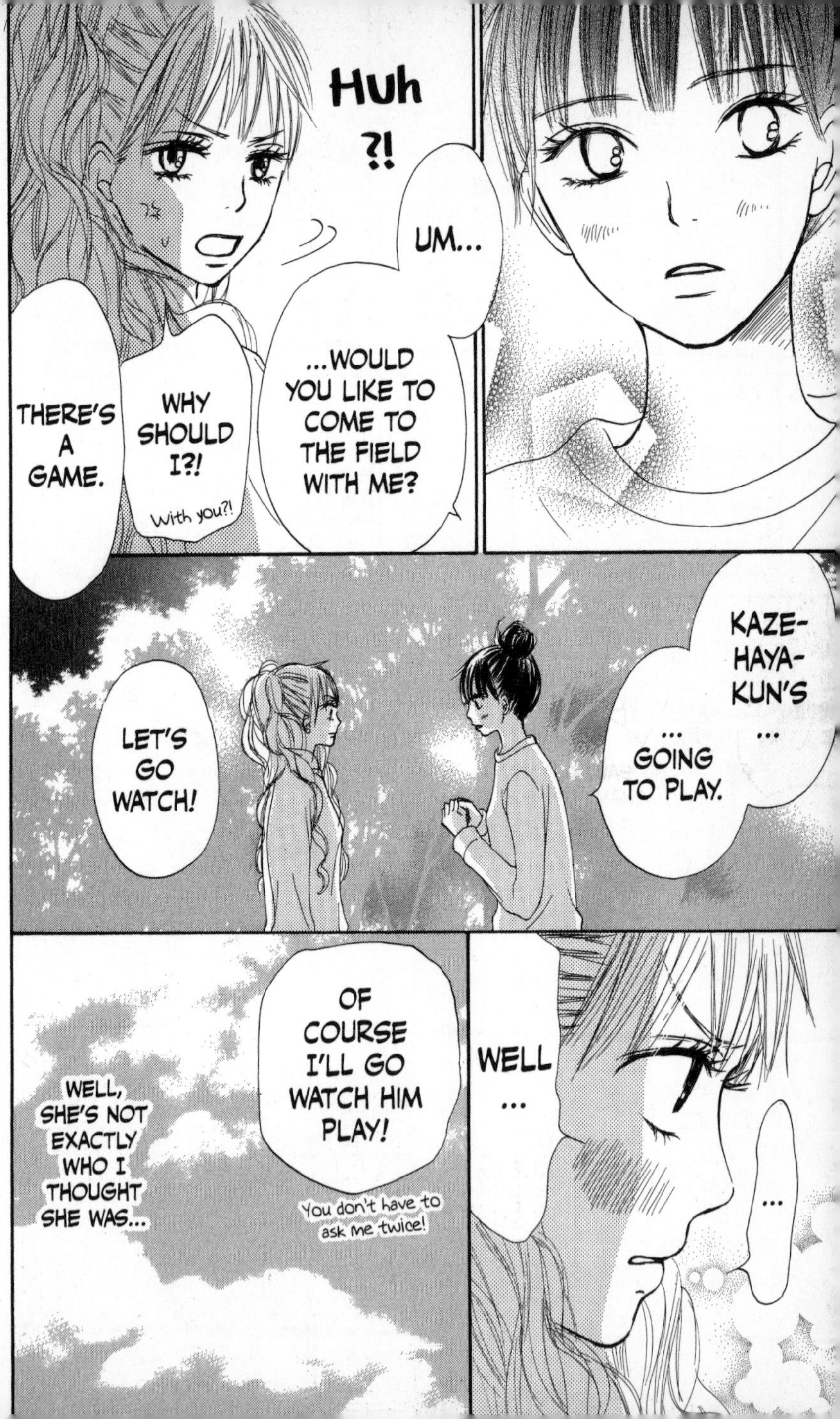
UM...
...WOULD YOU LIKE TO COME TO THE FIELD WITH ME?
Huh ?!
WHY SHOULD I?!
With you?!
THERE'S A GAME.
KAZE-HAYA-KUN'S ... ... GOING TO PLAY.
LET'S GO WATCH!
WELL ...
...
OF COURSE I'LL GO WATCH HIM PLAY!
You don't have to ask me twice!
WELL, SHE'S NOT EXACTLY WHO I THOUGHT SHE WAS...

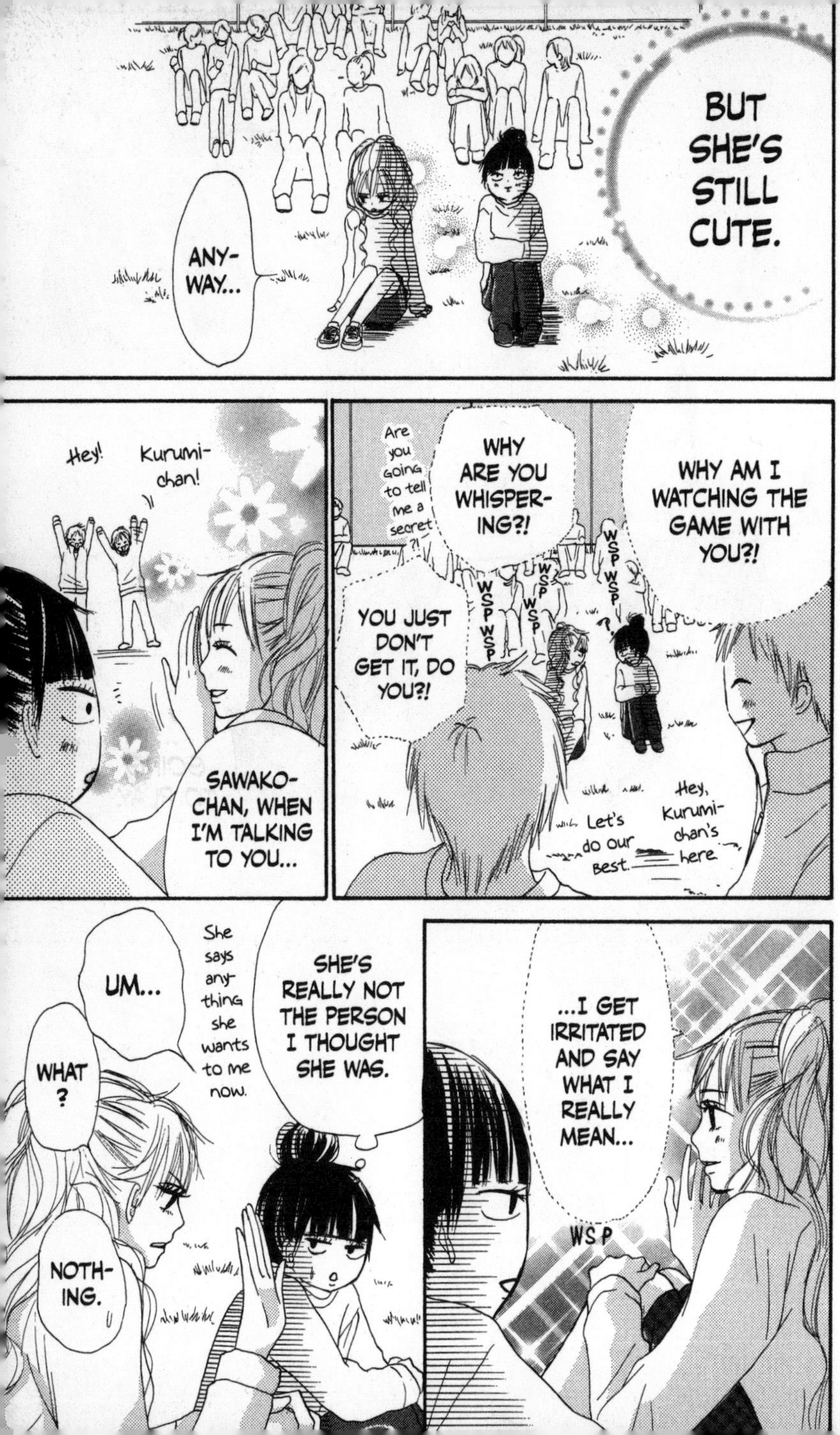
BUT SHE'S STILL CUTE.
ANY-WAY...
WHY AM I WATCHING THE GAME WITH YOU?!
WHY ARE YOU WHISPER-ING?!
Are you going to tell me a secret ?!
WSP WSP
WSP WSP
WSP WSP
YOU JUST DON'T GET IT, DO YOU?!
Hey, Kurumi-chan's here
Let's do our Best.
Hey! Kurumi-chan!
SAWAKO-CHAN, WHEN I'M TALKING TO YOU...
...I GET IRRITATED AND SAY WHAT I REALLY MEAN...
WSP
SHE'S REALLY NOT THE PERSON I THOUGHT SHE WAS.
She says any-thing she wants to me now.
UM...
WHAT ?
NOTH-ING.

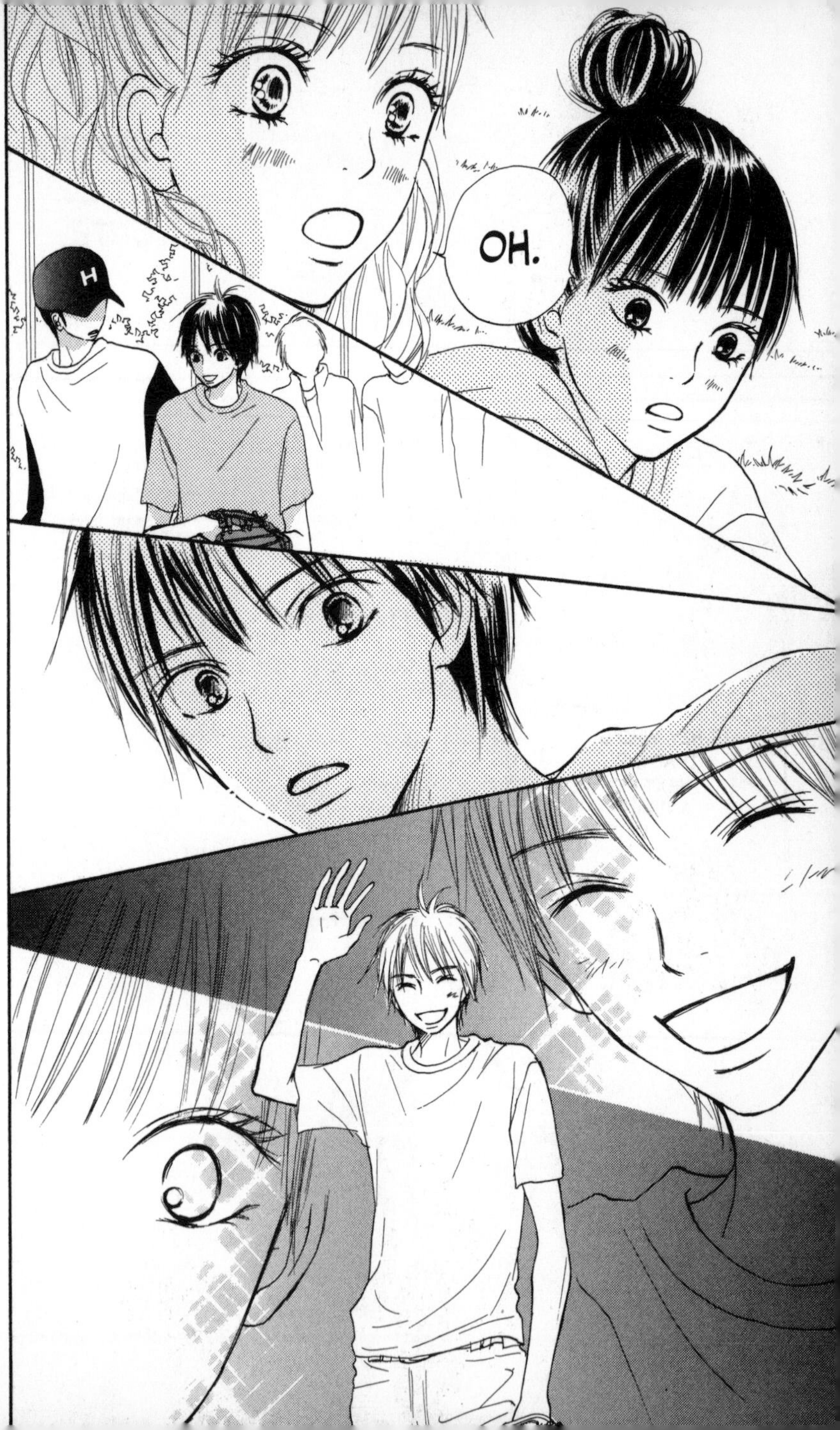
OH.

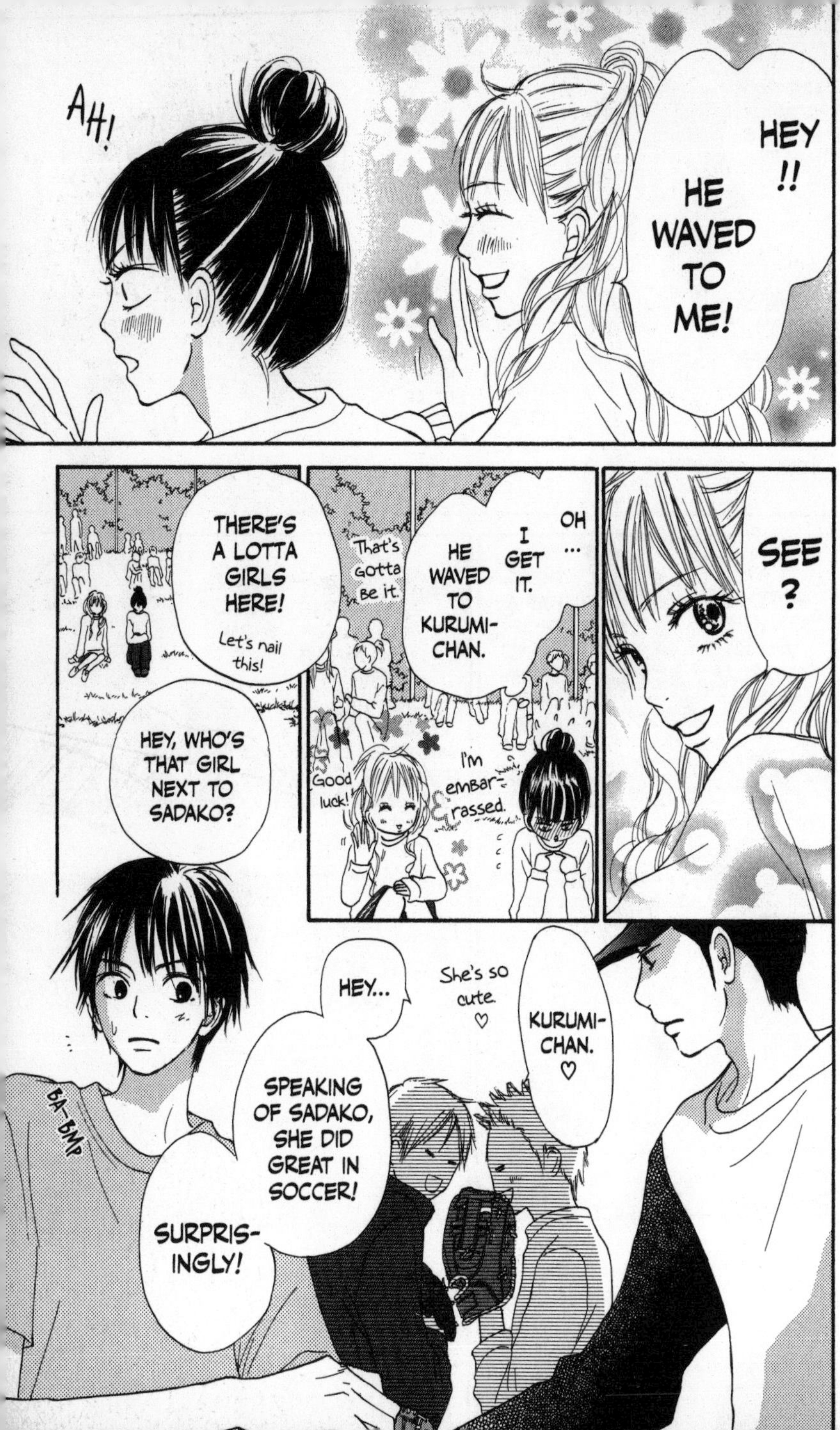
HEY!!
HE WAVED TO ME!
AH!
SEE?
OH... I GET IT.
HE WAVED TO KURUMI-CHAN.
That's gotta be it.
I'm embarrassed.
Good luck!
THERE'S A LOTTA GIRLS HERE!
Let's nail this!
HEY, WHO'S THAT GIRL NEXT TO SADAKO?
KURUMI-CHAN. ♡
She's so cute. ♡
HEY...
SPEAKING OF SADAKO, SHE DID GREAT IN SOCCER!
SURPRISINGLY!
BA-BMP

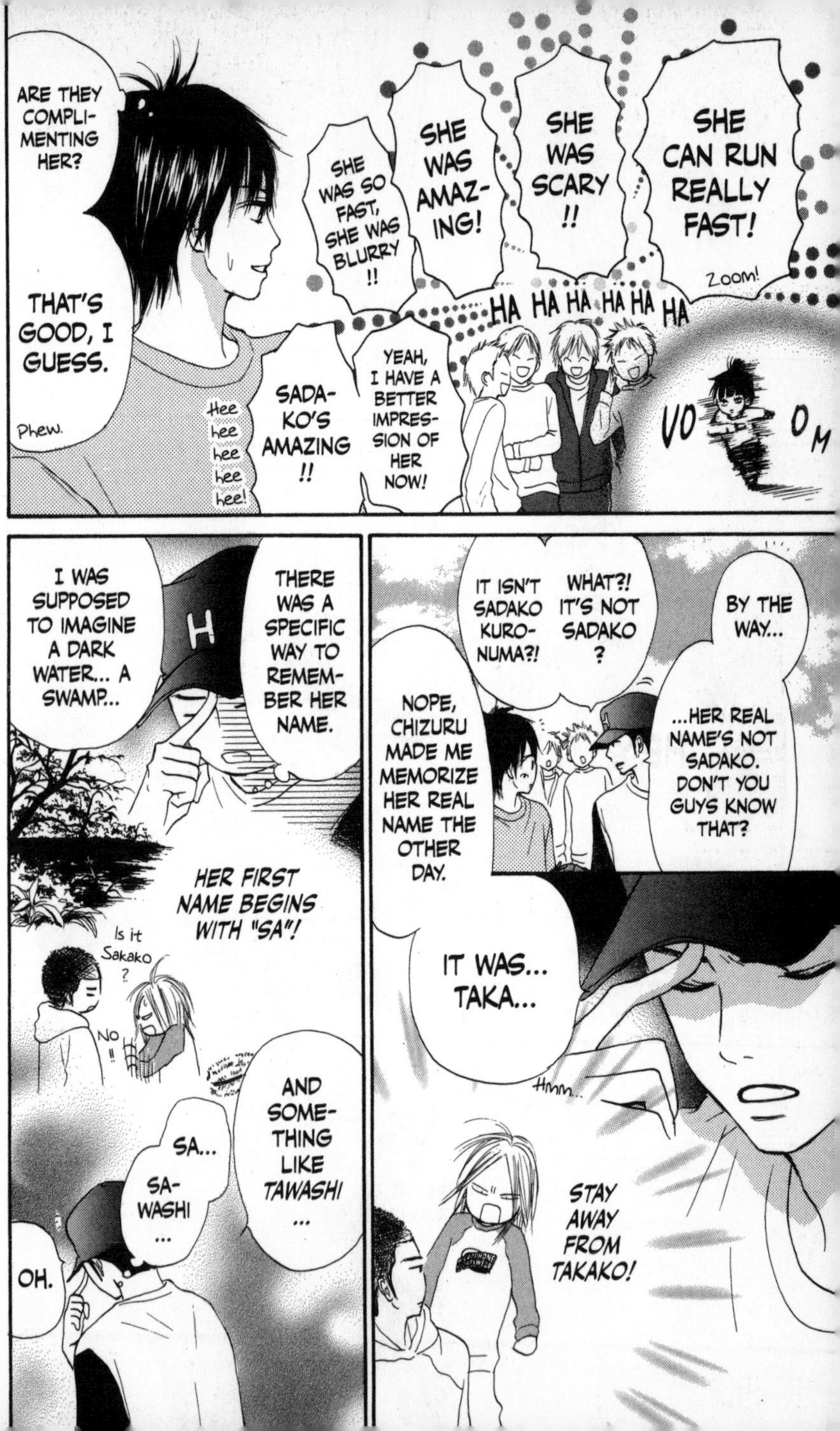
SHE CAN RUN REALLY FAST!
Zoom!
SHE WAS SCARY!!
SHE WAS AMAZING!
SHE WAS SO FAST, SHE WAS BLURRY!!
HA HA HA HA HA HA
VOOM
YEAH, I HAVE A BETTER IMPRESSION OF HER NOW!
SADAKO'S AMAZING!!
ARE THEY COMPLIMENTING HER?
Hee hee hee hee hee!
THAT'S GOOD, I GUESS.
Phew.
BY THE WAY...
...HER REAL NAME'S NOT SADAKO. DON'T YOU GUYS KNOW THAT?
WHAT?! IT'S NOT SADAKO?
IT ISN'T SADAKO KURONUMA?!
NOPE, CHIZURU MADE ME MEMORIZE HER REAL NAME THE OTHER DAY.
IT WAS... TAKA...
Hmm...
STAY AWAY FROM TAKAKO!
THERE WAS A SPECIFIC WAY TO REMEMBER HER NAME.
I WAS SUPPOSED TO IMAGINE A DARK WATER... A SWAMP...
HER FIRST NAME BEGINS WITH "SA"!
Is it Sakako?
No!!
AND SOMETHING LIKE TAWASHI...
SA... SA-WASHI...
OH.

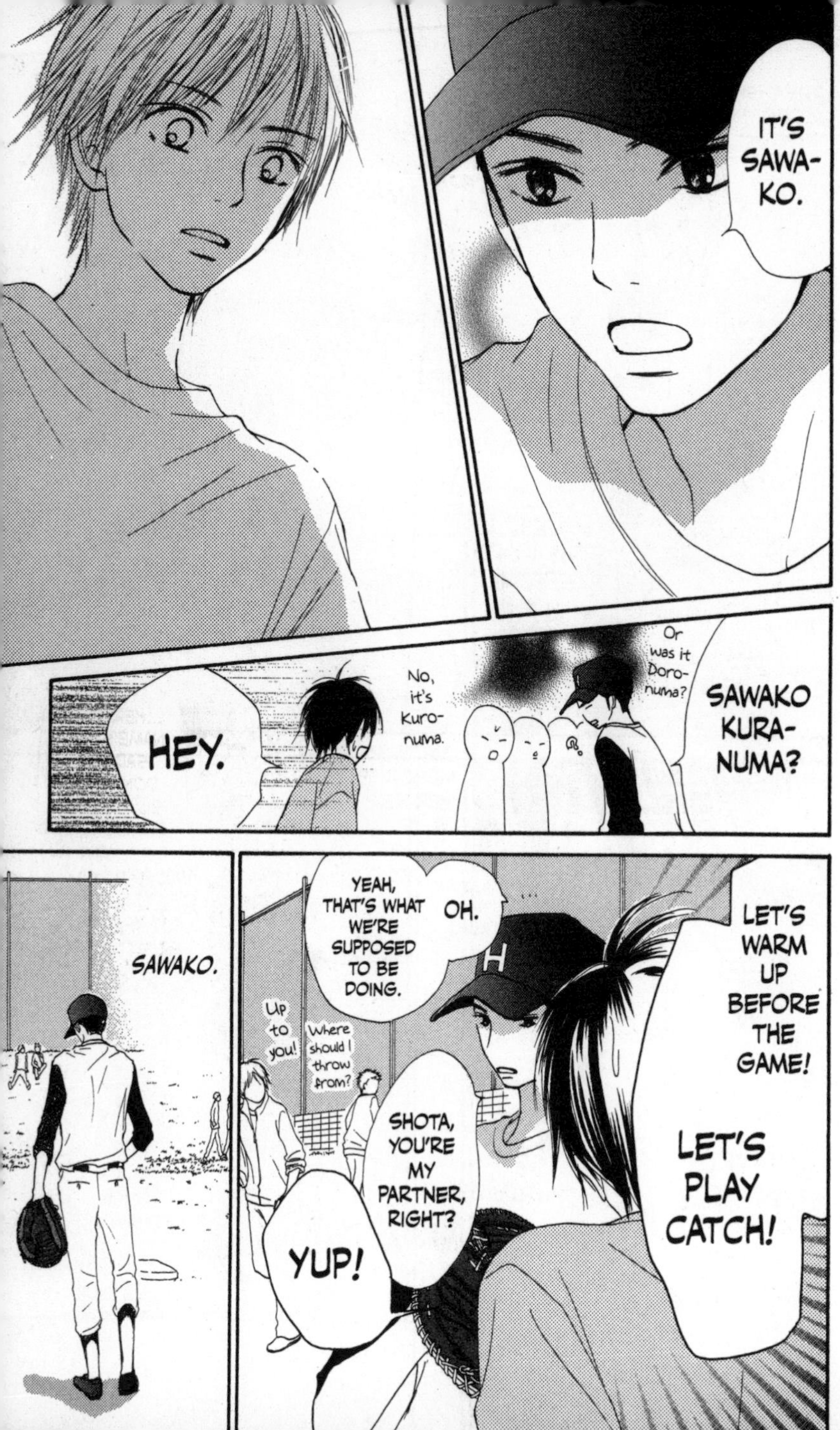
IT'S SAWAKO.
SAWAKO KURANUMA?
Or was it Doronuma?
No, it's Kuronuma.
HEY.
LET'S WARM UP BEFORE THE GAME!
LET'S PLAY CATCH!
OH.
YEAH, THAT'S WHAT WE'RE SUPPOSED TO BE DOING.
Where should I throw from?
Up to you!
SHOTA, YOU'RE MY PARTNER, RIGHT?
YUP!
SAWAKO.

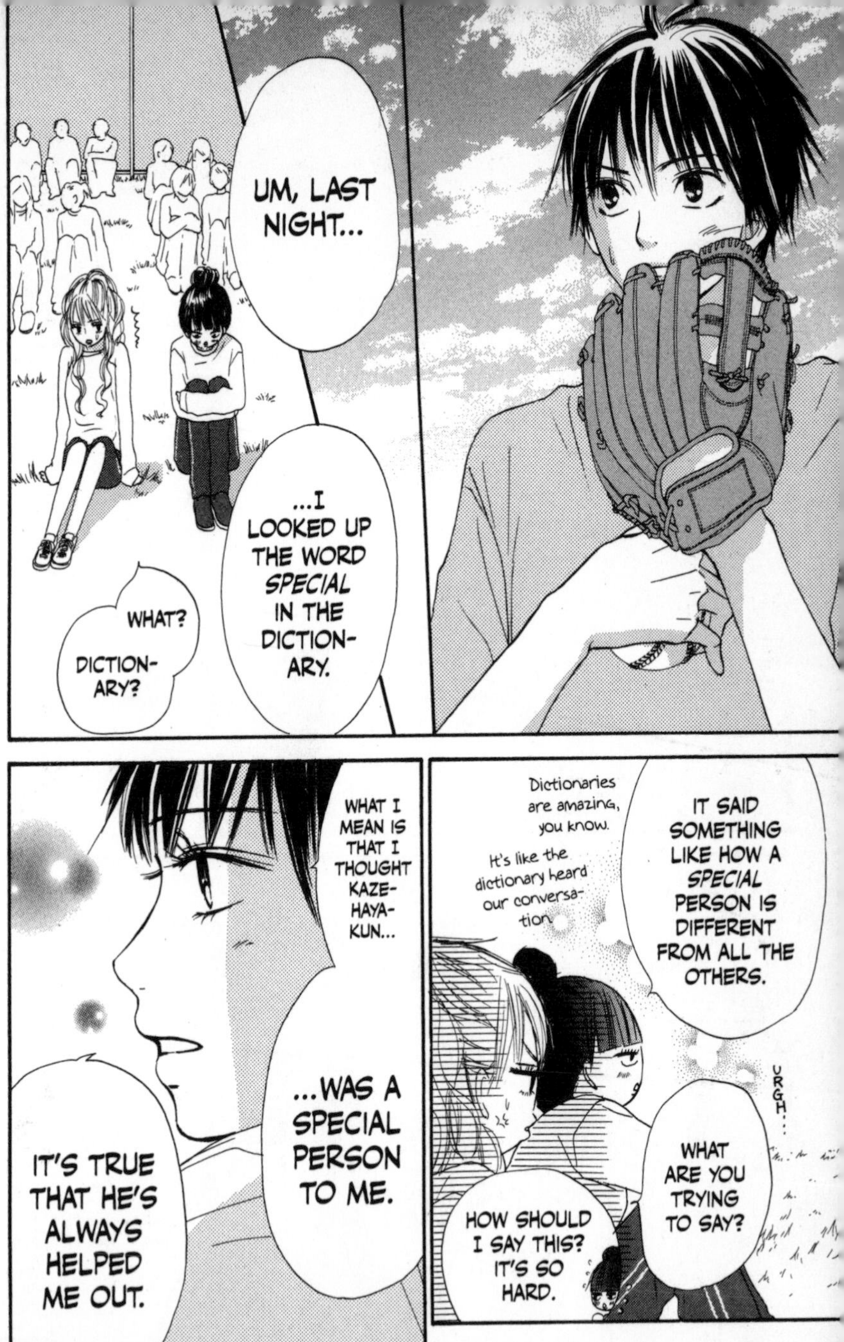
UM, LAST NIGHT...
...I LOOKED UP THE WORD *SPECIAL* IN THE DICTIONARY.
WHAT? DICTIONARY?
IT SAID SOMETHING LIKE HOW A *SPECIAL* PERSON IS DIFFERENT FROM ALL THE OTHERS.
Dictionaries are amazing, you know.
It's like the dictionary heard our conversation.
URGH...
WHAT ARE YOU TRYING TO SAY?
HOW SHOULD I SAY THIS? IT'S SO HARD.
WHAT I MEAN IS THAT I THOUGHT KAZEHAYA-KUN...
...WAS A SPECIAL PERSON TO ME.
IT'S TRUE THAT HE'S ALWAYS HELPED ME OUT.

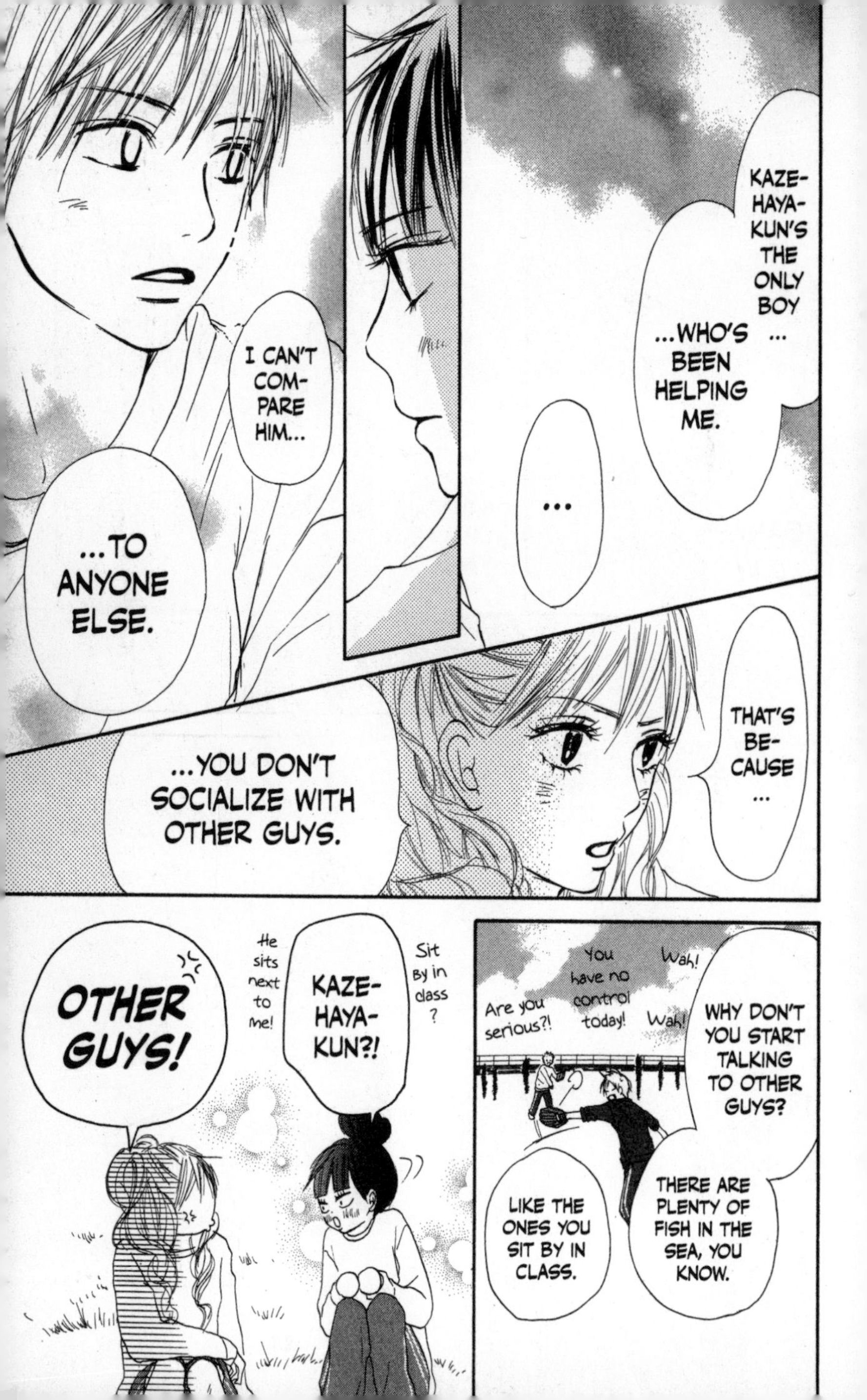
KAZE-HAYA-KUN'S THE ONLY BOY ...
...WHO'S BEEN HELPING ME.
...
I CAN'T COMPARE HIM...
...TO ANYONE ELSE.
THAT'S BECAUSE ...
...YOU DON'T SOCIALIZE WITH OTHER GUYS.
WHY DON'T YOU START TALKING TO OTHER GUYS?
Wah!
Wah!
You have no control today!
Are you serious?!
THERE ARE PLENTY OF FISH IN THE SEA, YOU KNOW.
LIKE THE ONES YOU SIT BY IN CLASS.
Sit by in class?
KAZE-HAYA-KUN?!
He sits next to me!
OTHER GUYS!

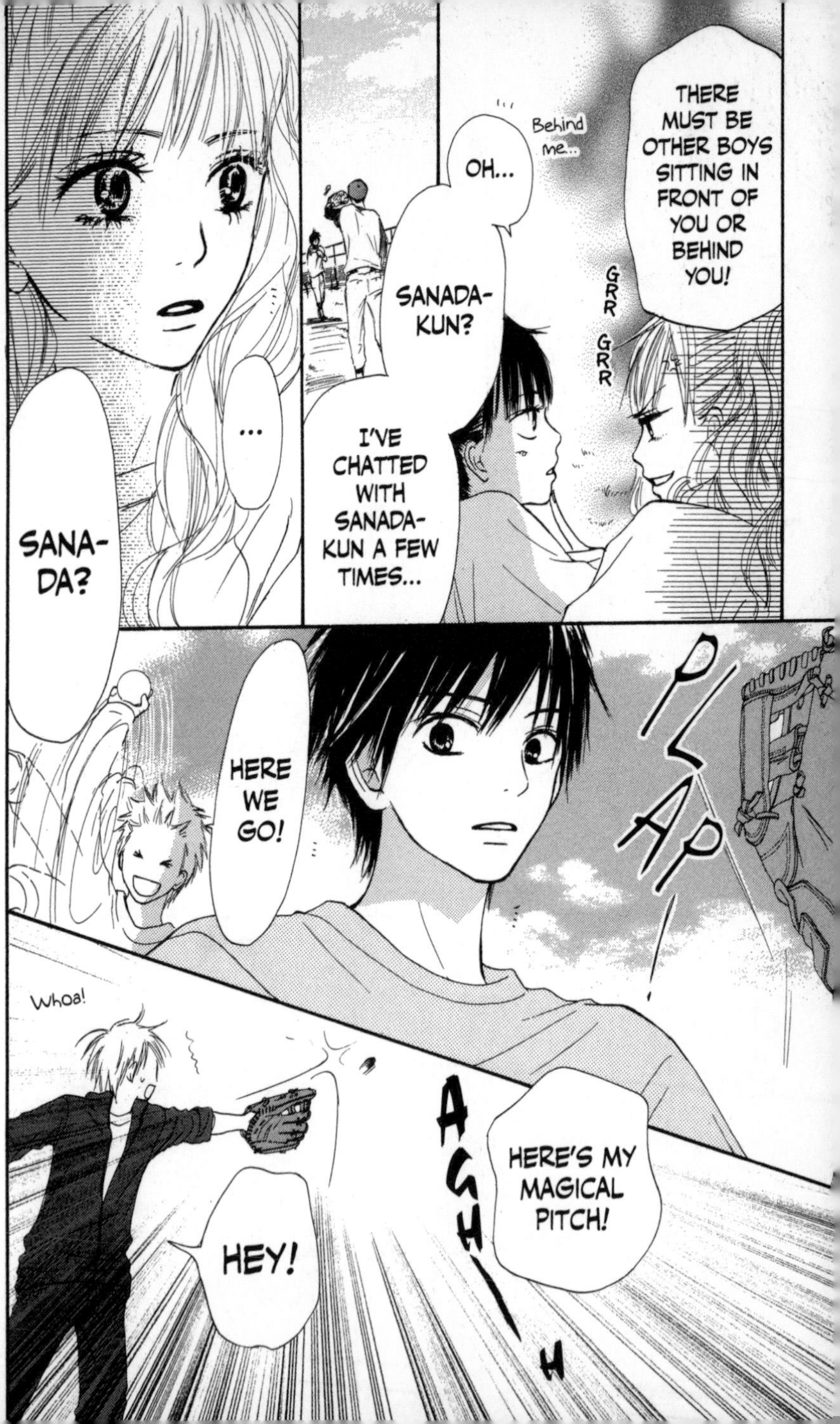
THERE MUST BE OTHER BOYS SITTING IN FRONT OF YOU OR BEHIND YOU!
GRR GRR
Behind me...
OH...
SANADA-KUN?
I'VE CHATTED WITH SANADA-KUN A FEW TIMES...
...
SANA-DA?
PLAP!
HERE WE GO!
HERE'S MY MAGICAL PITCH!
AGH!
HEY!
Whoa!

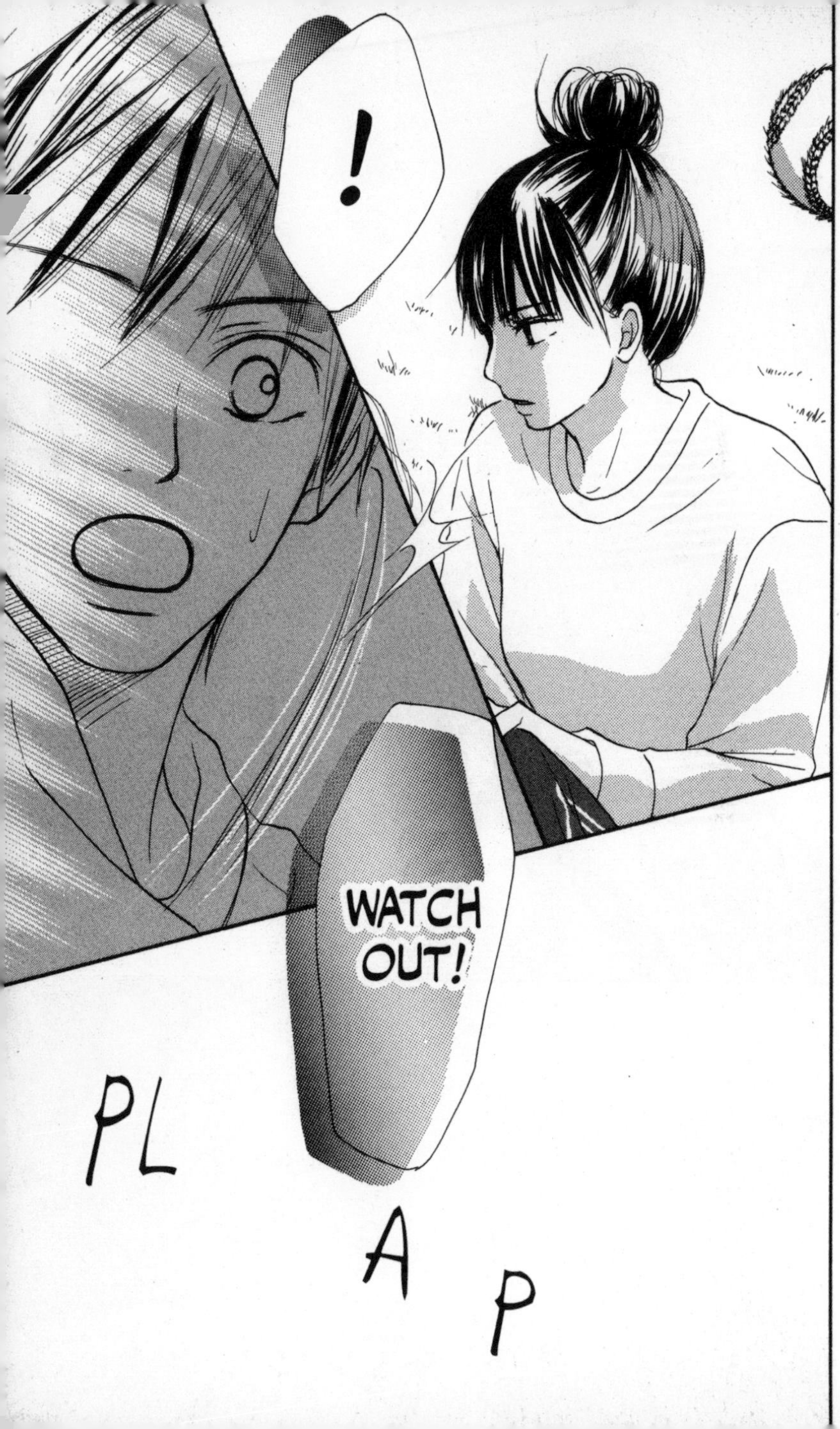
!
WATCH OUT!
PLAP

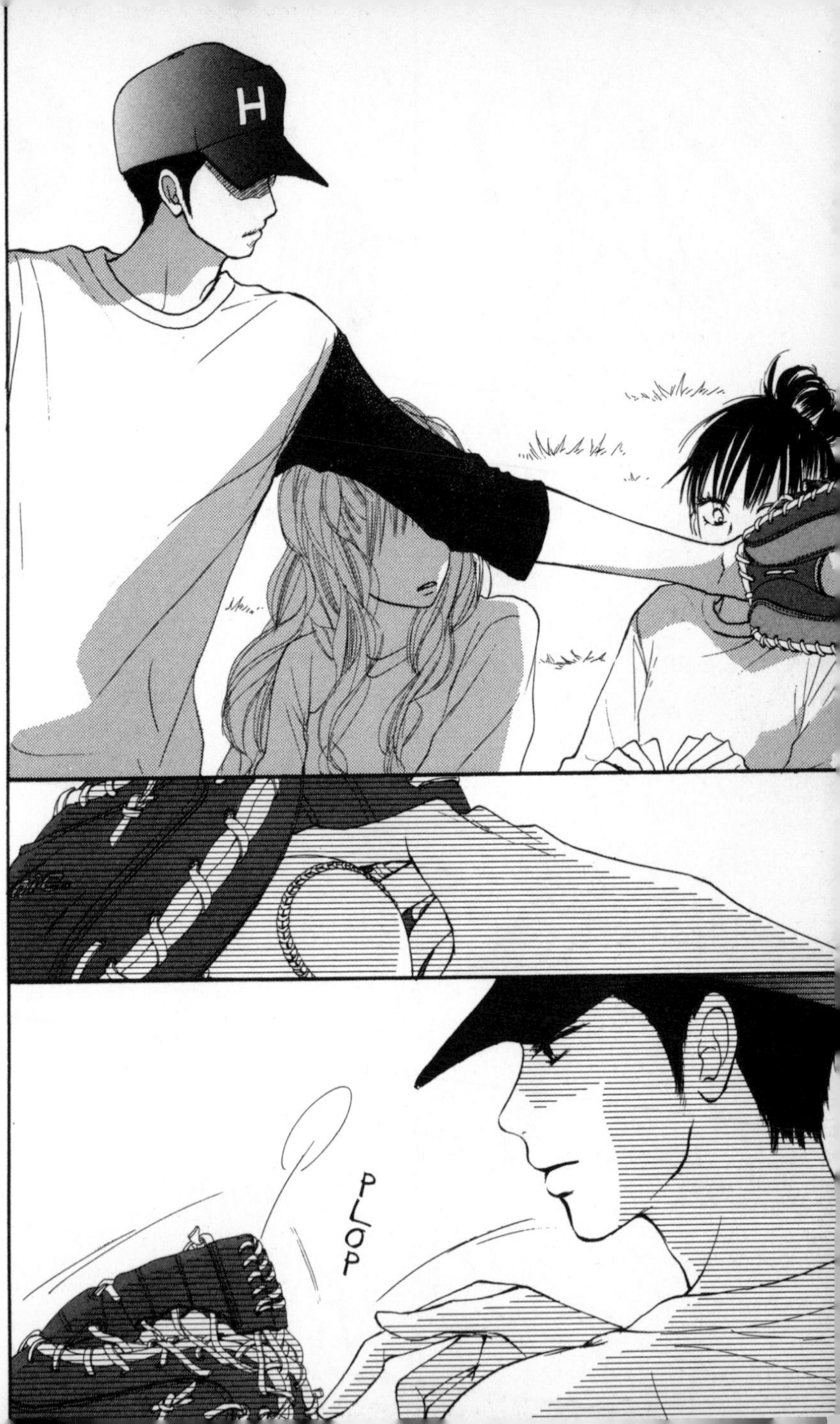
PLOP

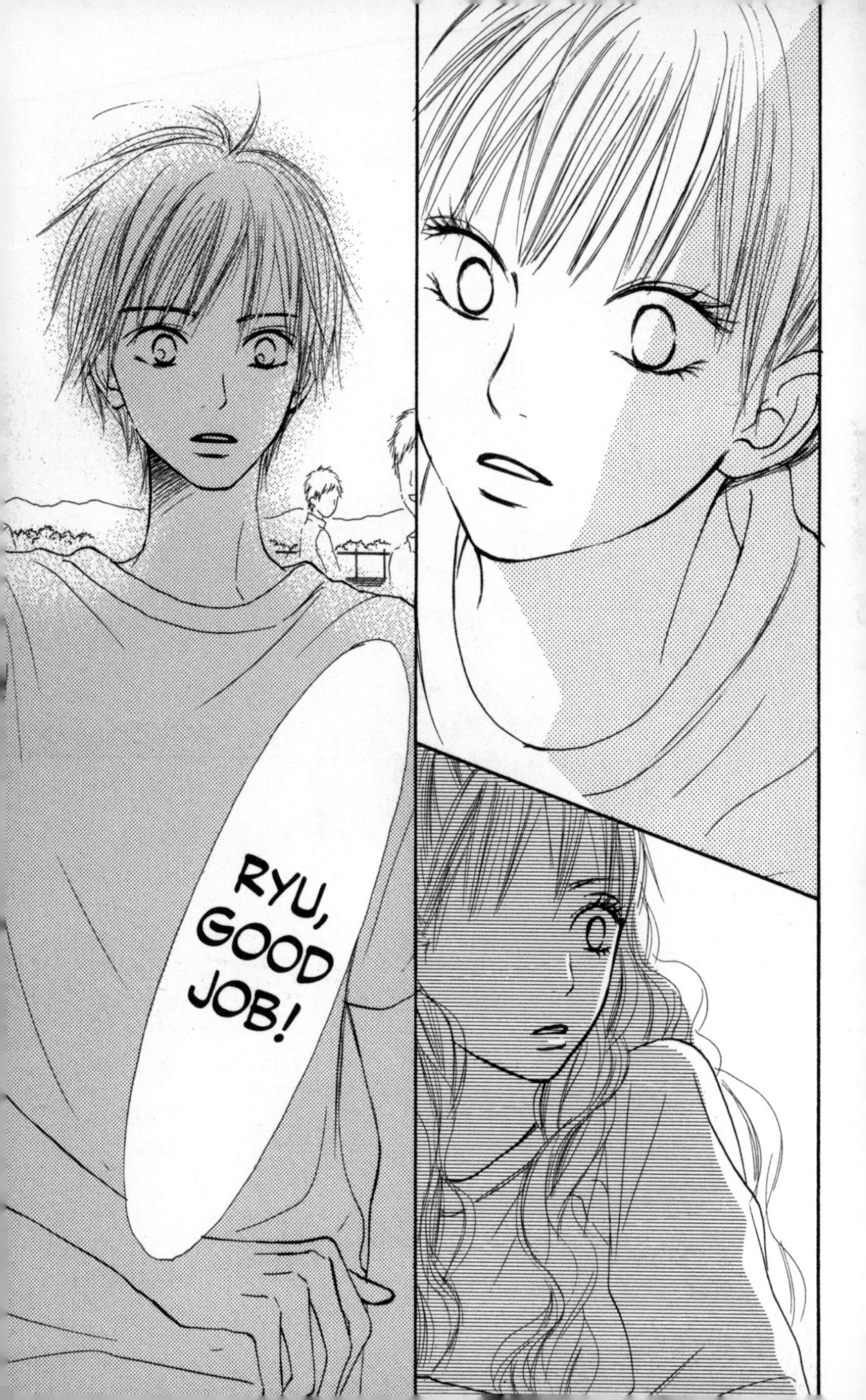
RYU, GOOD JOB!

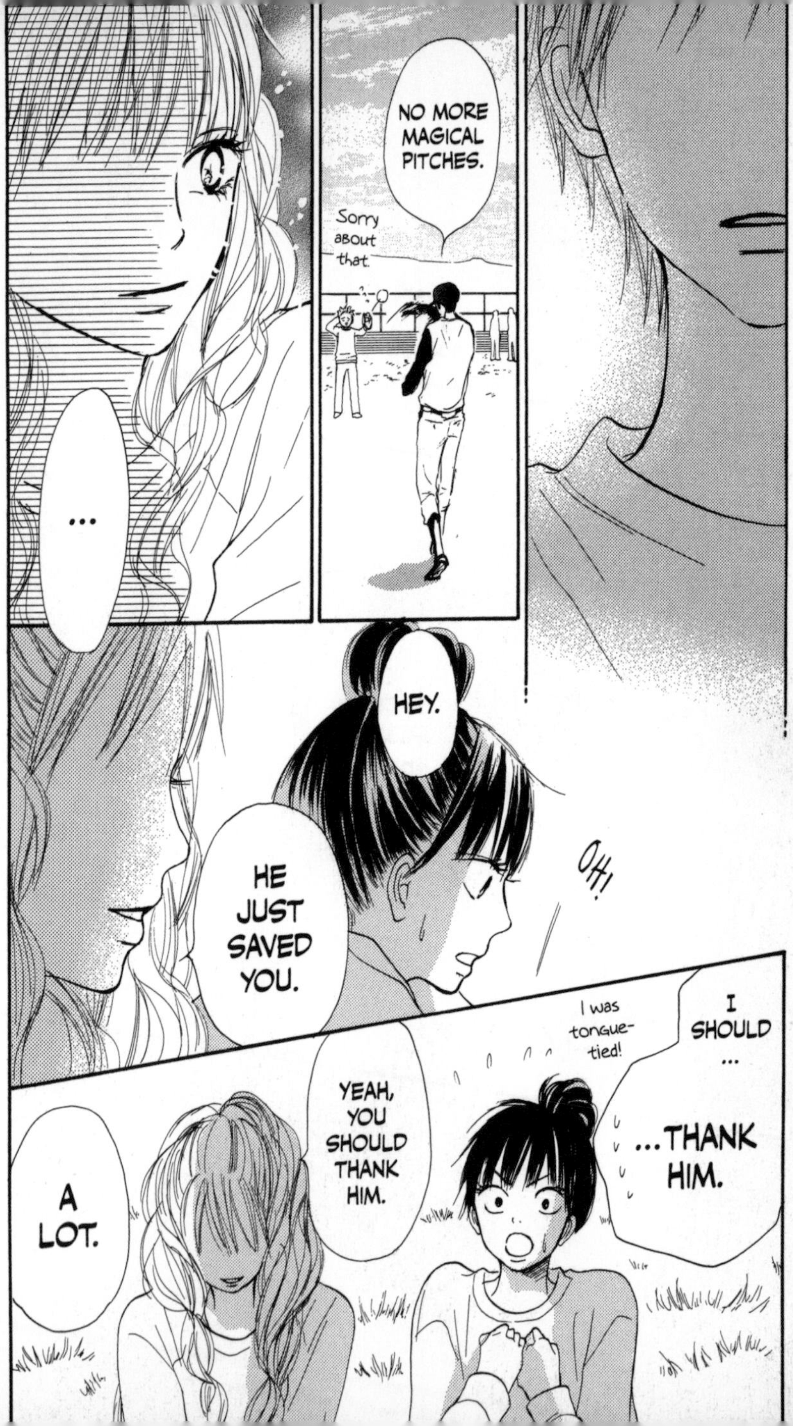
NO MORE MAGICAL PITCHES.
Sorry about that.
...
HEY.
OH!
HE JUST SAVED YOU.
I SHOULD ...
...THANK HIM.
I was tongue-tied!
YEAH, YOU SHOULD THANK HIM.
A LOT.

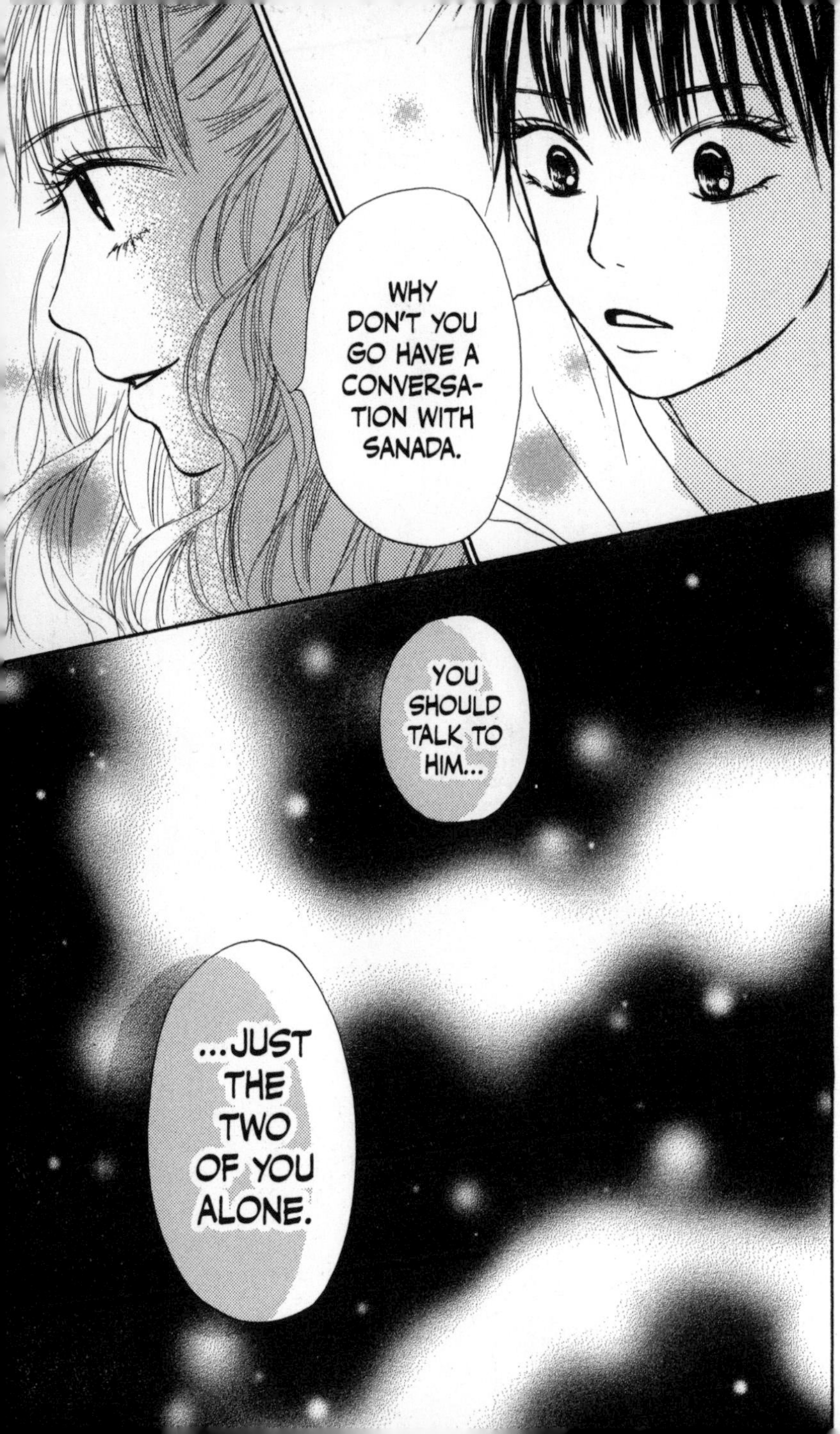
WHY DON'T YOU GO HAVE A CONVERSA-TION WITH SANADA.
YOU SHOULD TALK TO HIM...
...JUST THE TWO OF YOU ALONE.

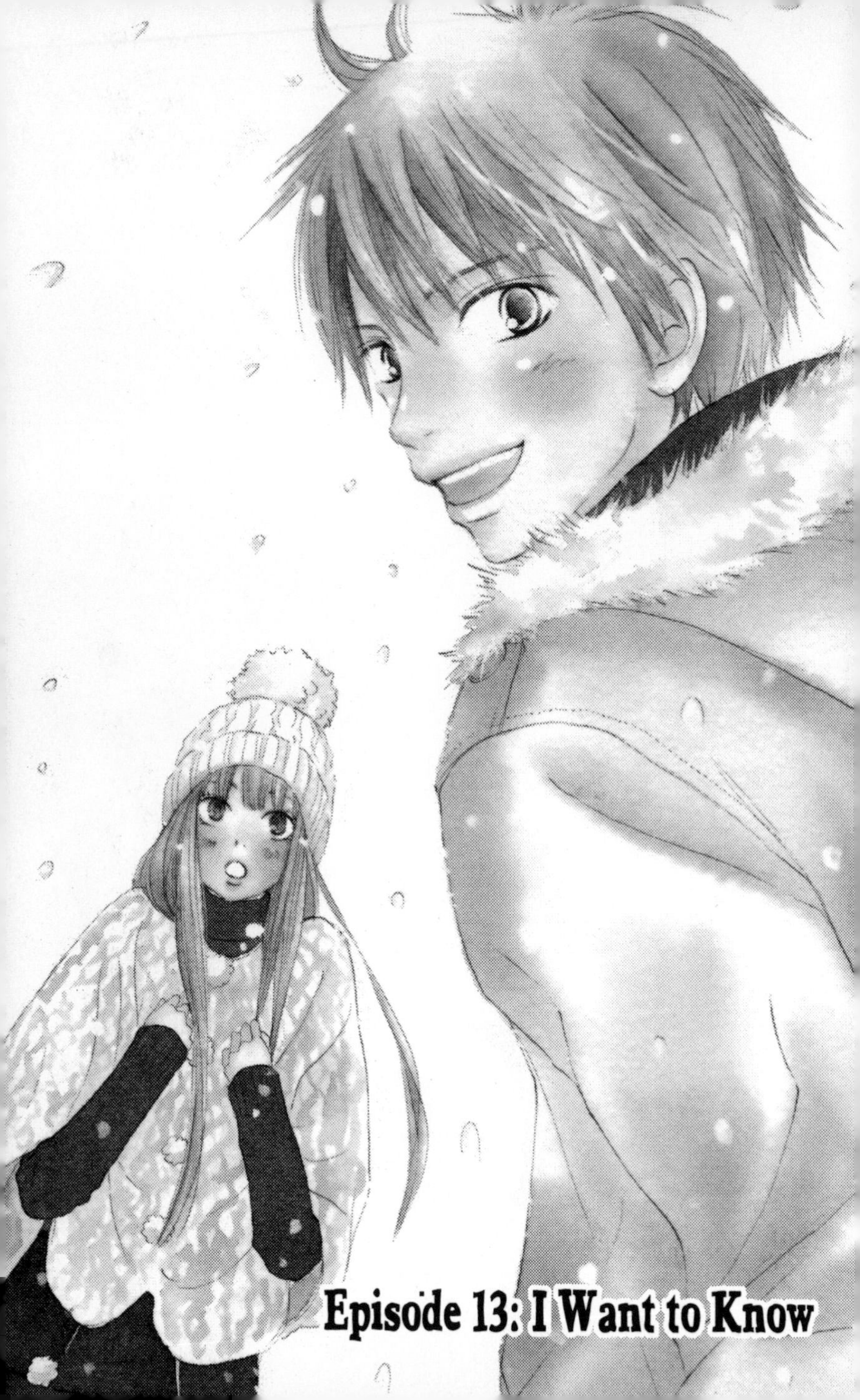

Episode 13: I Want to Know

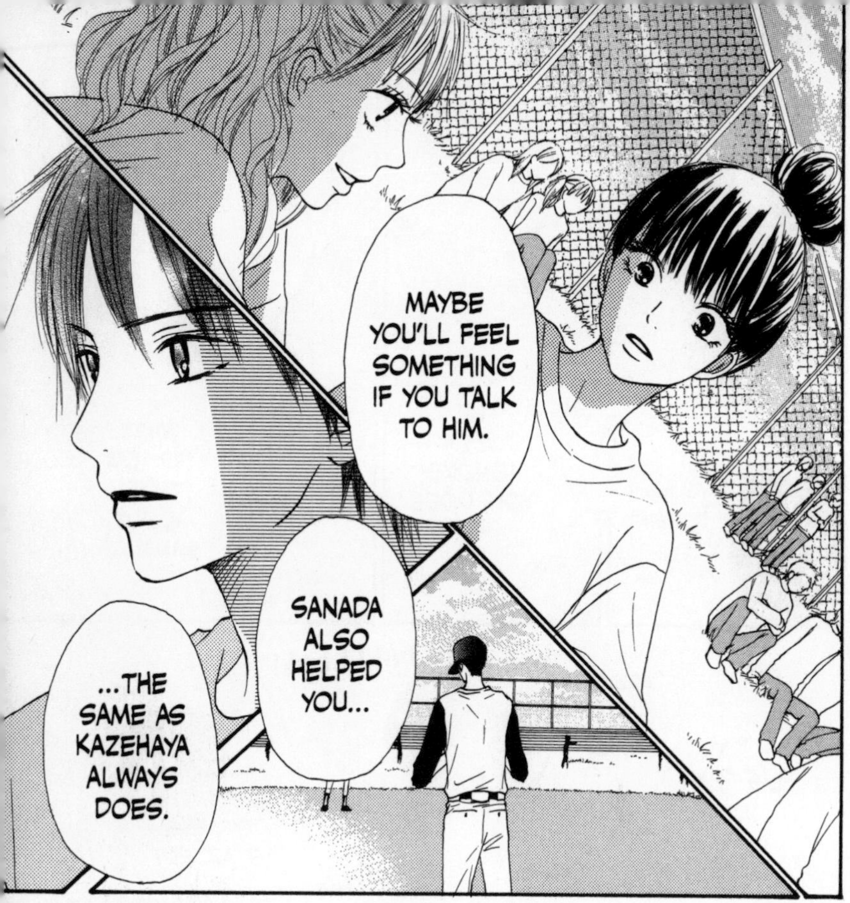
MAYBE YOU'LL FEEL SOMETHING IF YOU TALK TO HIM.
SANADA ALSO HELPED YOU...
...THE SAME AS KAZEHAYA ALWAYS DOES.

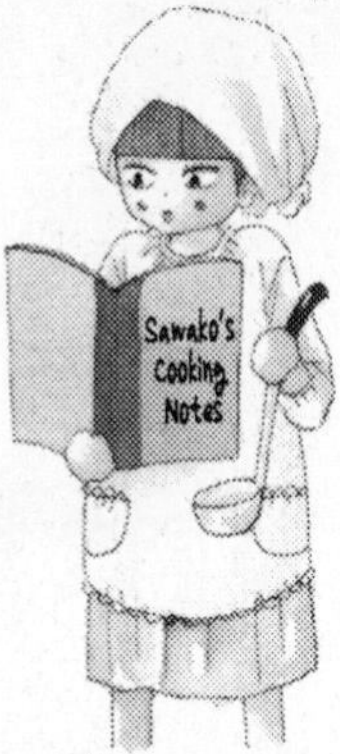
Sawako's Cooking Notes

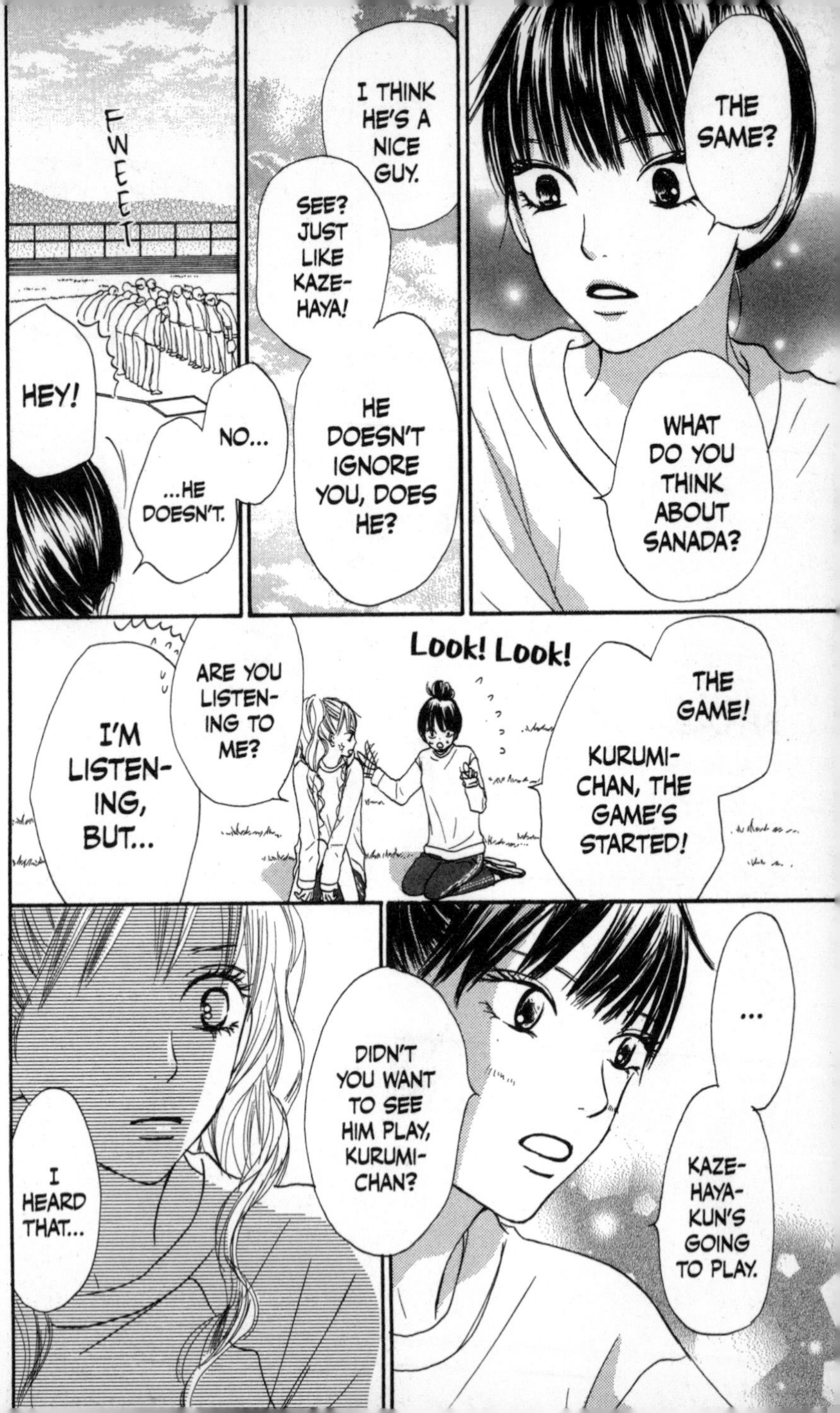
THE SAME?
WHAT DO YOU THINK ABOUT SANADA?
I THINK HE'S A NICE GUY.
SEE? JUST LIKE KAZE-HAYA!
HE DOESN'T IGNORE YOU, DOES HE?
FWEET
NO...
...HE DOESN'T.
HEY!
THE GAME!
KURUMI-CHAN, THE GAME'S STARTED!
Look! Look!
ARE YOU LISTENING TO ME?
I'M LISTENING, BUT...
...
KAZE-HAYA-KUN'S GOING TO PLAY.
DIDN'T YOU WANT TO SEE HIM PLAY, KURUMI-CHAN?
I HEARD THAT...

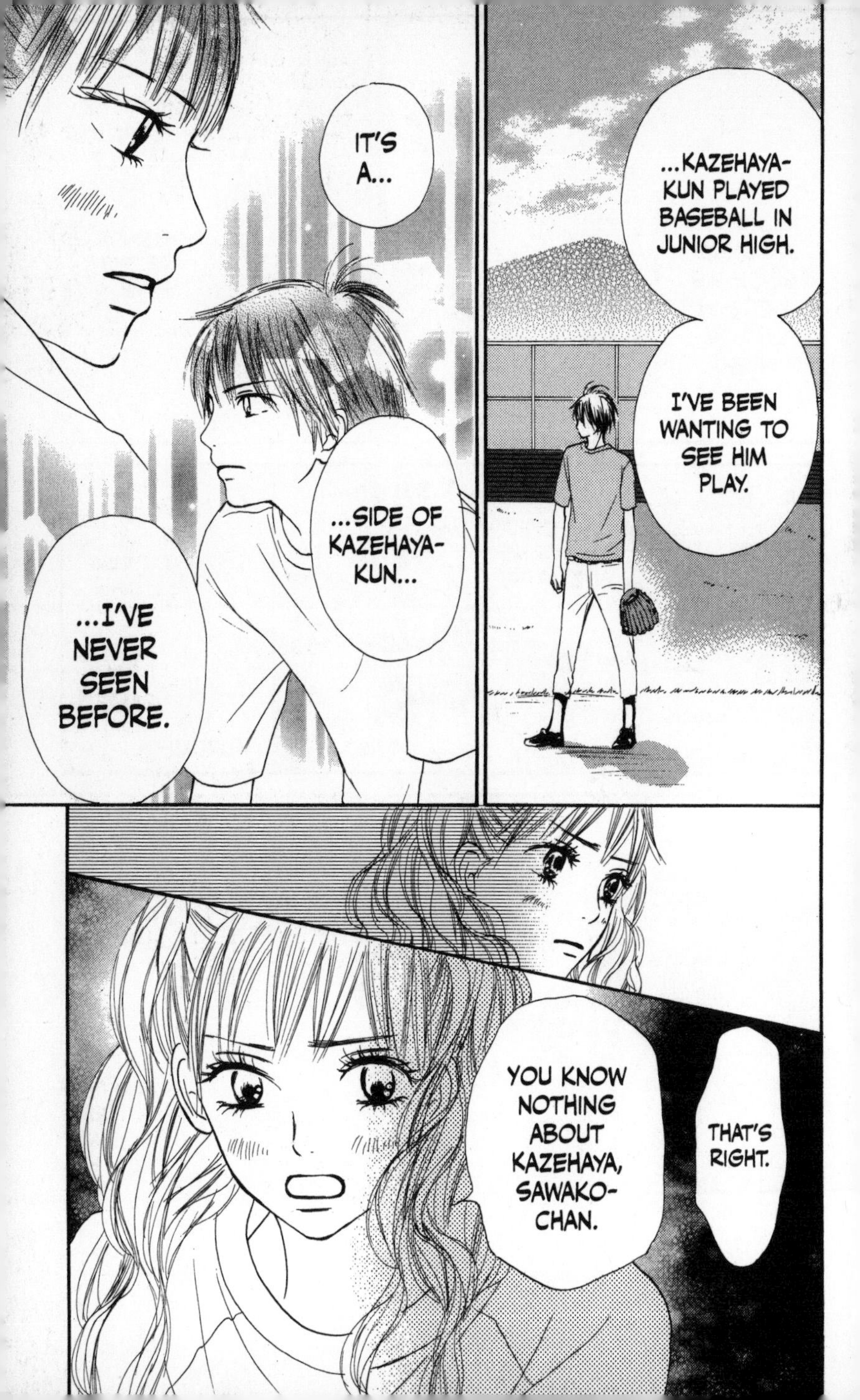
...KAZEHAYA-KUN PLAYED BASEBALL IN JUNIOR HIGH.
I'VE BEEN WANTING TO SEE HIM PLAY.
IT'S A...
...SIDE OF KAZEHAYA-KUN...
...I'VE NEVER SEEN BEFORE.
THAT'S RIGHT.
YOU KNOW NOTHING ABOUT KAZEHAYA, SAWAKO-CHAN.

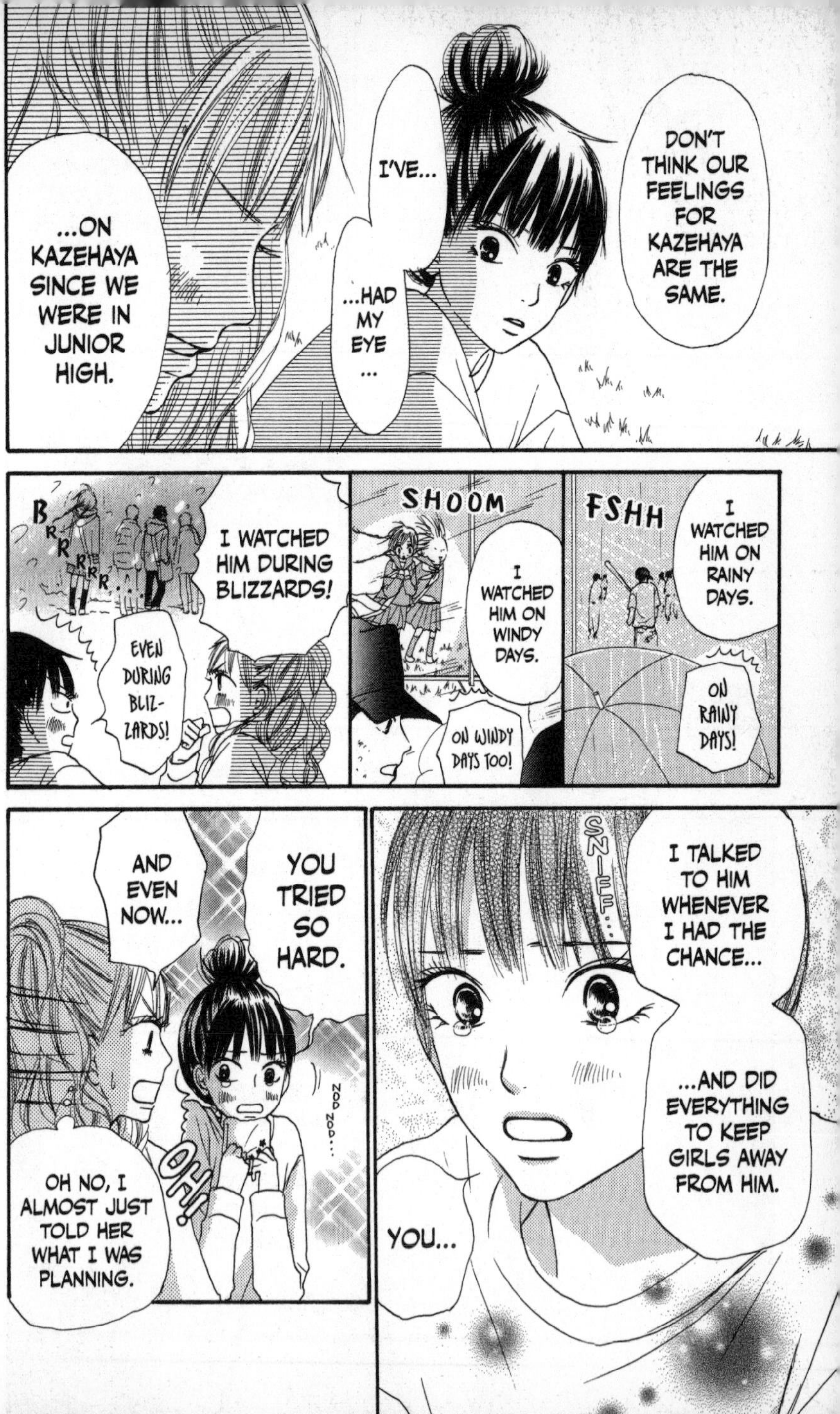
DON'T THINK OUR FEELINGS FOR KAZEHAYA ARE THE SAME.
I'VE...
...HAD MY EYE...
...ON KAZEHAYA SINCE WE WERE IN JUNIOR HIGH.
FSHH
I WATCHED HIM ON RAINY DAYS.
ON RAINY DAYS!
SHOOM
I WATCHED HIM ON WINDY DAYS.
ON WINDY DAYS TOO!
I WATCHED HIM DURING BLIZZARDS!
BRRRRRR
EVEN DURING BLIZ-ZARDS!
SNIFF...
I TALKED TO HIM WHENEVER I HAD THE CHANCE...
...AND DID EVERYTHING TO KEEP GIRLS AWAY FROM HIM.
YOU...
YOU TRIED SO HARD.
AND EVEN NOW...
NOD NOD...
OH!
OH NO, I ALMOST JUST TOLD HER WHAT I WAS PLANNING.

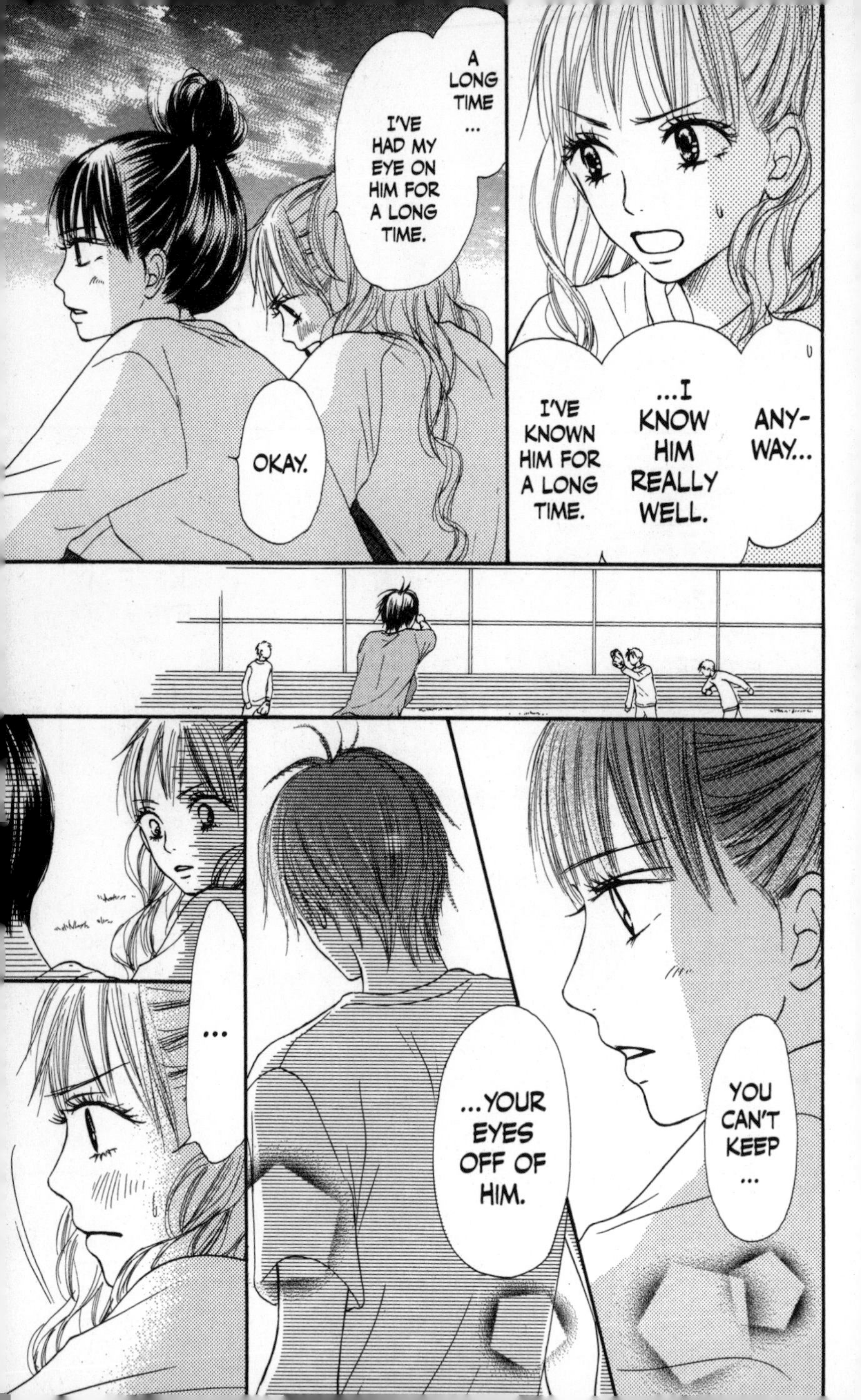
ANYWAY...
...I KNOW HIM REALLY WELL.
I'VE KNOWN HIM FOR A LONG TIME.
A LONG TIME...
I'VE HAD MY EYE ON HIM FOR A LONG TIME.
OKAY.
YOU CAN'T KEEP...
...YOUR EYES OFF OF HIM.
...

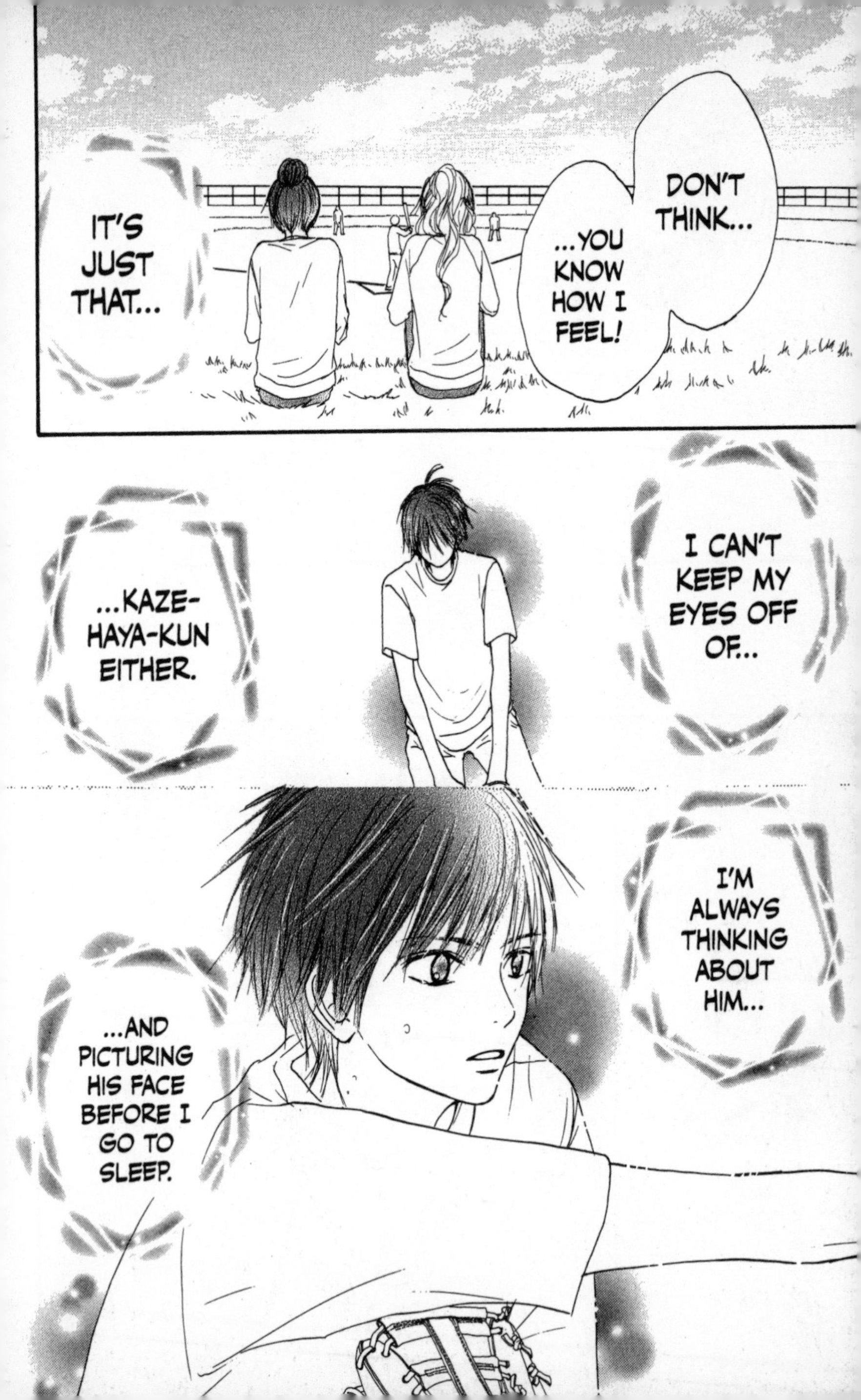
DON'T THINK...
...YOU KNOW HOW I FEEL!
IT'S JUST THAT...
I CAN'T KEEP MY EYES OFF OF...
...KAZE-HAYA-KUN EITHER.
I'M ALWAYS THINKING ABOUT HIM...
...AND PICTURING HIS FACE BEFORE I GO TO SLEEP.

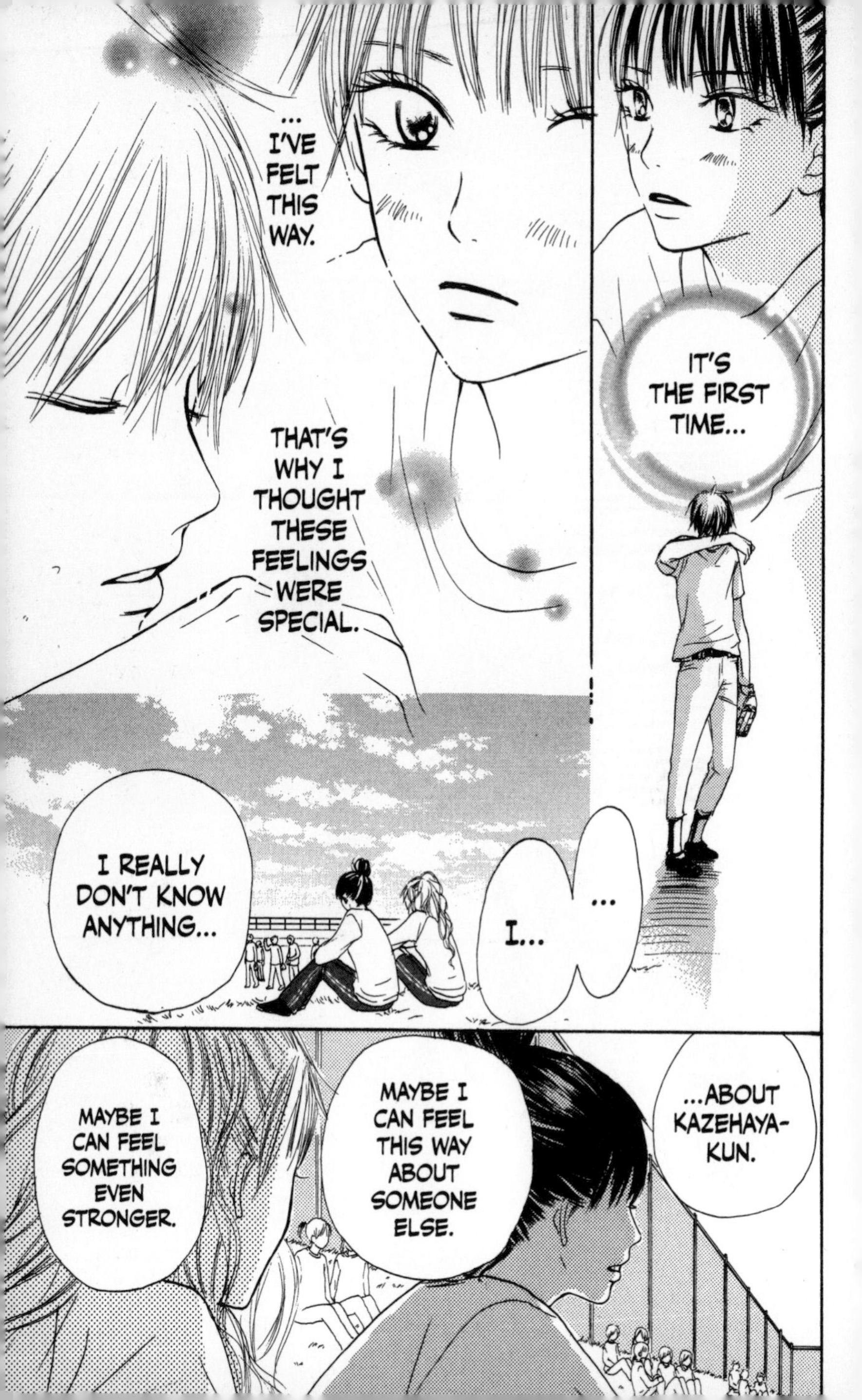
IT'S THE FIRST TIME...
...I'VE FELT THIS WAY.
THAT'S WHY I THOUGHT THESE FEELINGS WERE SPECIAL.
... I...
I REALLY DON'T KNOW ANYTHING...
...ABOUT KAZEHAYA-KUN.
MAYBE I CAN FEEL THIS WAY ABOUT SOMEONE ELSE.
MAYBE I CAN FEEL SOMETHING EVEN STRONGER.

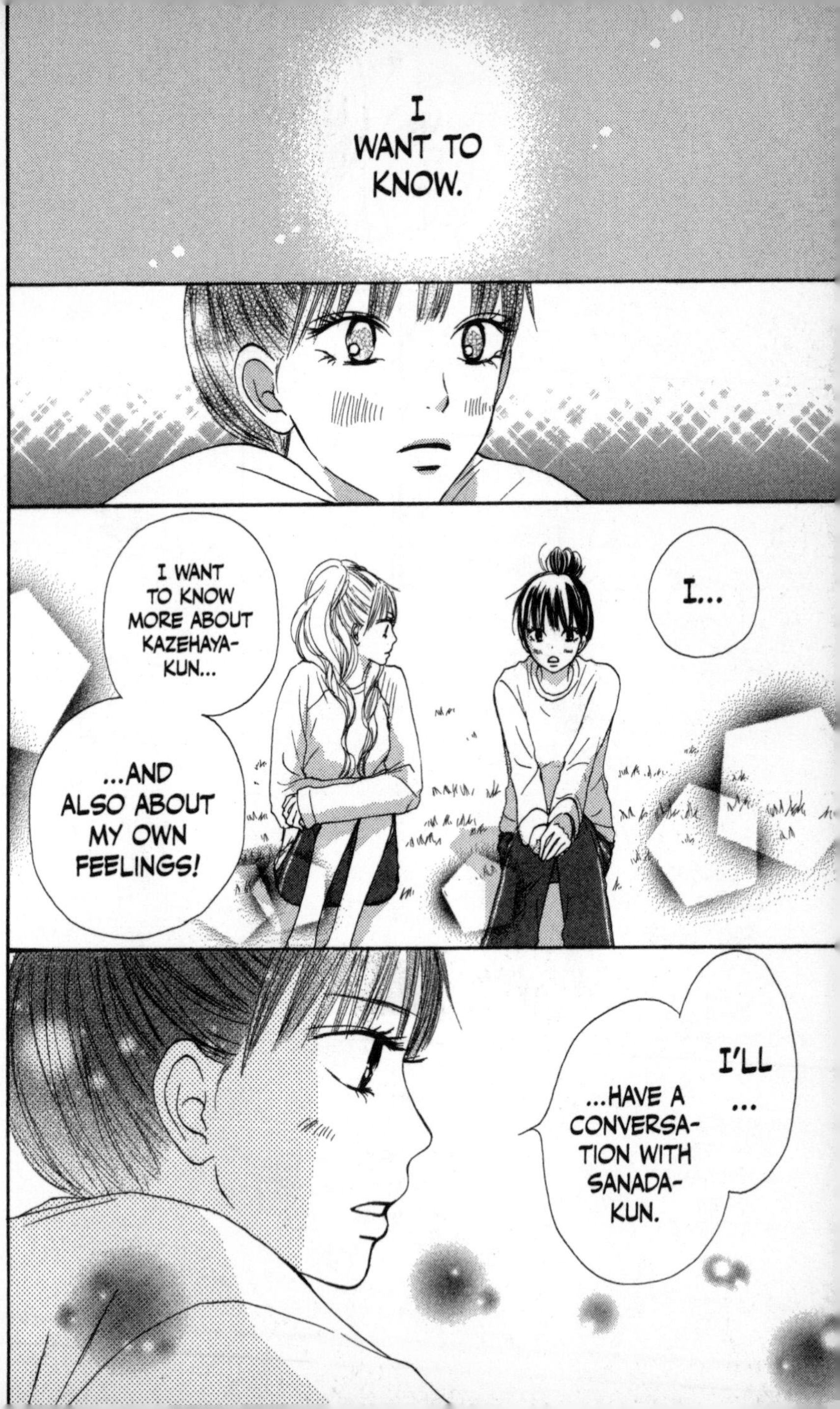
I WANT TO KNOW.
I...
I WANT TO KNOW MORE ABOUT KAZEHAYA-KUN...
...AND ALSO ABOUT MY OWN FEELINGS!
I'LL...
...HAVE A CONVERSATION WITH SANADA-KUN.

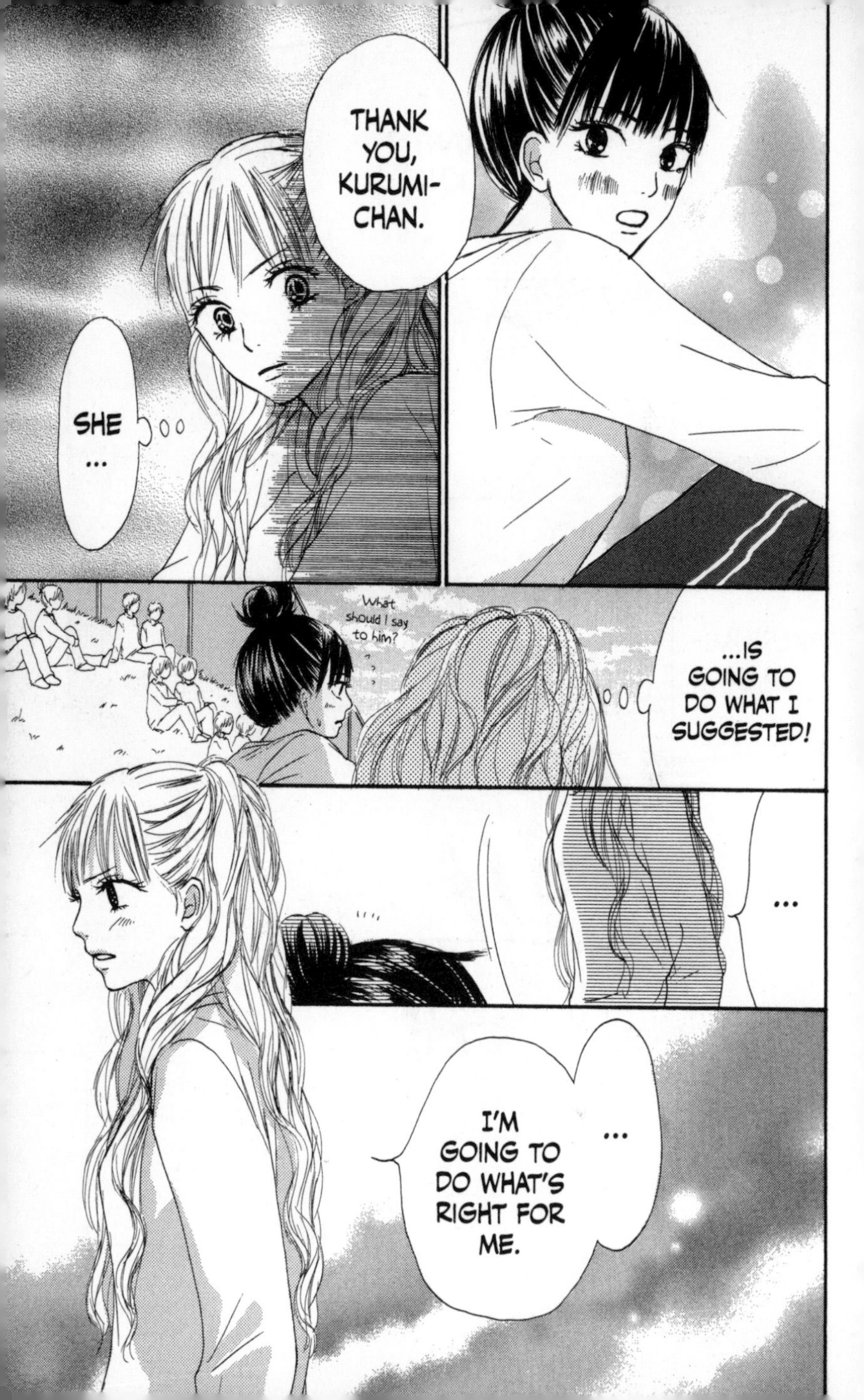
THANK YOU, KURUMI-CHAN.
SHE ...
...IS GOING TO DO WHAT I SUGGESTED!
What should I say to him?
...
... I'M GOING TO DO WHAT'S RIGHT FOR ME.

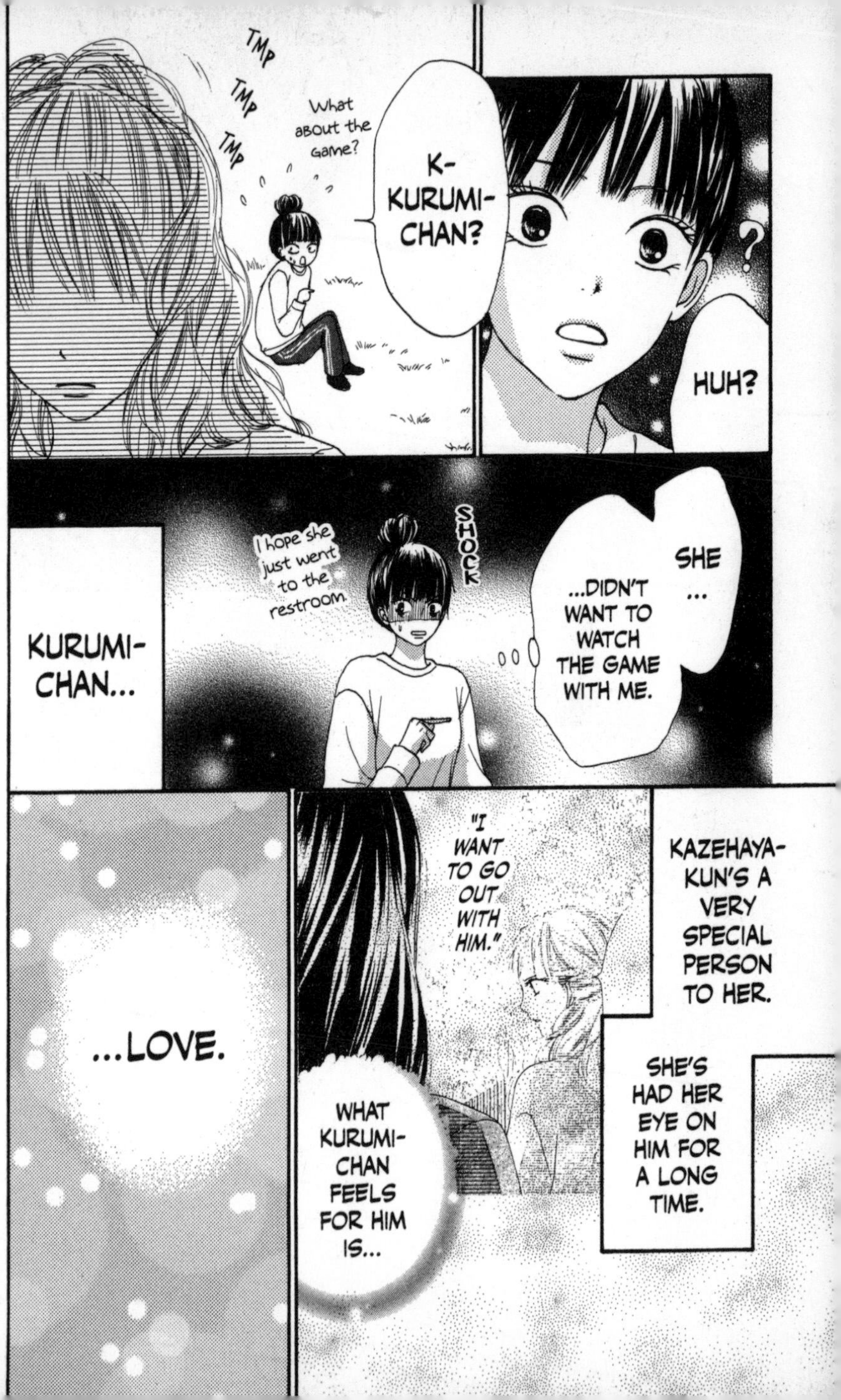

K-KURUMI-CHAN?
HUH?
TMP TMP TMP
What about the game?
SHE ...
...DIDN'T WANT TO WATCH THE GAME WITH ME.
SHOCK
I hope she just went to the restroom.
KURUMI-CHAN...
KAZEHAYA-KUN'S A VERY SPECIAL PERSON TO HER.
SHE'S HAD HER EYE ON HIM FOR A LONG TIME.
"I WANT TO GO OUT WITH HIM."
WHAT KURUMI-CHAN FEELS FOR HIM IS...
...LOVE.

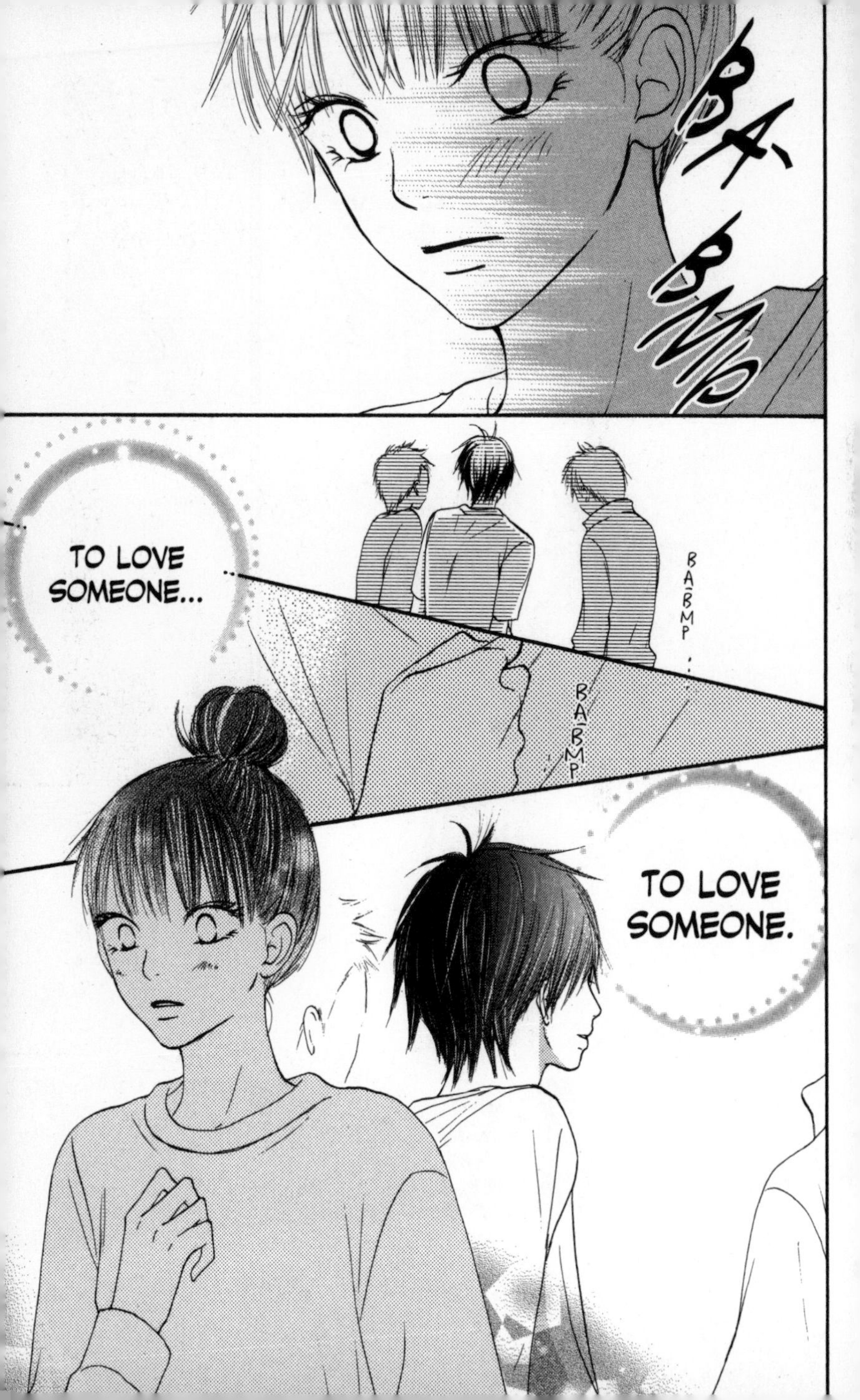
BA-BMP
BA-BMP
BA-BMP
TO LOVE SOMEONE...
TO LOVE SOMEONE.

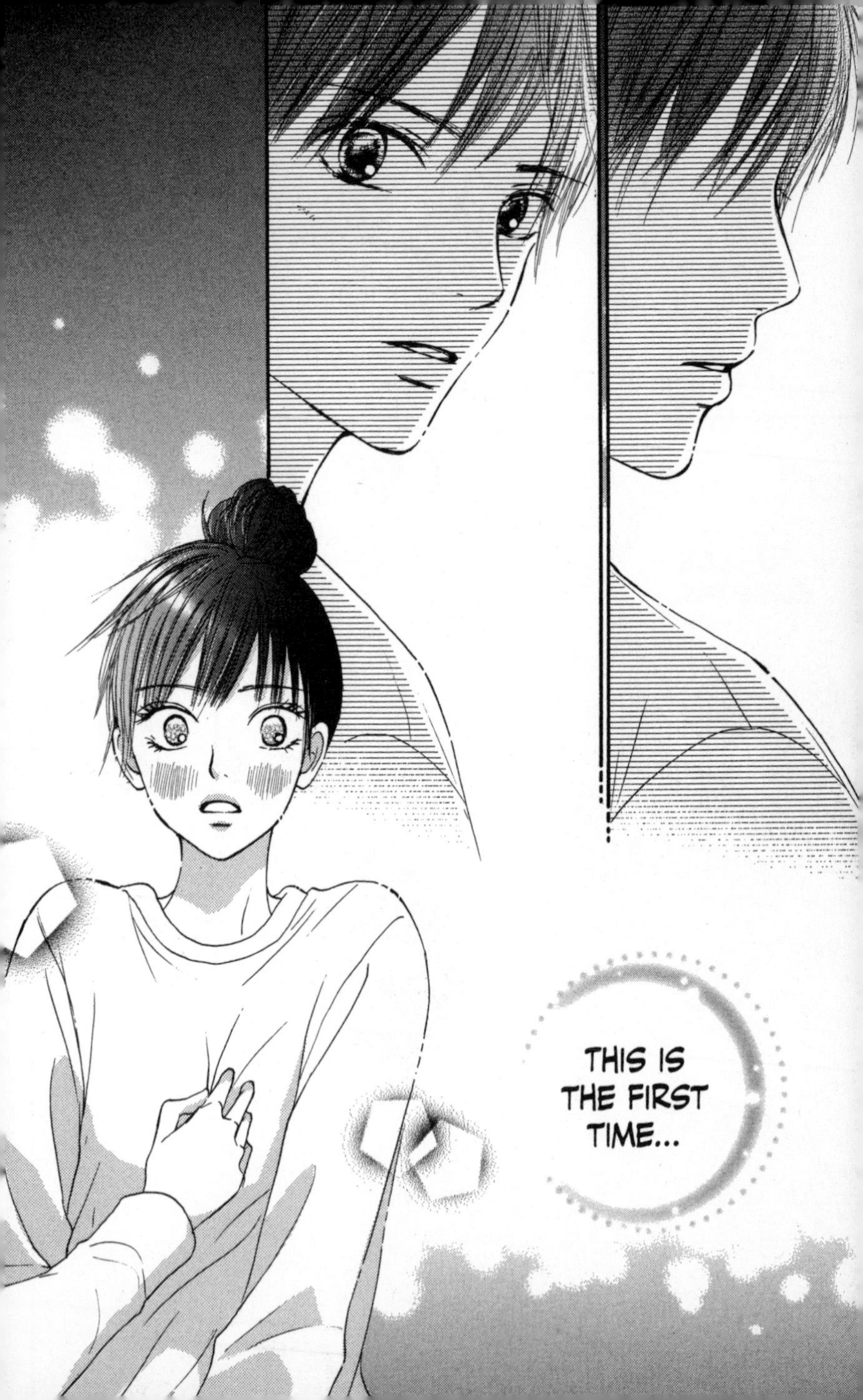
THIS IS THE FIRST TIME...

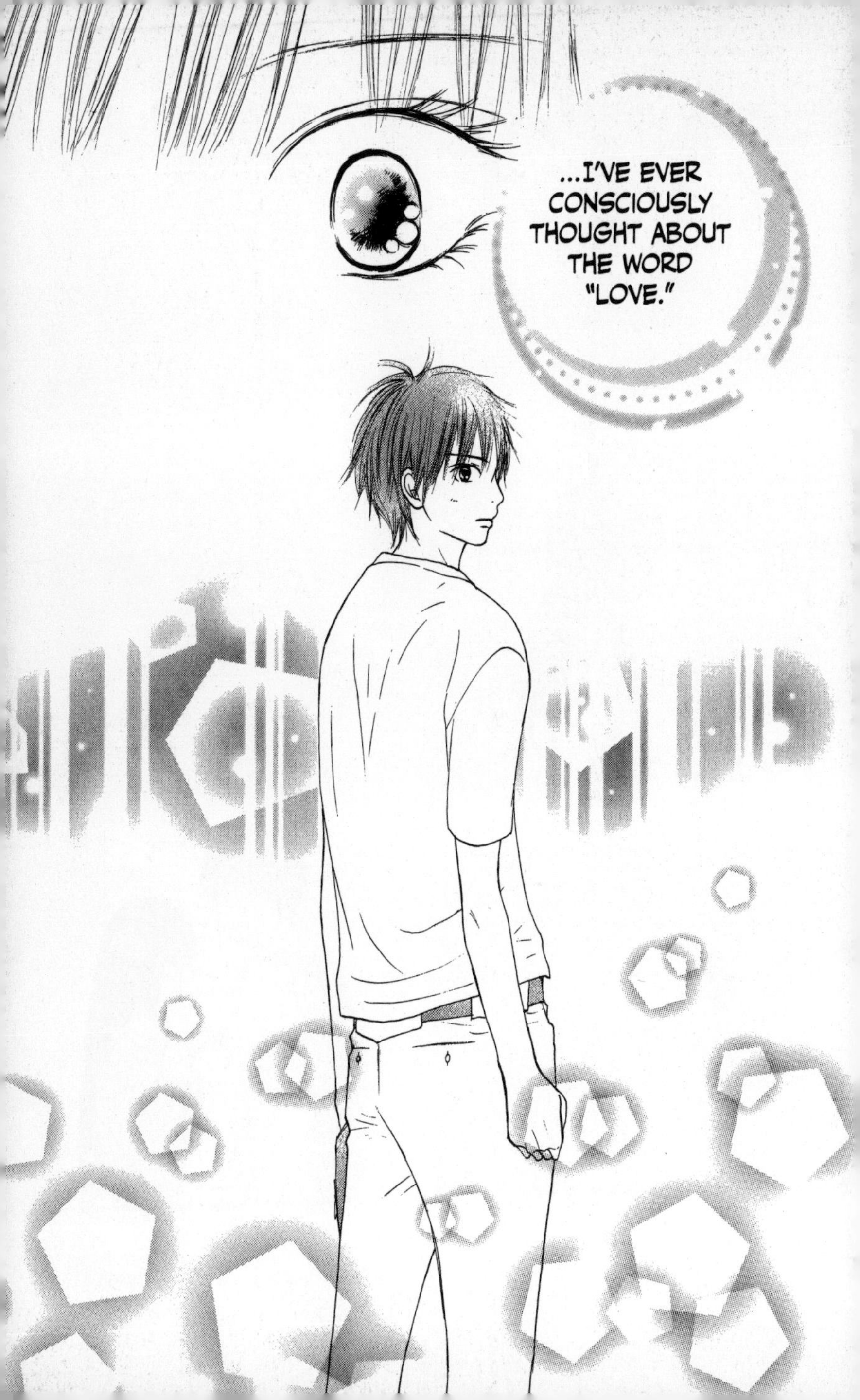
...I'VE EVER CONSCIOUSLY THOUGHT ABOUT THE WORD "LOVE."

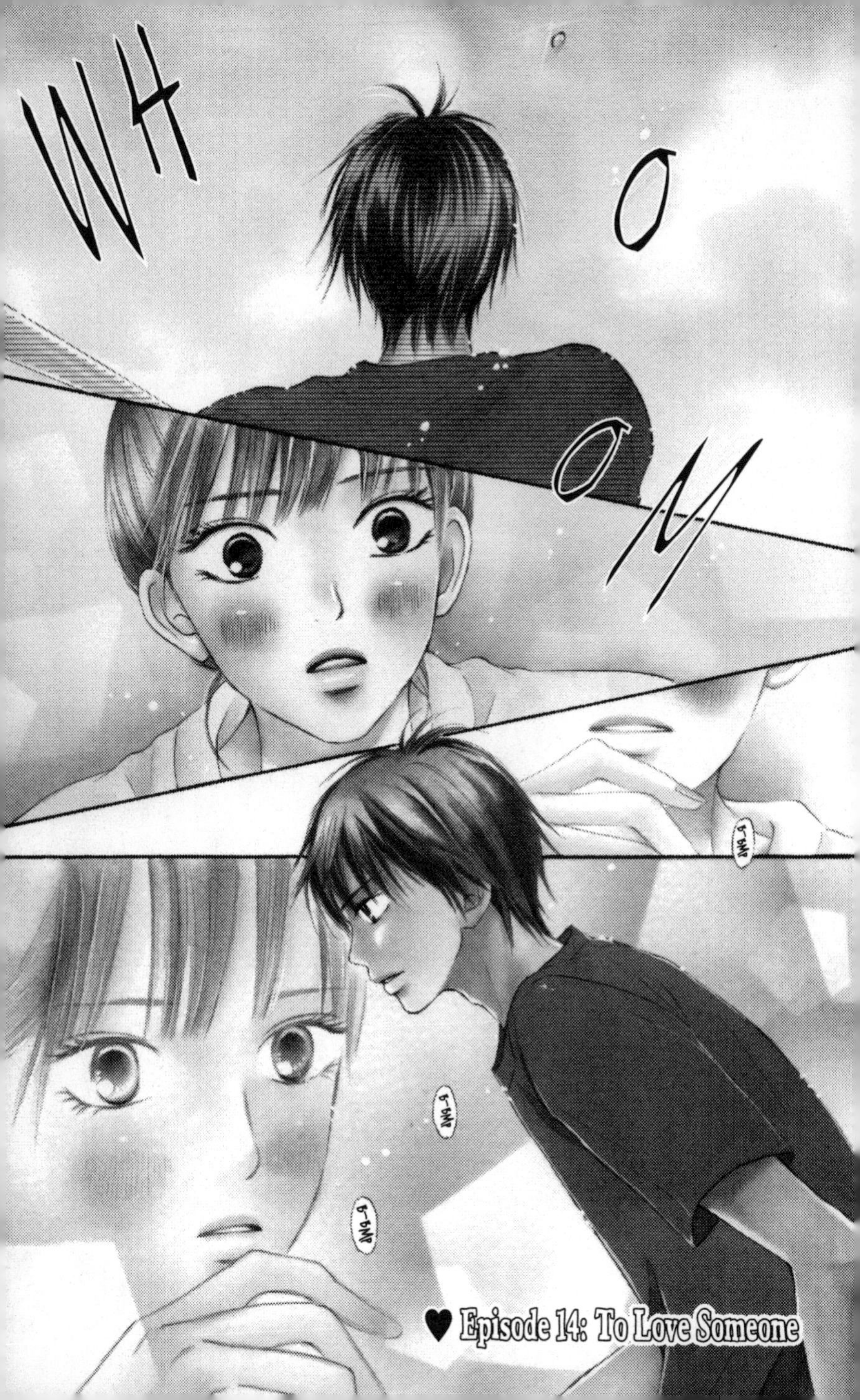
WHOOM
B-BMP
B-BMP
B-BMP
♥ Episode 14: To Love Someone

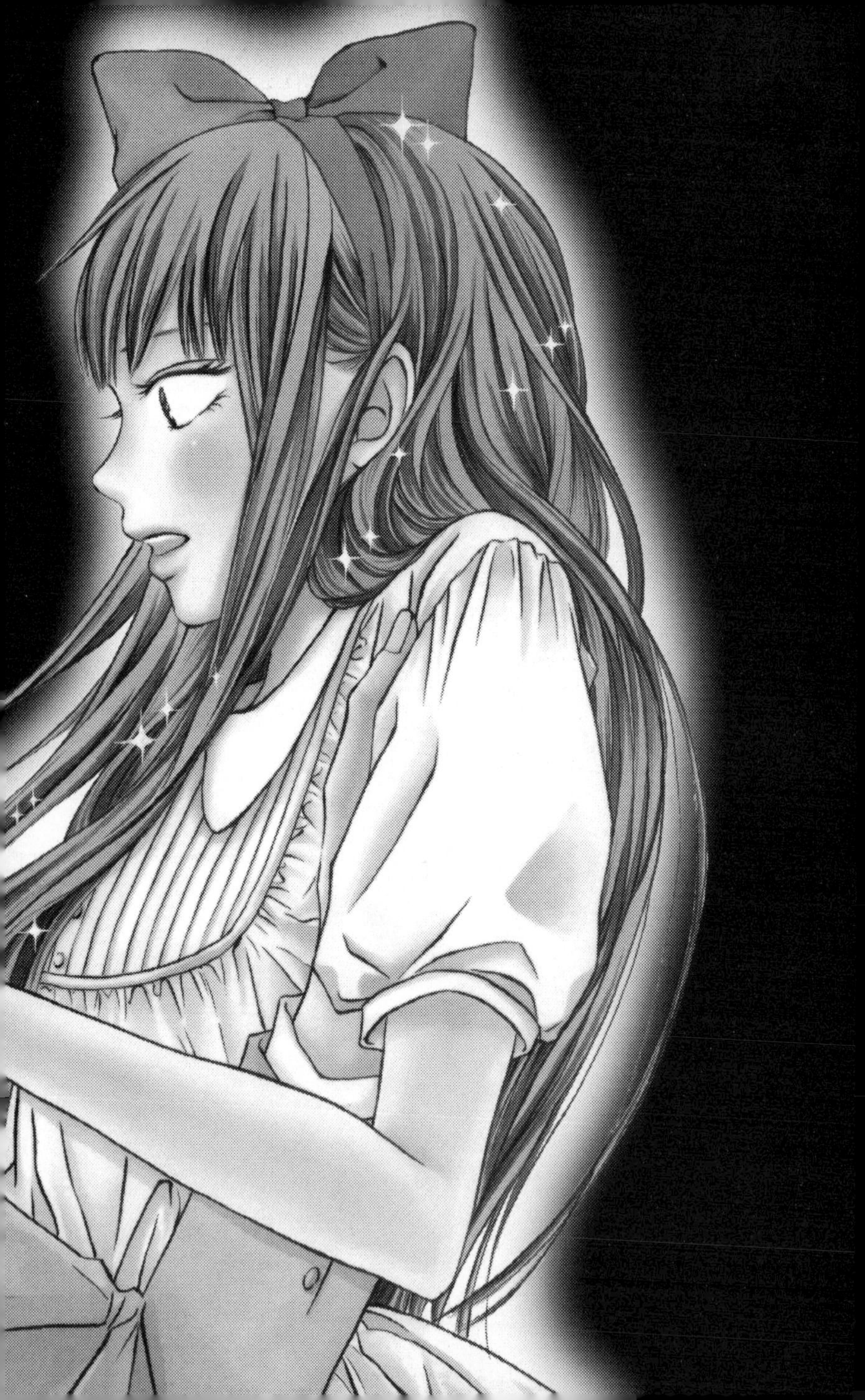

Episode 14: To Love Someone

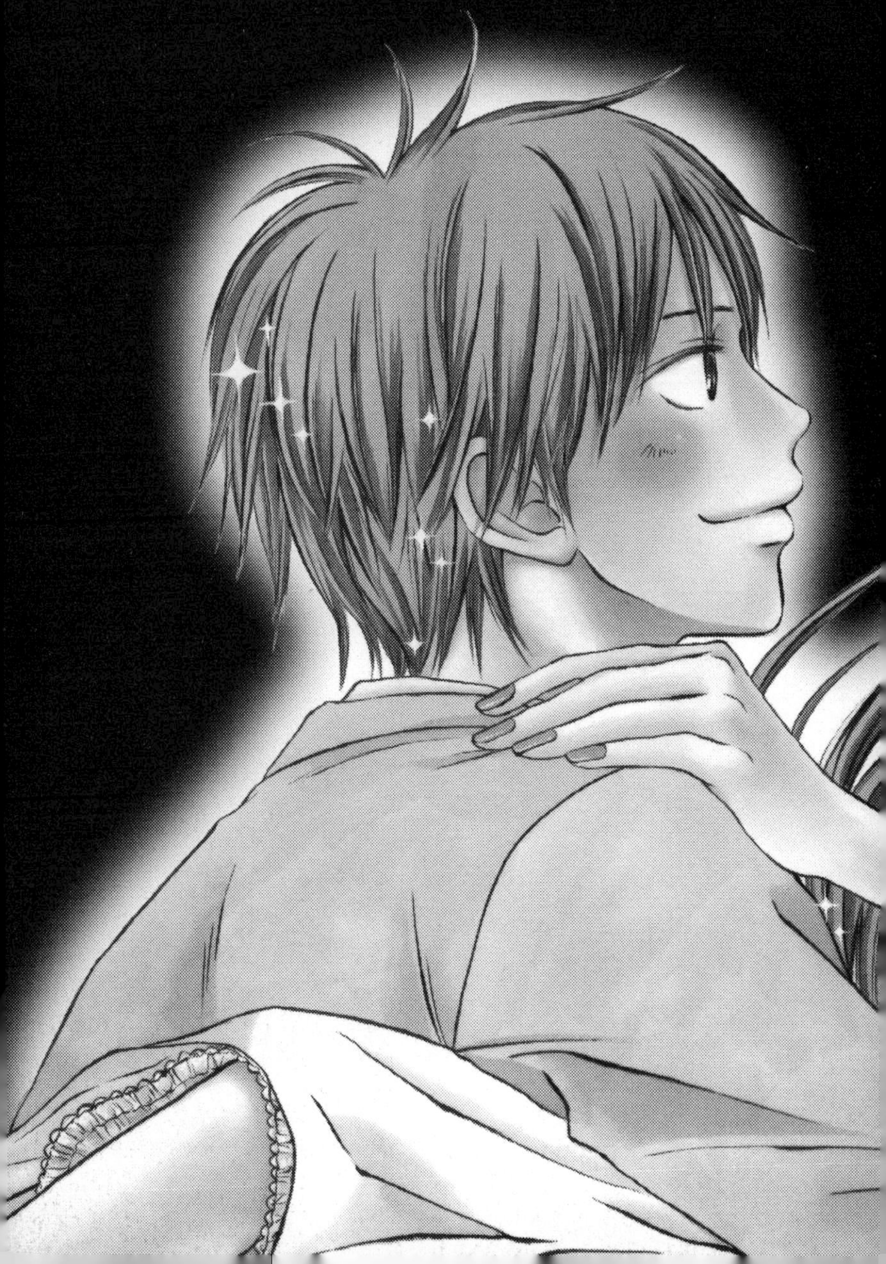

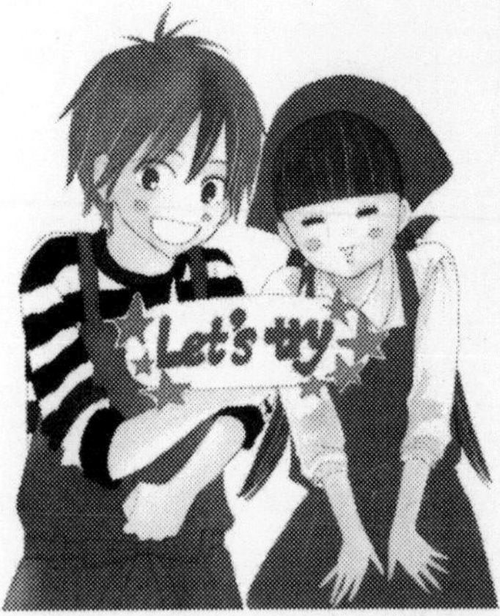
Let's try

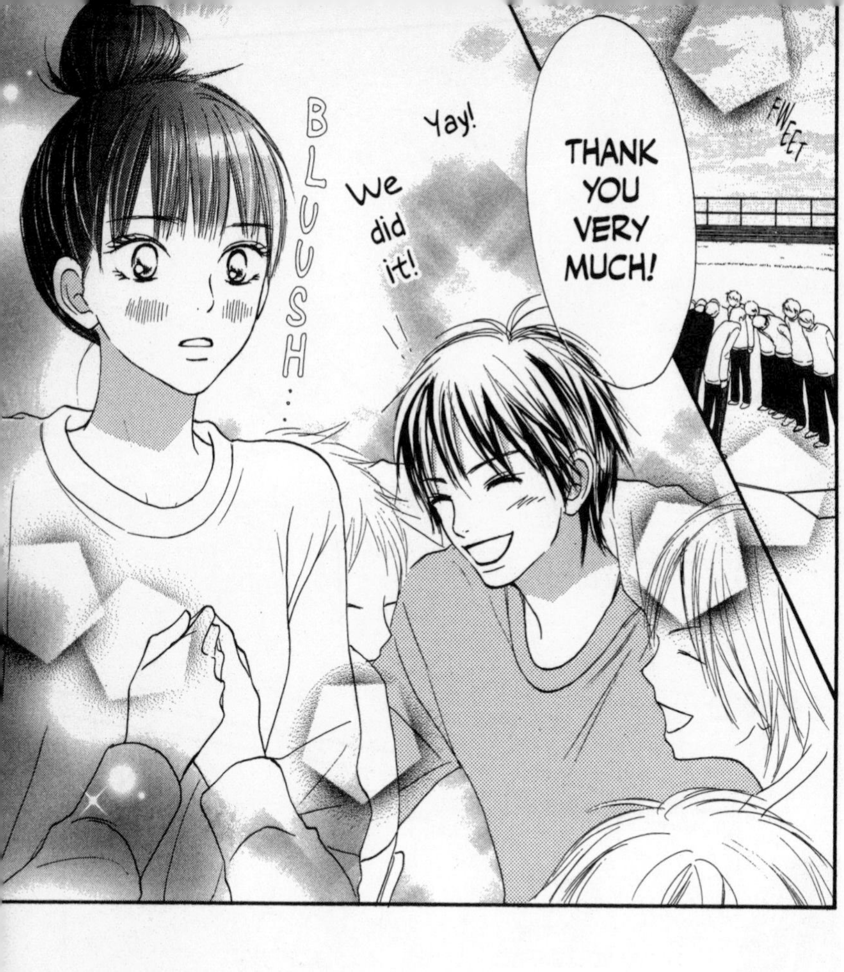
FWEEET
THANK YOU VERY MUCH!
Yay!
We did it!
BLUUSH...

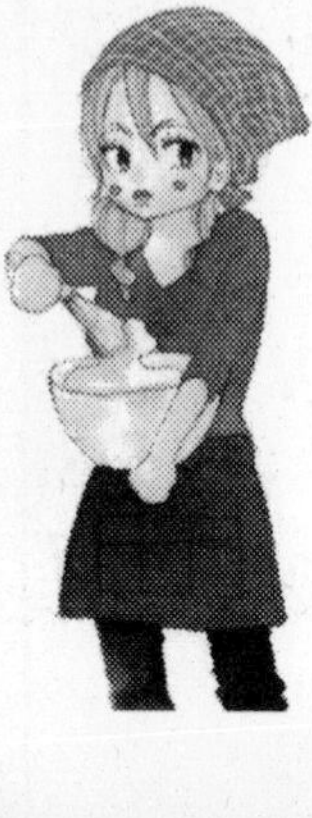

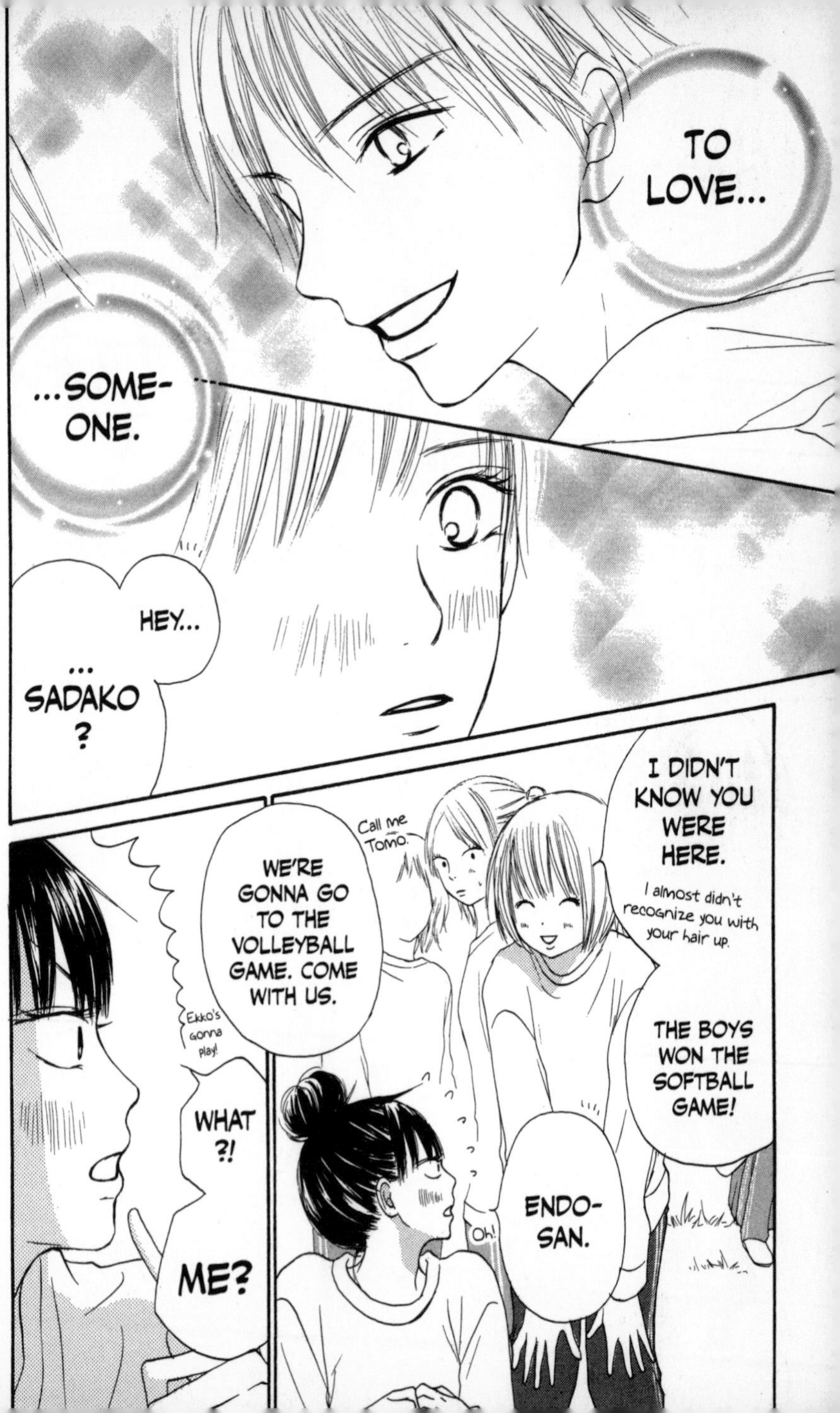
TO LOVE...
...SOME-ONE.
HEY...
...SADAKO?
I DIDN'T KNOW YOU WERE HERE.
I almost didn't recognize you with your hair up.
THE BOYS WON THE SOFTBALL GAME!
ENDO-SAN.
Oh!
Call me Tomo.
WE'RE GONNA GO TO THE VOLLEYBALL GAME. COME WITH US.
Ekko's gonna play!
WHAT?!
ME?

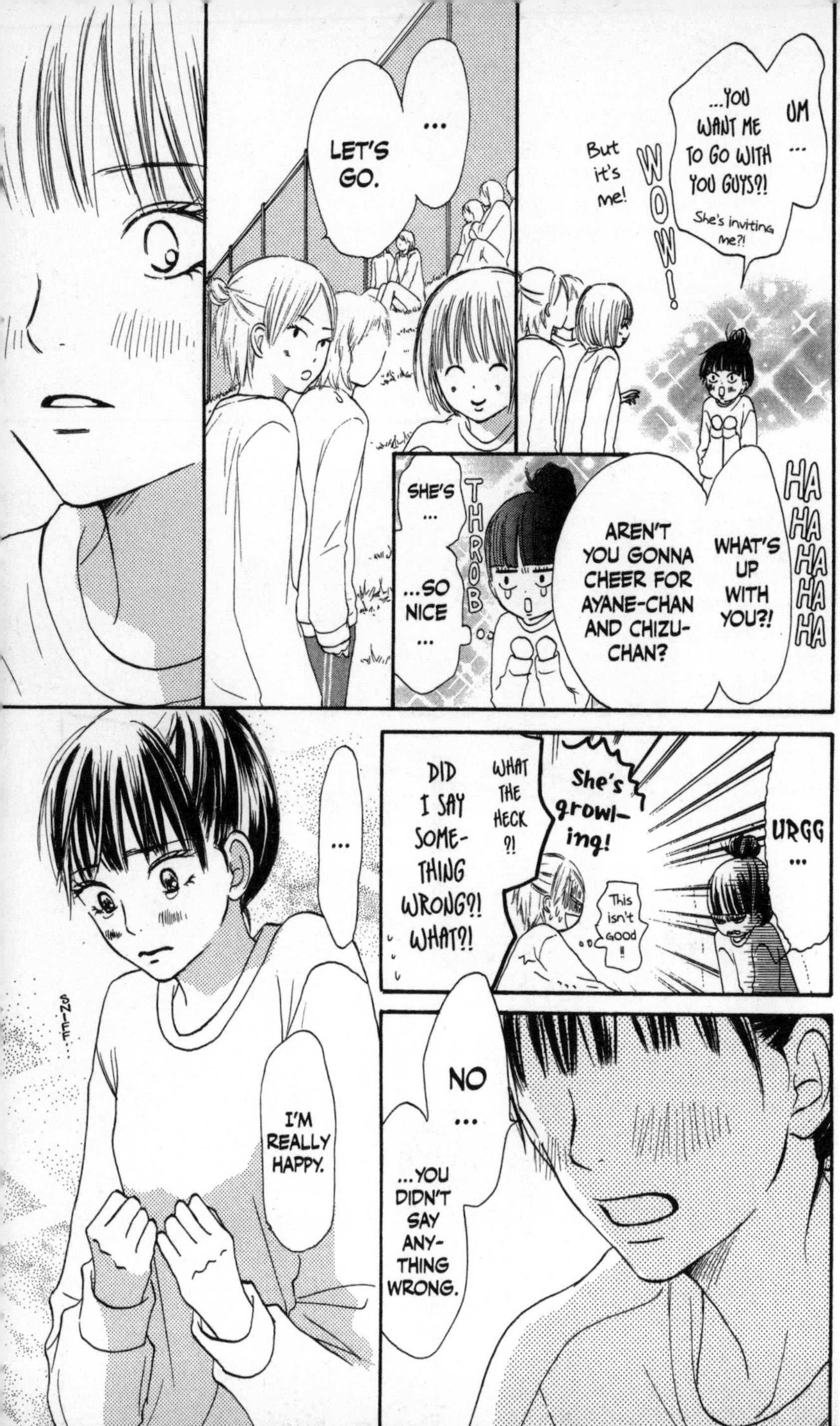
UM ...
...YOU WANT ME TO GO WITH YOU GUYS?!
She's inviting me?!
WOW!
But it's me!
HA HA HA HA HA
WHAT'S UP WITH YOU?!
AREN'T YOU GONNA CHEER FOR AYANE-CHAN AND CHIZU-CHAN?
THROB
SHE'S ...
...SO NICE ...
... LET'S GO.
URGG ...
This isn't good !!
She's growl-ing!
WHAT THE HECK ?!
DID I SAY SOME-THING WRONG?! WHAT?!
NO ...
...YOU DIDN'T SAY ANY-THING WRONG.
...
I'M REALLY HAPPY.

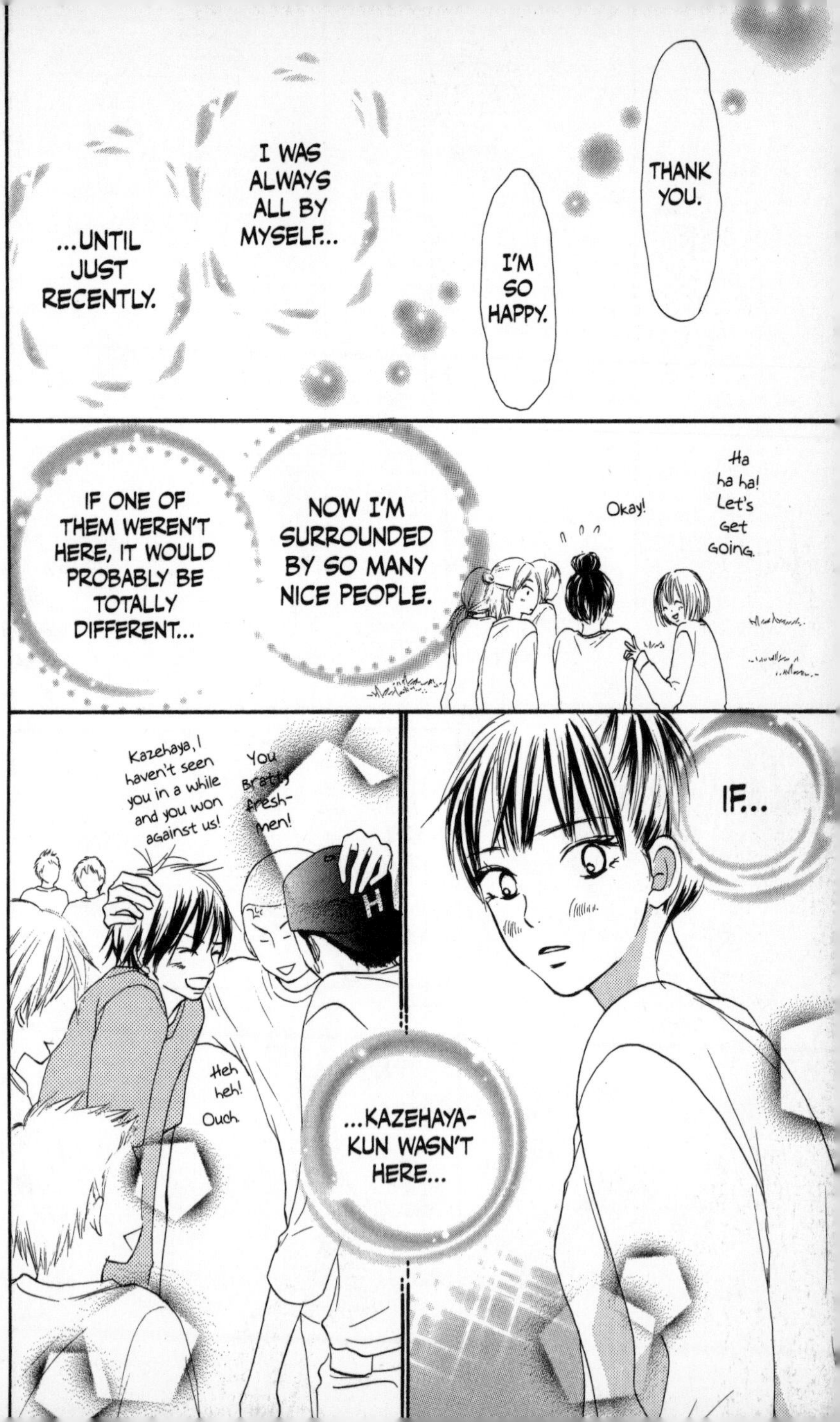
THANK YOU.
I'M SO HAPPY.
I WAS ALWAYS ALL BY MYSELF...
...UNTIL JUST RECENTLY.
Ha ha ha! Let's get going.
Okay!
NOW I'M SURROUNDED BY SO MANY NICE PEOPLE.
IF ONE OF THEM WEREN'T HERE, IT WOULD PROBABLY BE TOTALLY DIFFERENT...
IF...
...KAZEHAYA-KUN WASN'T HERE...
You bratty freshmen!
Kazehaya, I haven't seen you in a while and you won against us!
Heh heh!
Ouch.

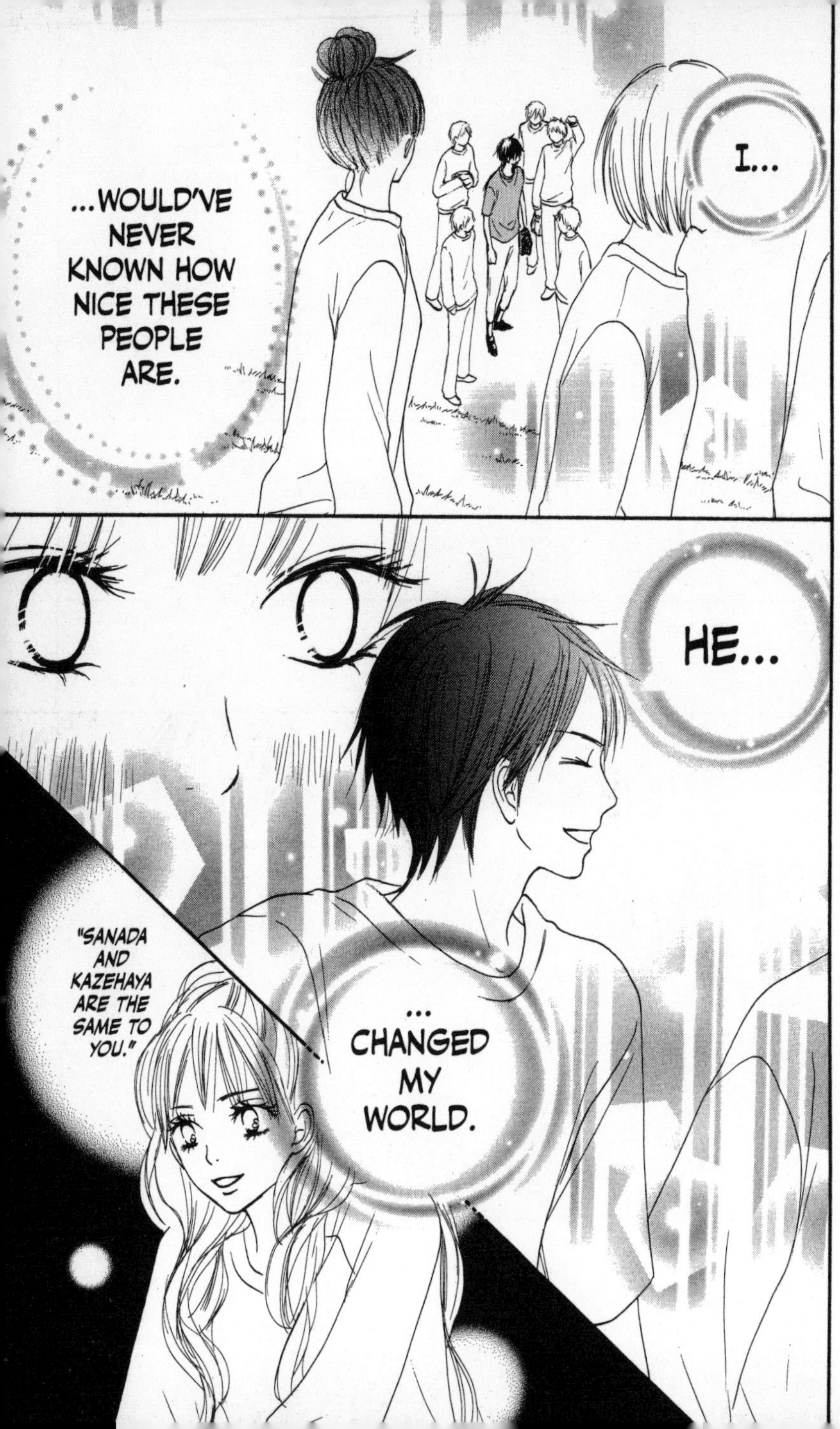
I...
...WOULD'VE NEVER KNOWN HOW NICE THESE PEOPLE ARE.
HE...
...CHANGED MY WORLD.
"SANADA AND KAZEHAYA ARE THE SAME TO YOU."

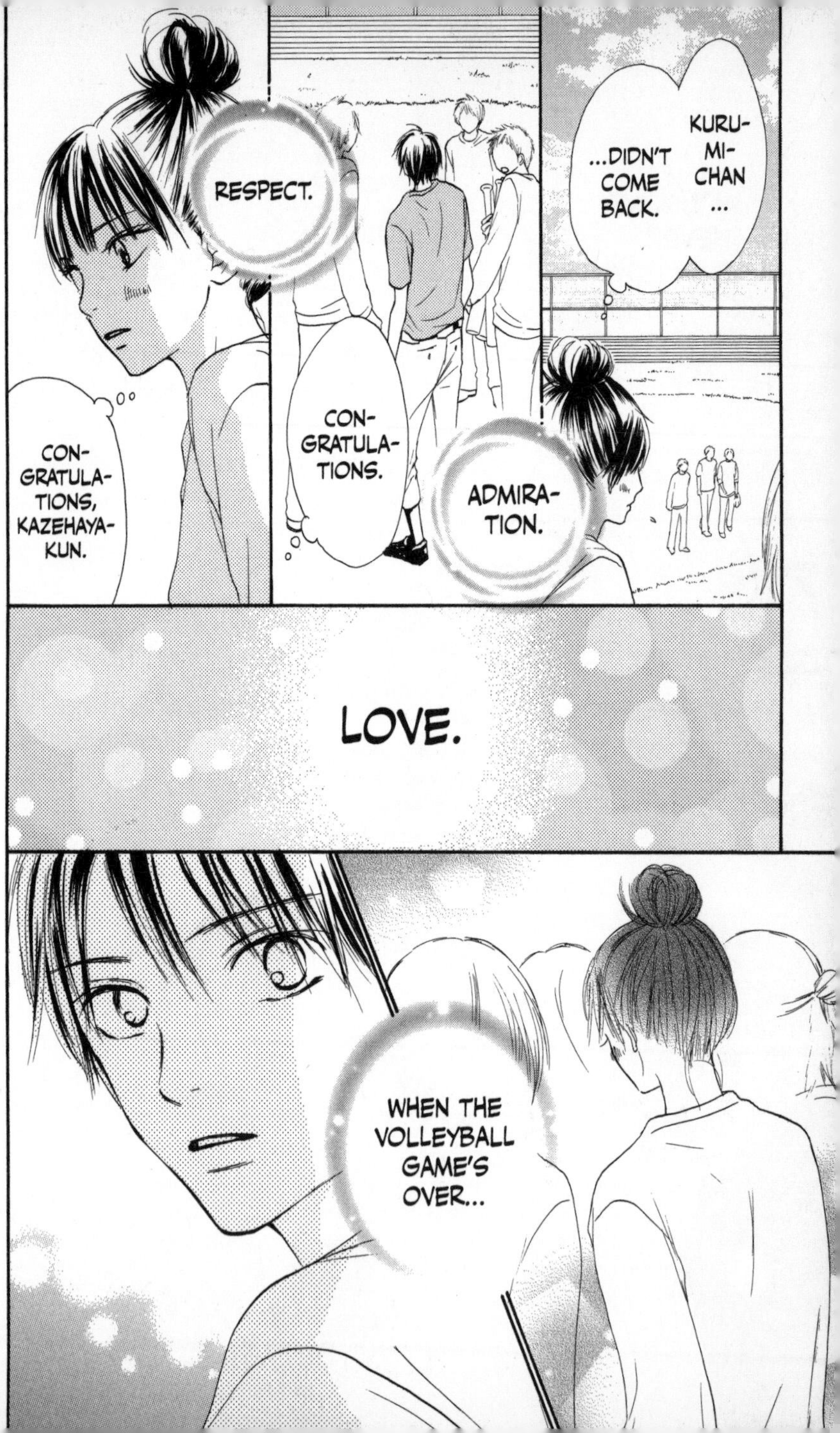
KURU-MI-CHAN...
...DIDN'T COME BACK.
ADMIRA-TION.
RESPECT.
CON-GRATULA-TIONS.
CON-GRATULA-TIONS, KAZEHAYA-KUN.
LOVE.
WHEN THE VOLLEYBALL GAME'S OVER...

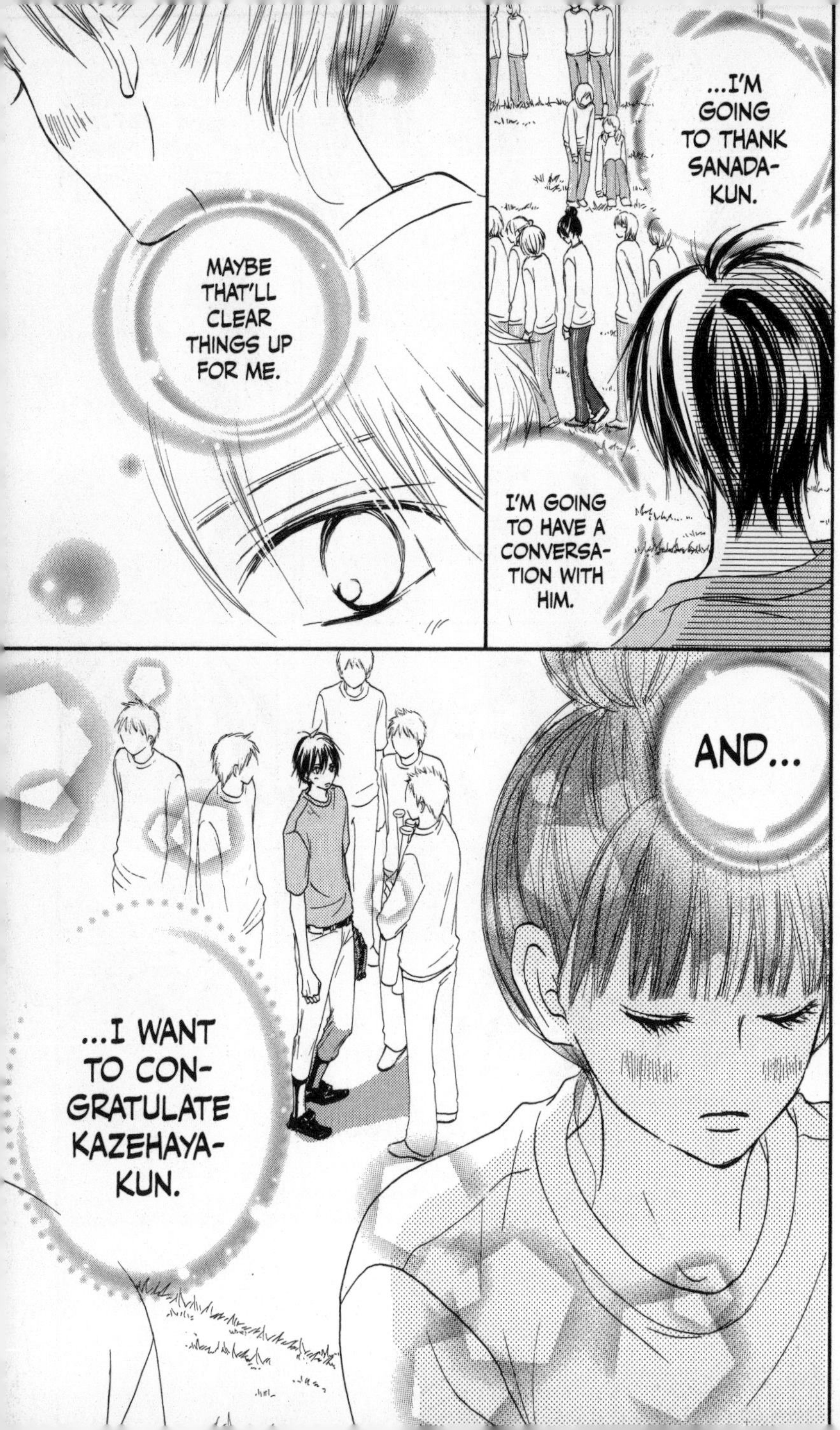
...I'M GOING TO THANK SANADA-KUN.
I'M GOING TO HAVE A CONVERSA-TION WITH HIM.
MAYBE THAT'LL CLEAR THINGS UP FOR ME.
AND...
...I WANT TO CON-GRATULATE KAZEHAYA-KUN.

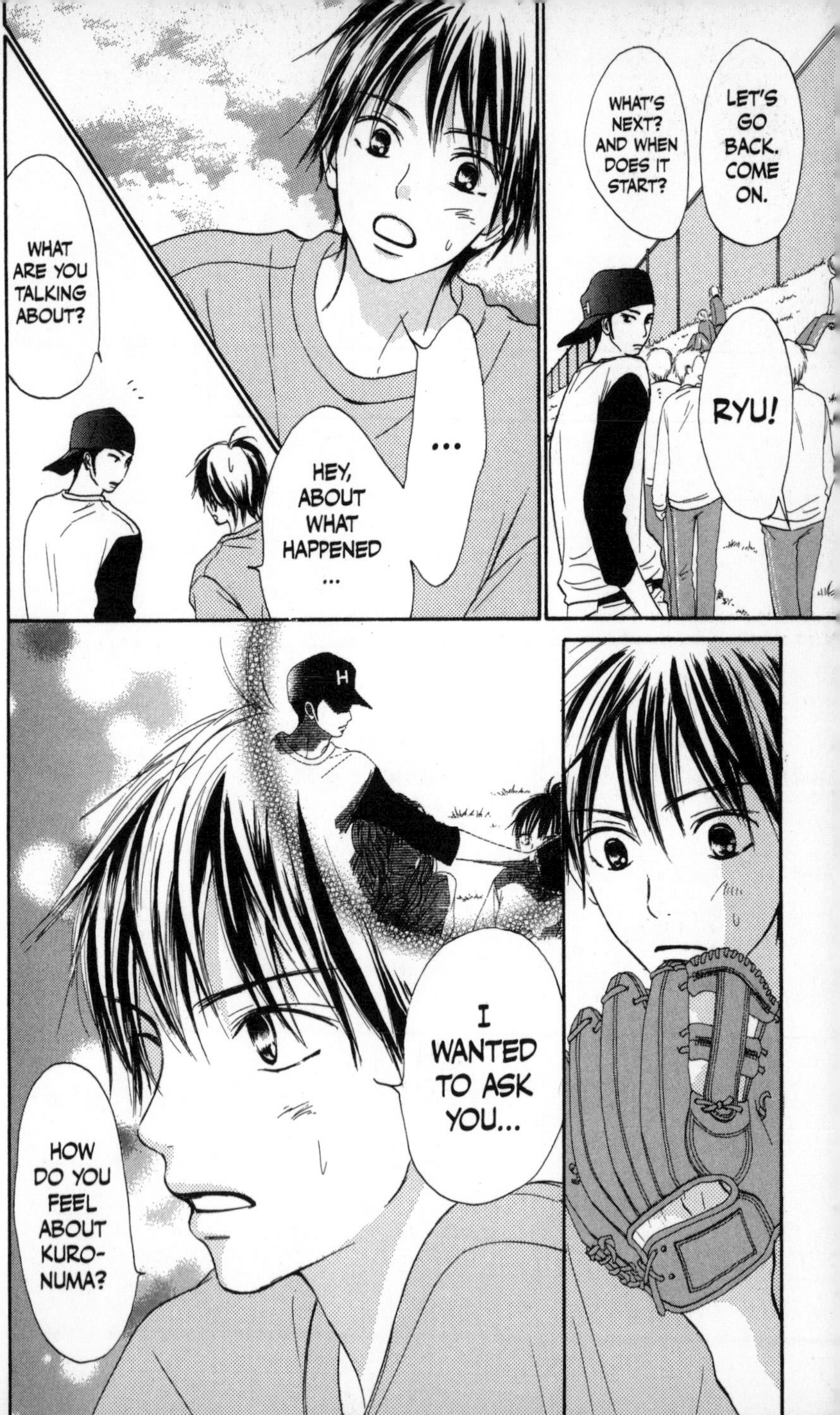
LET'S GO BACK. COME ON.
WHAT'S NEXT? AND WHEN DOES IT START?
RYU!
...
HEY, ABOUT WHAT HAPPENED...
WHAT ARE YOU TALKING ABOUT?
I WANTED TO ASK YOU...
HOW DO YOU FEEL ABOUT KURO-NUMA?

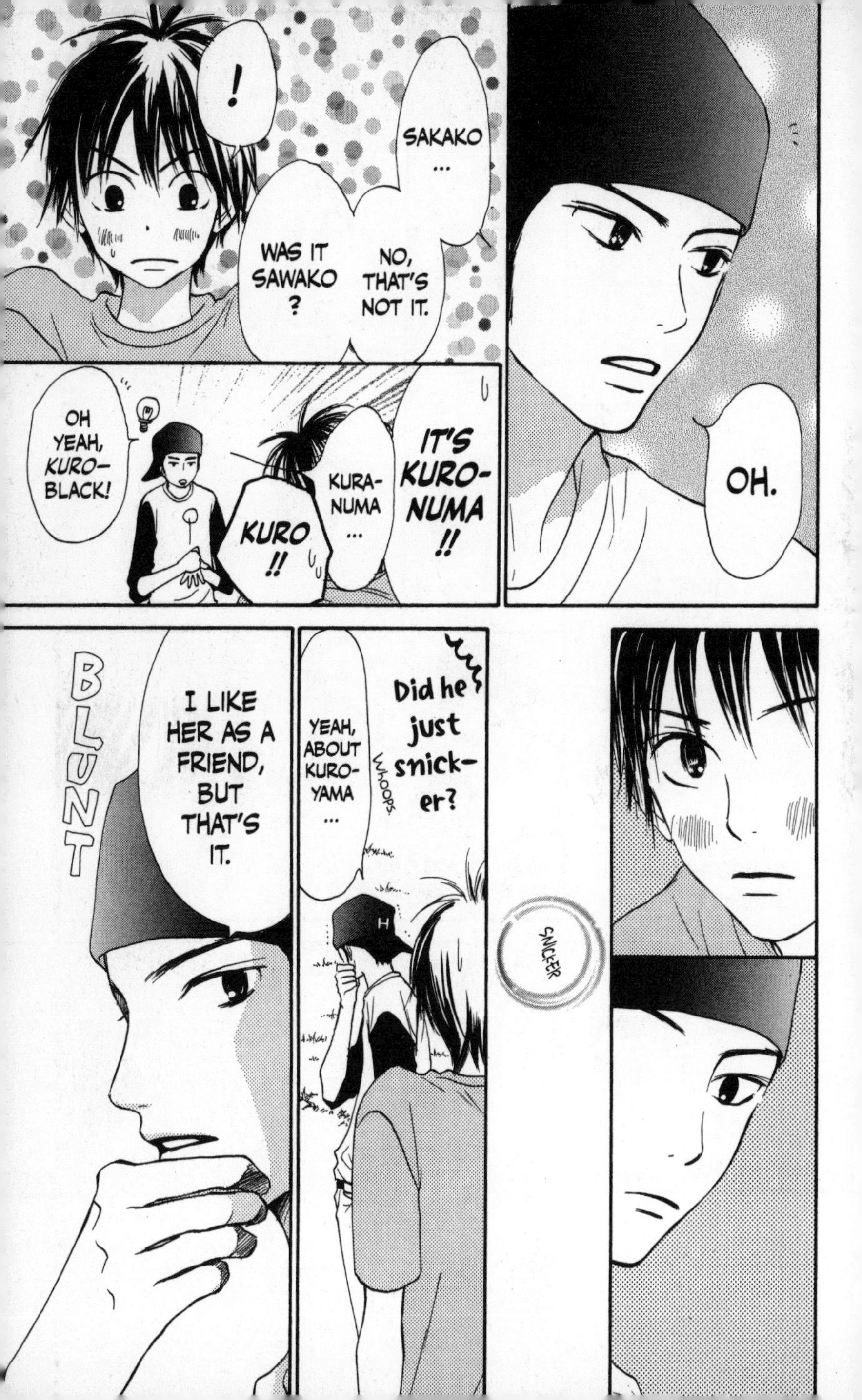
OH.
!
SAKAKO ...
NO, THAT'S NOT IT.
WAS IT SAWAKO?
IT'S KURONUMA!!
KURANUMA ...
KURO!!
OH YEAH, KURO-BLACK!
SNICKER
Did he just snicker?
YEAH, ABOUT KUROYAMA ...
WHOOPS.
I LIKE HER AS A FRIEND, BUT THAT'S IT.
BLUNT

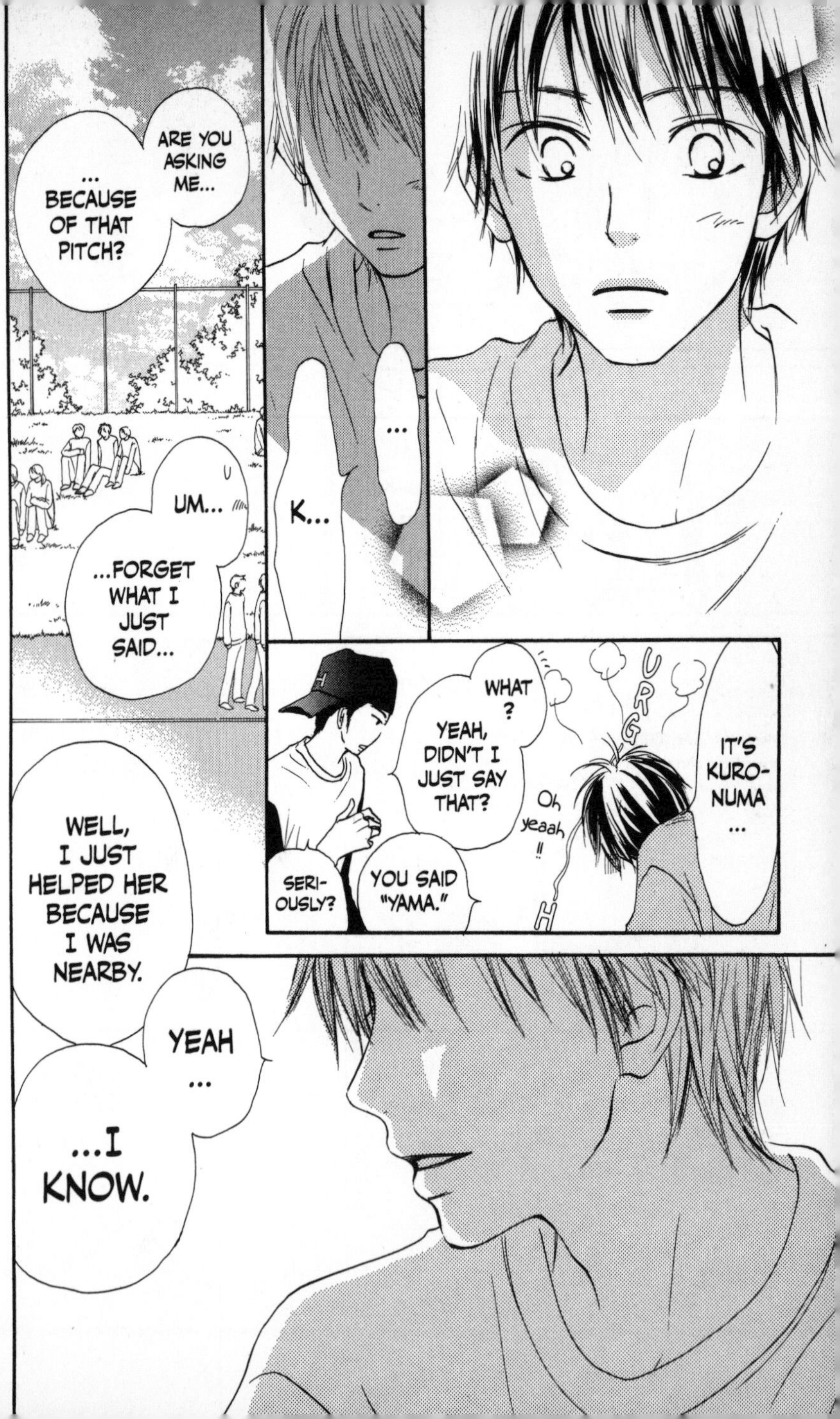
...
K...
IT'S KURO-NUMA...
URG
H
Oh yeaah!!
WHAT?
YEAH, DIDN'T I JUST SAY THAT?
YOU SAID "YAMA."
SERI-OUSLY?
ARE YOU ASKING ME...
...BECAUSE OF THAT PITCH?
UM...
...FORGET WHAT I JUST SAID...
WELL, I JUST HELPED HER BECAUSE I WAS NEARBY.
YEAH...
...I KNOW.

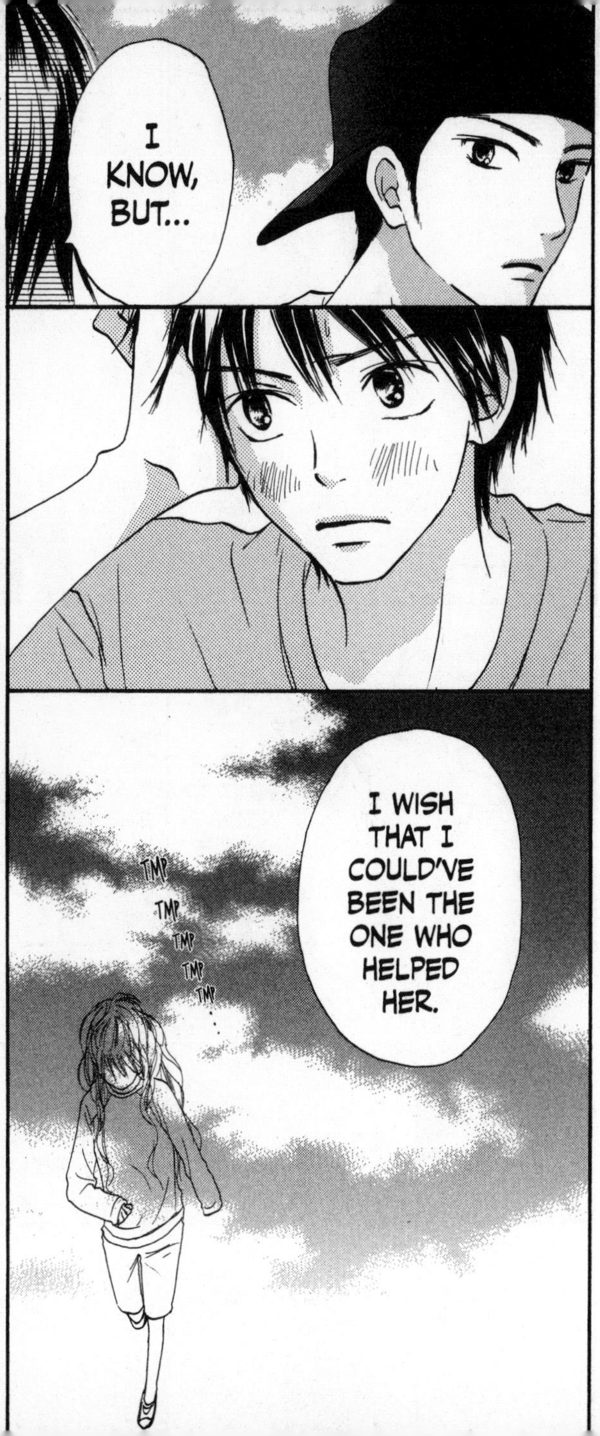
I KNOW, BUT...
I WISH THAT I COULD'VE BEEN THE ONE WHO HELPED HER.
TMP TMP TMP TMP TMP

KARUPIN on JAPAN

2

I admire people who are natural. They're wonderful. ♡

My editor is a very natural person.

You really think so?

Maybe she doesn't know this, but just being around her relaxes me a lot.

• • • • • • • •

The other day, I was on a program with Sakura Merry Men-san. They're a wonderful three-piece band. I think many of you might have heard some of their music in commercials. They have a song called "Margaret," which is the name of the magazine *Kimi ni Todoke* is published in, and they even feature the phrase "kimi ni todoke" in their lyrics, so we mutually thought that it would be interesting to do a program together.

They're still young, but very wonderful, professional people!

They seemed so mature!

To be continued...

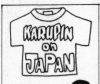

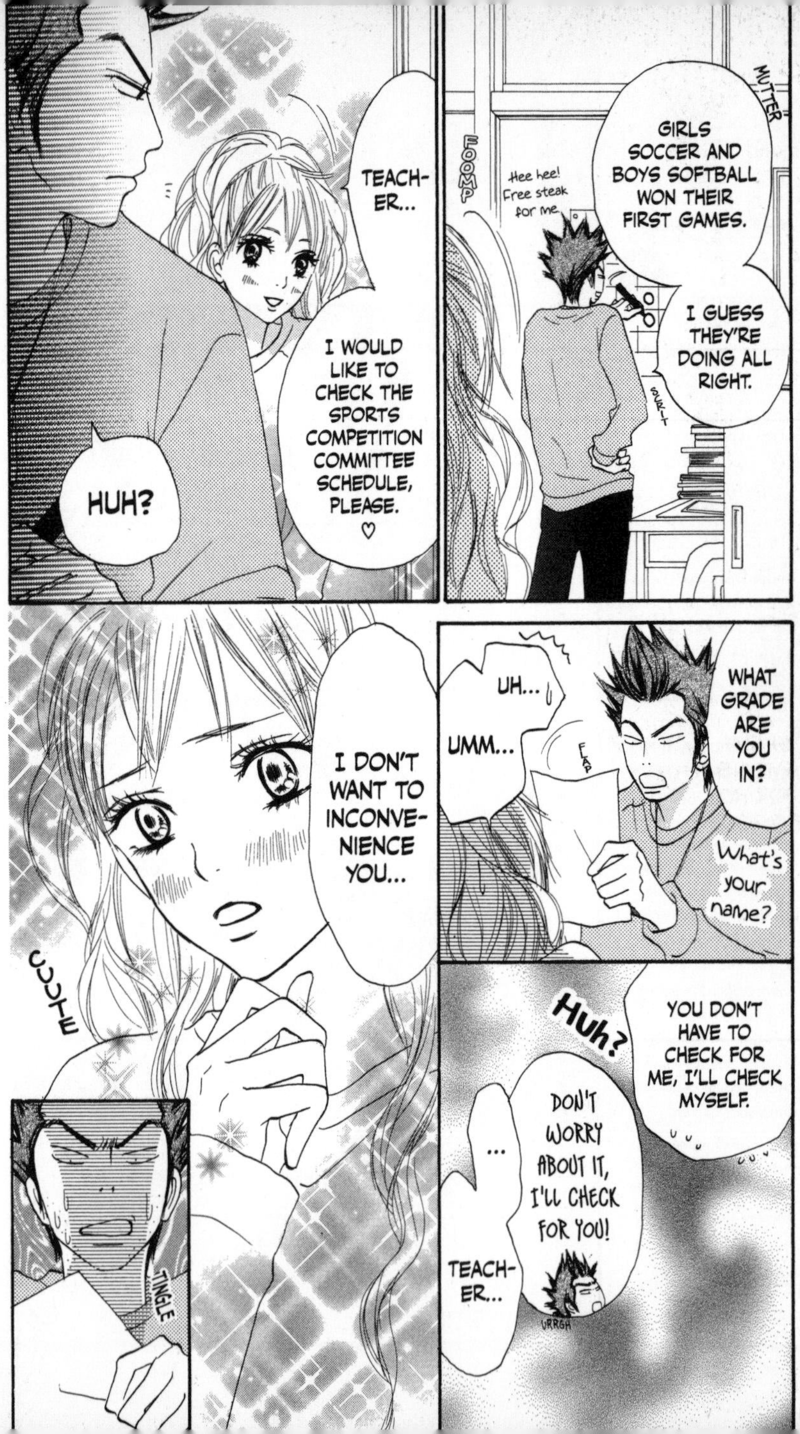
MUTTER
GIRLS SOCCER AND BOYS SOFTBALL WON THEIR FIRST GAMES.
I GUESS THEY'RE DOING ALL RIGHT.
SURIT
Hee hee! Free steak for me.
FOOMP
TEACHER...
I WOULD LIKE TO CHECK THE SPORTS COMPETITION COMMITTEE SCHEDULE, PLEASE. ♡
HUH?
WHAT GRADE ARE YOU IN?
What's your name?
FLAP
UH...
UMM...
YOU DON'T HAVE TO CHECK FOR ME, I'LL CHECK MYSELF.
Huh?
DON'T WORRY ABOUT IT, I'LL CHECK FOR YOU!
...
TEACHER...
URRGH
I DON'T WANT TO INCONVENIENCE YOU...
CUUTE
TINGLE

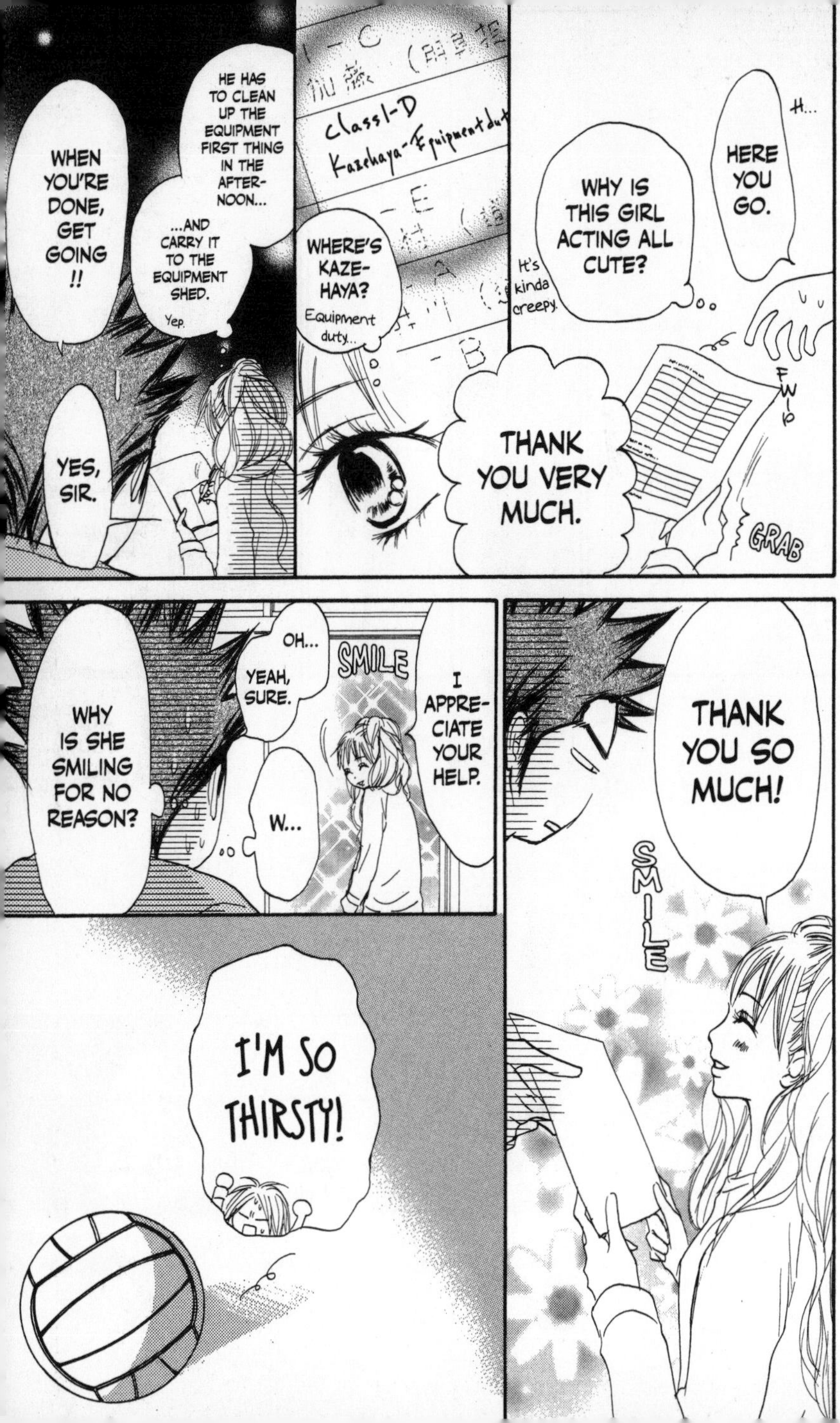
H...
HERE YOU GO.
WHY IS THIS GIRL ACTING ALL CUTE?
It's kinda creepy.
FWIP
THANK YOU VERY MUCH.
GRAB
Class 1-D
Kazehaya-Equipment duty
WHERE'S KAZEHAYA?
Equipment duty...
HE HAS TO CLEAN UP THE EQUIPMENT FIRST THING IN THE AFTERNOON...
...AND CARRY IT TO THE EQUIPMENT SHED.
Yep.
WHEN YOU'RE DONE, GET GOING!!
YES, SIR.
THANK YOU SO MUCH!
SMILE
I APPRECIATE YOUR HELP.
SMILE
OH... YEAH, SURE.
W...
WHY IS SHE SMILING FOR NO REASON?
I'M SO THIRSTY!

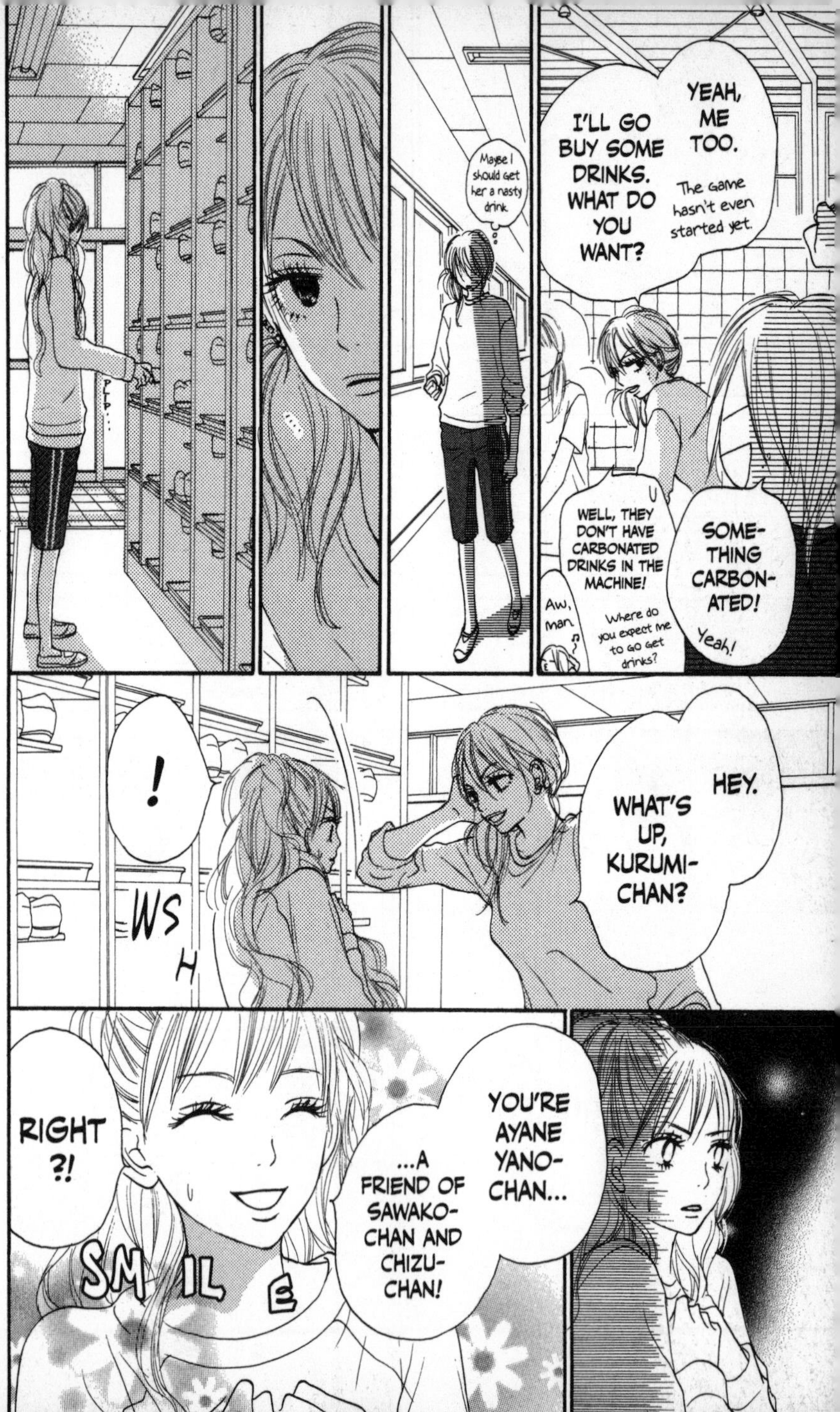
YEAH, ME TOO.
The game hasn't even started yet.
I'LL GO BUY SOME DRINKS. WHAT DO YOU WANT?
SOMETHING CARBONATED!
Yeah!
WELL, THEY DON'T HAVE CARBONATED DRINKS IN THE MACHINE!
Where do you expect me to go get drinks?
Aw, man.
Maybe I should get her a nasty drink.
...
PLIP...
HEY.
WHAT'S UP, KURUMI-CHAN?
!
WSH
YOU'RE AYANE YANO-CHAN...
...A FRIEND OF SAWAKO-CHAN AND CHIZU-CHAN!
RIGHT?!
SMILE

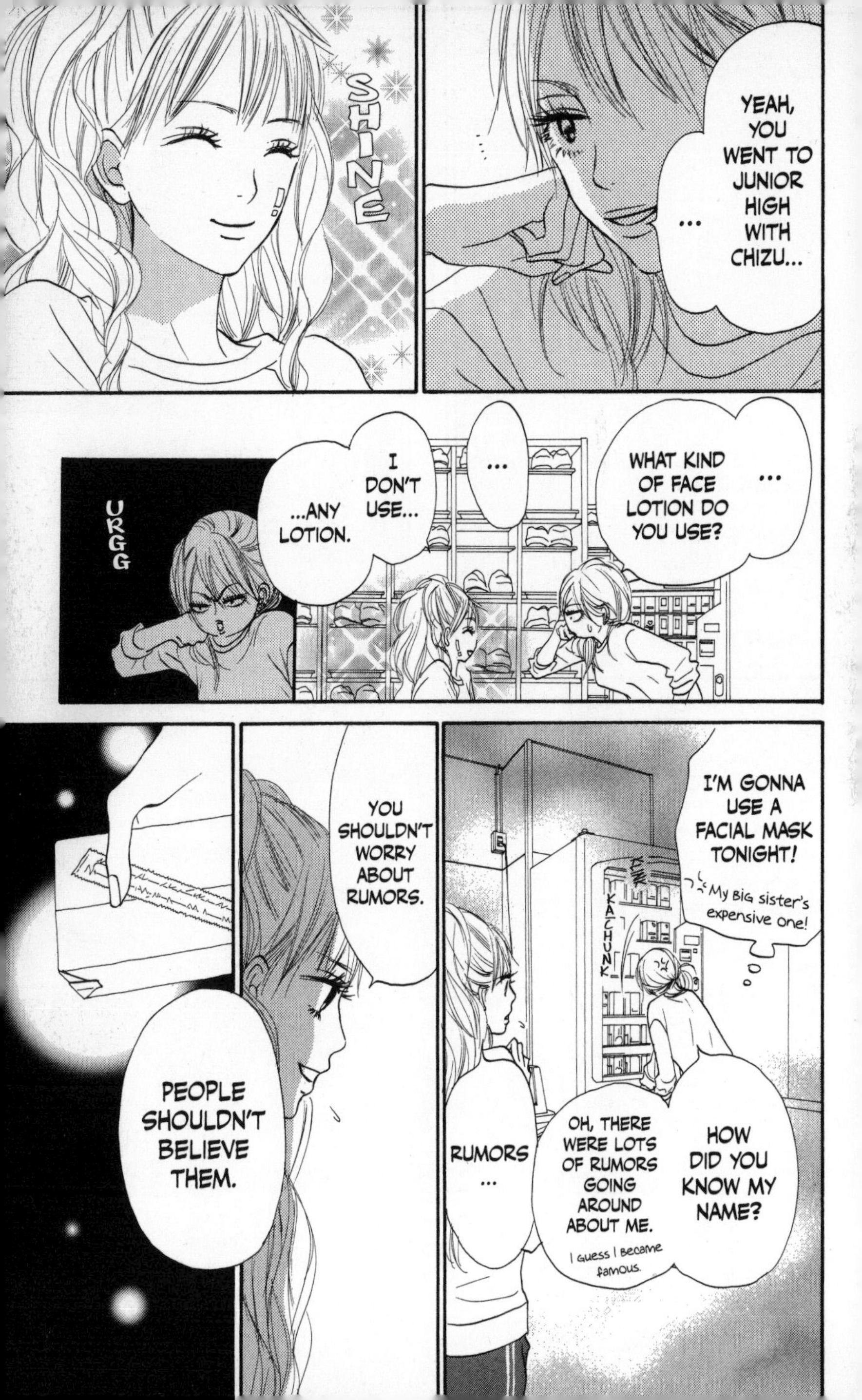
YEAH, YOU WENT TO JUNIOR HIGH WITH CHIZU...
...
SHINE
...
WHAT KIND OF FACE LOTION DO YOU USE?
...
I DON'T USE...
...ANY LOTION.
URGG
I'M GONNA USE A FACIAL MASK TONIGHT!
My BIG sister's expensive one!
KACHUNK
HOW DID YOU KNOW MY NAME?
OH, THERE WERE LOTS OF RUMORS GOING AROUND ABOUT ME.
I guess I became famous.
RUMORS...
YOU SHOULDN'T WORRY ABOUT RUMORS.
PEOPLE SHOULDN'T BELIEVE THEM.

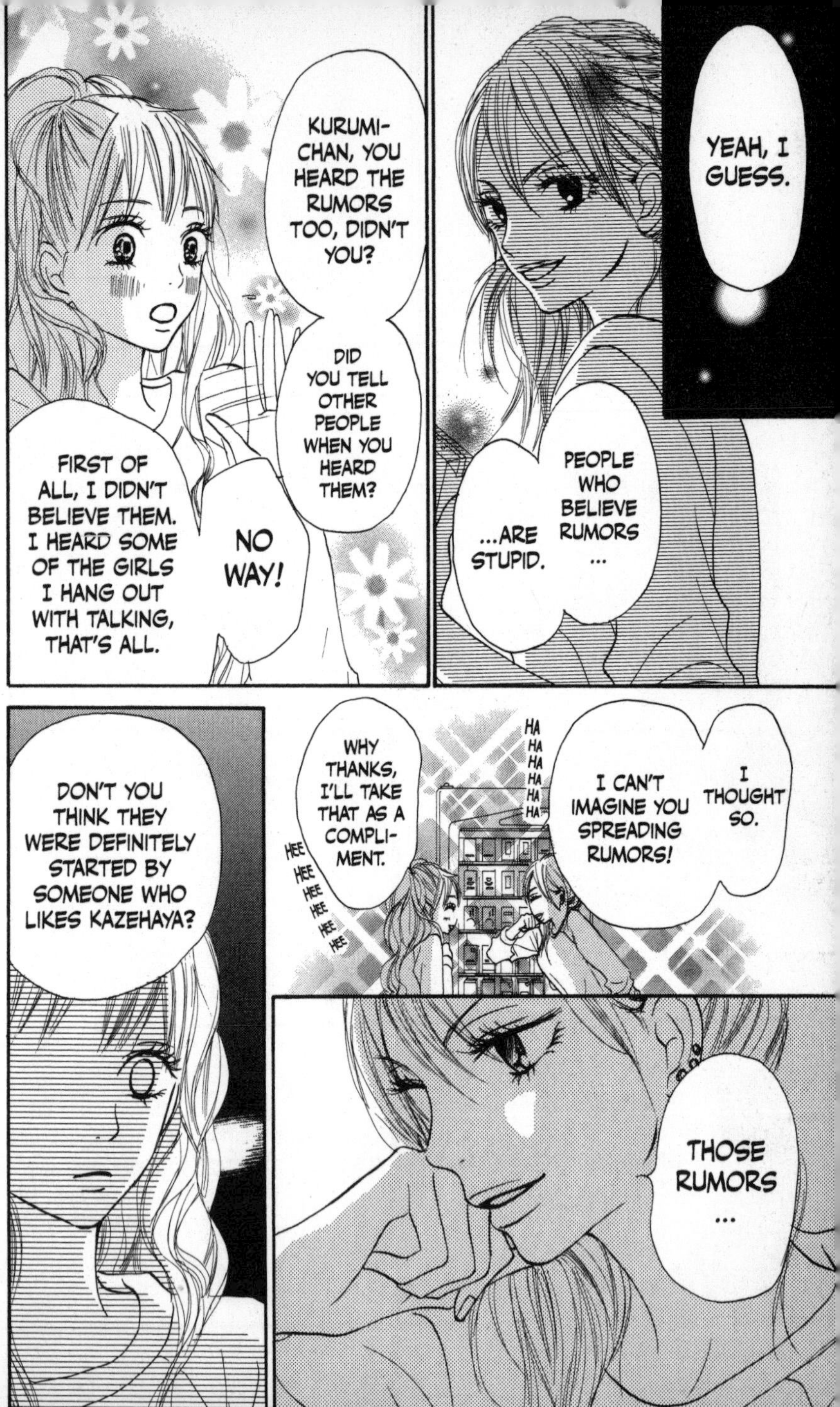
YEAH, I GUESS.
PEOPLE WHO BELIEVE RUMORS ...
...ARE STUPID.
KURUMI-CHAN, YOU HEARD THE RUMORS TOO, DIDN'T YOU?
DID YOU TELL OTHER PEOPLE WHEN YOU HEARD THEM?
NO WAY!
FIRST OF ALL, I DIDN'T BELIEVE THEM. I HEARD SOME OF THE GIRLS I HANG OUT WITH TALKING, THAT'S ALL.
I THOUGHT SO.
I CAN'T IMAGINE YOU SPREADING RUMORS!
HA HA HA HA HA HA
WHY THANKS, I'LL TAKE THAT AS A COMPLIMENT.
HEE HEE HEE HEE HEE HEE
THOSE RUMORS ...
DON'T YOU THINK THEY WERE DEFINITELY STARTED BY SOMEONE WHO LIKES KAZEHAYA?

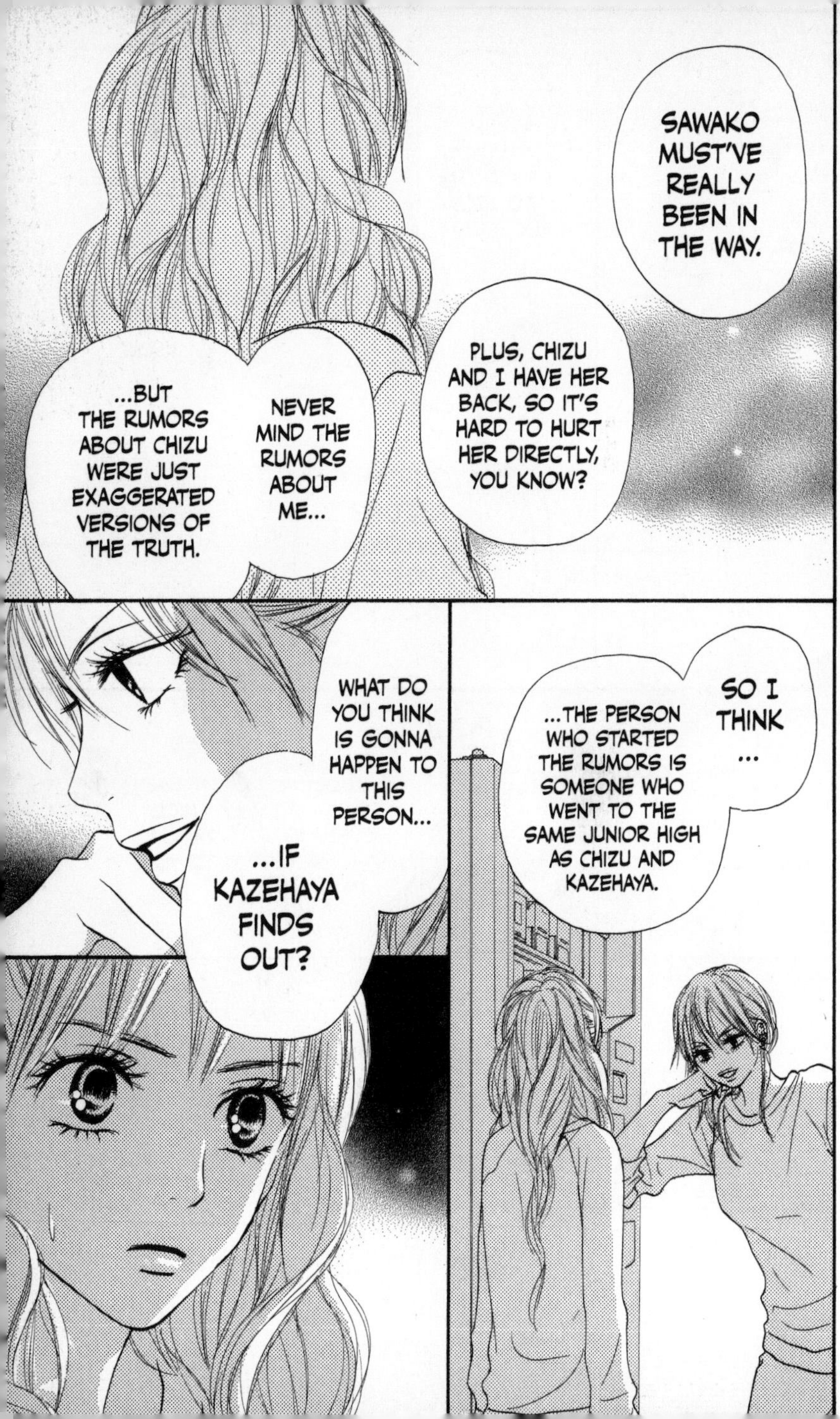
SAWAKO MUST'VE REALLY BEEN IN THE WAY.
PLUS, CHIZU AND I HAVE HER BACK, SO IT'S HARD TO HURT HER DIRECTLY, YOU KNOW?
NEVER MIND THE RUMORS ABOUT ME...
...BUT THE RUMORS ABOUT CHIZU WERE JUST EXAGGERATED VERSIONS OF THE TRUTH.
SO I THINK...
...THE PERSON WHO STARTED THE RUMORS IS SOMEONE WHO WENT TO THE SAME JUNIOR HIGH AS CHIZU AND KAZEHAYA.
WHAT DO YOU THINK IS GONNA HAPPEN TO THIS PERSON...
...IF KAZEHAYA FINDS OUT?

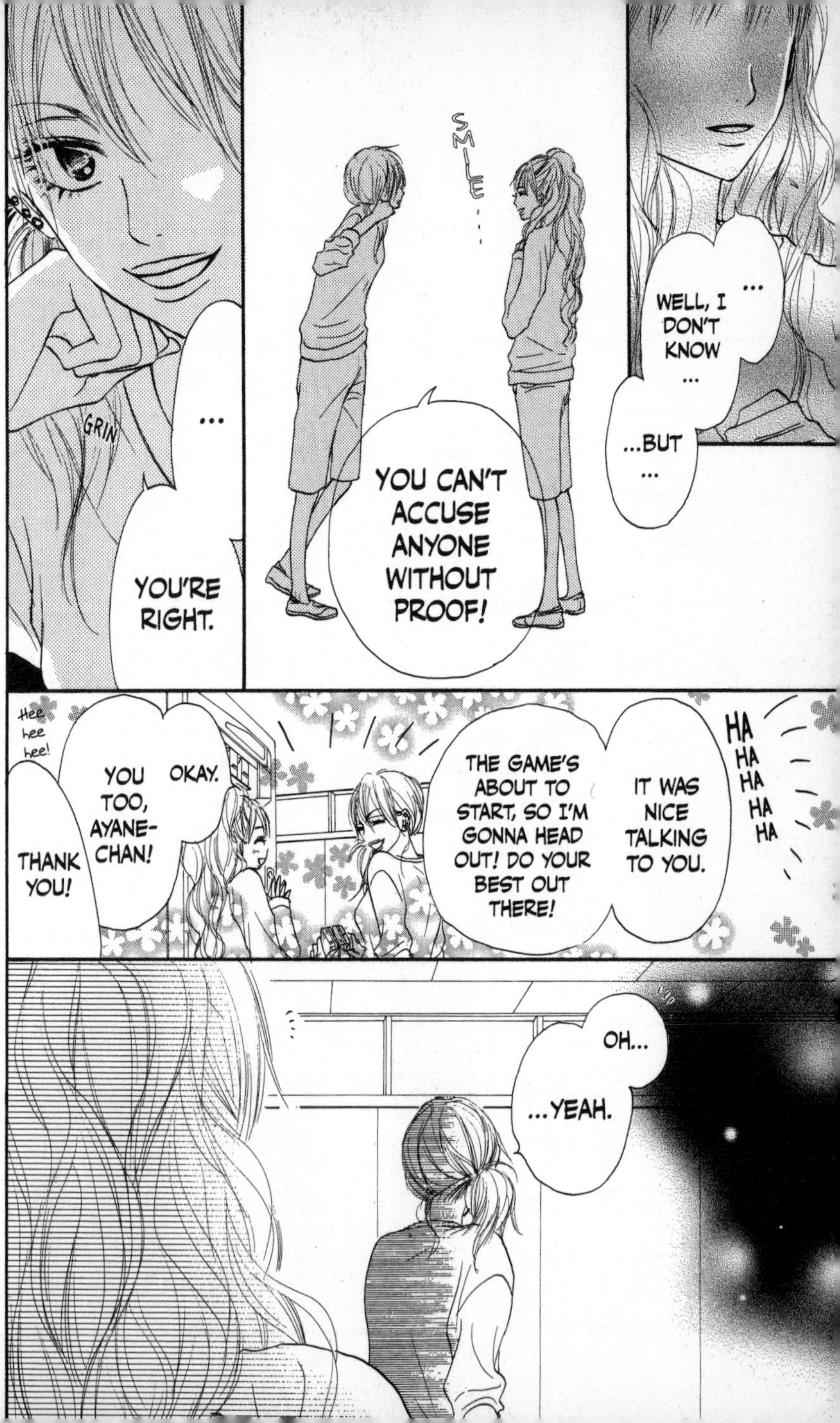
...
WELL, I DON'T KNOW ...
...BUT ...
SMILE...
YOU CAN'T ACCUSE ANYONE WITHOUT PROOF!
GRIN
...
YOU'RE RIGHT.
HA HA HA HA HA
IT WAS NICE TALKING TO YOU.
THE GAME'S ABOUT TO START, SO I'M GONNA HEAD OUT! DO YOUR BEST OUT THERE!
OKAY.
YOU TOO, AYANE-CHAN!
Hee hee hee!
THANK YOU!
OH...
...YEAH.

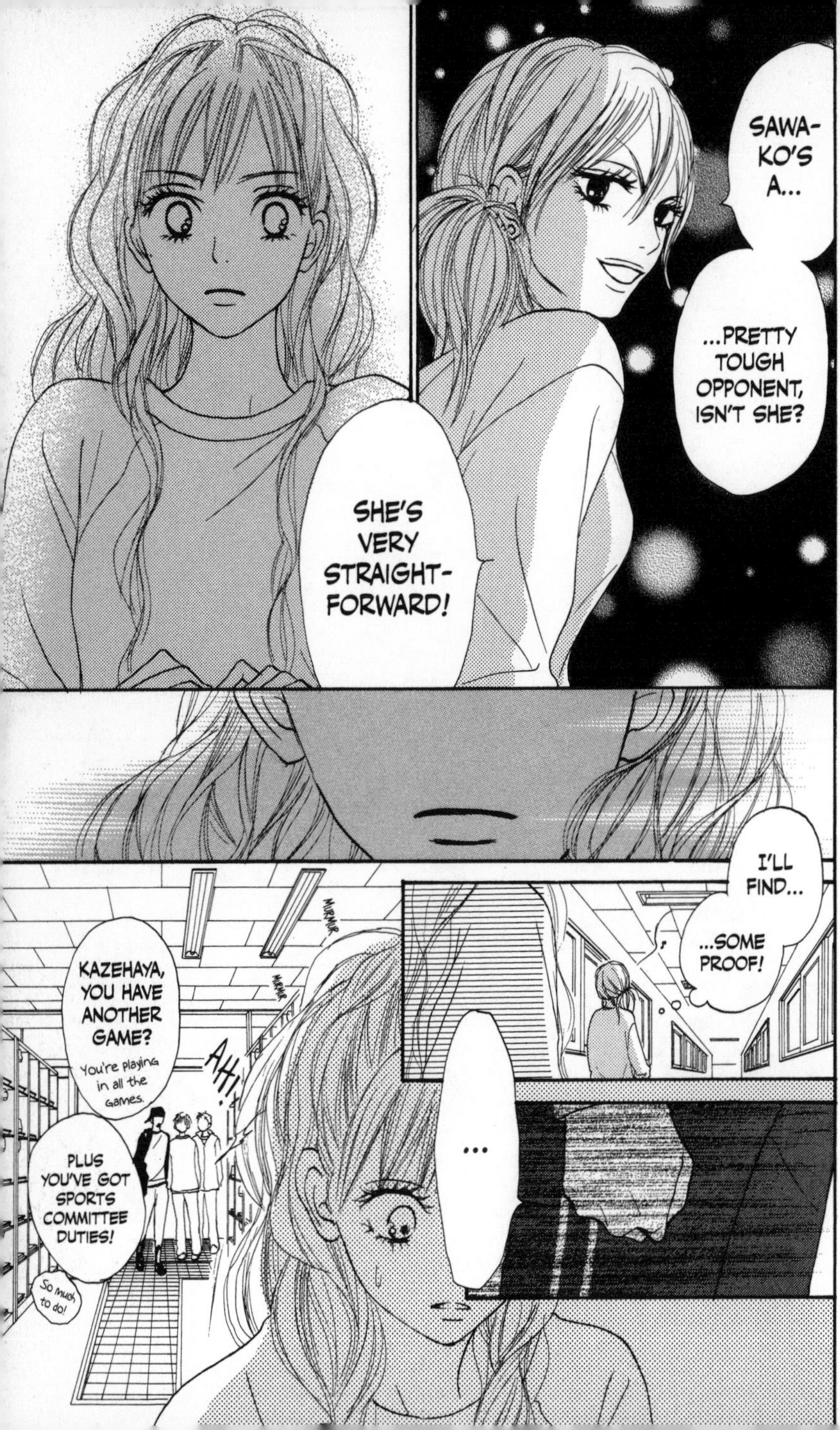
SAWAKO'S A...
...PRETTY TOUGH OPPONENT, ISN'T SHE?
SHE'S VERY STRAIGHTFORWARD!
I'LL FIND...
...SOME PROOF!
...
MURMUR
MURMUR
KAZEHAYA, YOU HAVE ANOTHER GAME?
You're playing in all the games.
AH!
PLUS YOU'VE GOT SPORTS COMMITTEE DUTIES!
So much to do!

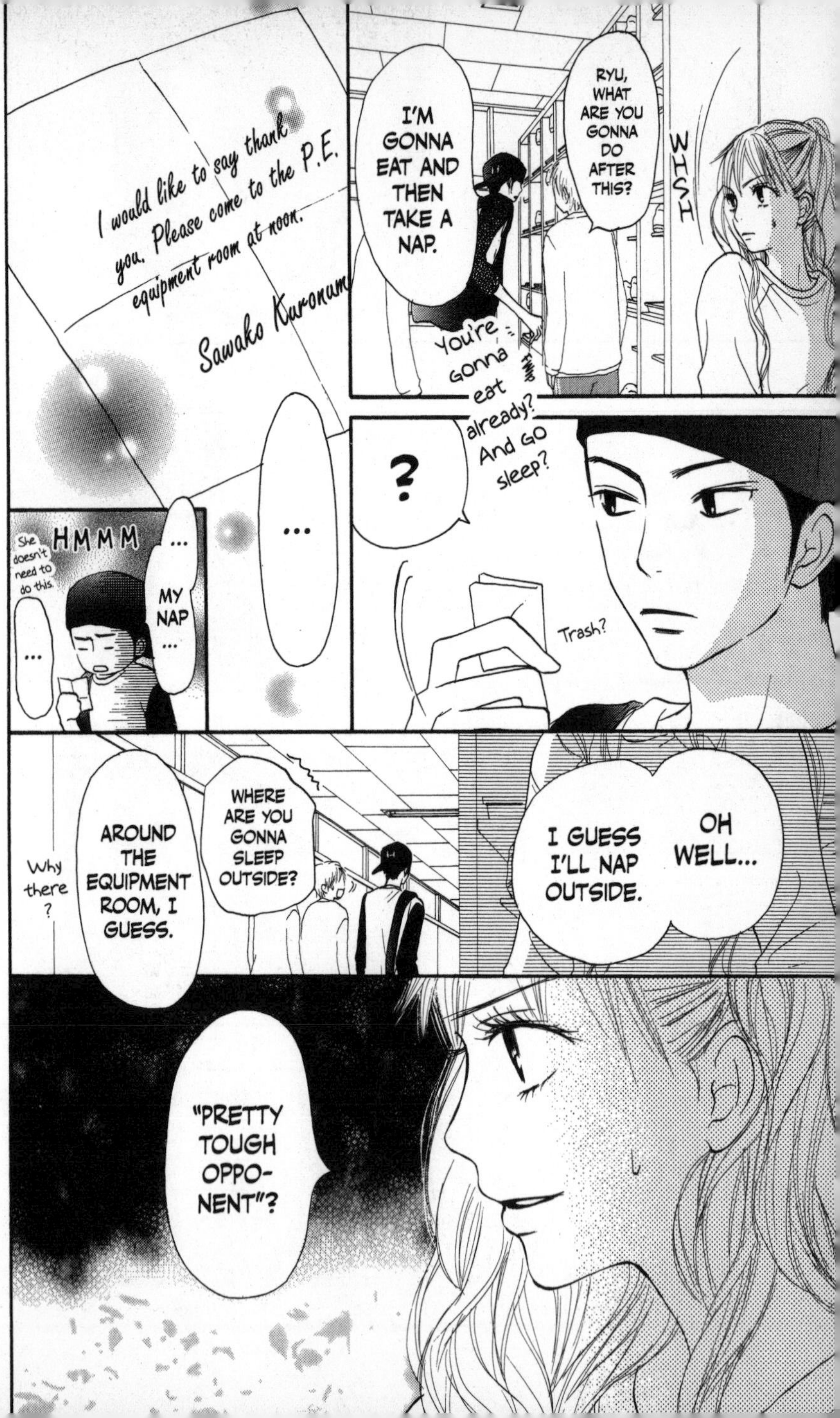
WHSH
RYU, WHAT ARE YOU GONNA DO AFTER THIS?
I'M GONNA EAT AND THEN TAKE A NAP.
You're gonna eat already? And go sleep?
?
...
Trash?
I would like to say thank you. Please come to the P.E. equipment room at noon.
Sawako Kuronum
HMMM
... MY NAP ...
She doesn't need to do this.
...
OH WELL...
I GUESS I'LL NAP OUTSIDE.
WHERE ARE YOU GONNA SLEEP OUTSIDE?
AROUND THE EQUIPMENT ROOM, I GUESS.
Why there?
"PRETTY TOUGH OPPONENT"?

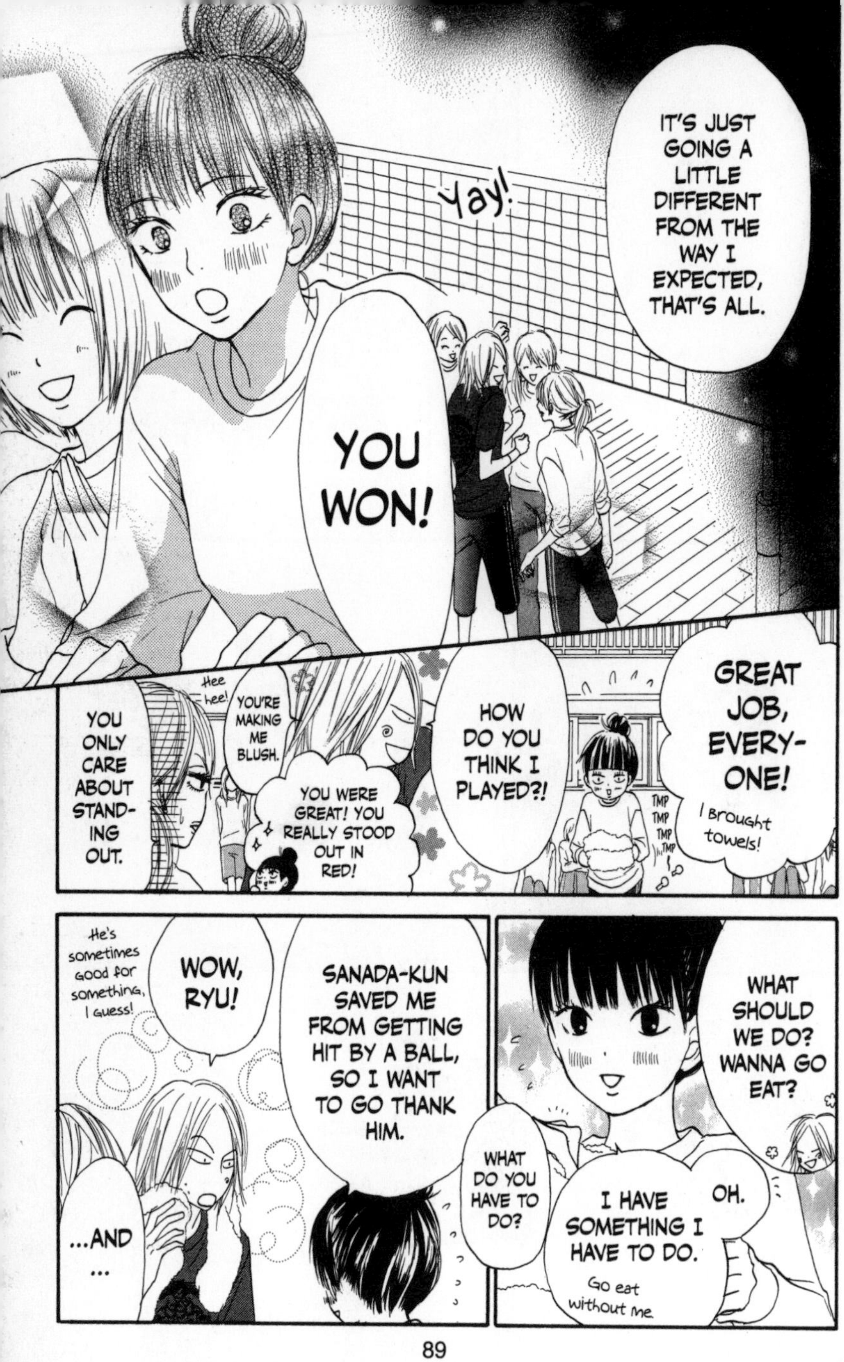
IT'S JUST GOING A LITTLE DIFFERENT FROM THE WAY I EXPECTED, THAT'S ALL.
Yay!
YOU WON!
GREAT JOB, EVERY-ONE!
I brought towels!
TMP TMP TMP TMP
HOW DO YOU THINK I PLAYED?!
YOU WERE GREAT! YOU REALLY STOOD OUT IN RED!
YOU'RE MAKING ME BLUSH.
Hee hee!
YOU ONLY CARE ABOUT STAND-ING OUT.
WHAT SHOULD WE DO? WANNA GO EAT?
OH.
I HAVE SOMETHING I HAVE TO DO.
Go eat without me
WHAT DO YOU HAVE TO DO?
SANADA-KUN SAVED ME FROM GETTING HIT BY A BALL, SO I WANT TO GO THANK HIM.
WOW, RYU!
He's sometimes good for something, I guess!
...AND ...

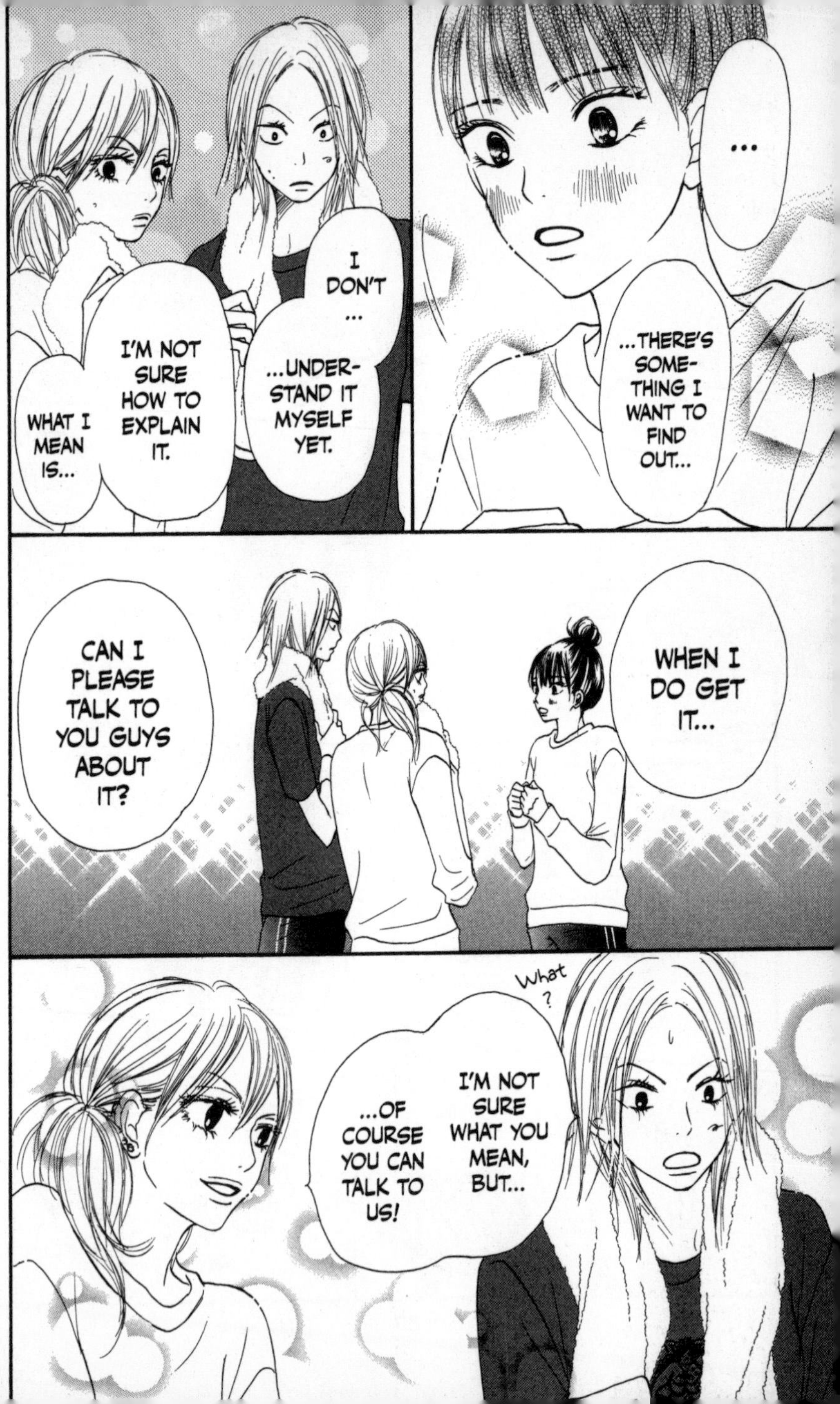
...
...THERE'S SOME-THING I WANT TO FIND OUT...
I DON'T ...
...UNDER-STAND IT MYSELF YET.
I'M NOT SURE HOW TO EXPLAIN IT.
WHAT I MEAN IS...
WHEN I DO GET IT...
CAN I PLEASE TALK TO YOU GUYS ABOUT IT?
What?
I'M NOT SURE WHAT YOU MEAN, BUT...
...OF COURSE YOU CAN TALK TO US!

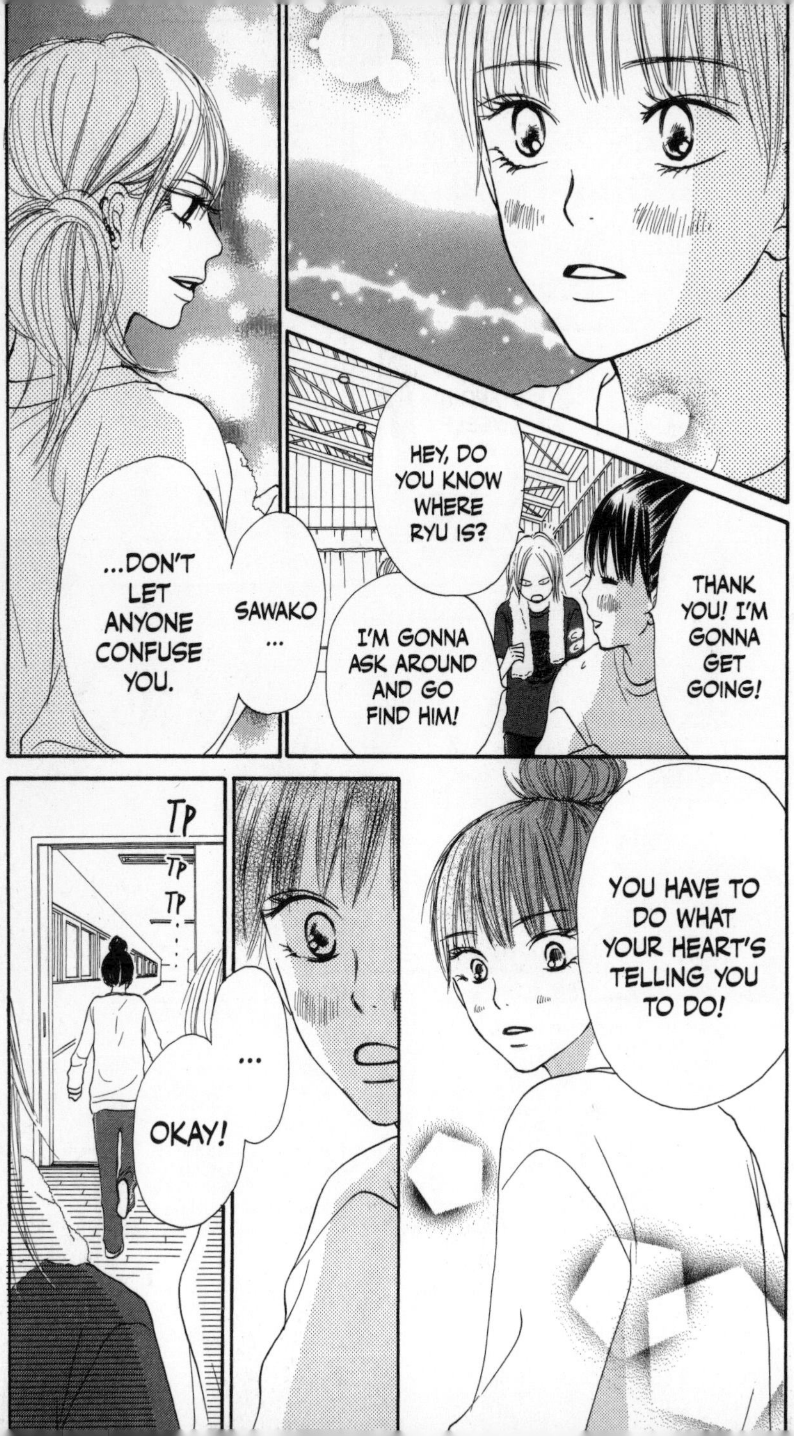
HEY, DO YOU KNOW WHERE RYU IS?
THANK YOU! I'M GONNA GET GOING!
I'M GONNA ASK AROUND AND GO FIND HIM!
SAWAKO ...
...DON'T LET ANYONE CONFUSE YOU.
YOU HAVE TO DO WHAT YOUR HEART'S TELLING YOU TO DO!
...
OKAY!
TP
TP
TP

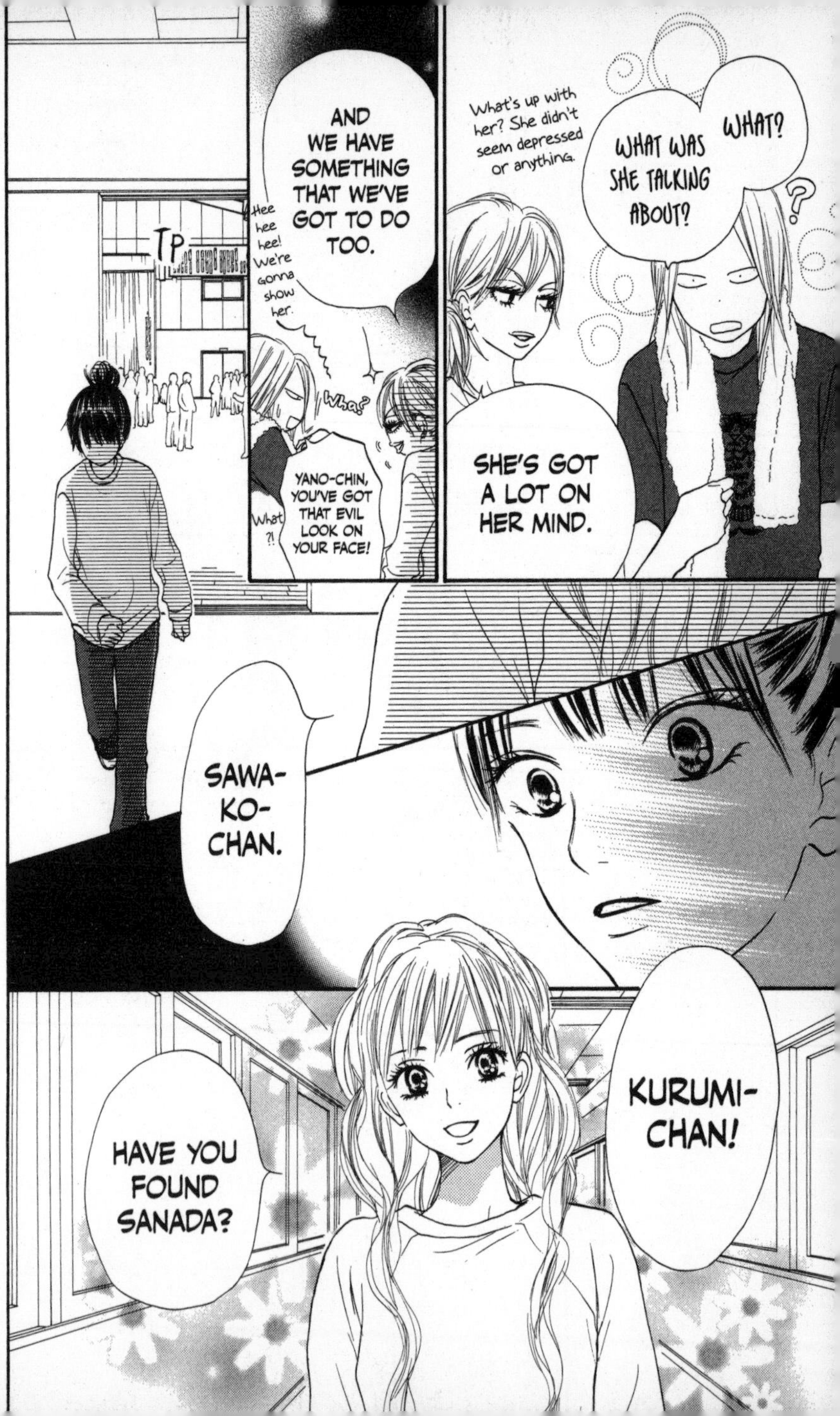
WHAT?
WHAT WAS SHE TALKING ABOUT?
What's up with her? She didn't seem depressed or anything.
SHE'S GOT A LOT ON HER MIND.
AND WE HAVE SOMETHING THAT WE'VE GOT TO DO TOO.
Hee hee hee! We're gonna show her.
Wha?
YANO-CHIN, YOU'VE GOT THAT EVIL LOOK ON YOUR FACE!
What?!
TP
SAWA-KO-CHAN.
KURUMI-CHAN!
HAVE YOU FOUND SANADA?

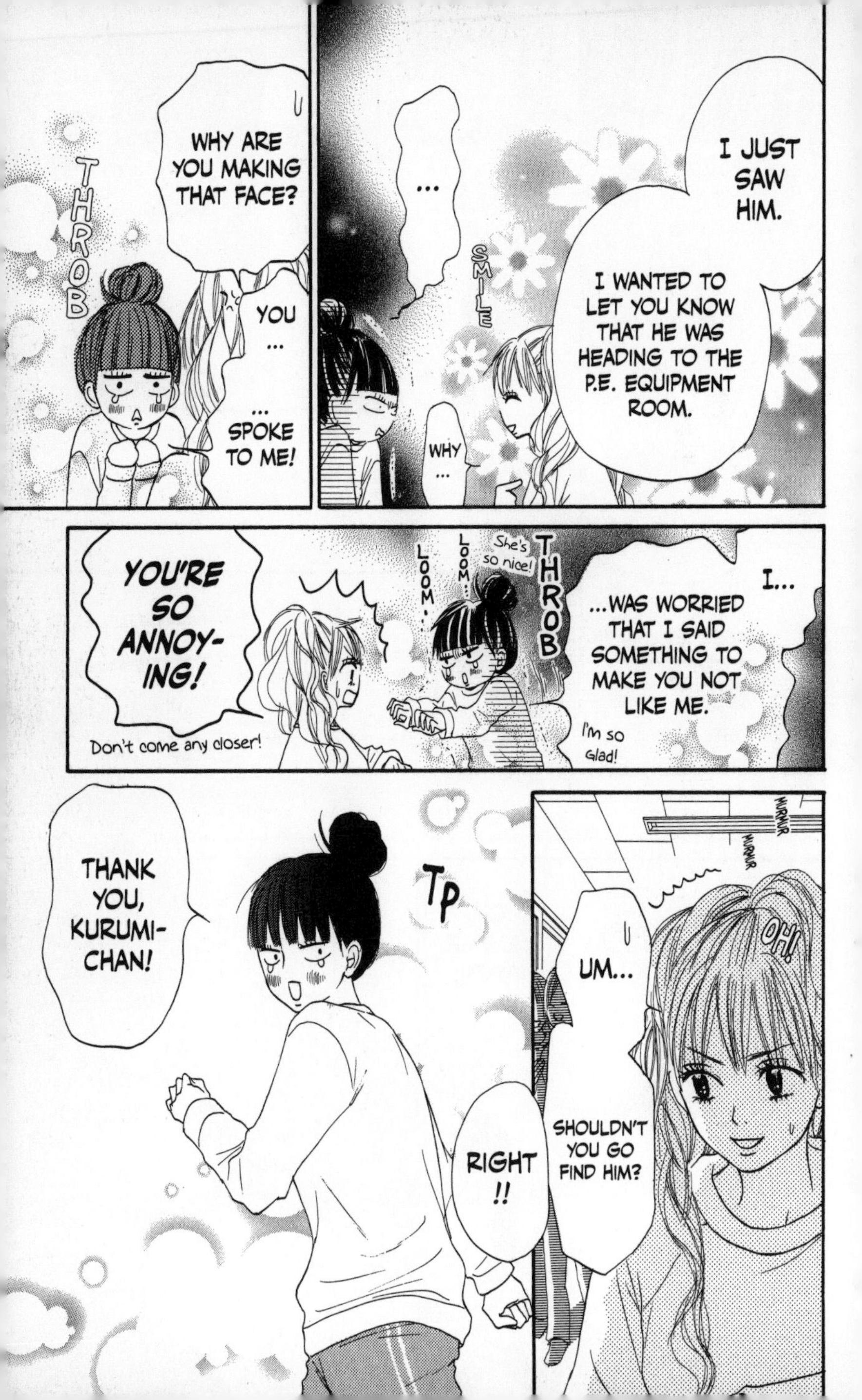
I JUST SAW HIM.
I WANTED TO LET YOU KNOW THAT HE WAS HEADING TO THE P.E. EQUIPMENT ROOM.
...
SMILE
WHY ...
WHY ARE YOU MAKING THAT FACE?
YOU ... ... SPOKE TO ME!
THROB
I...
...WAS WORRIED THAT I SAID SOMETHING TO MAKE YOU NOT LIKE ME.
I'm so Glad!
THROB
She's so nice!
LOOM...
LOOM...
YOU'RE SO ANNOY-ING!
Don't come any closer!
MURMUR
MURMUR
OH!
UM...
SHOULDN'T YOU GO FIND HIM?
RIGHT !!
TP
THANK YOU, KURUMI-CHAN!

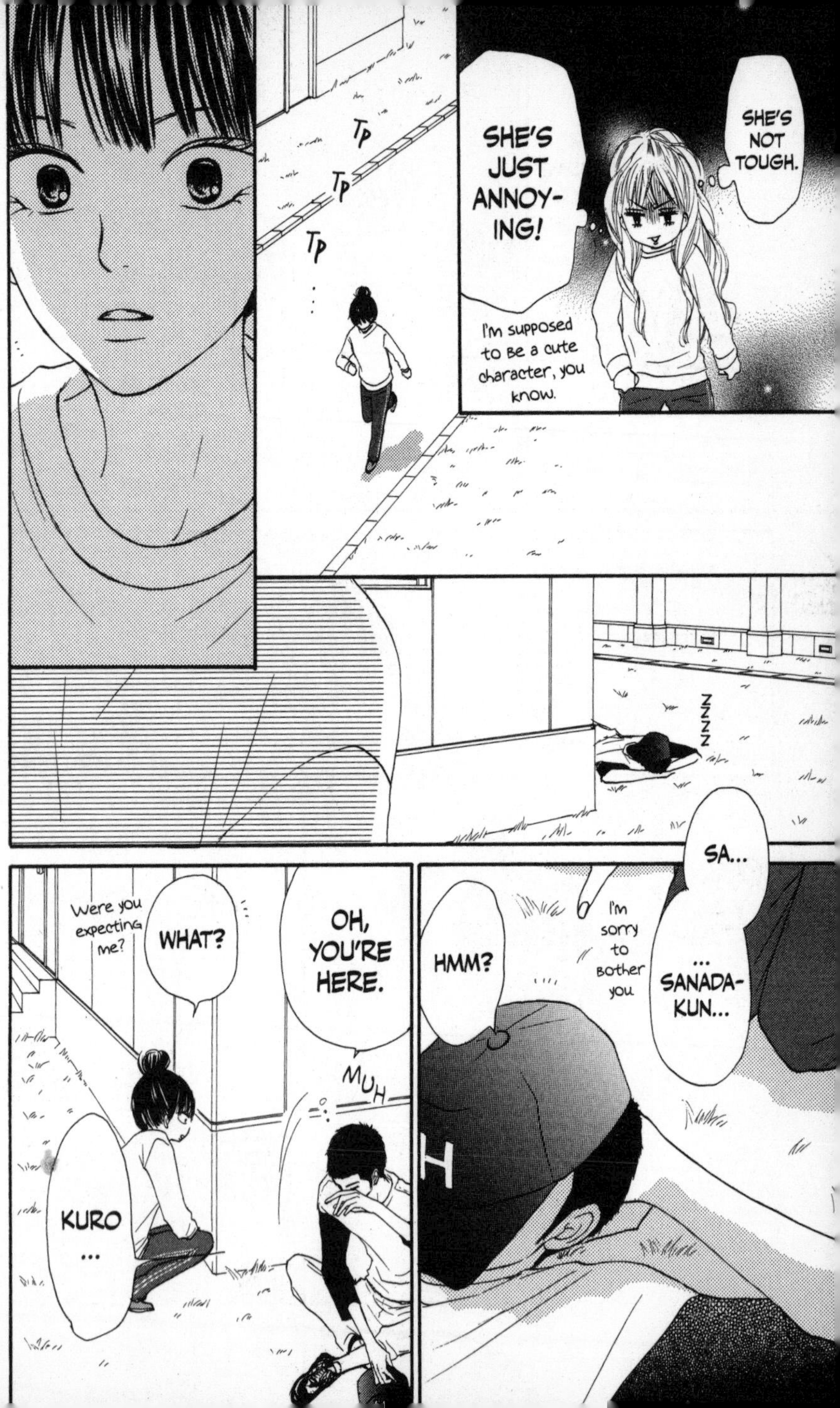
SHE'S NOT TOUGH.
SHE'S JUST ANNOYING!
I'm supposed to be a cute character, you know.
TP
TP
TP
ZZZZ
SA...
...SANADA-KUN...
I'm sorry to bother you
HMM?
OH, YOU'RE HERE.
MUH
WHAT?
Were you expecting me?
KURO...

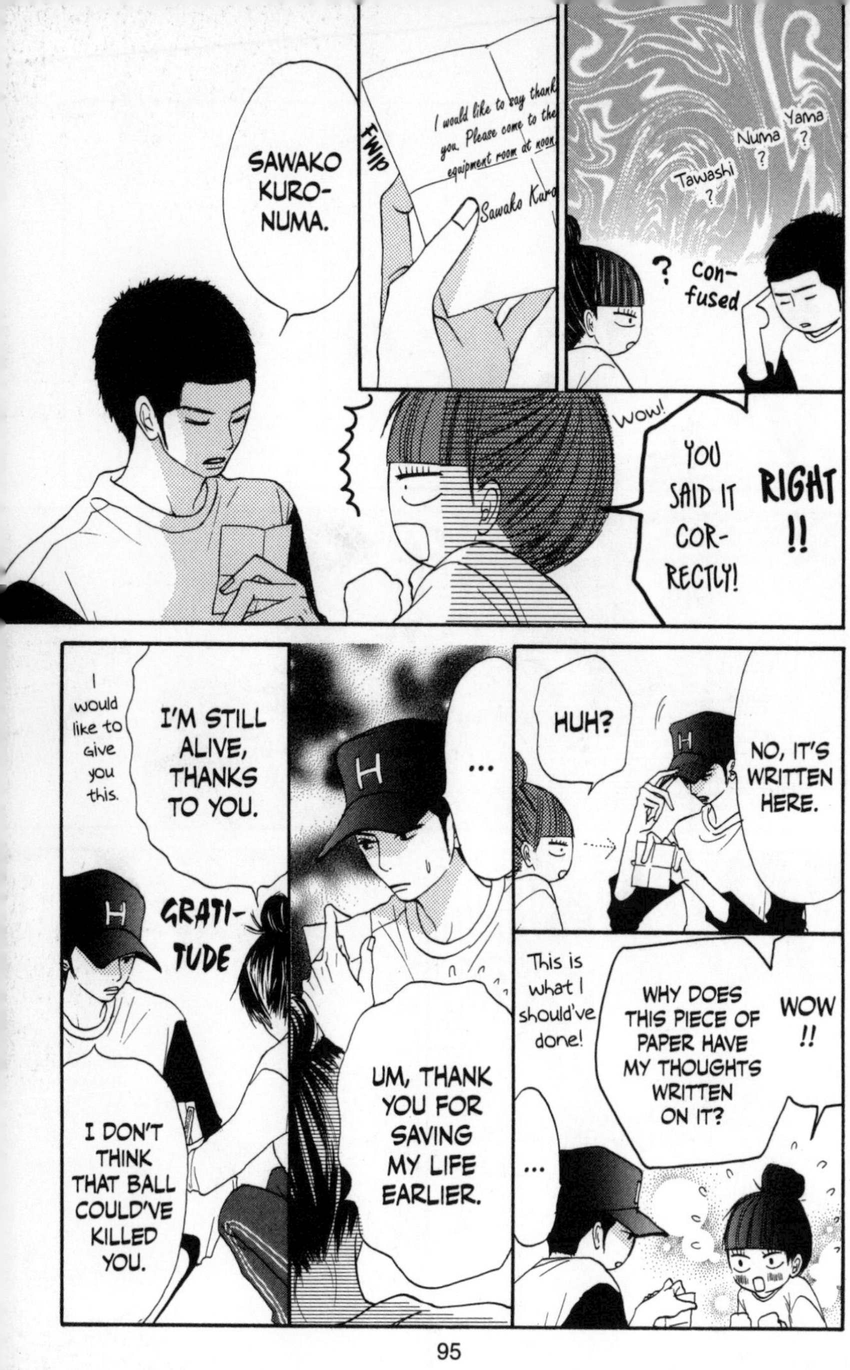
Yama ?
Numa ?
Tawashi ?
?
Con-fused
FWIP
I would like to say thank
you. Please come to the
equipment room at noon.
Sawako Kuro
SAWAKO KURO-NUMA.
WOW!
YOU SAID IT COR-RECTLY!
RIGHT !!
HUH?
NO, IT'S WRITTEN HERE.
WOW !!
WHY DOES THIS PIECE OF PAPER HAVE MY THOUGHTS WRITTEN ON IT?
This is what I should've done!
...
...
UM, THANK YOU FOR SAVING MY LIFE EARLIER.
I'M STILL ALIVE, THANKS TO YOU.
I would like to give you this.
GRATI-TUDE
I DON'T THINK THAT BALL COULD'VE KILLED YOU.

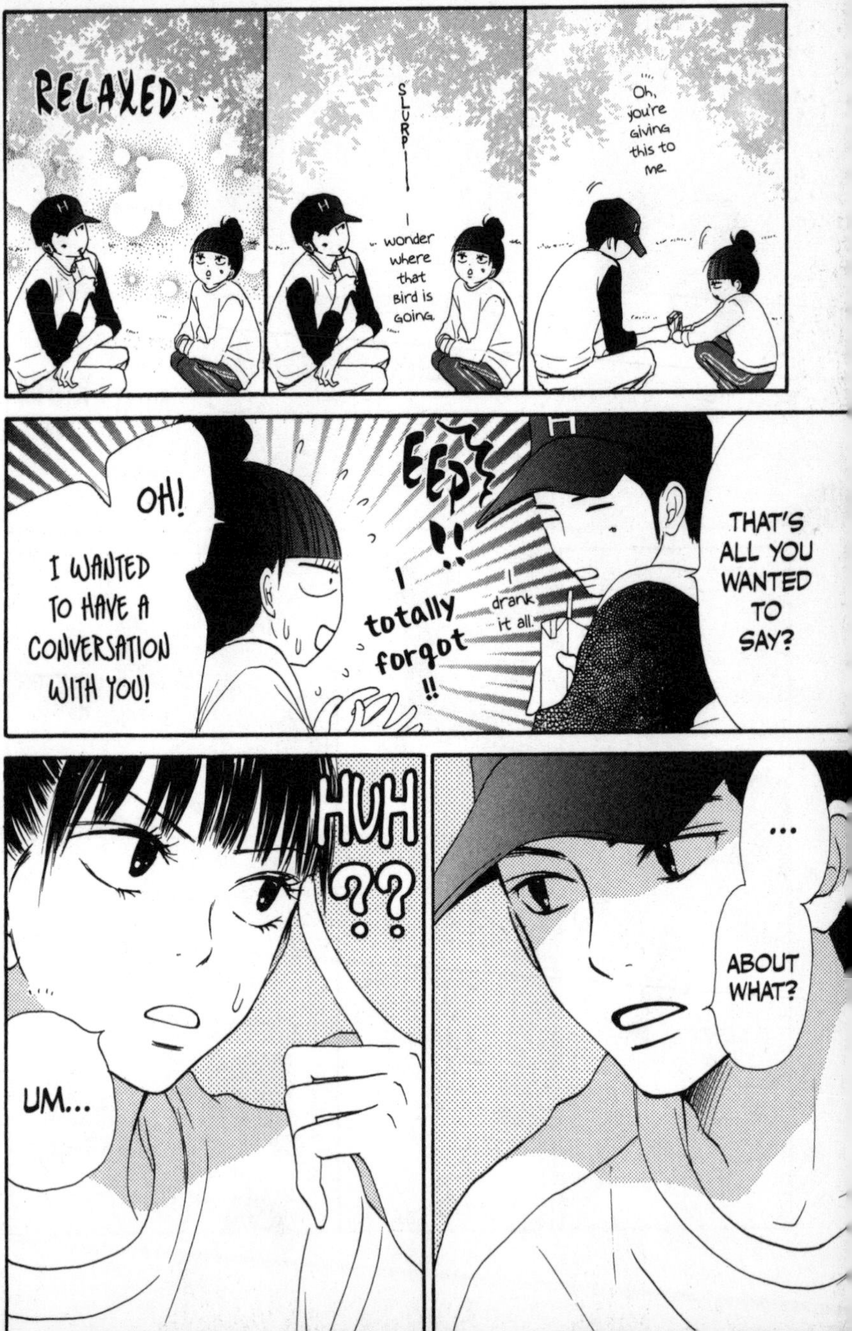

.... Oh, you're giving this to me.
SLURP
I wonder where that bird is going.
RELAXED...
THAT'S ALL YOU WANTED TO SAY?
I drank it all.
EEP!!
I totally forgot!!
OH!
I WANTED TO HAVE A CONVERSATION WITH YOU!
...
ABOUT WHAT?
HUH??
UM...

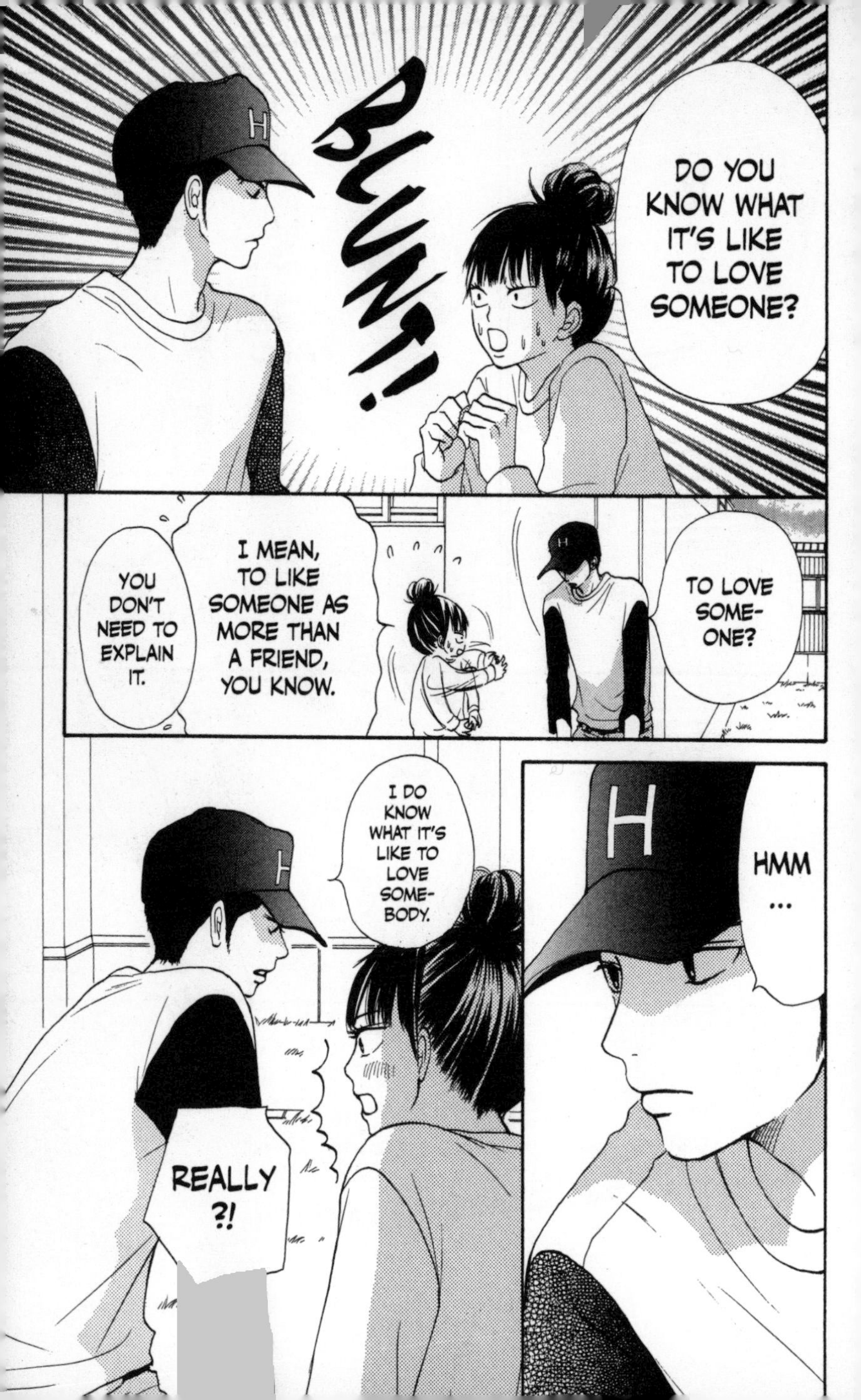
DO YOU KNOW WHAT IT'S LIKE TO LOVE SOMEONE?
BLUNT!!
TO LOVE SOME-ONE?
I MEAN, TO LIKE SOMEONE AS MORE THAN A FRIEND, YOU KNOW.
YOU DON'T NEED TO EXPLAIN IT.
HMM ...
I DO KNOW WHAT IT'S LIKE TO LOVE SOME-BODY.
REALLY ?!

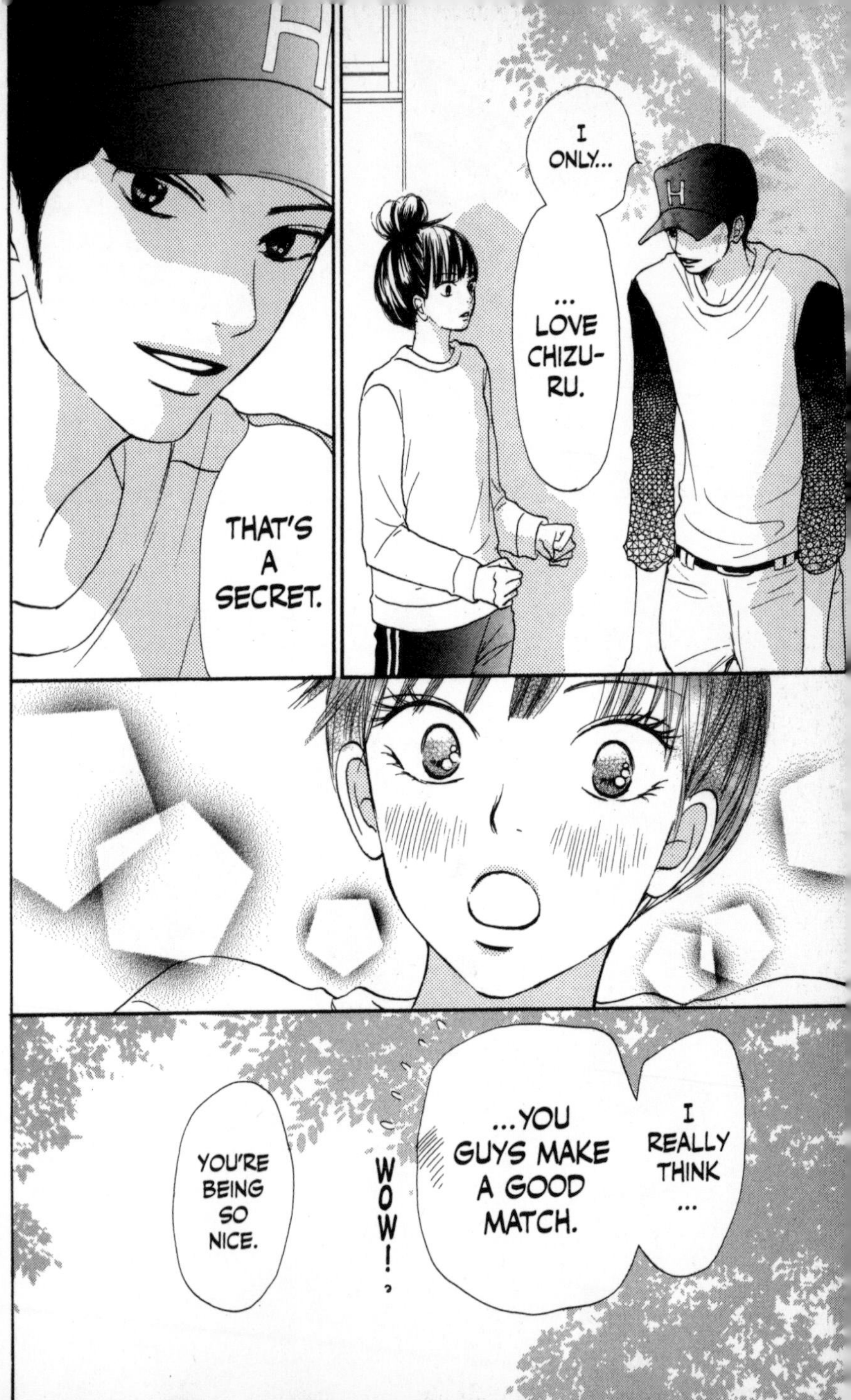
I ONLY...
... LOVE CHIZURU.
THAT'S A SECRET.
I REALLY THINK ...
...YOU GUYS MAKE A GOOD MATCH.
WOW!
YOU'RE BEING SO NICE.

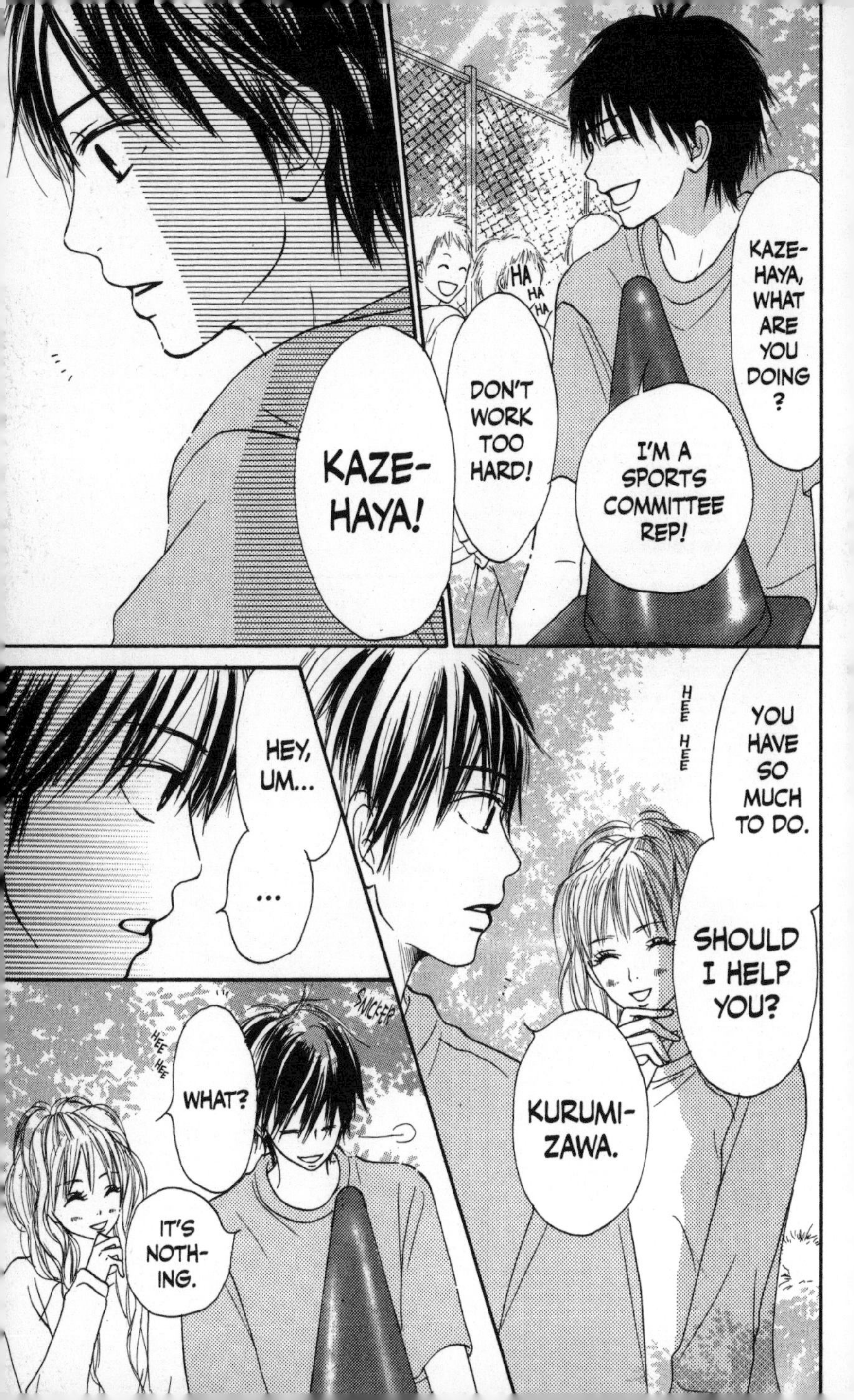
KAZE-HAYA, WHAT ARE YOU DOING?
I'M A SPORTS COMMITTEE REP!
HA HA HA
DON'T WORK TOO HARD!
KAZE-HAYA!
HEE HEE
YOU HAVE SO MUCH TO DO.
SHOULD I HELP YOU?
KURUMI-ZAWA.
HEY, UM...
...
SNICKER
HEE HEE
WHAT?
IT'S NOTH-ING.

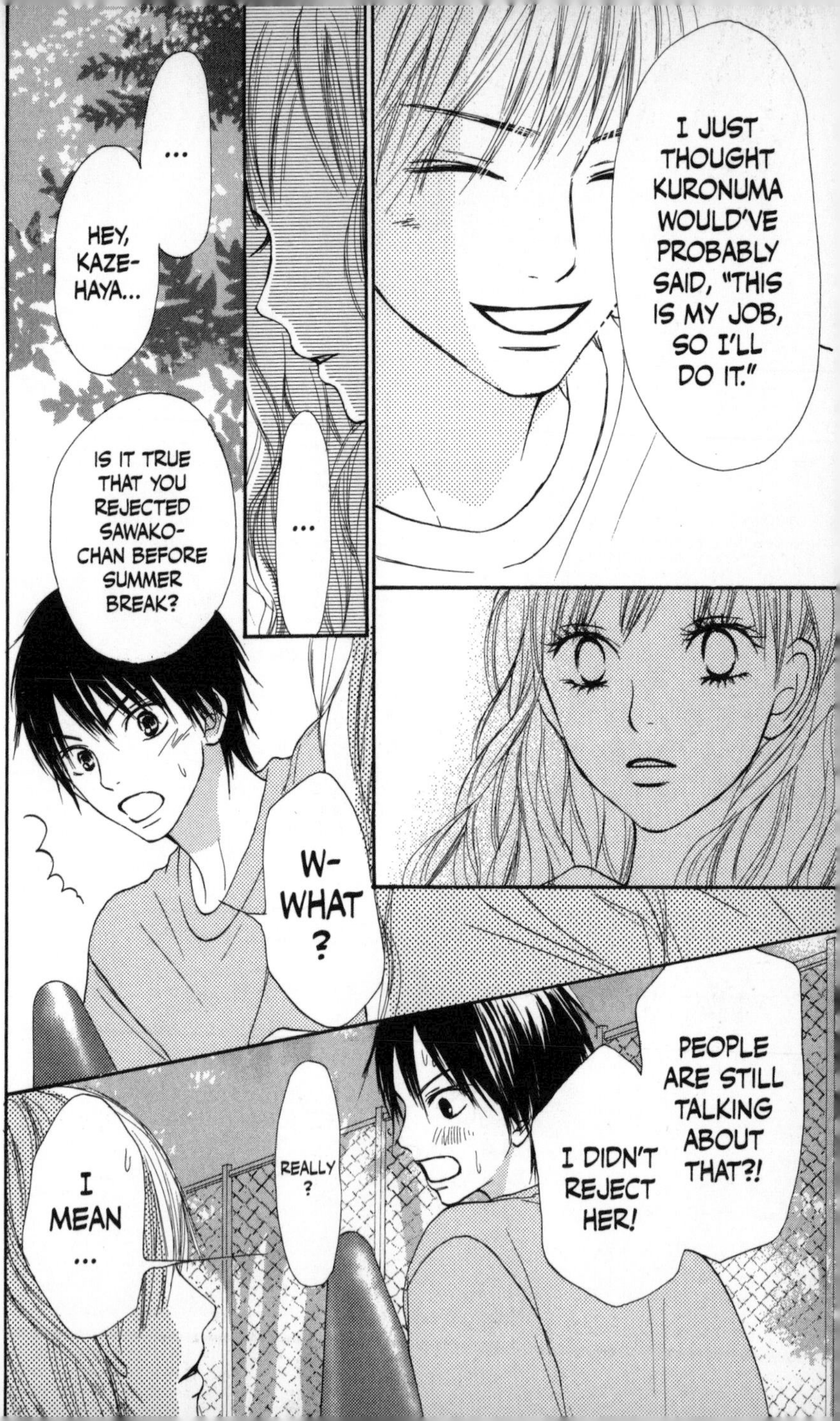
I JUST THOUGHT KURONUMA WOULD'VE PROBABLY SAID, "THIS IS MY JOB, SO I'LL DO IT."
...
...
HEY, KAZE-HAYA...
IS IT TRUE THAT YOU REJECTED SAWAKO-CHAN BEFORE SUMMER BREAK?
W-WHAT?
PEOPLE ARE STILL TALKING ABOUT THAT?!
I DIDN'T REJECT HER!
REALLY?
I MEAN...

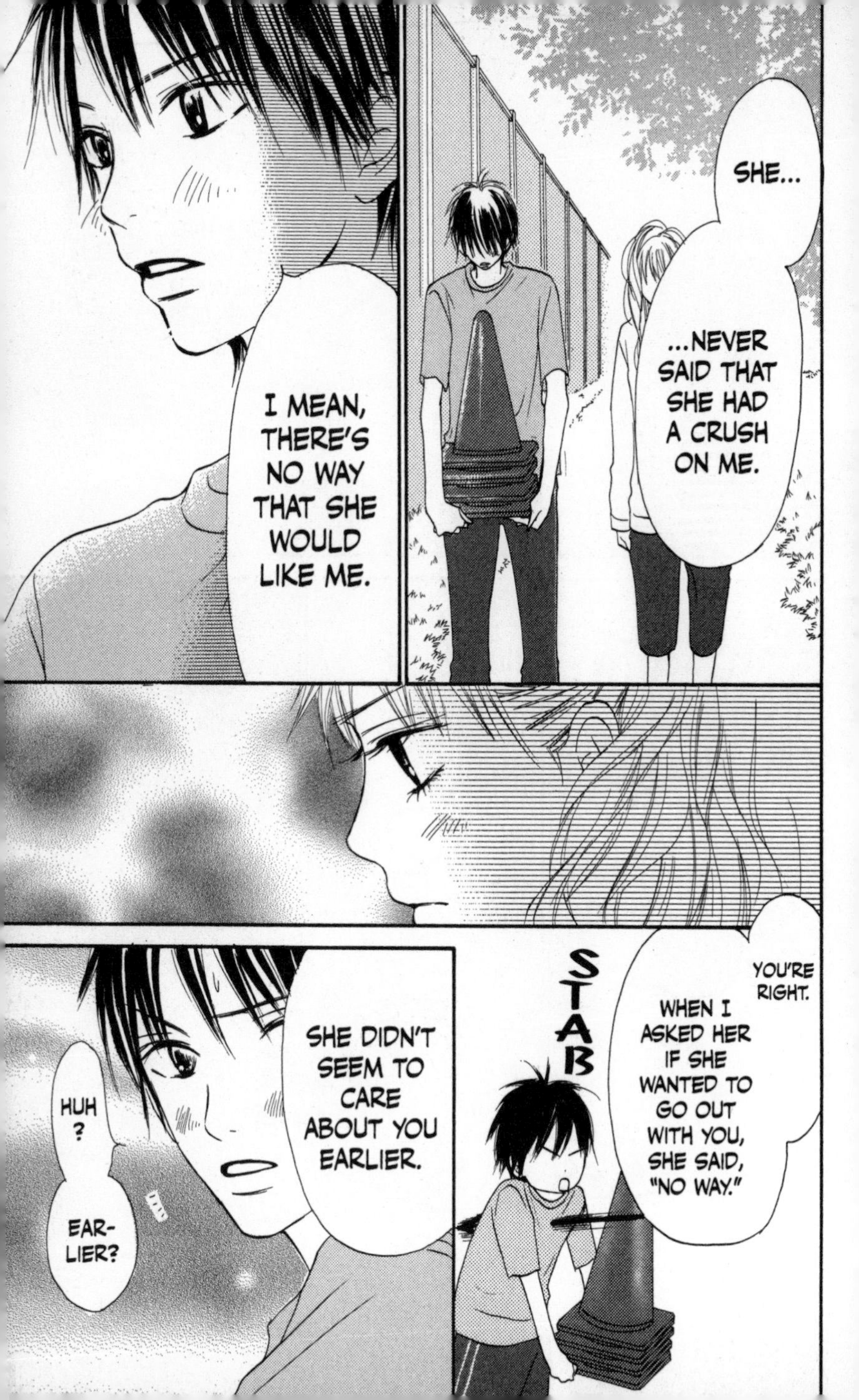
SHE...
...NEVER SAID THAT SHE HAD A CRUSH ON ME.
I MEAN, THERE'S NO WAY THAT SHE WOULD LIKE ME.
YOU'RE RIGHT.
WHEN I ASKED HER IF SHE WANTED TO GO OUT WITH YOU, SHE SAID, "NO WAY."
STAB
SHE DIDN'T SEEM TO CARE ABOUT YOU EARLIER.
HUH?
...
EAR-LIER?

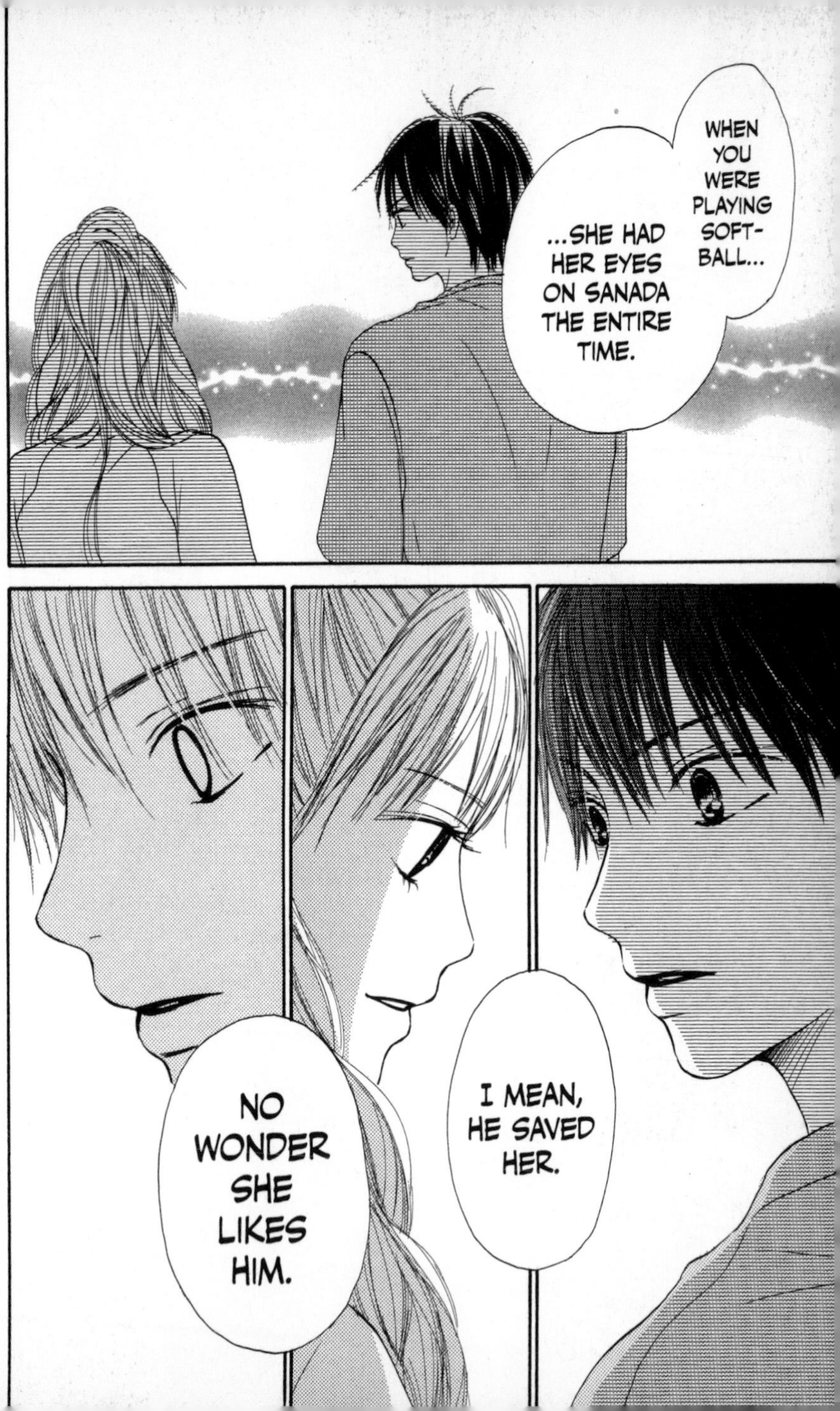
WHEN YOU WERE PLAYING SOFT-BALL...
...SHE HAD HER EYES ON SANADA THE ENTIRE TIME.
I MEAN, HE SAVED HER.
NO WONDER SHE LIKES HIM.

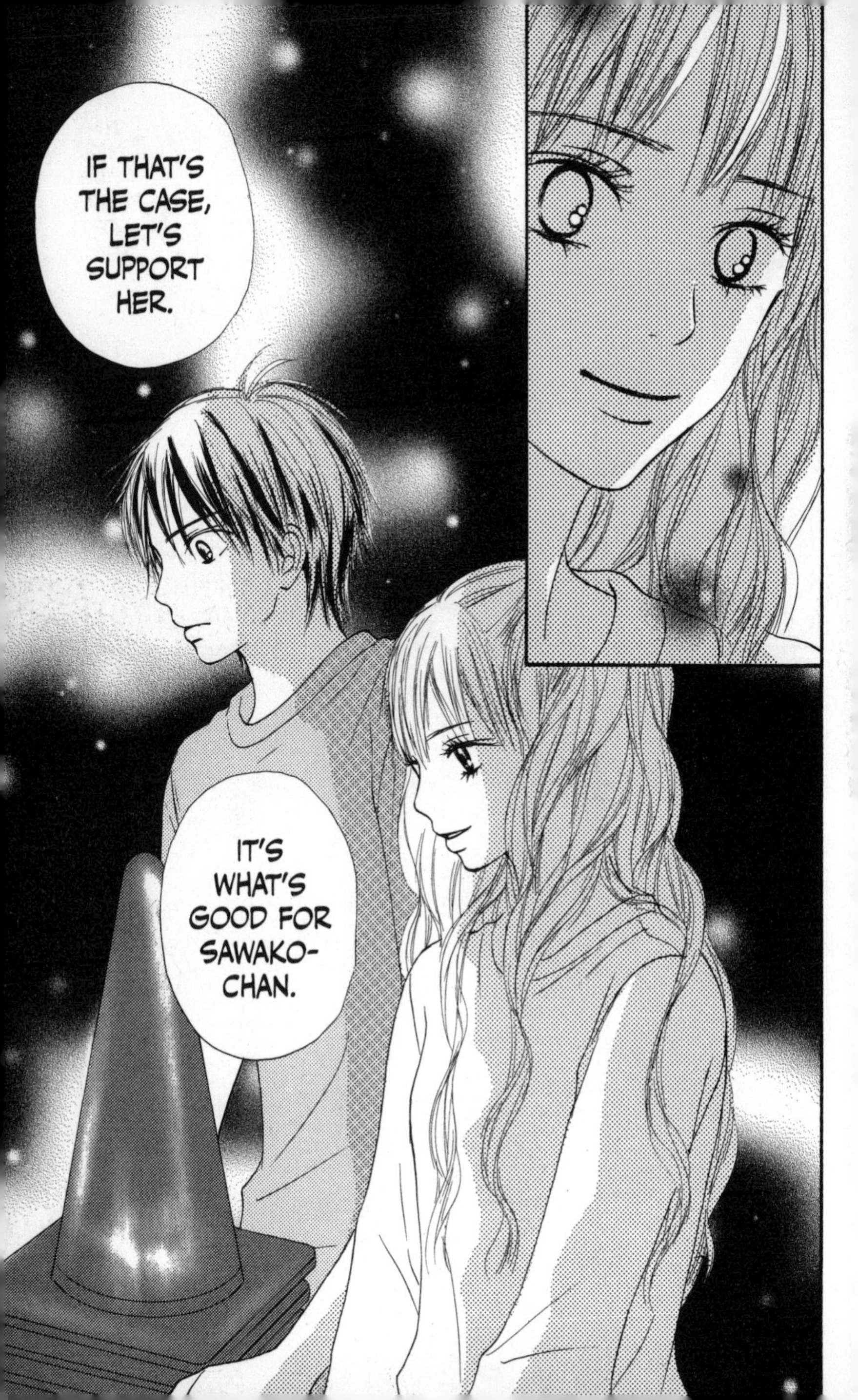
IF THAT'S THE CASE, LET'S SUPPORT HER.
IT'S WHAT'S GOOD FOR SAWAKO-CHAN.

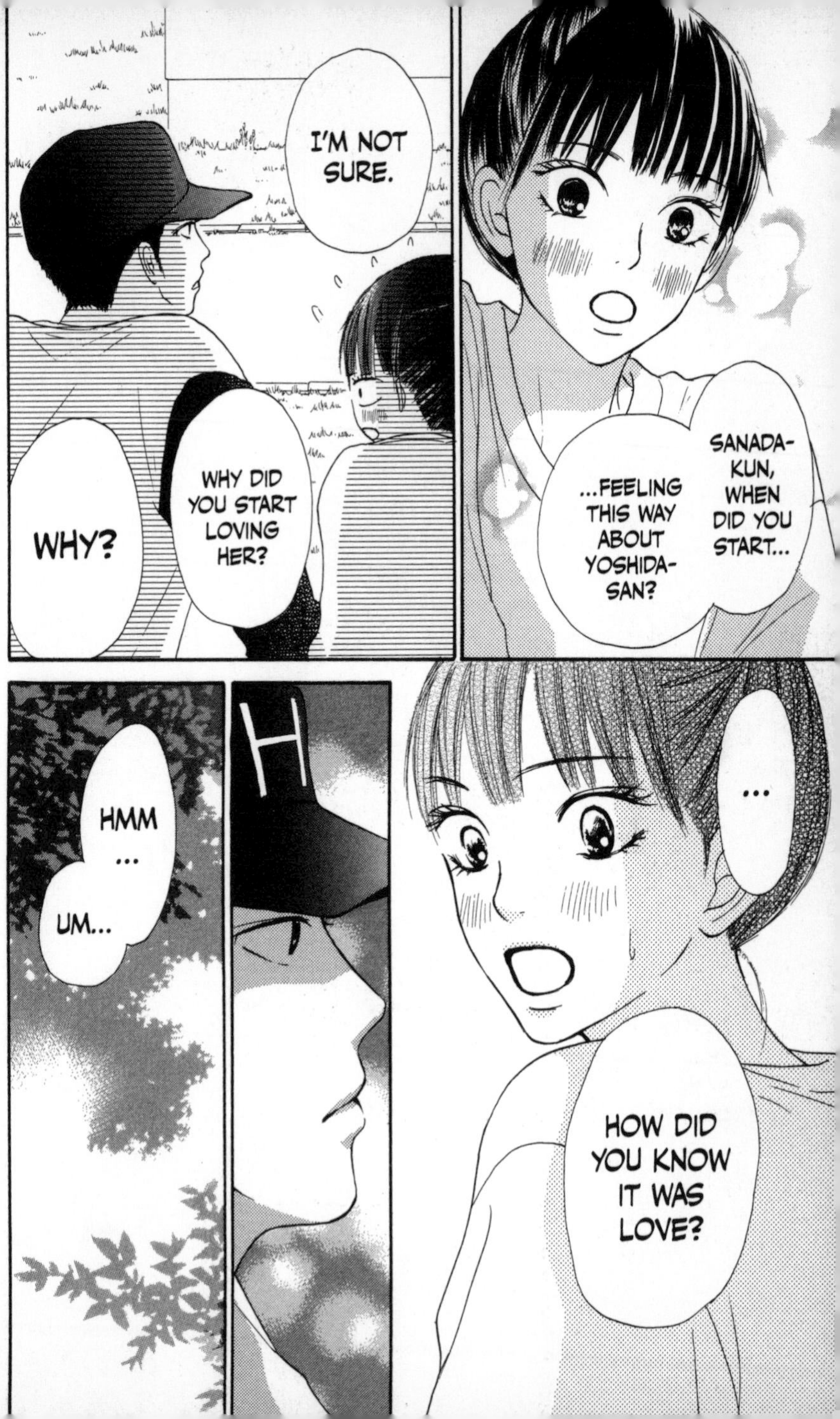
SANADA-KUN, WHEN DID YOU START...
...FEELING THIS WAY ABOUT YOSHIDA-SAN?
I'M NOT SURE.
WHY DID YOU START LOVING HER?
WHY?
...
HOW DID YOU KNOW IT WAS LOVE?
HMM ...
UM...

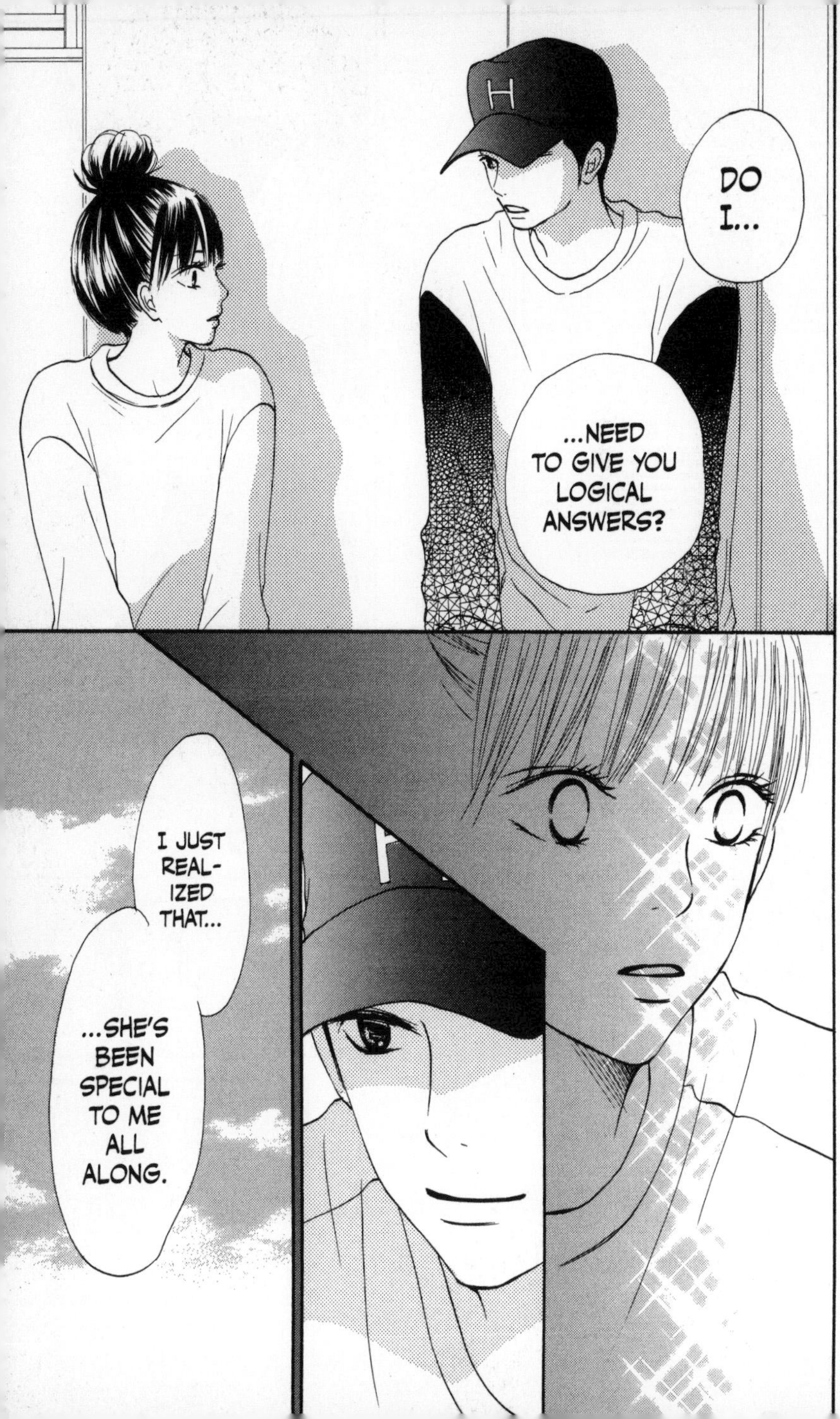
DO I...
...NEED TO GIVE YOU LOGICAL ANSWERS?
I JUST REALIZED THAT...
...SHE'S BEEN SPECIAL TO ME ALL ALONG.

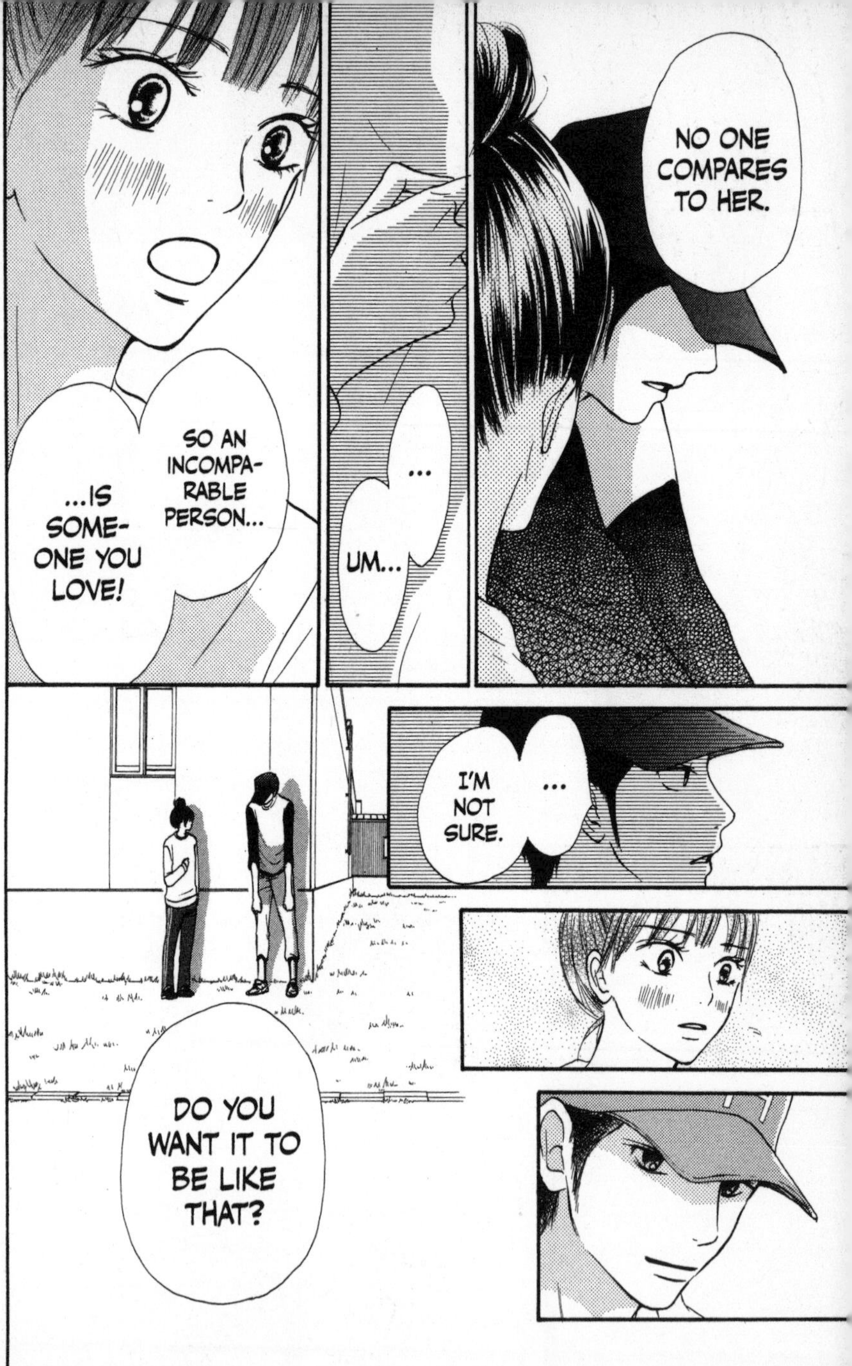
NO ONE COMPARES TO HER.
...
UM...
SO AN INCOMPARABLE PERSON...
...IS SOMEONE YOU LOVE!
...
I'M NOT SURE.
DO YOU WANT IT TO BE LIKE THAT?

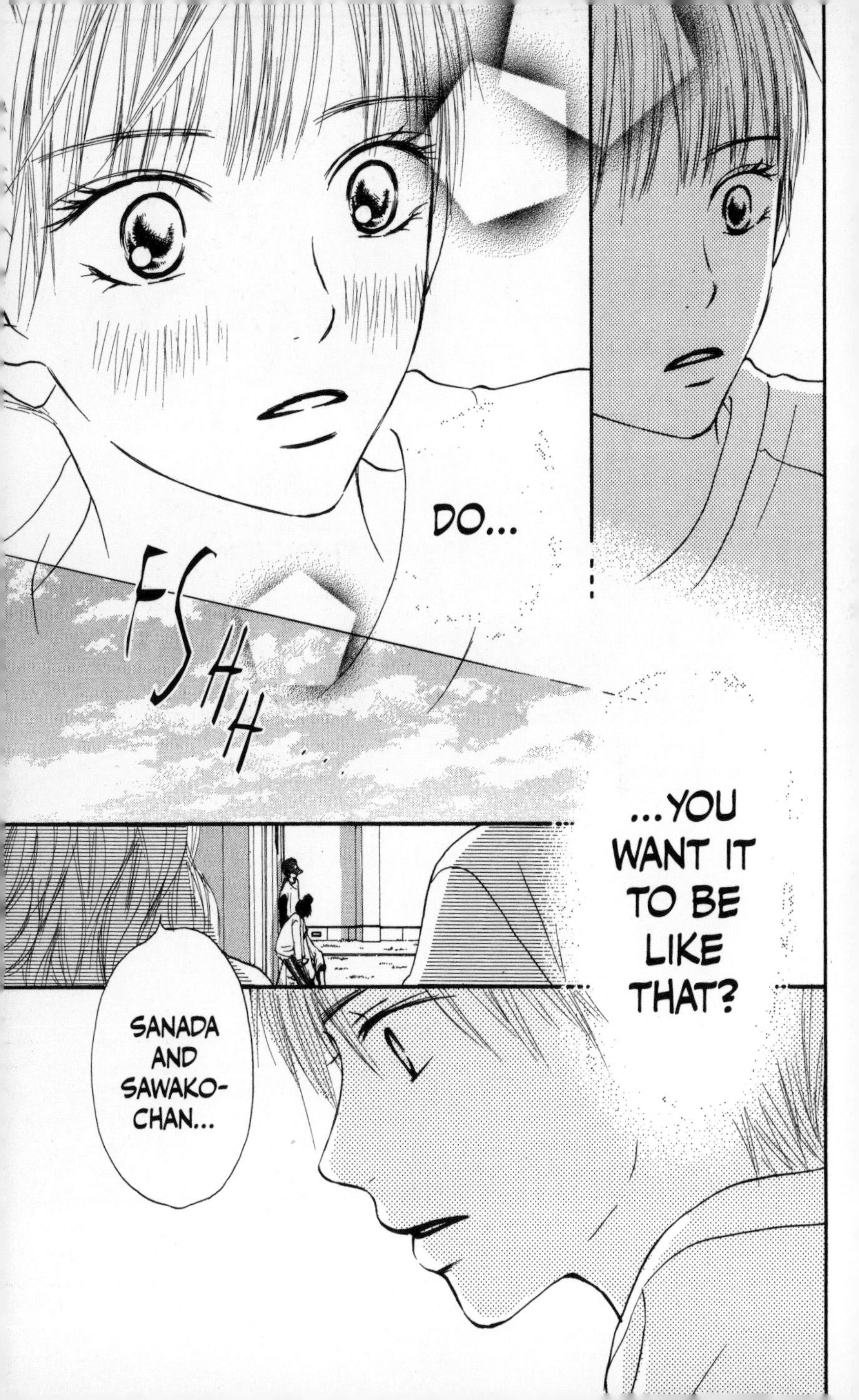
DO...
FSHH
...YOU WANT IT TO BE LIKE THAT?
SANADA AND SAWAKO-CHAN...

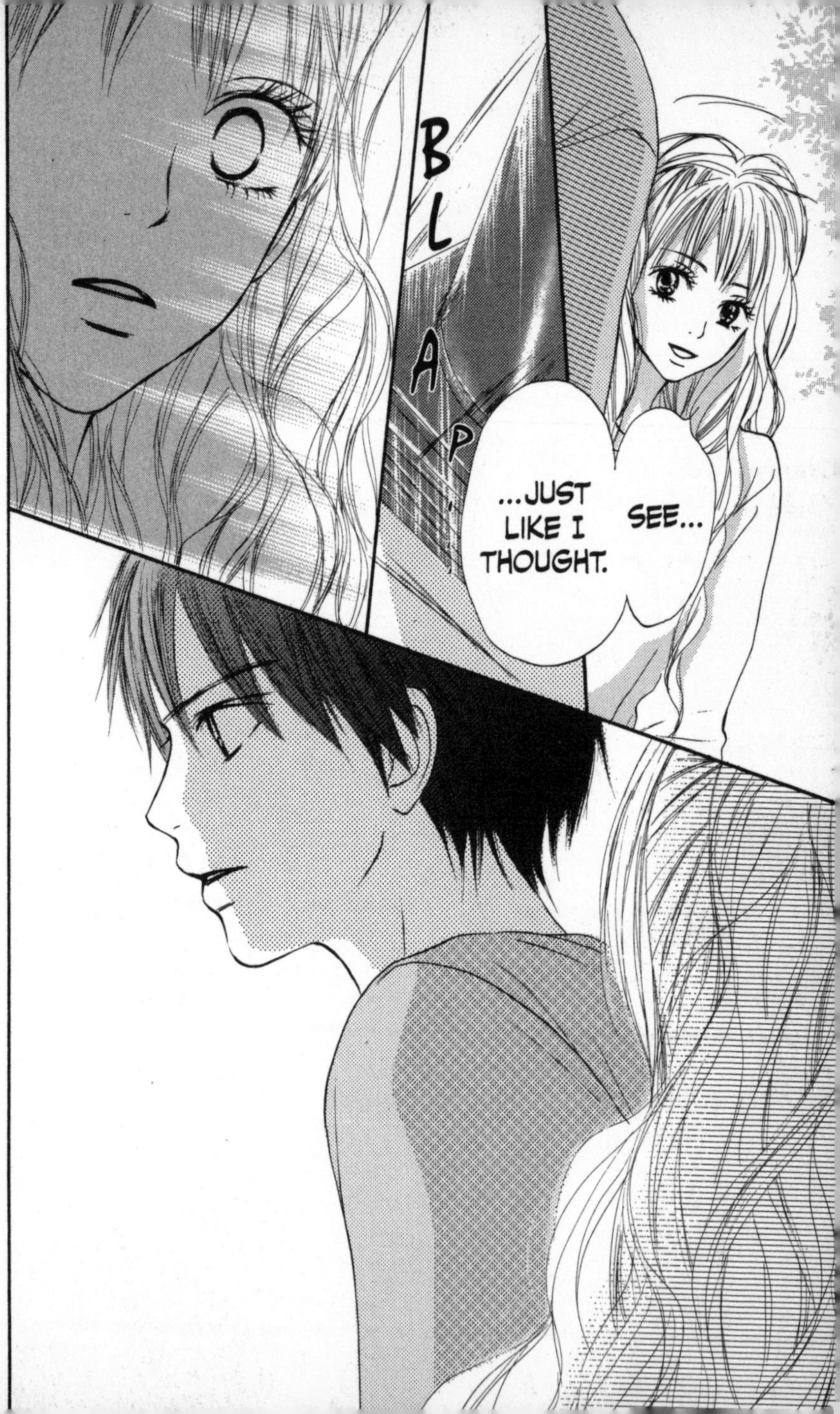
SEE...
...JUST LIKE I THOUGHT.
BLAP

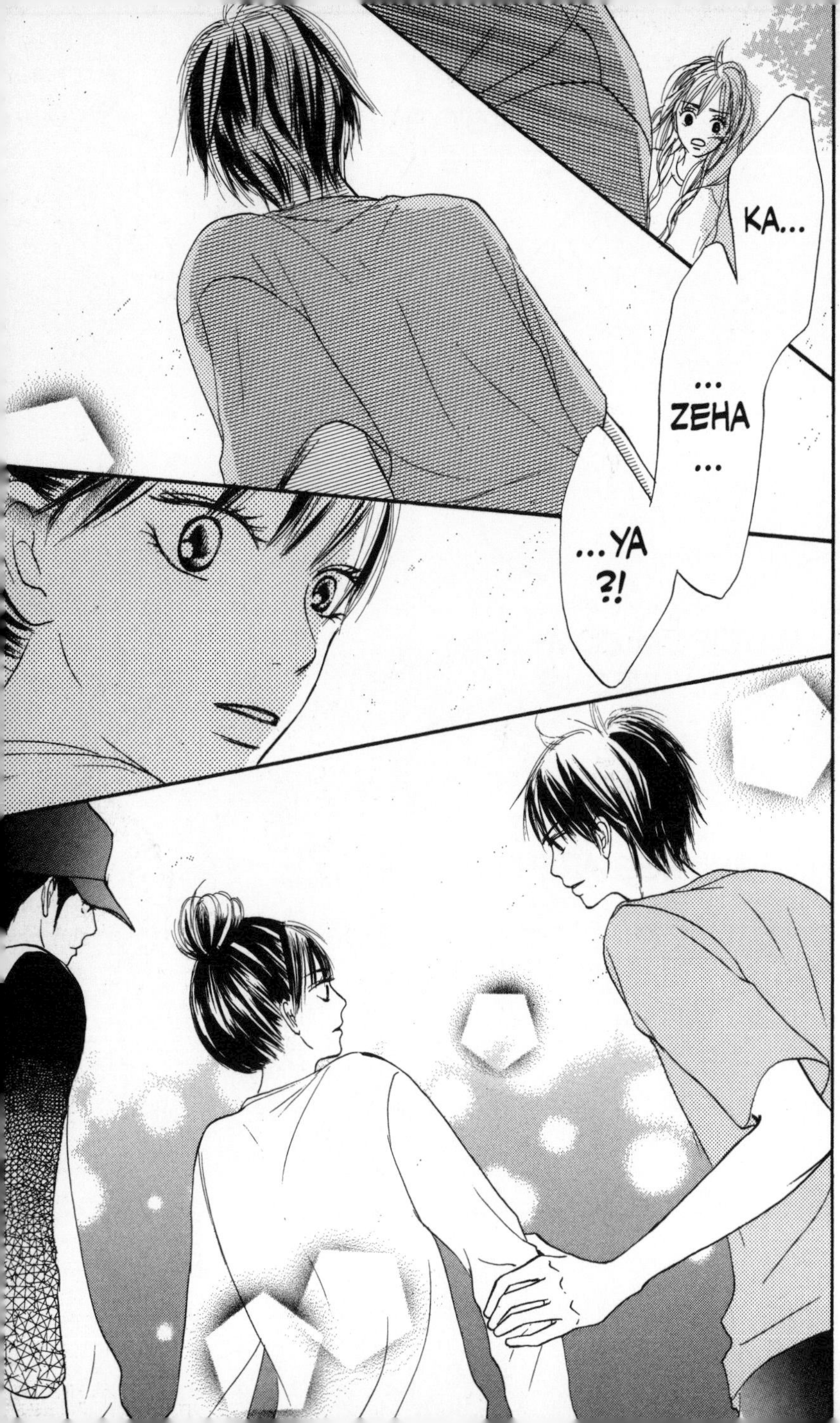
KA...
... ZEHA ...
...YA ?!

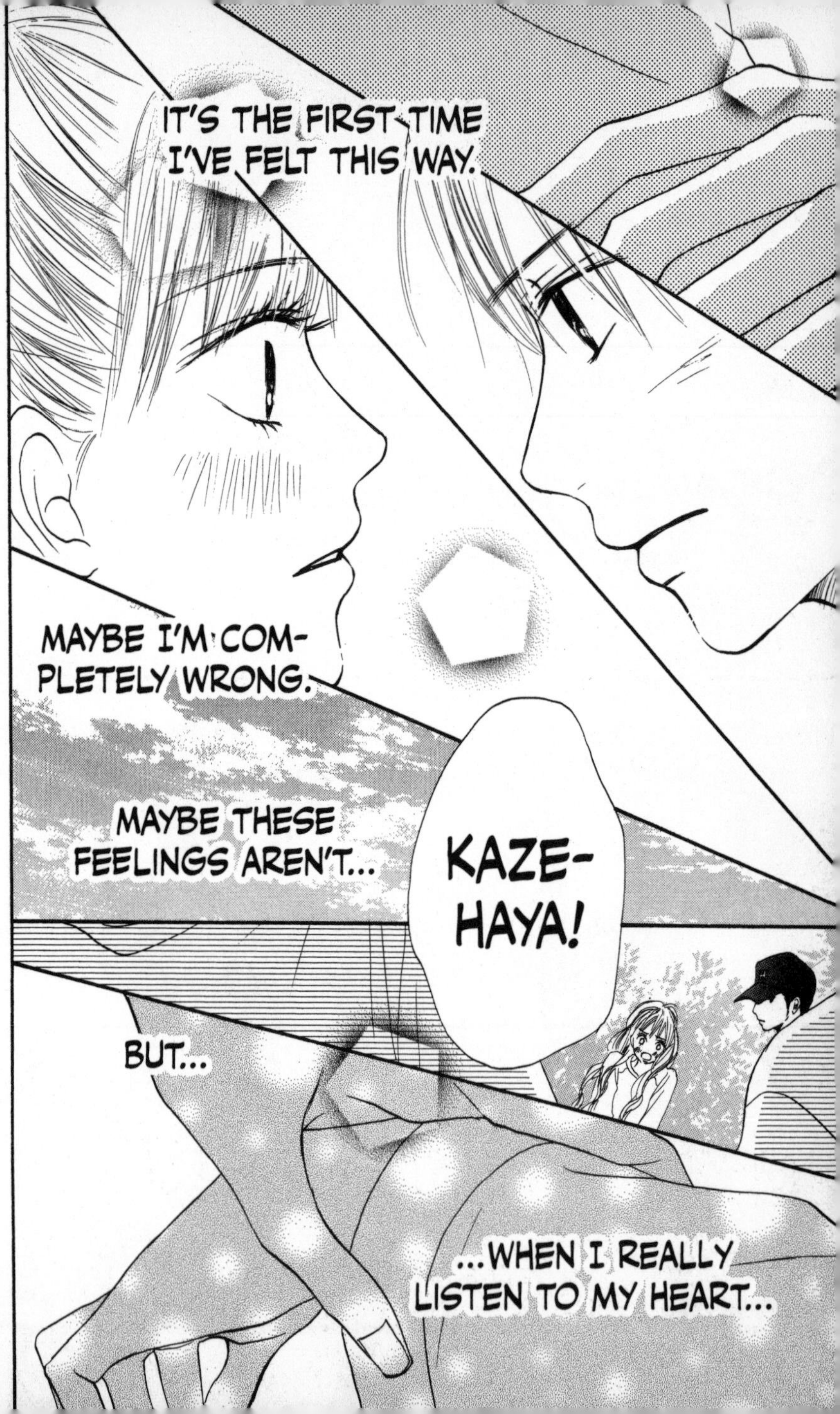
IT'S THE FIRST TIME I'VE FELT THIS WAY.
MAYBE I'M COMPLETELY WRONG.
MAYBE THESE FEELINGS AREN'T...
KAZE-HAYA!
BUT...
...WHEN I REALLY LISTEN TO MY HEART...

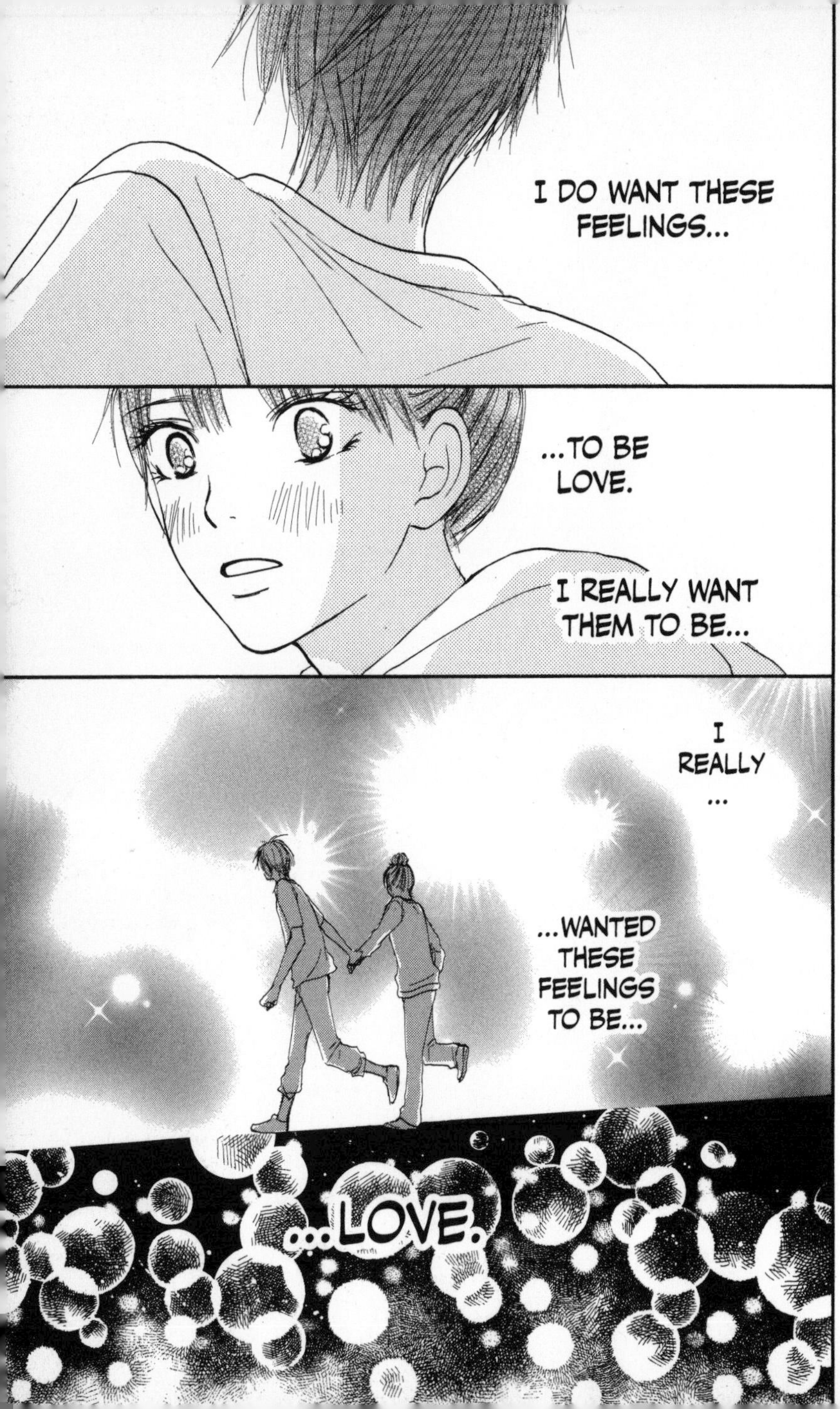
I DO WANT THESE FEELINGS...
...TO BE LOVE.
I REALLY WANT THEM TO BE...
I REALLY ...
...WANTED THESE FEELINGS TO BE...
...LOVE.

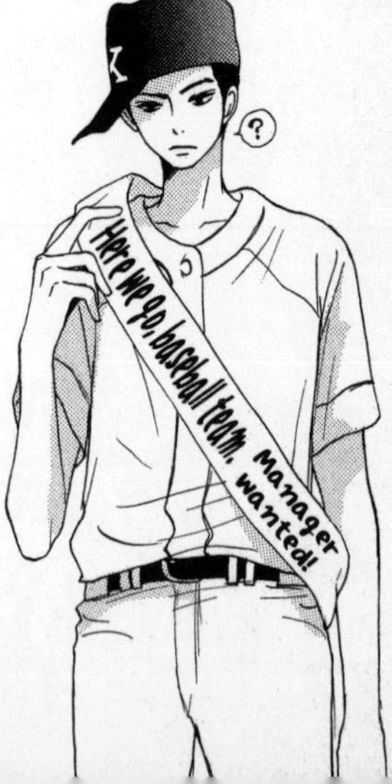
?
Here we go, baseball team.
Manager wanted!

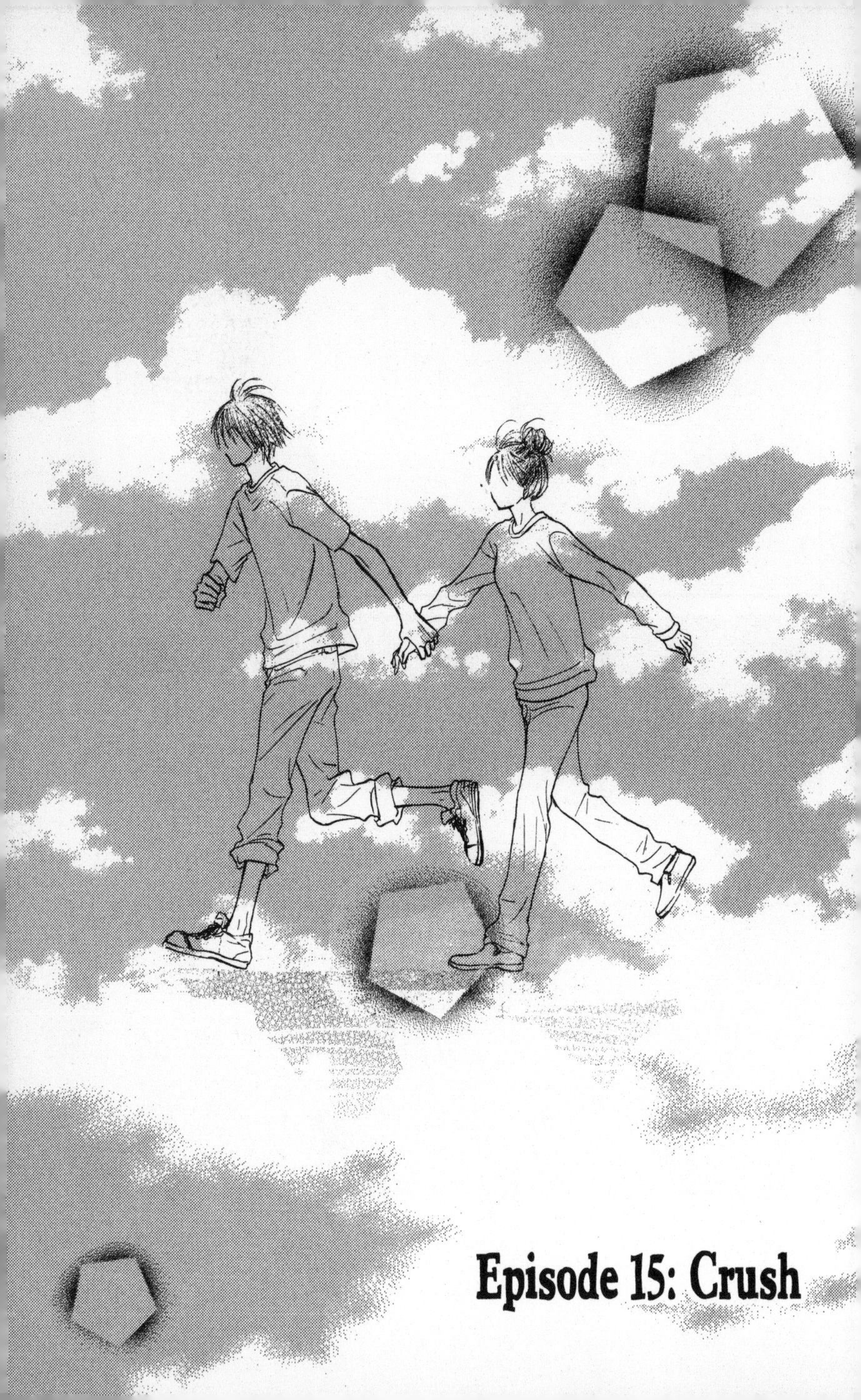

Episode 15: Crush

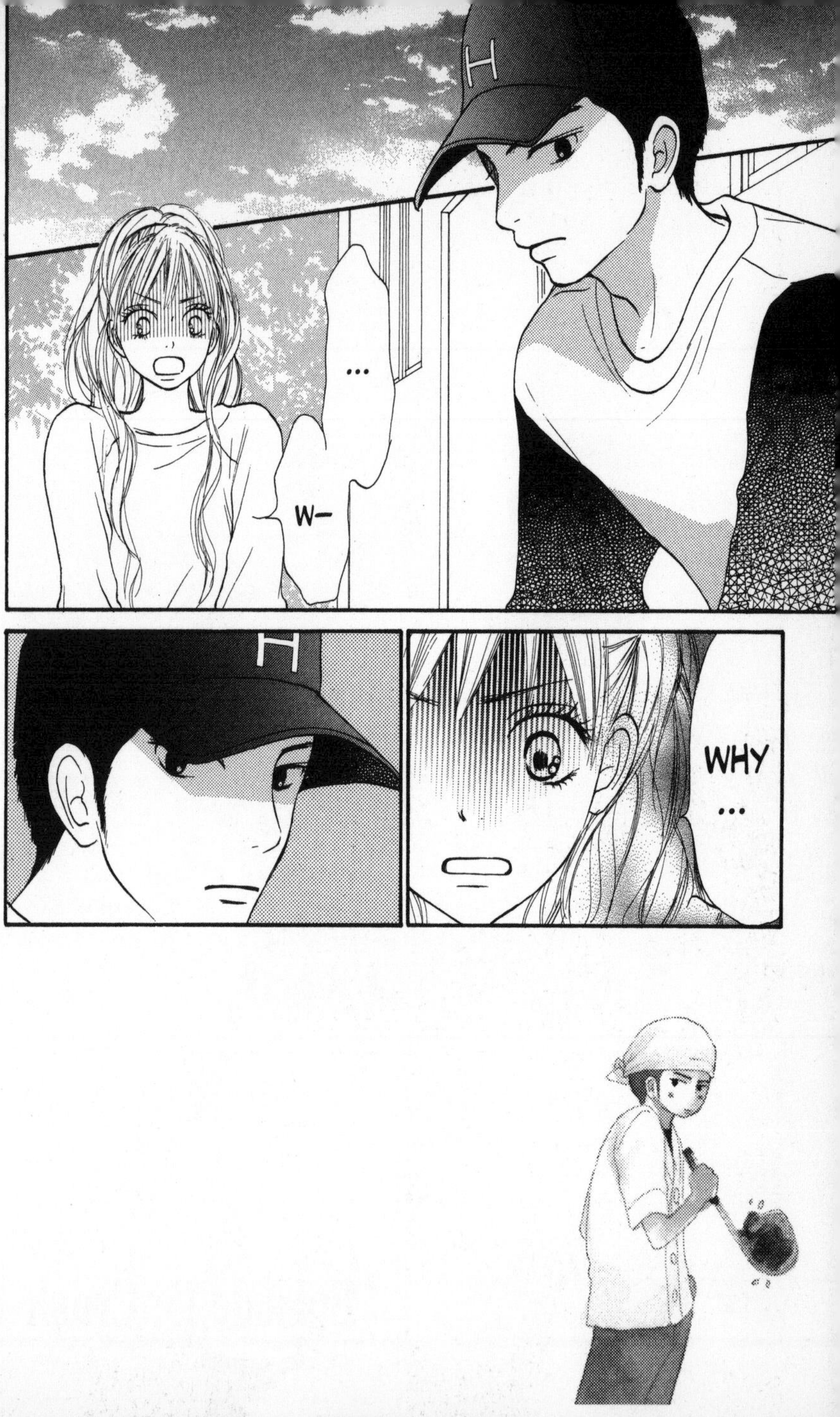
...
W-
WHY ...

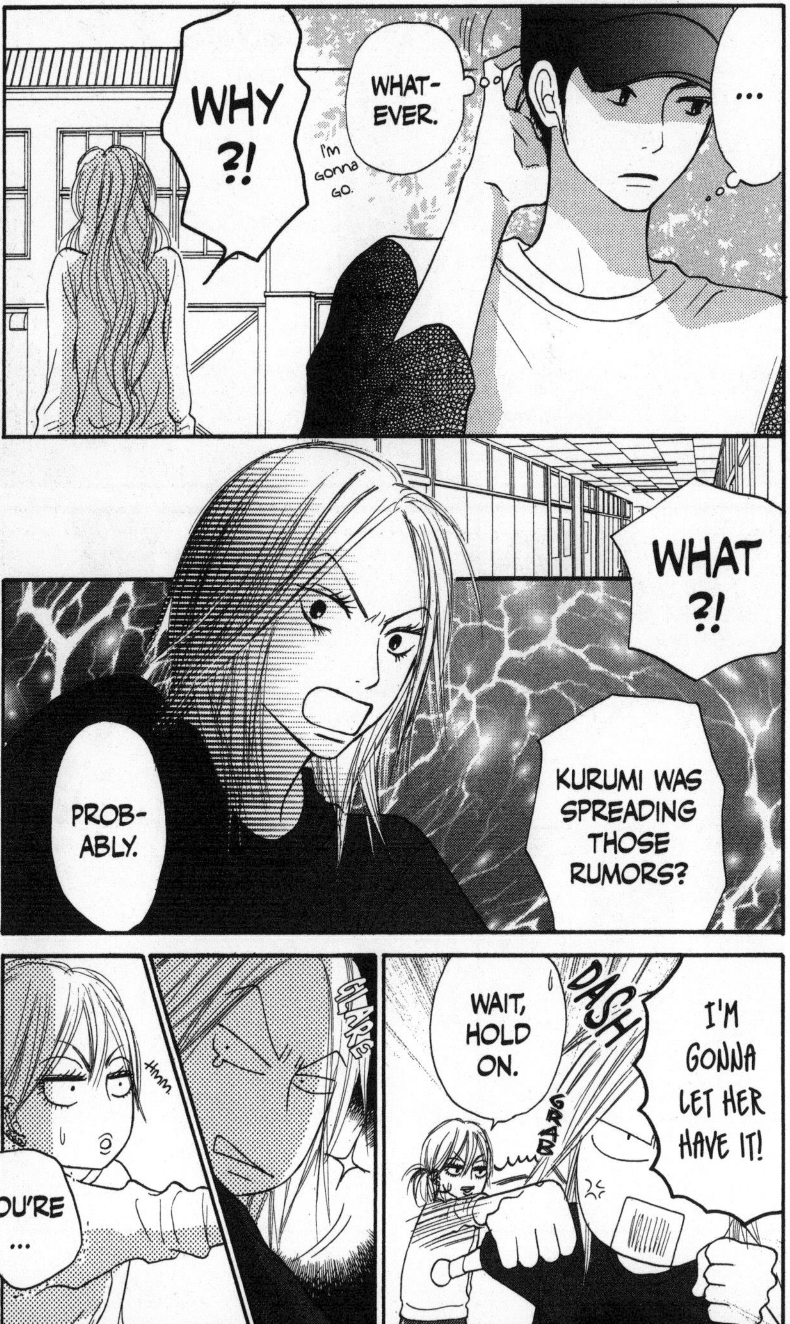
...
WHAT-EVER.
I'm gonna go.
WHY?!
WHAT?!
KURUMI WAS SPREADING THOSE RUMORS?
PROB-ABLY.
I'M GONNA LET HER HAVE IT!
DASH
WAIT, HOLD ON.
GRAB
GLARE
Hmm
YOU'RE ...

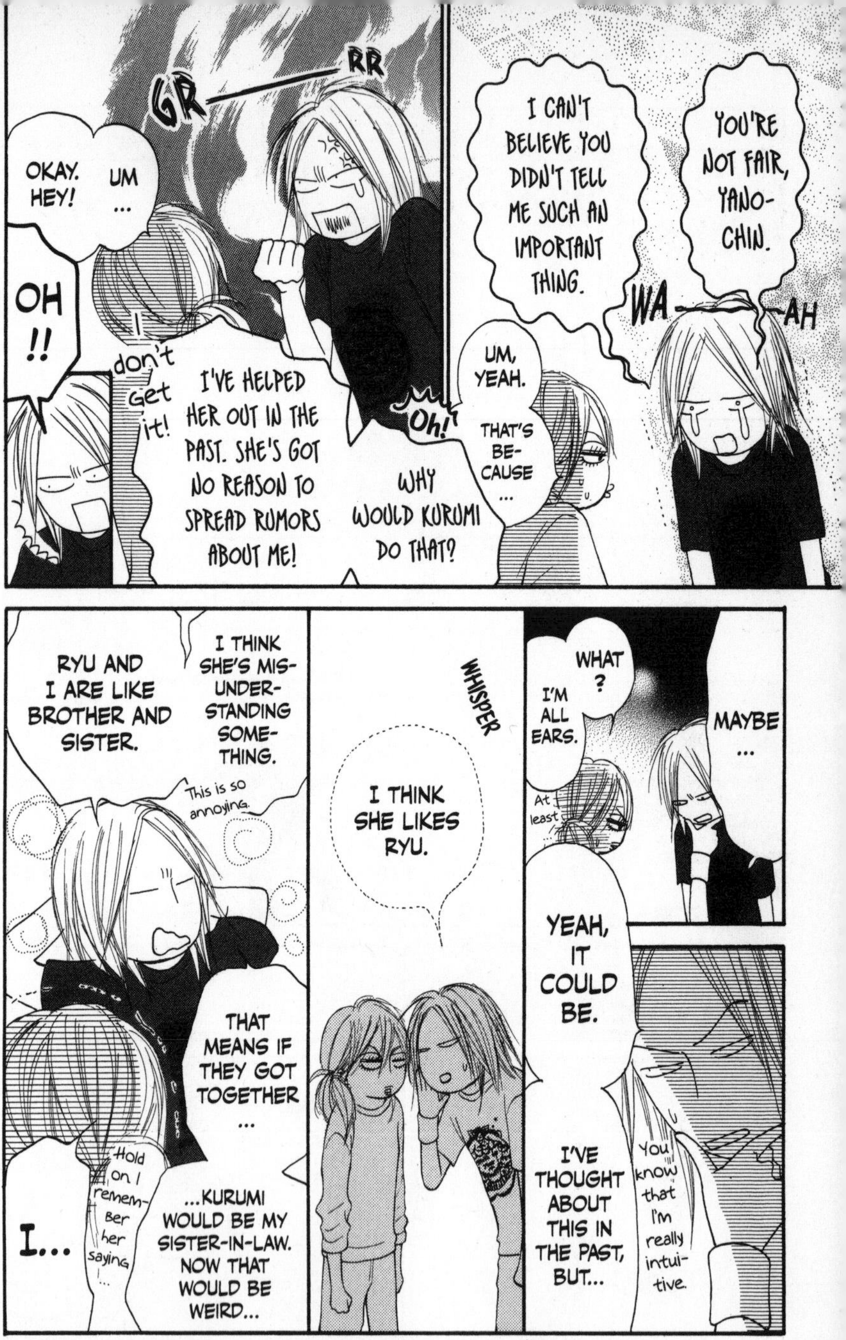
YOU'RE NOT FAIR, YANO-CHIN.
I CAN'T BELIEVE YOU DIDN'T TELL ME SUCH AN IMPORTANT THING.
WA—AH
UM, YEAH.
THAT'S BECAUSE ...
GR—RR
Oh!
WHY WOULD KURUMI DO THAT?
I'VE HELPED HER OUT IN THE PAST. SHE'S GOT NO REASON TO SPREAD RUMORS ABOUT ME!
I don't get it!
UM ...
OKAY. HEY!
OH !!
MAYBE ...
WHAT ?
I'M ALL EARS.
At least ...
You know that I'm really intuitive.
YEAH, IT COULD BE.
I'VE THOUGHT ABOUT THIS IN THE PAST, BUT...
WHISPER
I THINK SHE LIKES RYU.
I THINK SHE'S MISUNDERSTANDING SOMETHING.
RYU AND I ARE LIKE BROTHER AND SISTER.
This is so annoying.
THAT MEANS IF THEY GOT TOGETHER ...
...KURUMI WOULD BE MY SISTER-IN-LAW. NOW THAT WOULD BE WEIRD...
Hold on I remember her saying ...
I...

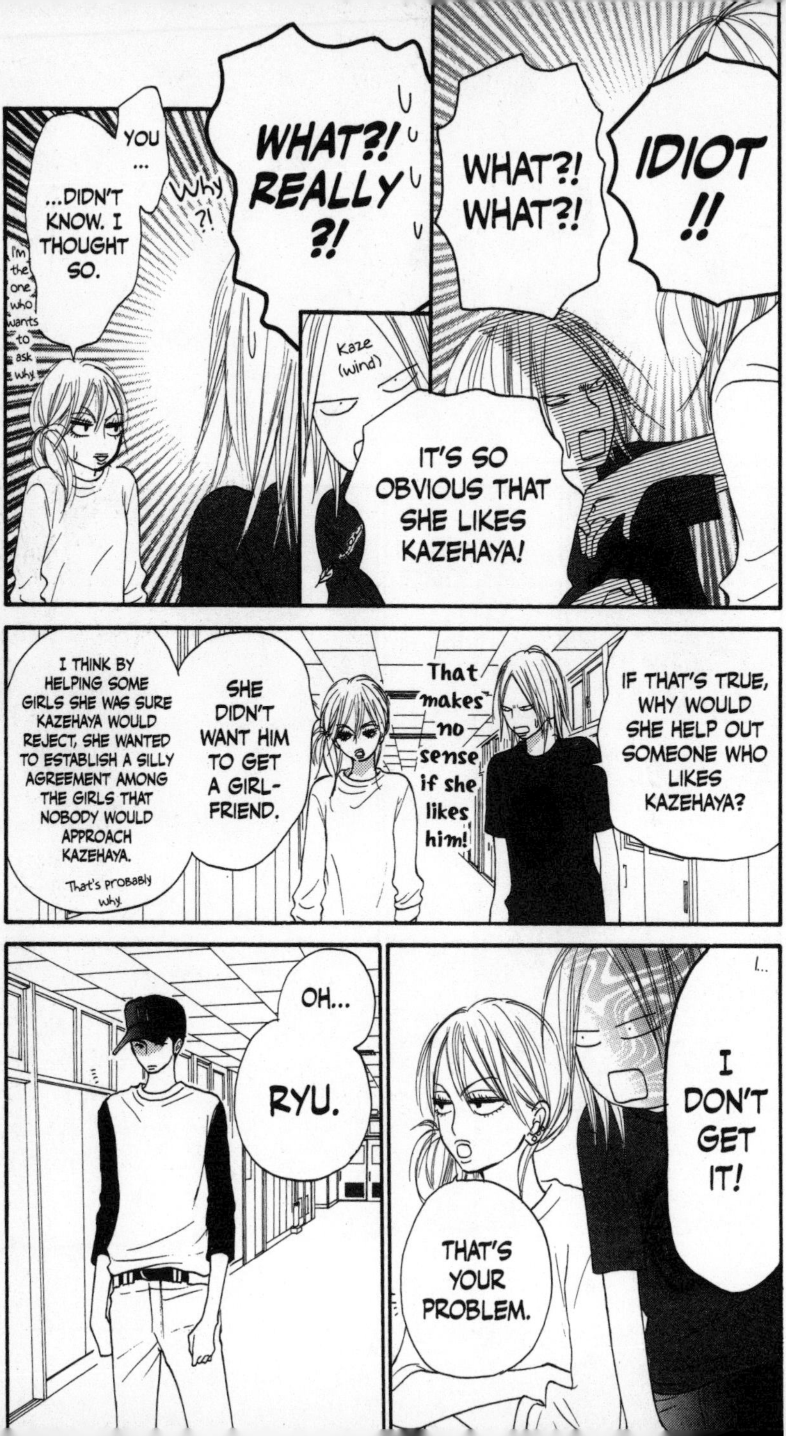
IDIOT!!
WHAT?! WHAT?!
Kaze (wind)
IT'S SO OBVIOUS THAT SHE LIKES KAZEHAYA!
WHAT?! REALLY?!
Why?!
YOU...
...DIDN'T KNOW. I THOUGHT SO.
I'm the one who wants to ask why!
IF THAT'S TRUE, WHY WOULD SHE HELP OUT SOMEONE WHO LIKES KAZEHAYA?
That makes no sense if she likes him!
SHE DIDN'T WANT HIM TO GET A GIRL-FRIEND.
I THINK BY HELPING SOME GIRLS SHE WAS SURE KAZEHAYA WOULD REJECT, SHE WANTED TO ESTABLISH A SILLY AGREEMENT AMONG THE GIRLS THAT NOBODY WOULD APPROACH KAZEHAYA.
That's probably why.
I...
I DON'T GET IT!
THAT'S YOUR PROBLEM.
OH...
RYU.

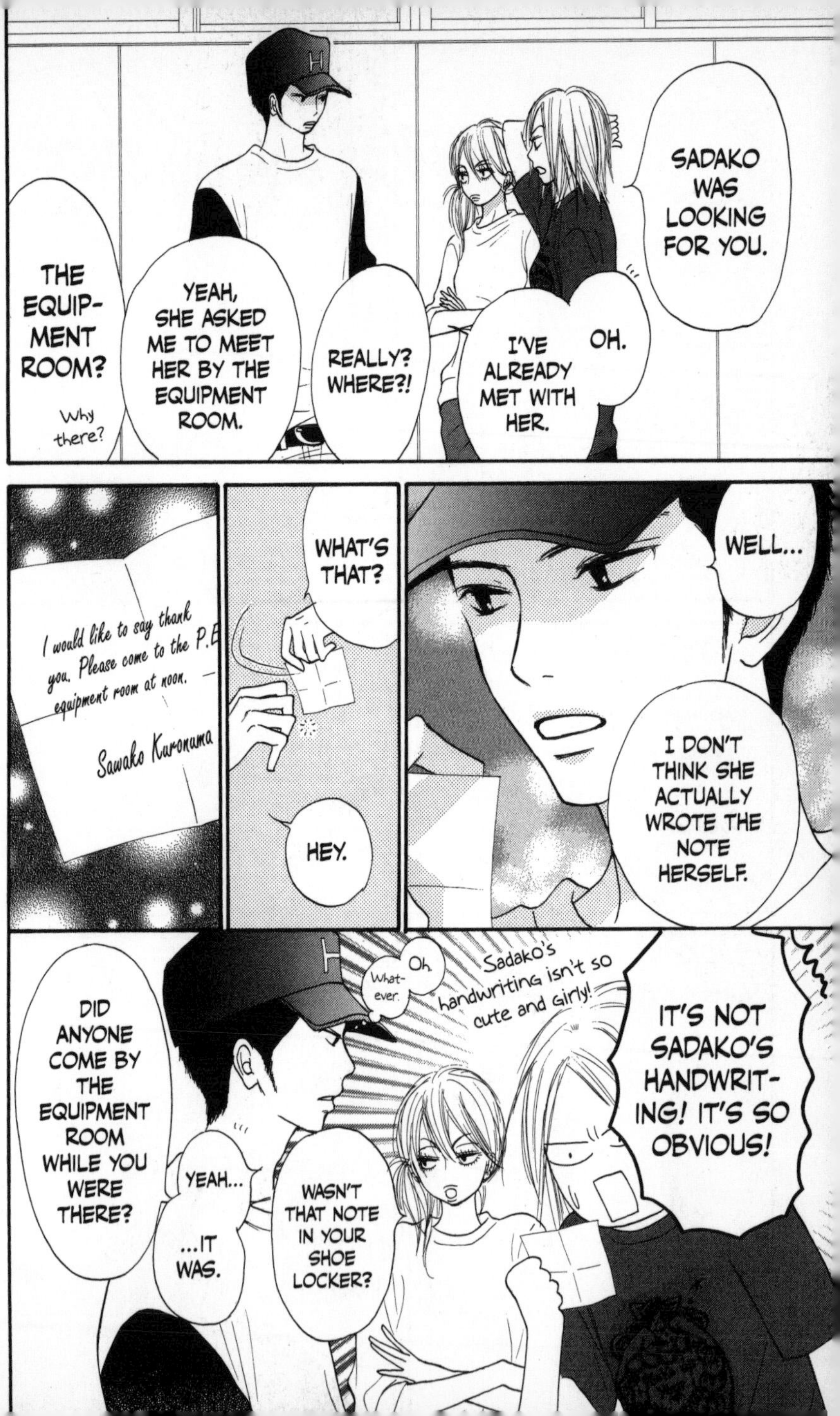
SADAKO WAS LOOKING FOR YOU.
OH.
I'VE ALREADY MET WITH HER.
REALLY? WHERE?!
YEAH, SHE ASKED ME TO MEET HER BY THE EQUIPMENT ROOM.
THE EQUIPMENT ROOM?
Why there?
WELL...
I DON'T THINK SHE ACTUALLY WROTE THE NOTE HERSELF.
WHAT'S THAT?
HEY.
I would like to say thank you. Please come to the P.E equipment room at noon.
Sawako Kuronuma
IT'S NOT SADAKO'S HANDWRITING! IT'S SO OBVIOUS!
Sadako's handwriting isn't so cute and girly!
Oh.
Whatever.
WASN'T THAT NOTE IN YOUR SHOE LOCKER?
YEAH...
...IT WAS.
DID ANYONE COME BY THE EQUIPMENT ROOM WHILE YOU WERE THERE?

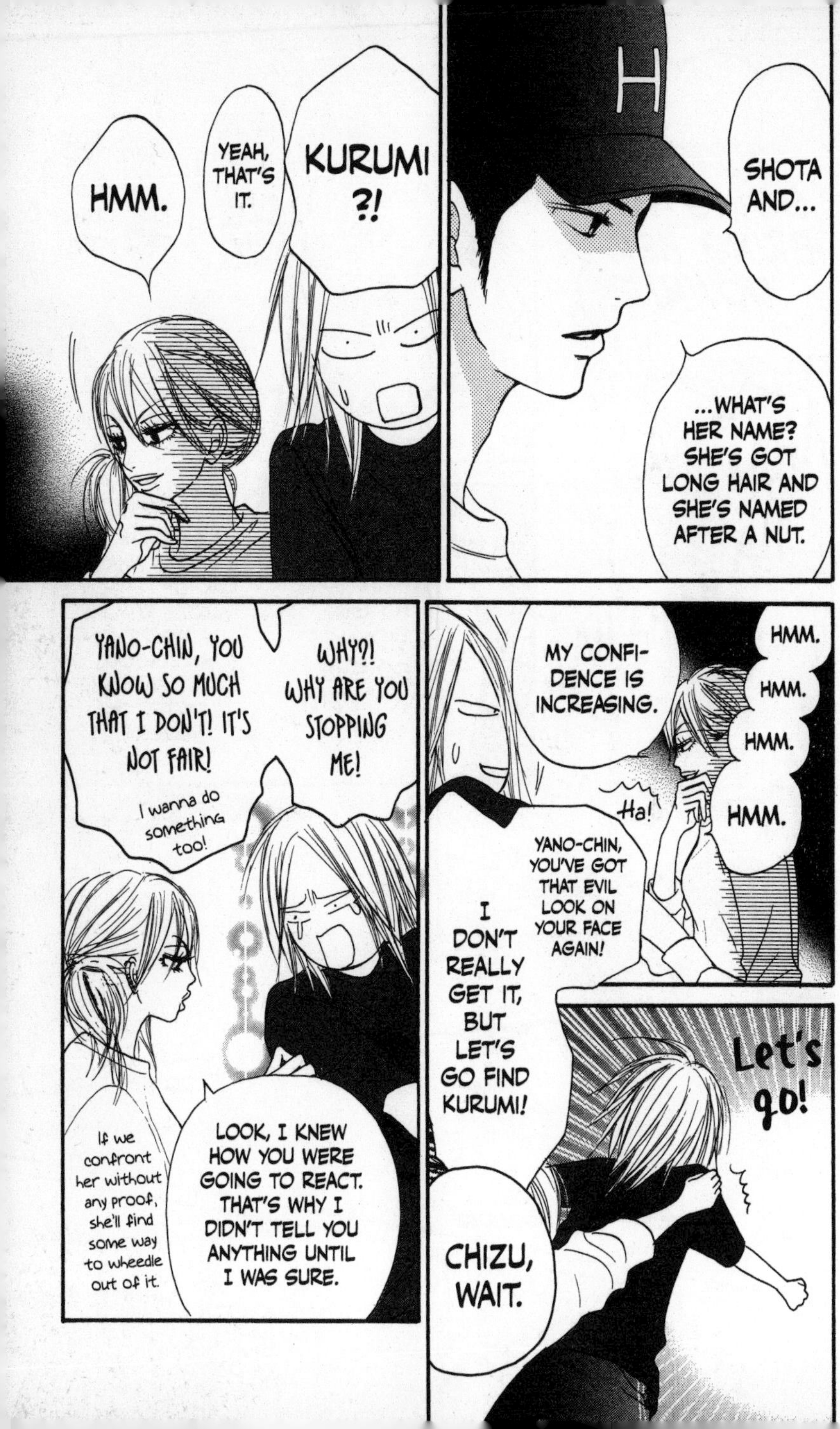
SHOTA AND...
...WHAT'S HER NAME? SHE'S GOT LONG HAIR AND SHE'S NAMED AFTER A NUT.
KURUMI ?!
YEAH, THAT'S IT.
HMM.
HMM.
HMM.
HMM.
HMM.
Ha!
MY CONFI-DENCE IS INCREASING.
YANO-CHIN, YOU'VE GOT THAT EVIL LOOK ON YOUR FACE AGAIN!
I DON'T REALLY GET IT, BUT LET'S GO FIND KURUMI!
Let's go!
CHIZU, WAIT.
WHY?! WHY ARE YOU STOPPING ME!
YANO-CHIN, YOU KNOW SO MUCH THAT I DON'T! IT'S NOT FAIR!
I wanna do something too!
LOOK, I KNEW HOW YOU WERE GOING TO REACT. THAT'S WHY I DIDN'T TELL YOU ANYTHING UNTIL I WAS SURE.
If we confront her without any proof, she'll find some way to wheedle out of it.

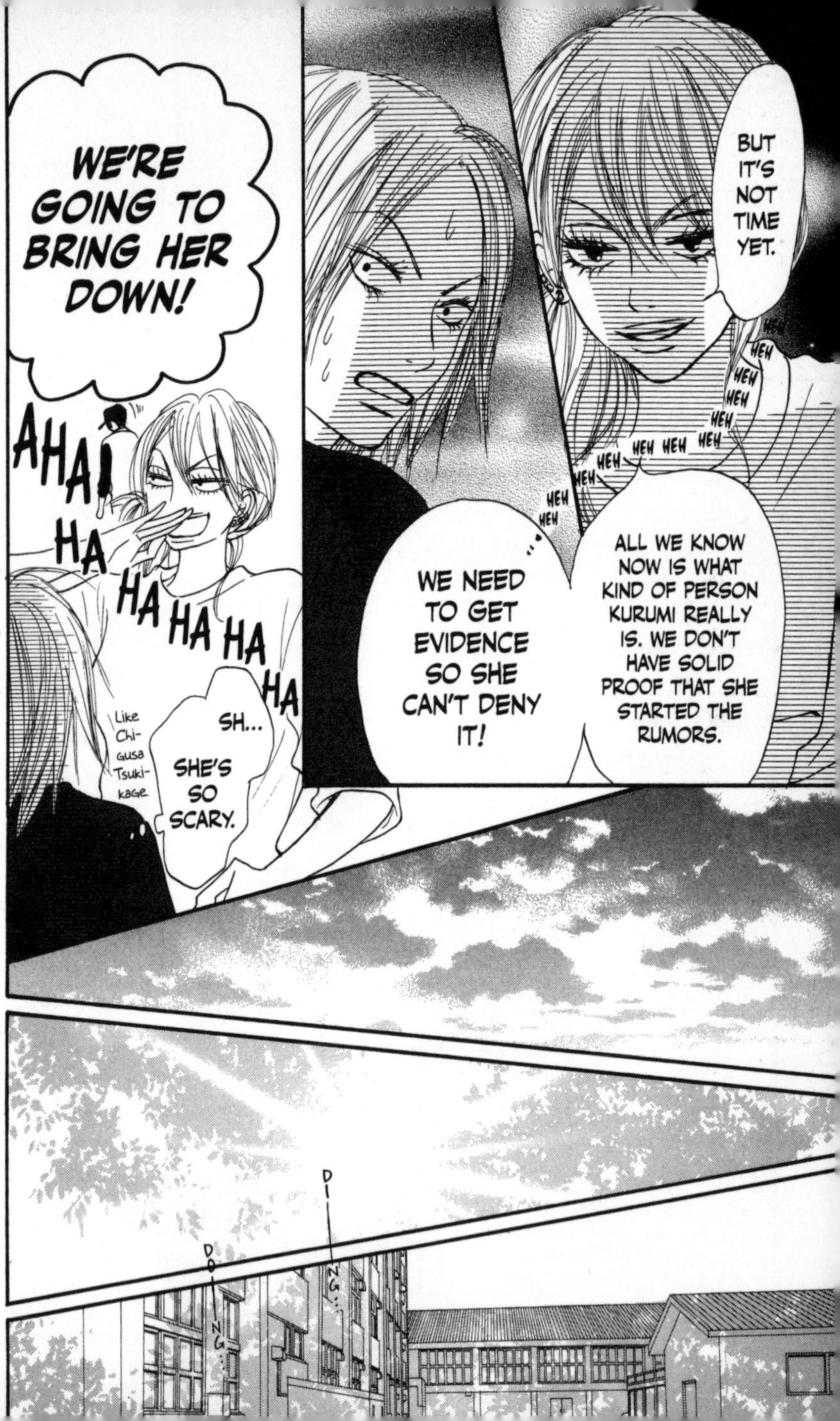
BUT IT'S NOT TIME YET.
HEH HEH HEH HEH HEH HEH HEH HEH HEH HEH HEH HEH
ALL WE KNOW NOW IS WHAT KIND OF PERSON KURUMI REALLY IS. WE DON'T HAVE SOLID PROOF THAT SHE STARTED THE RUMORS.
...
WE NEED TO GET EVIDENCE SO SHE CAN'T DENY IT!
WE'RE GOING TO BRING HER DOWN!
AHAHAHAHAHAHAHAHA
SH...
SHE'S SO SCARY.
Like Chi-gusa Tsuki-kage.
DING...
DONG...

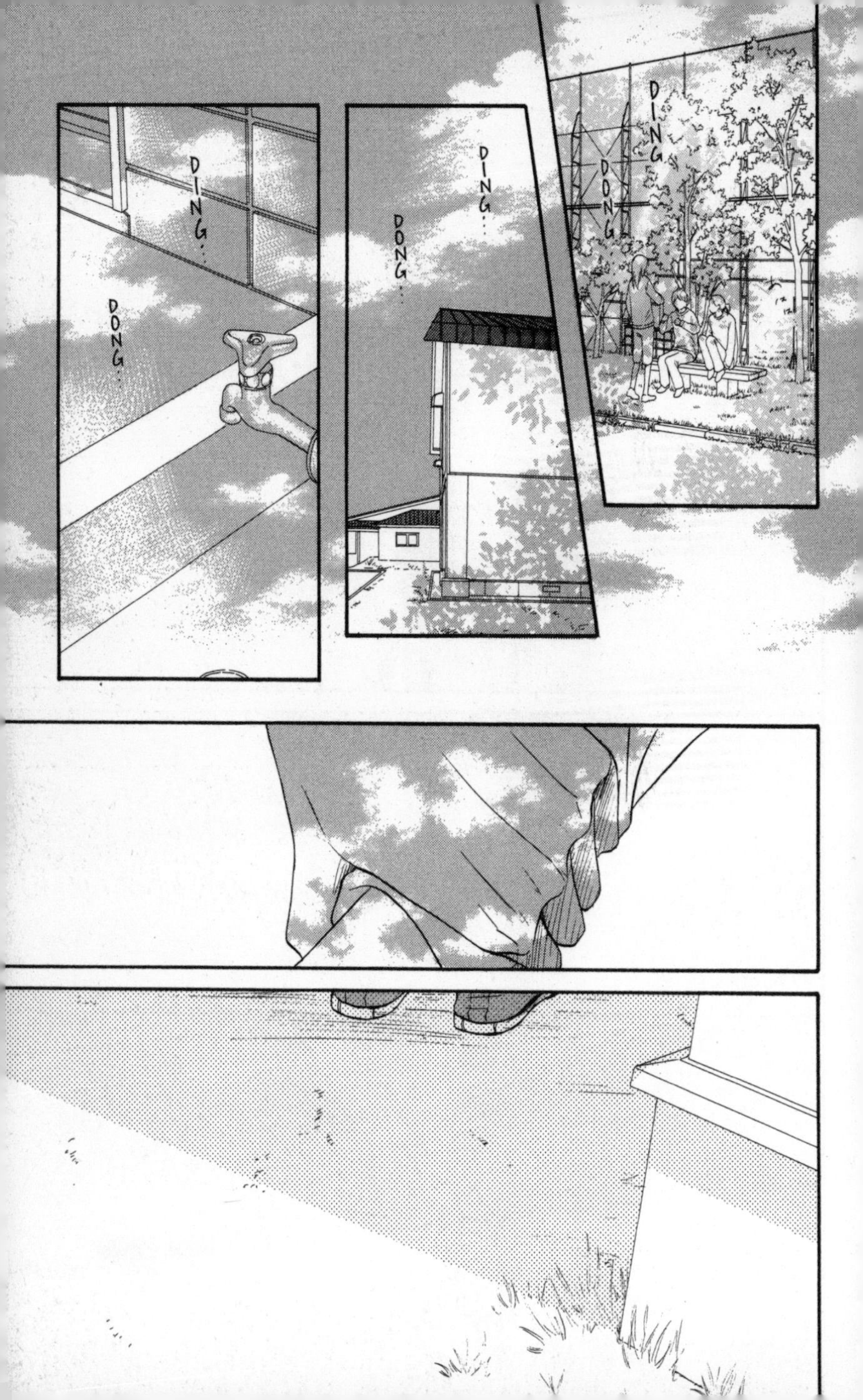
DING
DONG
DING...
DONG...
DING...
DONG...

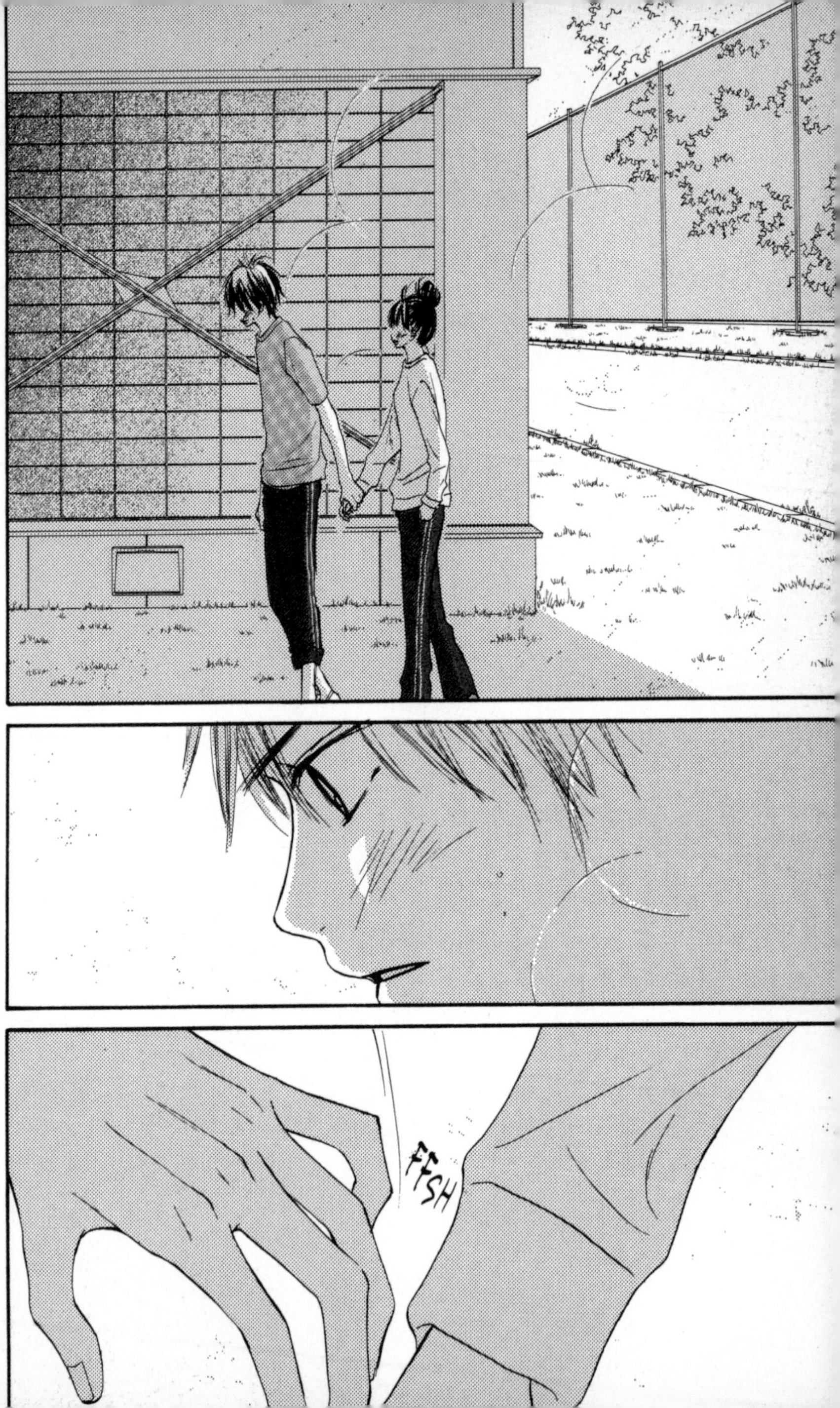
FFSH

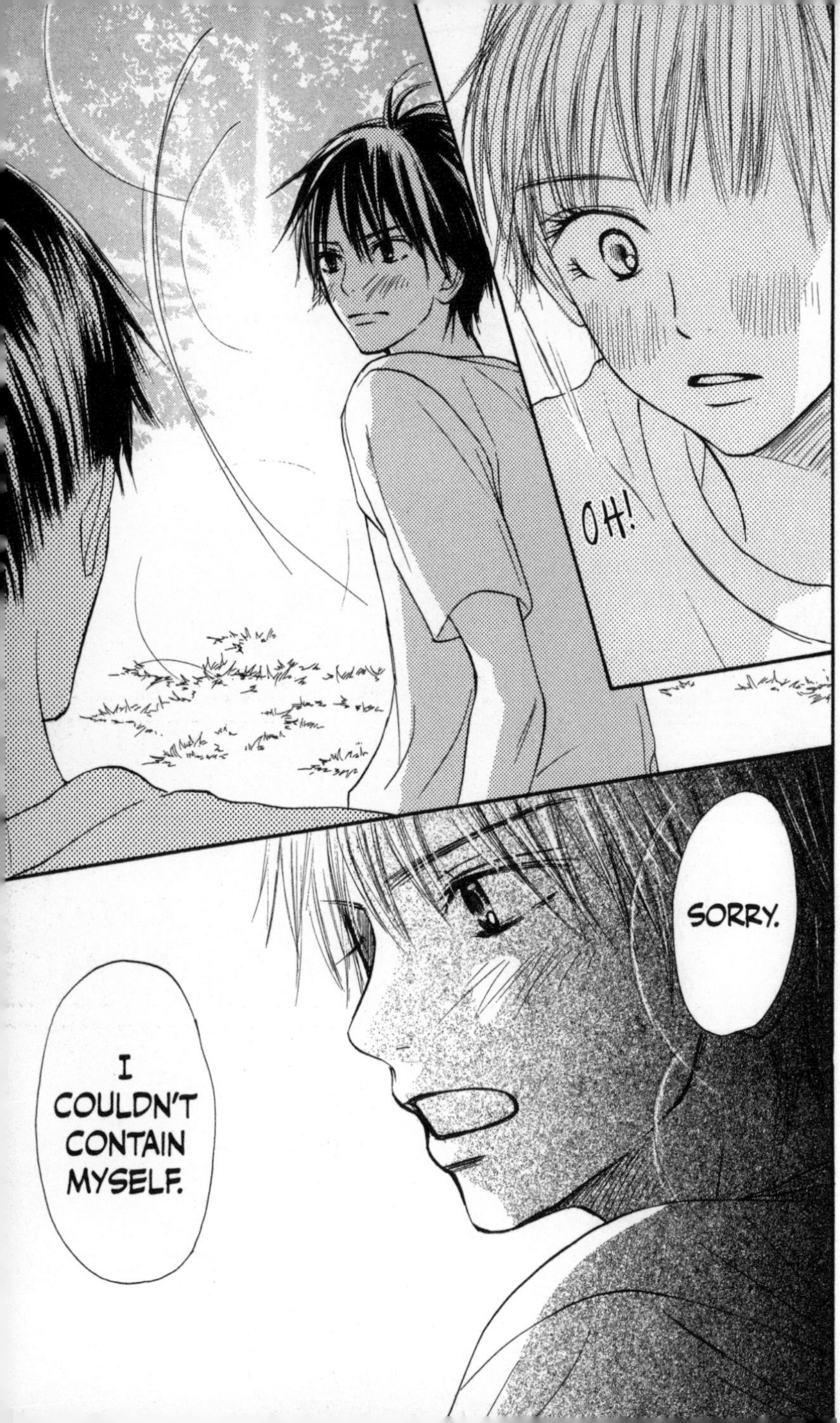
OH!
SORRY.
I COULDN'T CONTAIN MYSELF.

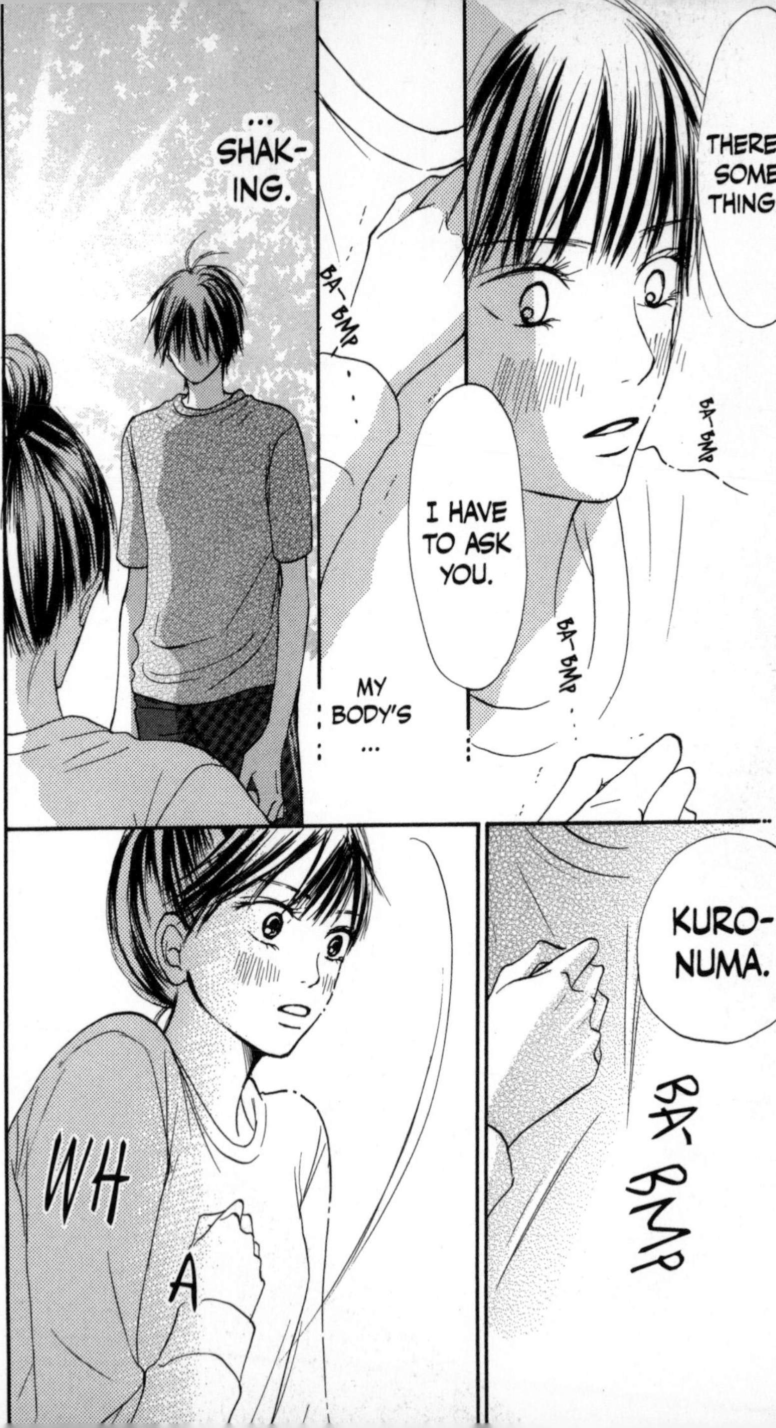
THERE'S SOME-THING...
BA-BMP
I HAVE TO ASK YOU.
BA-BMP
BA-BMP
MY BODY'S ...
... SHAK-ING.
KURO-NUMA.
BA-BMP
WH
A

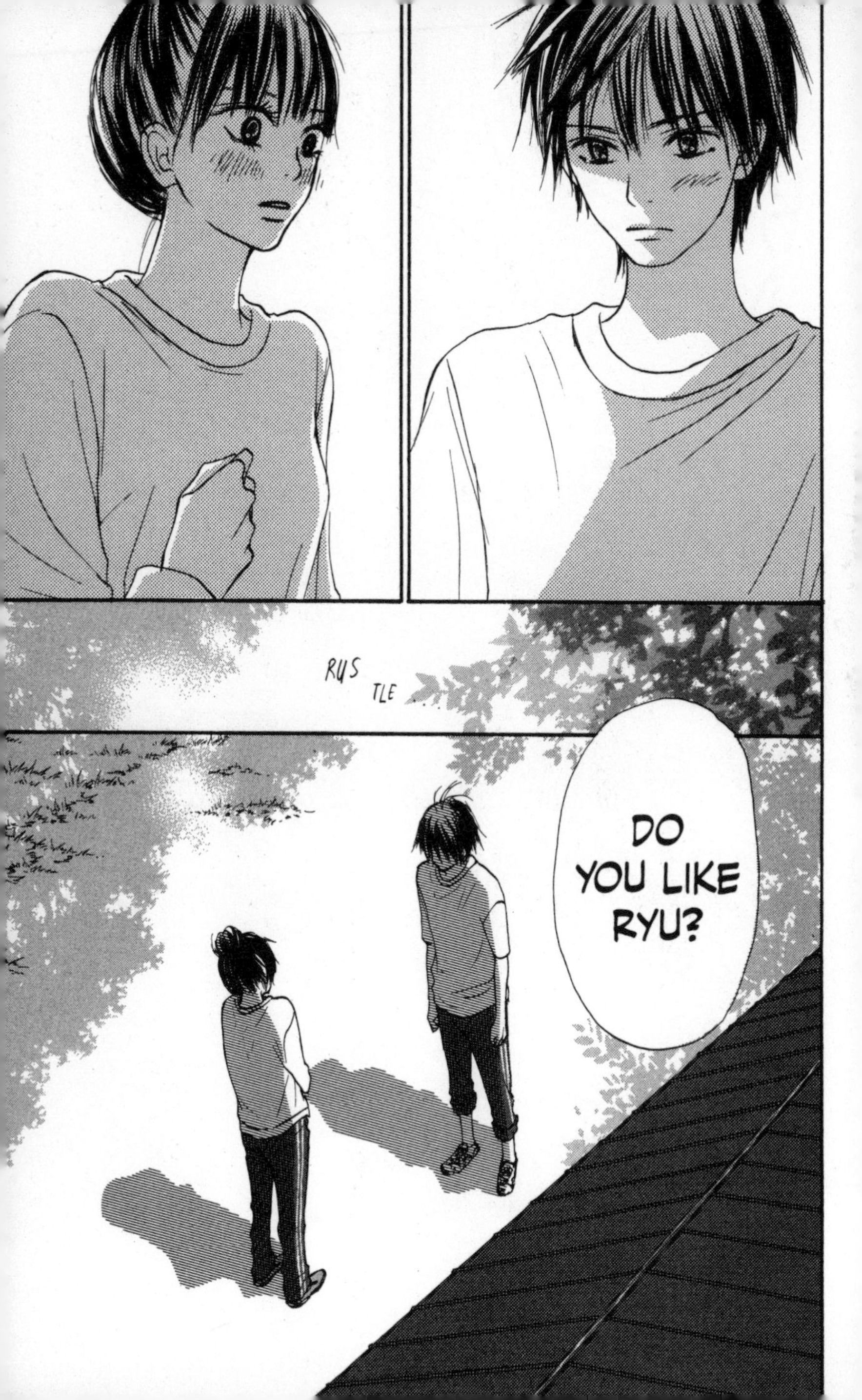
RUS TLE
DO YOU LIKE RYU?

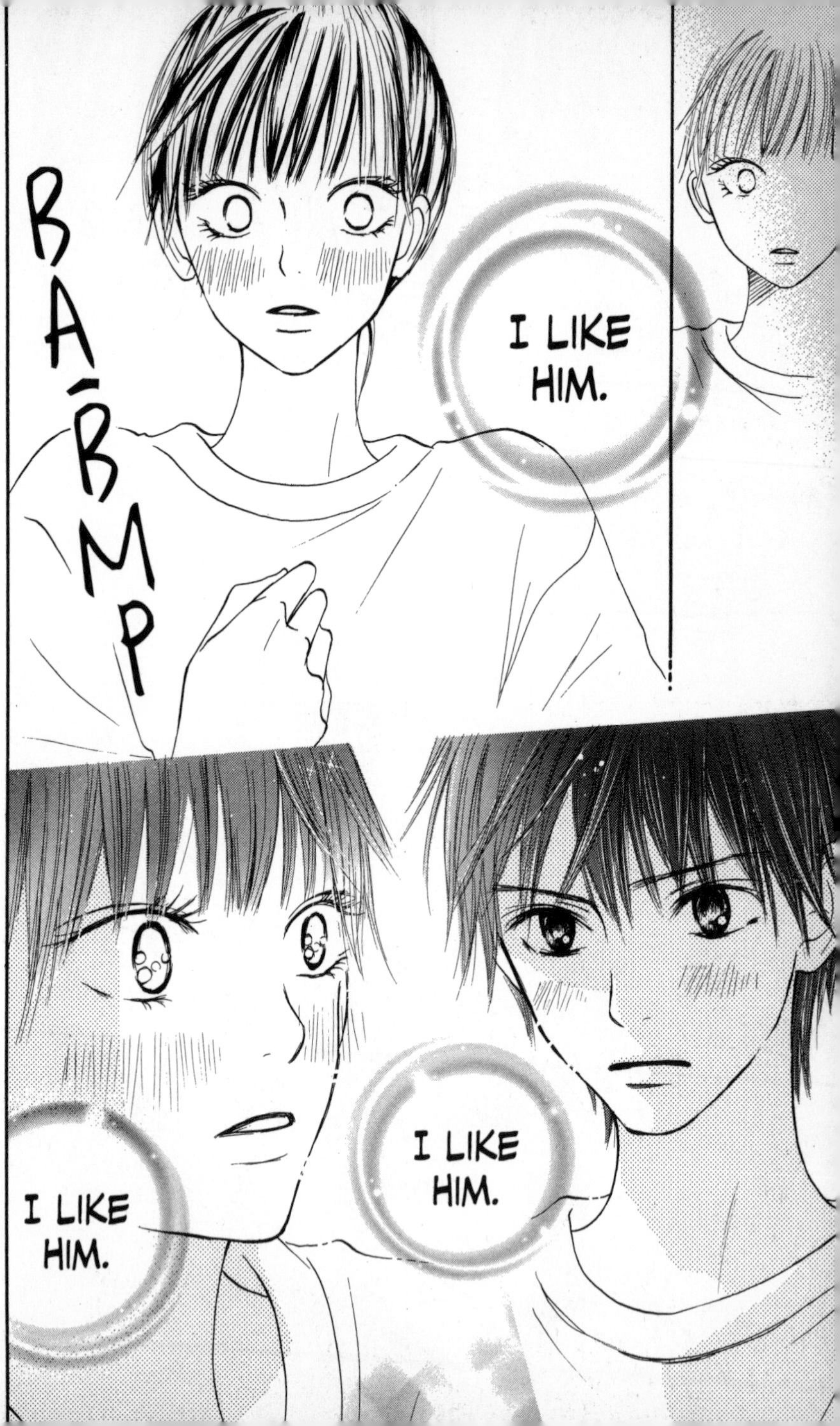
I LIKE HIM.
BA-BMP
I LIKE HIM.
I LIKE HIM.

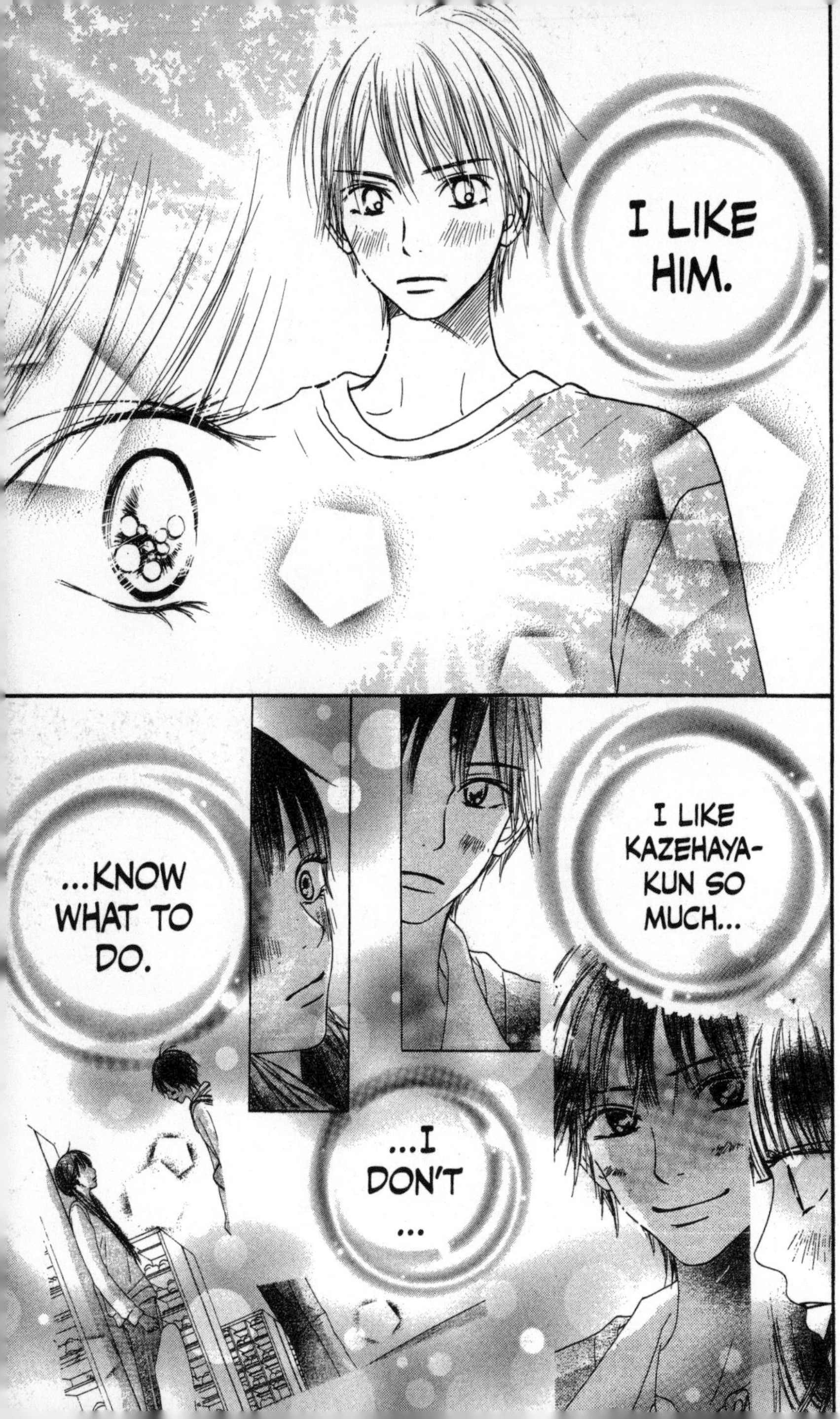
I LIKE HIM.
I LIKE KAZEHAYA-KUN SO MUCH...
...I DON'T ...
...KNOW WHAT TO DO.

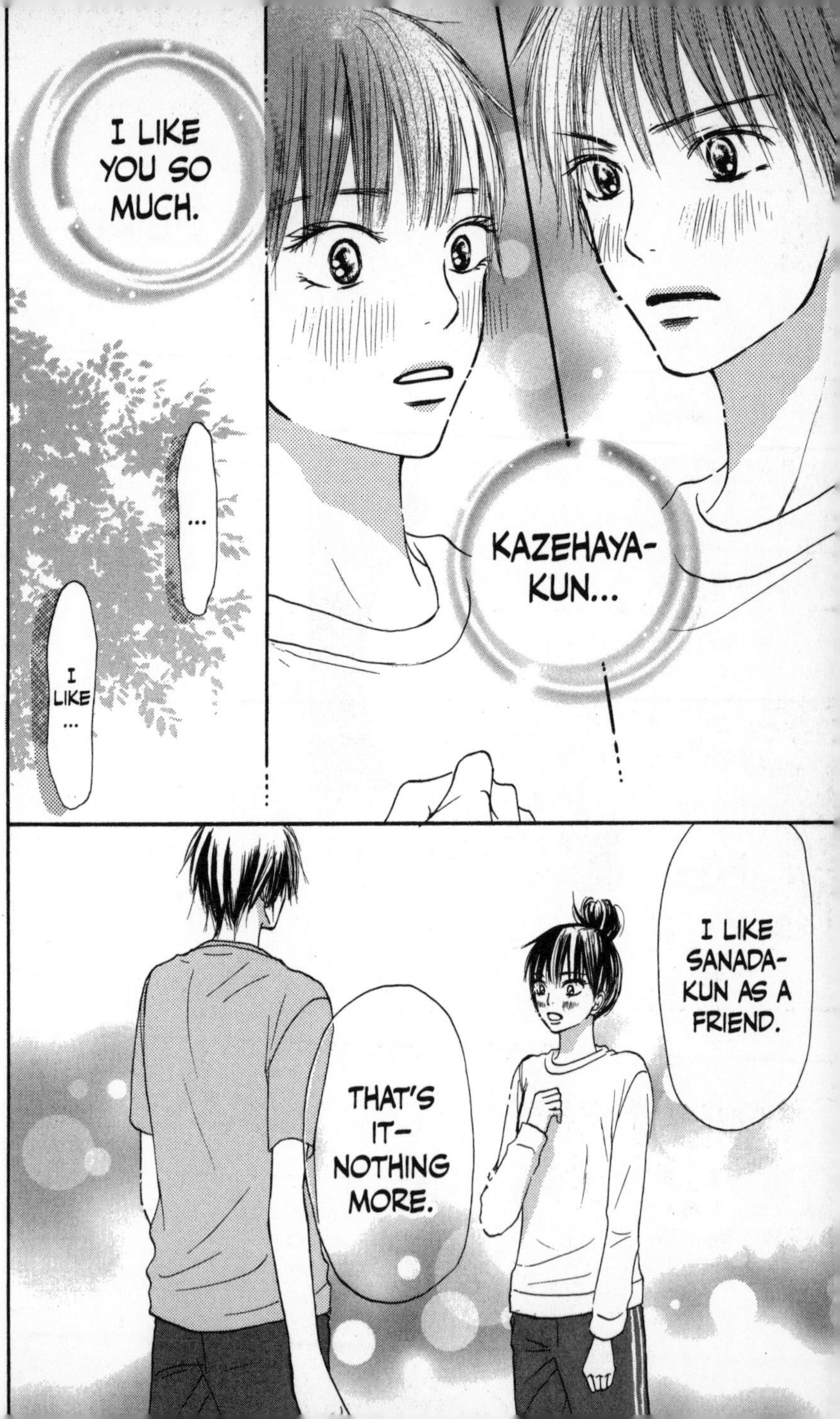
KAZEHAYA-KUN...
I LIKE YOU SO MUCH.
...
I LIKE ...
I LIKE SANADA-KUN AS A FRIEND.
THAT'S IT–NOTHING MORE.

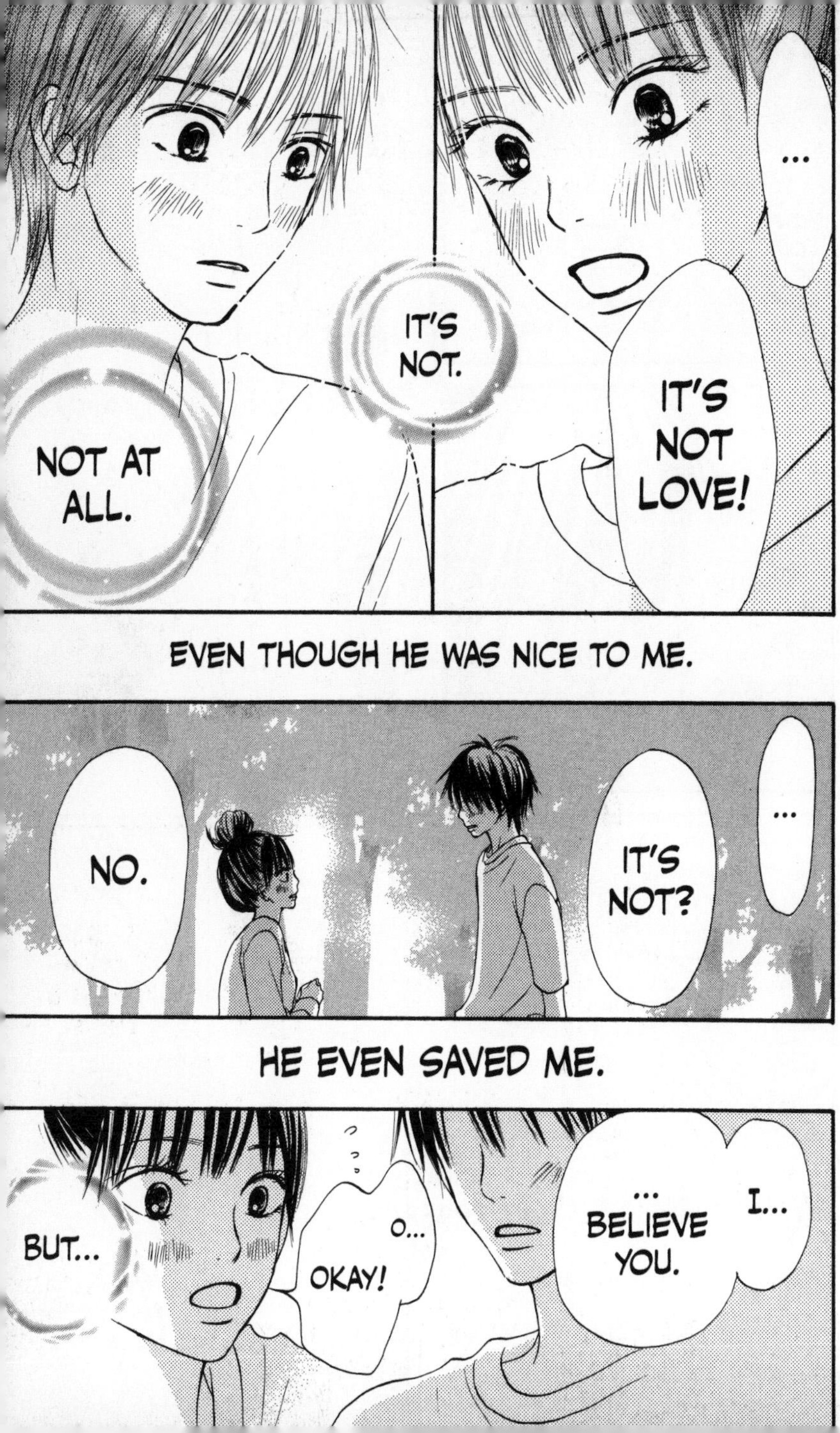
...
IT'S NOT LOVE!
IT'S NOT.
NOT AT ALL.
EVEN THOUGH HE WAS NICE TO ME.
...
IT'S NOT?
NO.
HE EVEN SAVED ME.
I...
... BELIEVE YOU.
O... OKAY!
BUT...

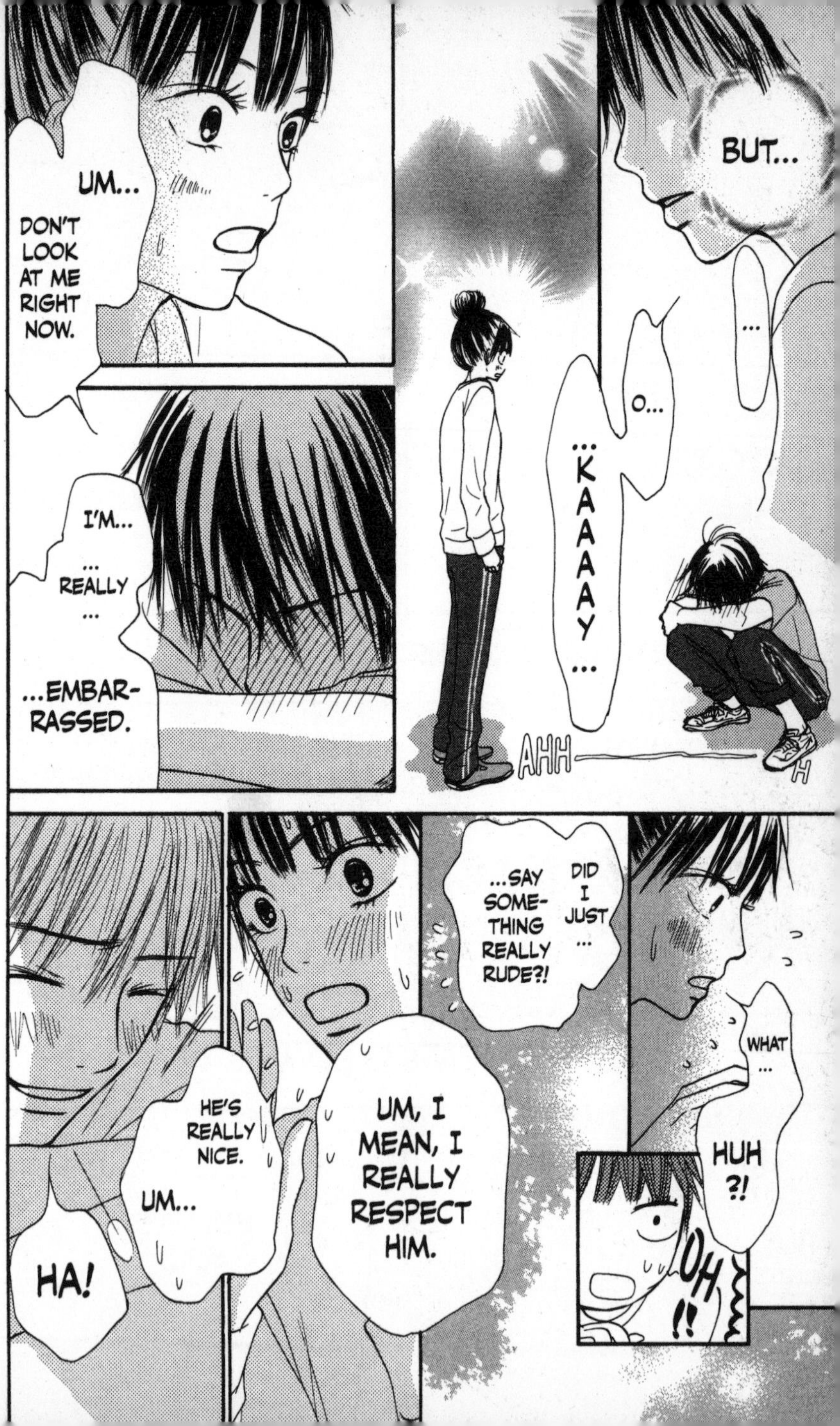
BUT...
...
O...
...KAAAAAY...
AHHHH
UM...
DON'T LOOK AT ME RIGHT NOW.
I'M...
...REALLY...
...EMBARRASSED.
WHAT...
HUH?!
OH!!
DID I JUST...
...SAY SOMETHING REALLY RUDE?!
UM, I MEAN, I REALLY RESPECT HIM.
UM...
HE'S REALLY NICE.
HA!

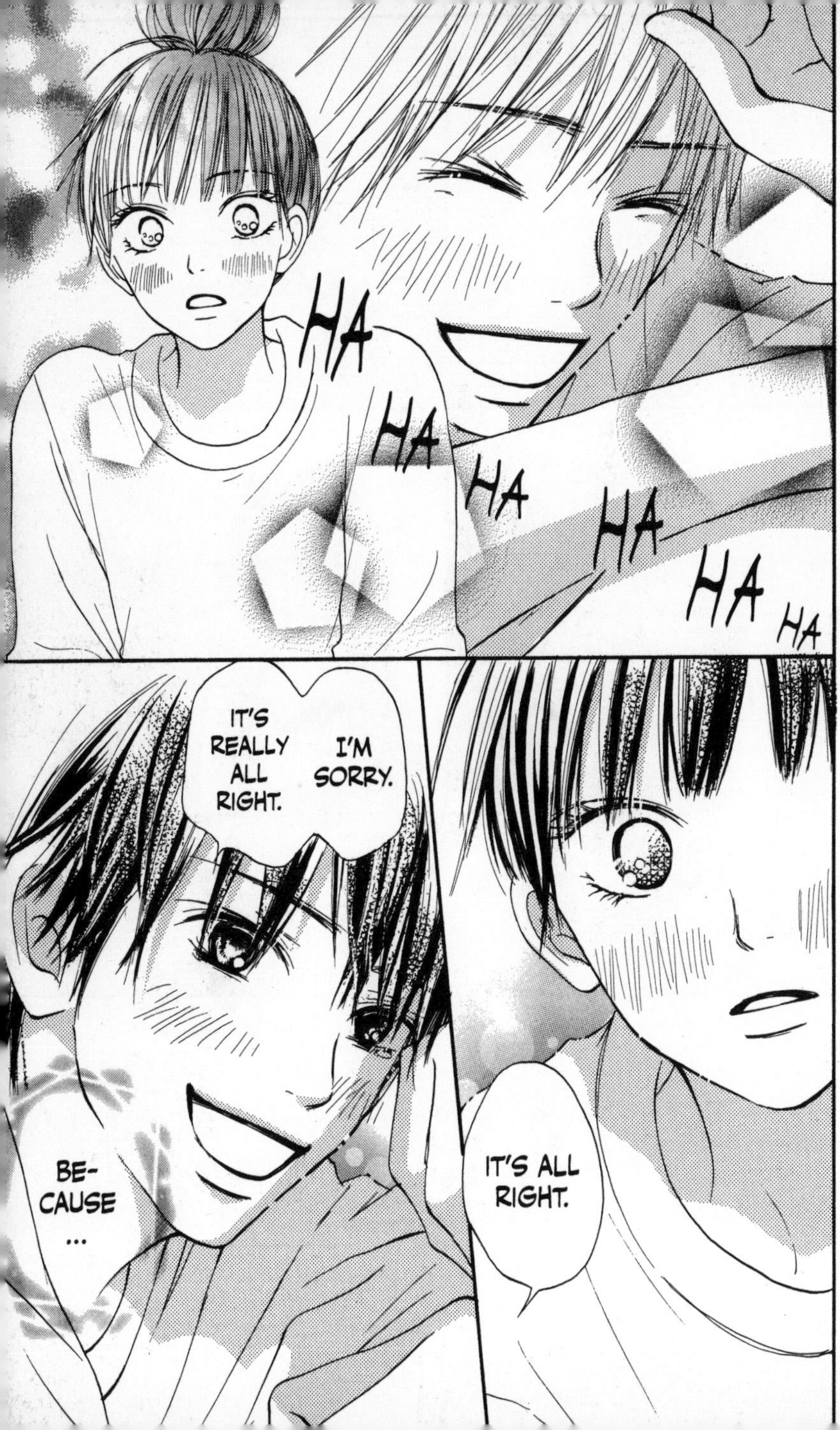
HA HA HA HA HA HA
IT'S ALL RIGHT.
I'M SORRY.
IT'S REALLY ALL RIGHT.
BE-CAUSE ...

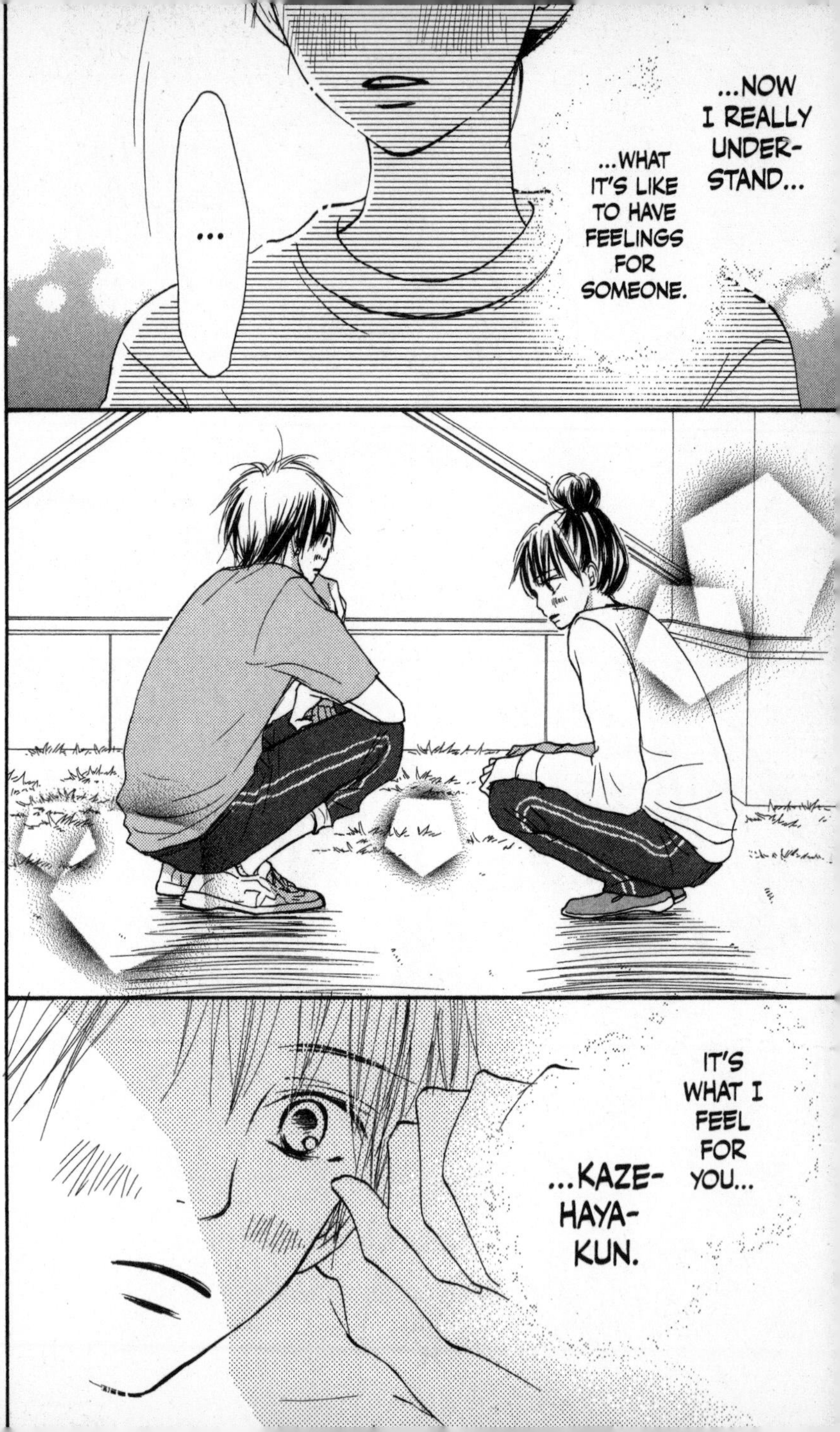
...NOW I REALLY UNDERSTAND...
...WHAT IT'S LIKE TO HAVE FEELINGS FOR SOMEONE.
...
IT'S WHAT I FEEL FOR YOU...
...KAZEHAYA-KUN.

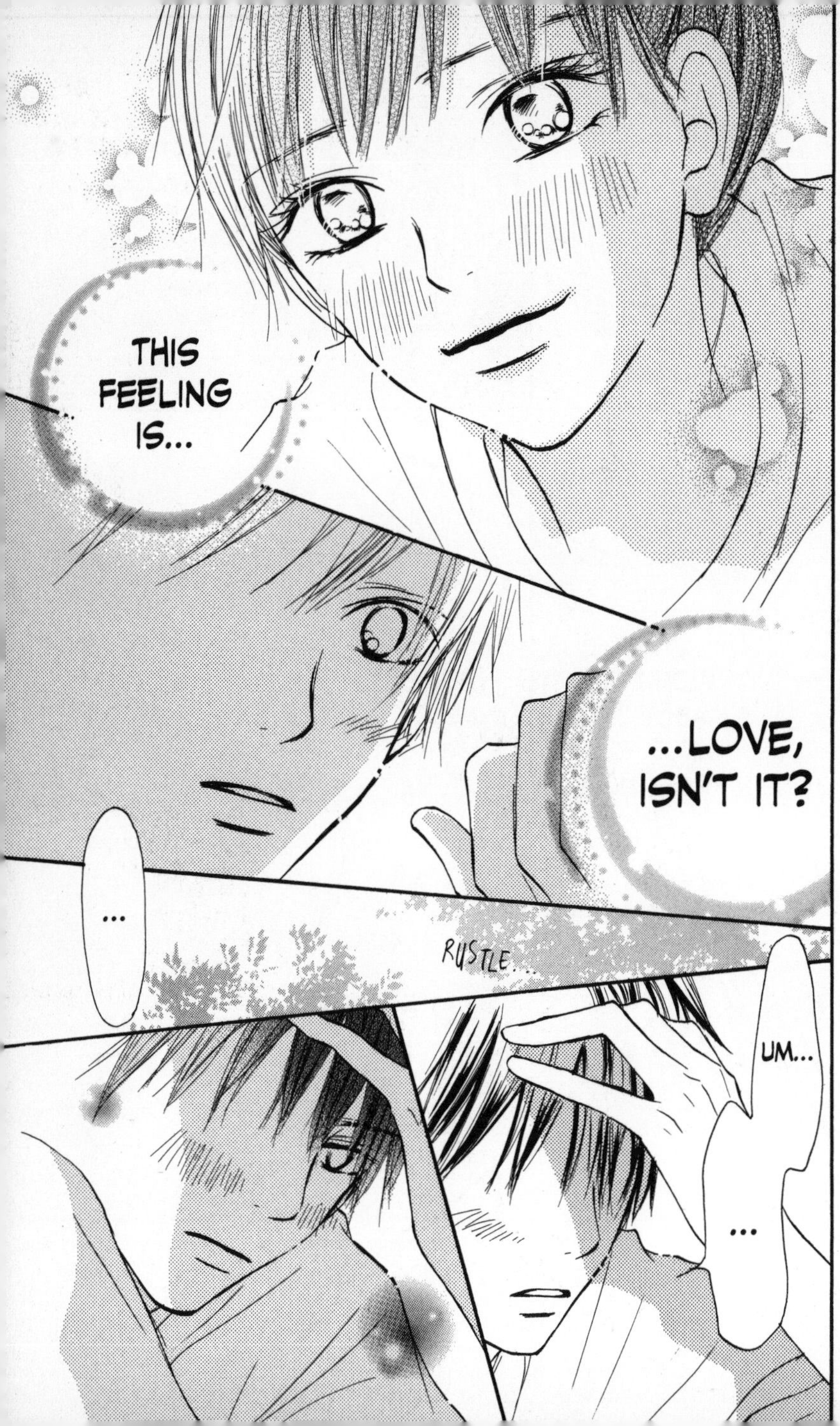
THIS FEELING IS...
...LOVE, ISN'T IT?
RUSTLE...
...
UM...
...

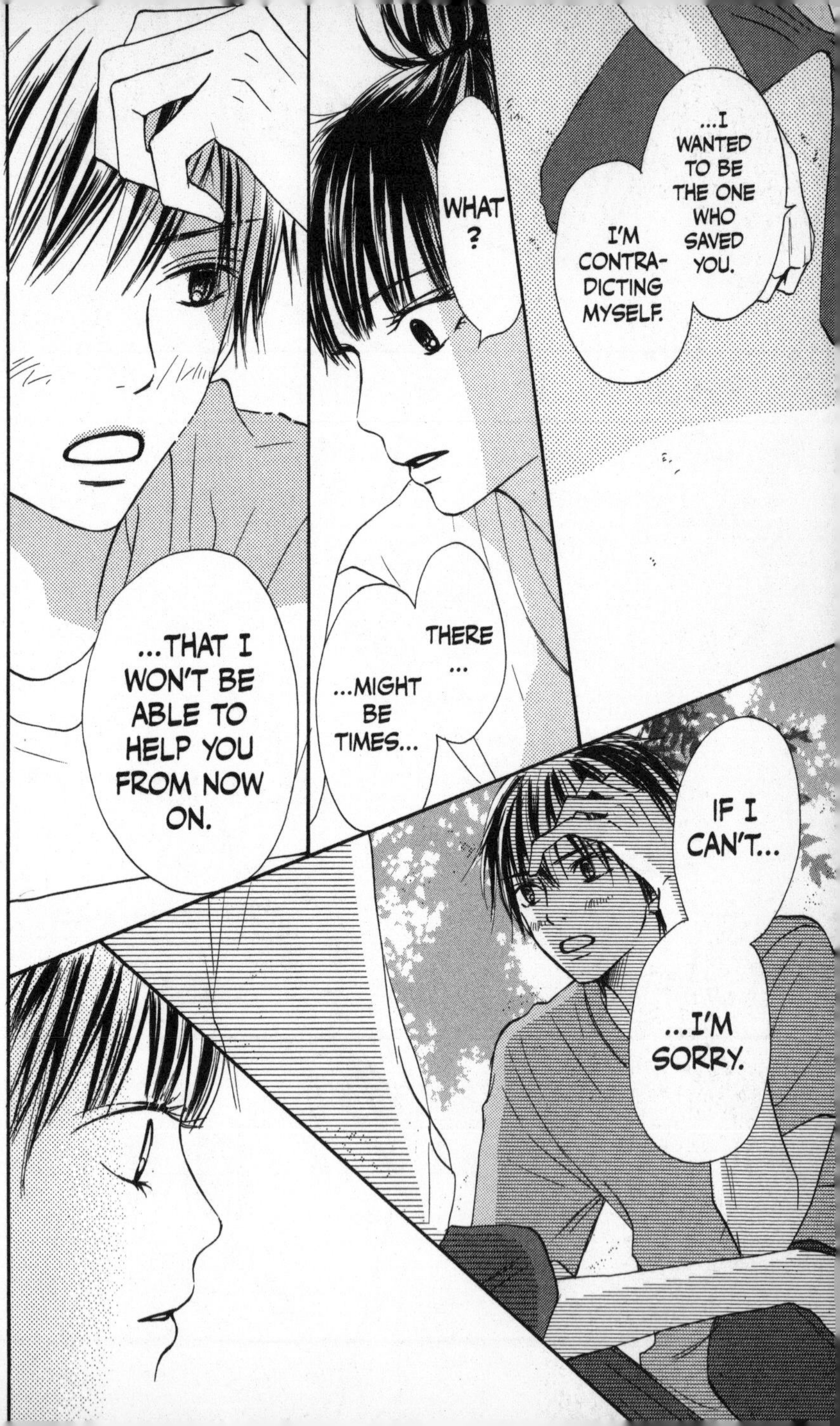
...I WANTED TO BE THE ONE WHO SAVED YOU.
I'M CONTRA-DICTING MYSELF.
WHAT?
THERE...
...MIGHT BE TIMES...
...THAT I WON'T BE ABLE TO HELP YOU FROM NOW ON.
IF I CAN'T...
...I'M SORRY.

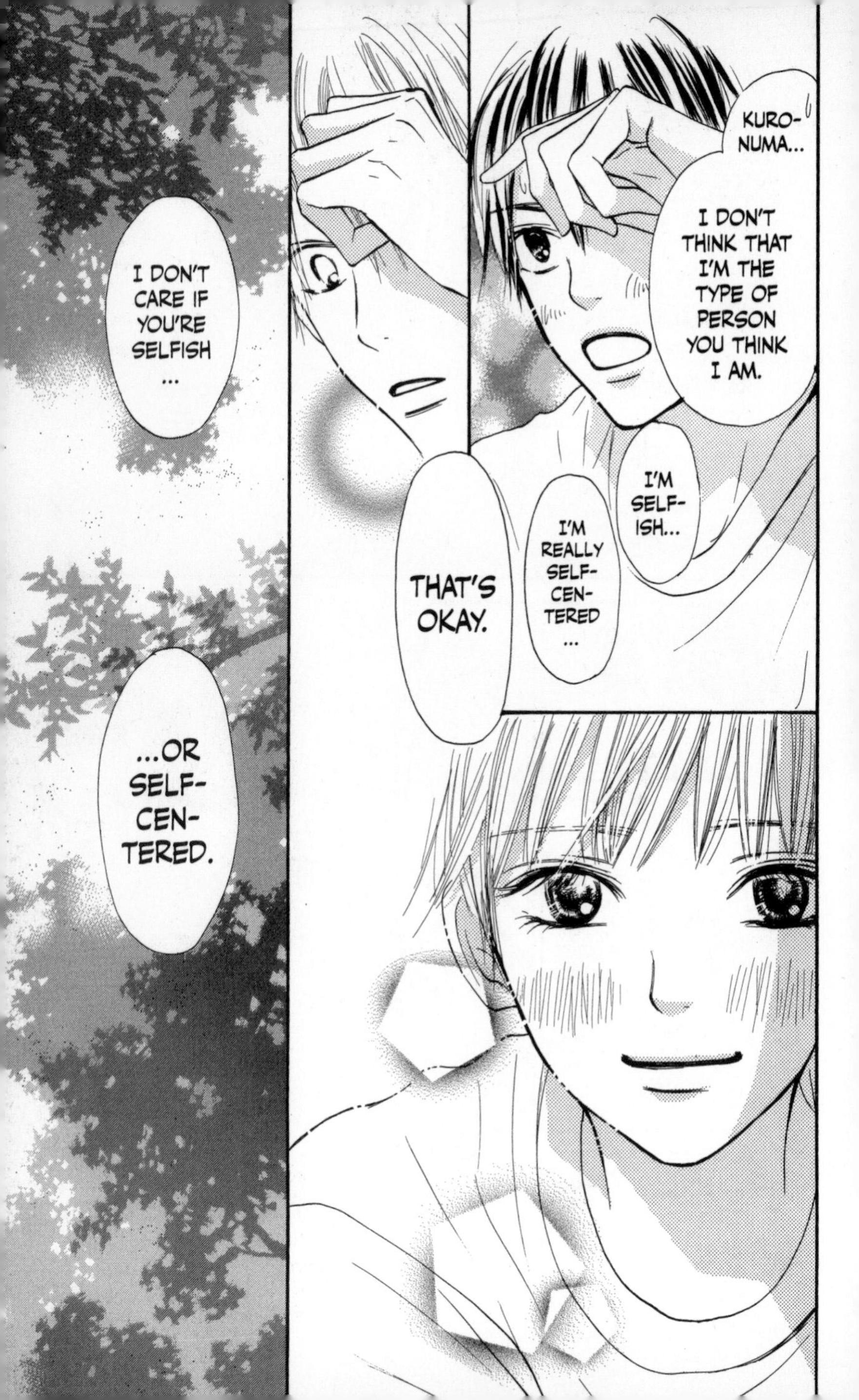
KURO-NUMA...
I DON'T THINK THAT I'M THE TYPE OF PERSON YOU THINK I AM.
I'M SELF-ISH...
I'M REALLY SELF-CEN-TERED...
THAT'S OKAY.
I DON'T CARE IF YOU'RE SELFISH...
...OR SELF-CEN-TERED.

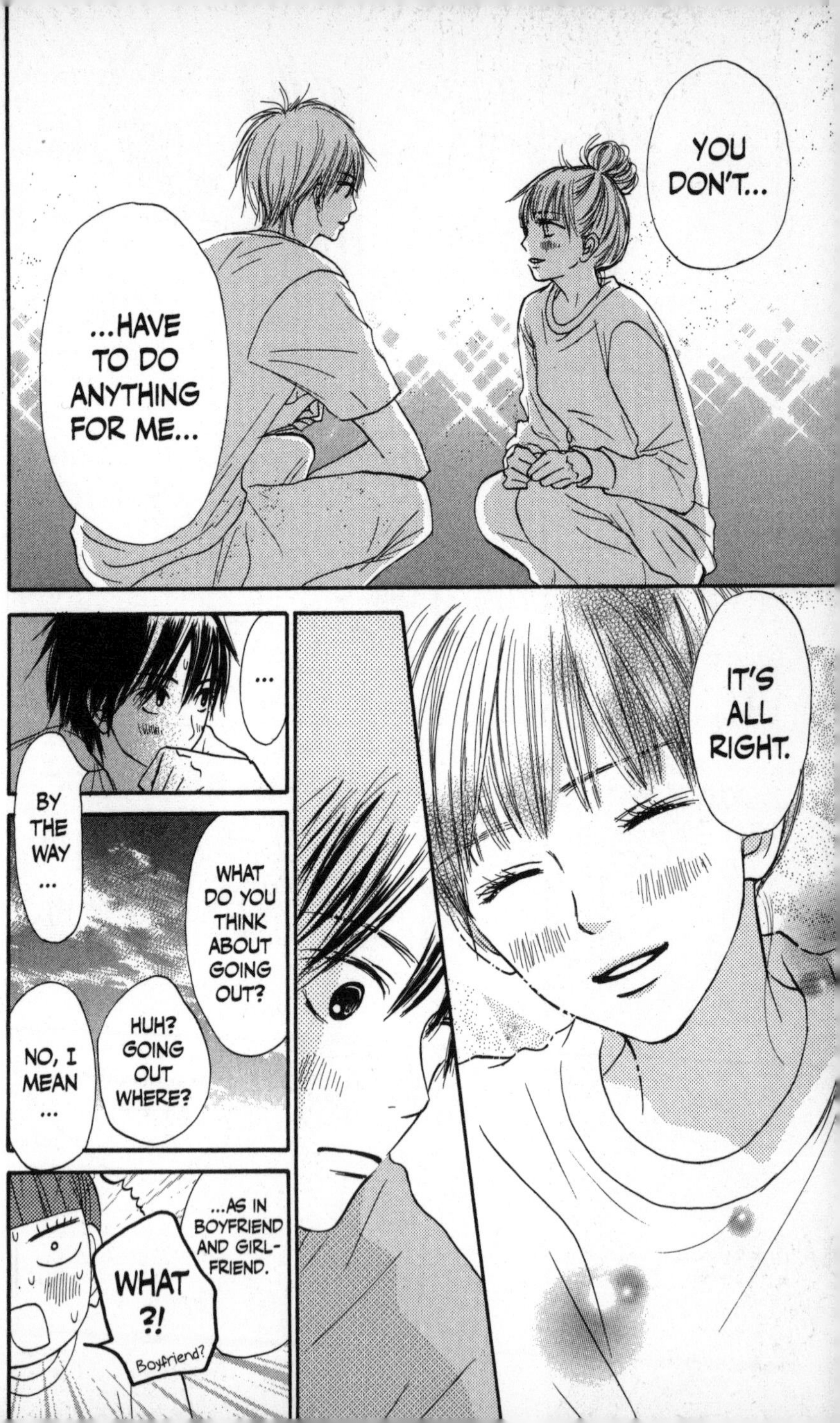
YOU DON'T...
...HAVE TO DO ANYTHING FOR ME...
IT'S ALL RIGHT.
...
BY THE WAY ...
WHAT DO YOU THINK ABOUT GOING OUT?
HUH? GOING OUT WHERE?
NO, I MEAN ...
...AS IN BOYFRIEND AND GIRL-FRIEND.
WHAT ?!
Boyfriend?

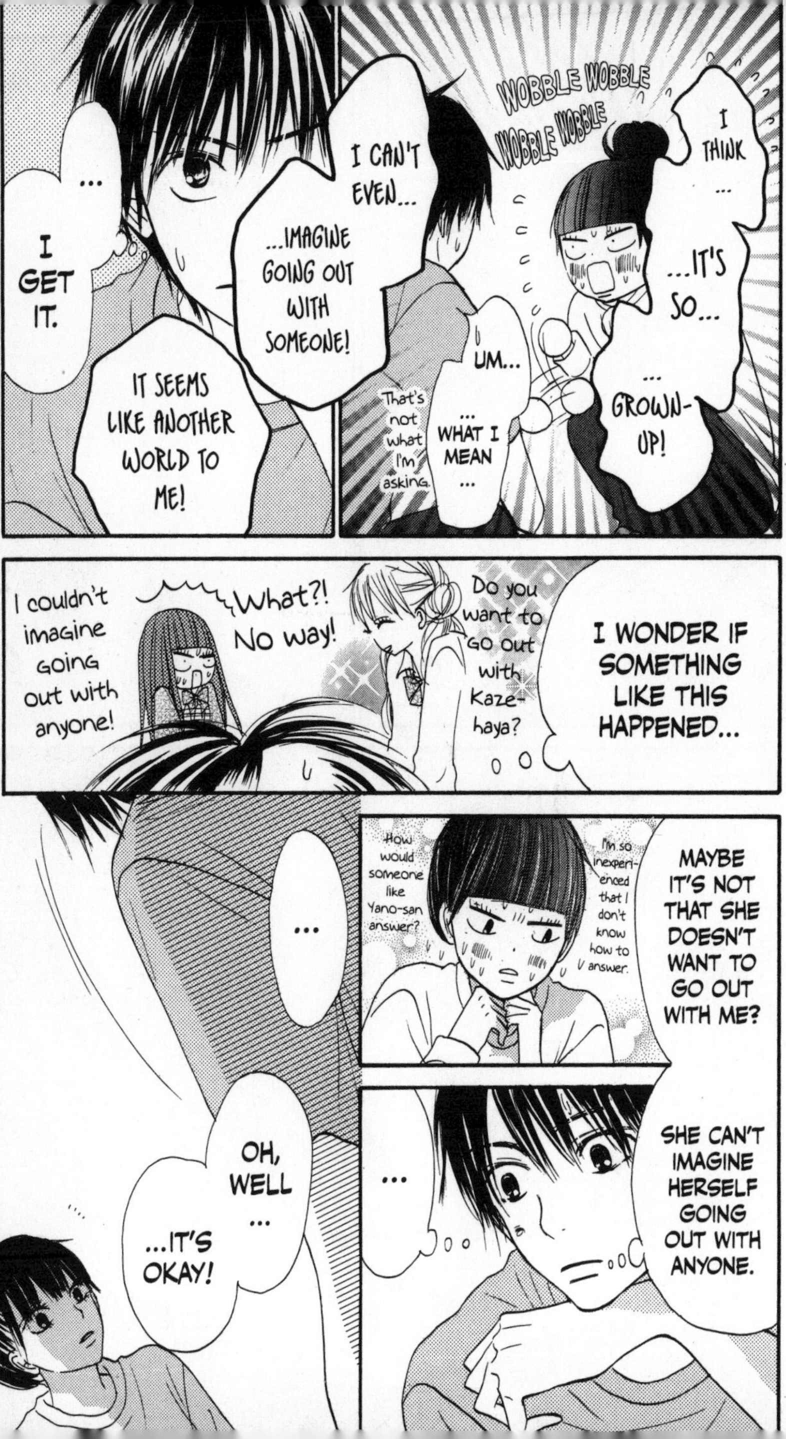
WOBBLE WOBBLE
WOBBLE WOBBLE
I THINK...
...IT'S SO...
...GROWN-UP!
UM...
...WHAT I MEAN...
That's not what I'm asking.
I CAN'T EVEN...
...IMAGINE GOING OUT WITH SOMEONE!
...
I GET IT.
IT SEEMS LIKE ANOTHER WORLD TO ME!
I WONDER IF SOMETHING LIKE THIS HAPPENED...
Do you want to go out with Kaze-haya?
What?! No way!
I couldn't imagine going out with anyone!
MAYBE IT'S NOT THAT SHE DOESN'T WANT TO GO OUT WITH ME?
I'm so inexperi-enced that I don't know how to answer.
How would someone like Yano-san answer?
SHE CAN'T IMAGINE HERSELF GOING OUT WITH ANYONE.
...
...
OH, WELL...
...IT'S OKAY!

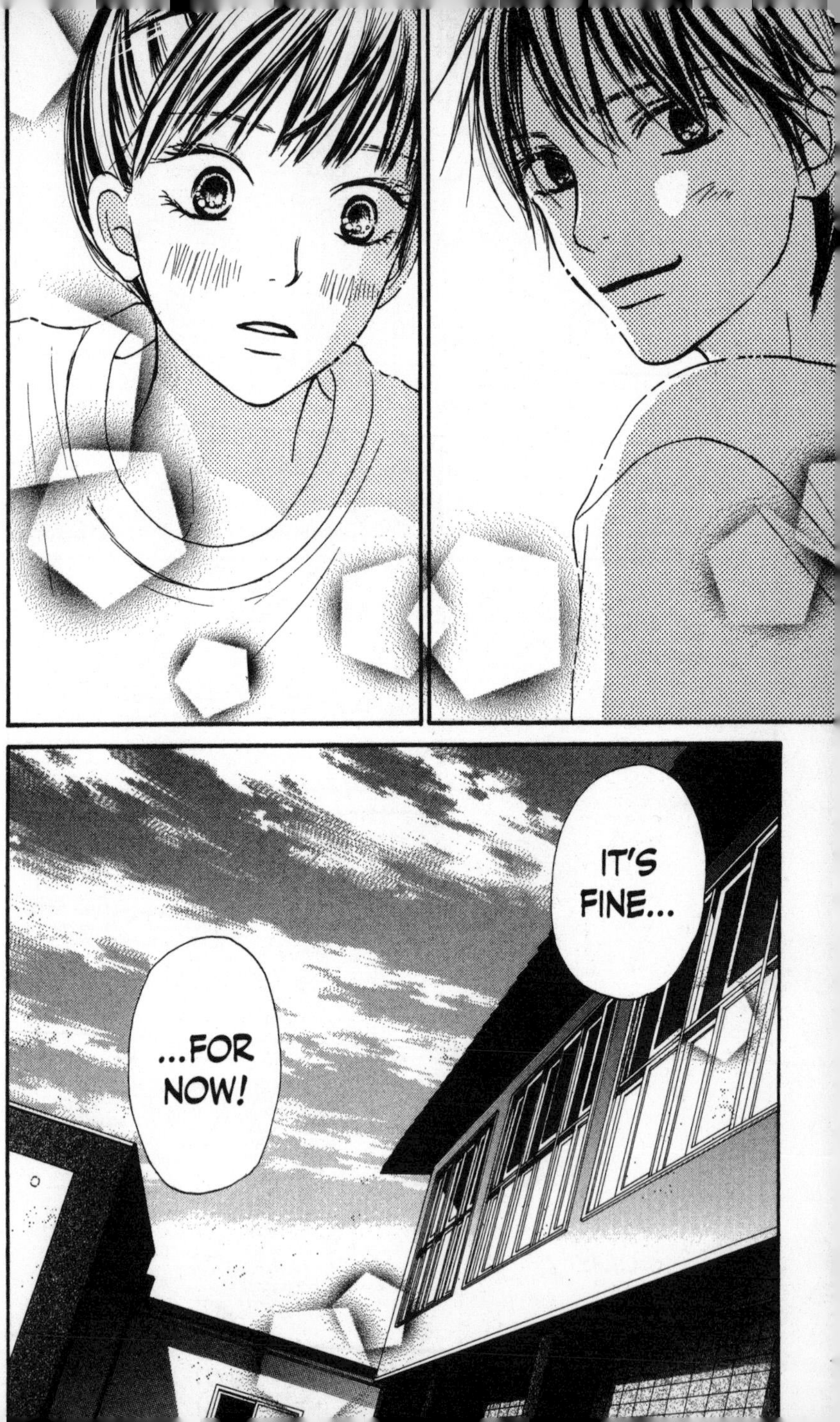
IT'S FINE...
...FOR NOW!

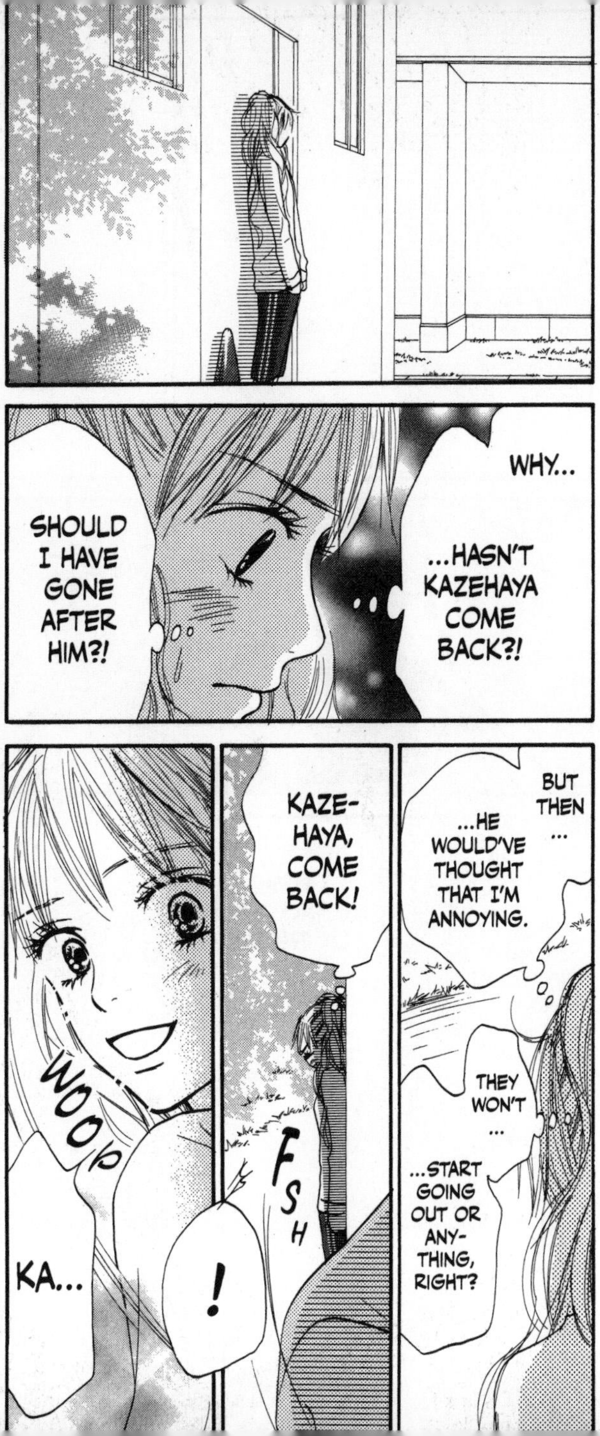
WHY...
...HASN'T KAZEHAYA COME BACK?!
SHOULD I HAVE GONE AFTER HIM?!
BUT THEN...
...HE WOULD'VE THOUGHT THAT I'M ANNOYING.
THEY WON'T...
...START GOING OUT OR ANYTHING, RIGHT?
KAZE-HAYA, COME BACK!
FSH
WOOP
!
KA...

KARUPIN on JAPAN 3

Continued → from before.

They were able to explain what they do and were fully conscious of their environment. They were extremely well-spoken and also made everyone laugh. I really respect the way they were able to express themselves, and I thought they were really positive people.

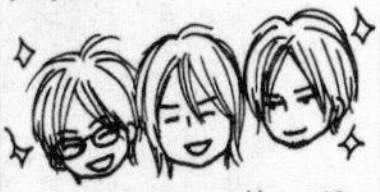

Sakura Merry Men-san

{ This doesn't really look like them! I surprised myself!

I told my husband about them when I got home.

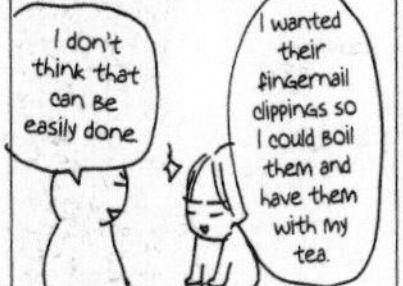
I don't think that can be easily done.
I wanted their fingernail clippings so I could boil them and have them with my tea.

I don't think that he quite got it.

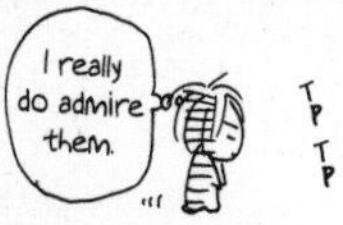
I really do admire them.
TP TP

I saw their live performance too, and it was great! Their album will probably be released when this comic comes out, so please support them! The songs besides "Margaret" are great too! ✧

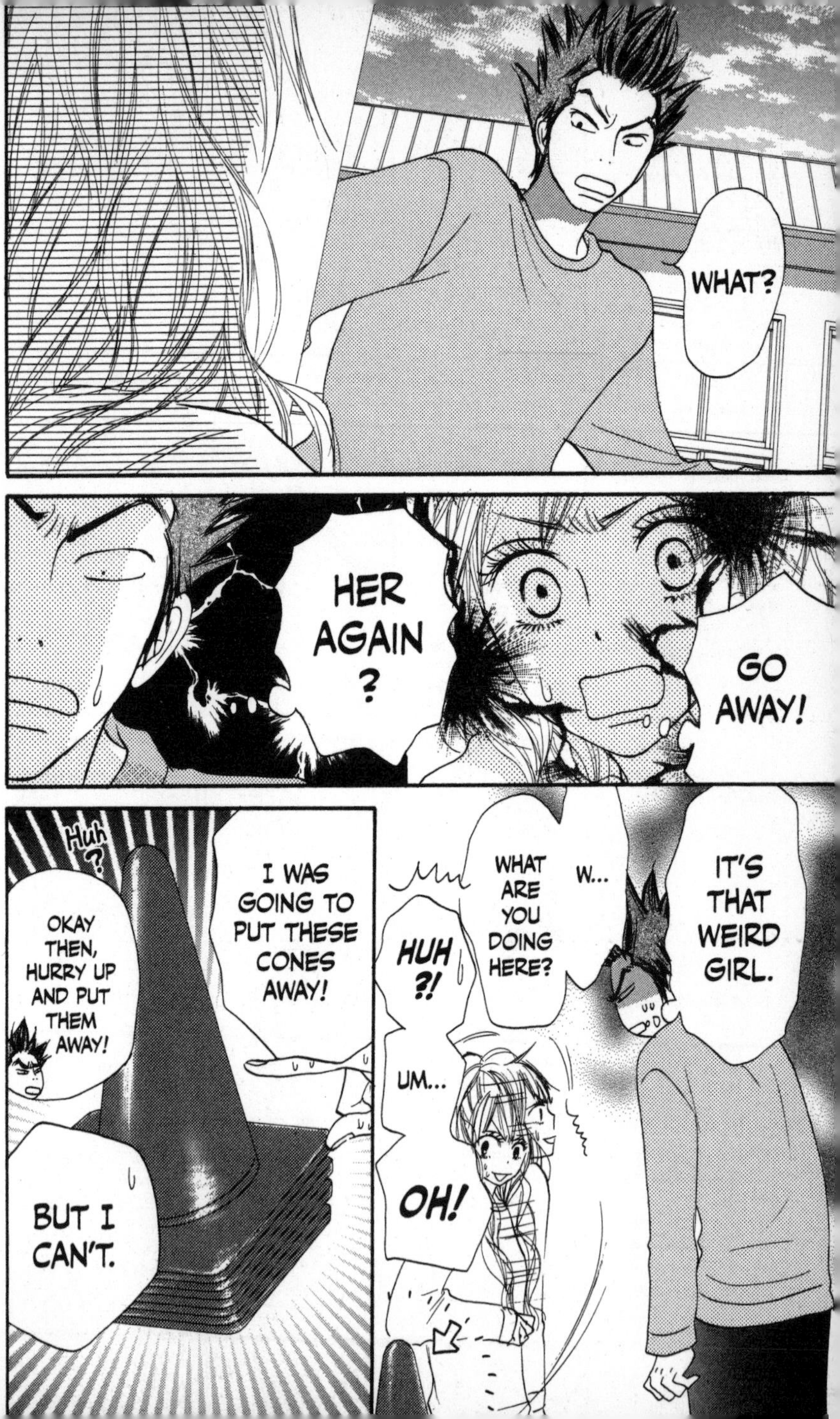
WHAT?
GO AWAY!
HER AGAIN?
IT'S THAT WEIRD GIRL.
W...
WHAT ARE YOU DOING HERE?
HUH?!
UM...
OH!
I WAS GOING TO PUT THESE CONES AWAY!
Huh?
OKAY THEN, HURRY UP AND PUT THEM AWAY!
BUT I CAN'T.

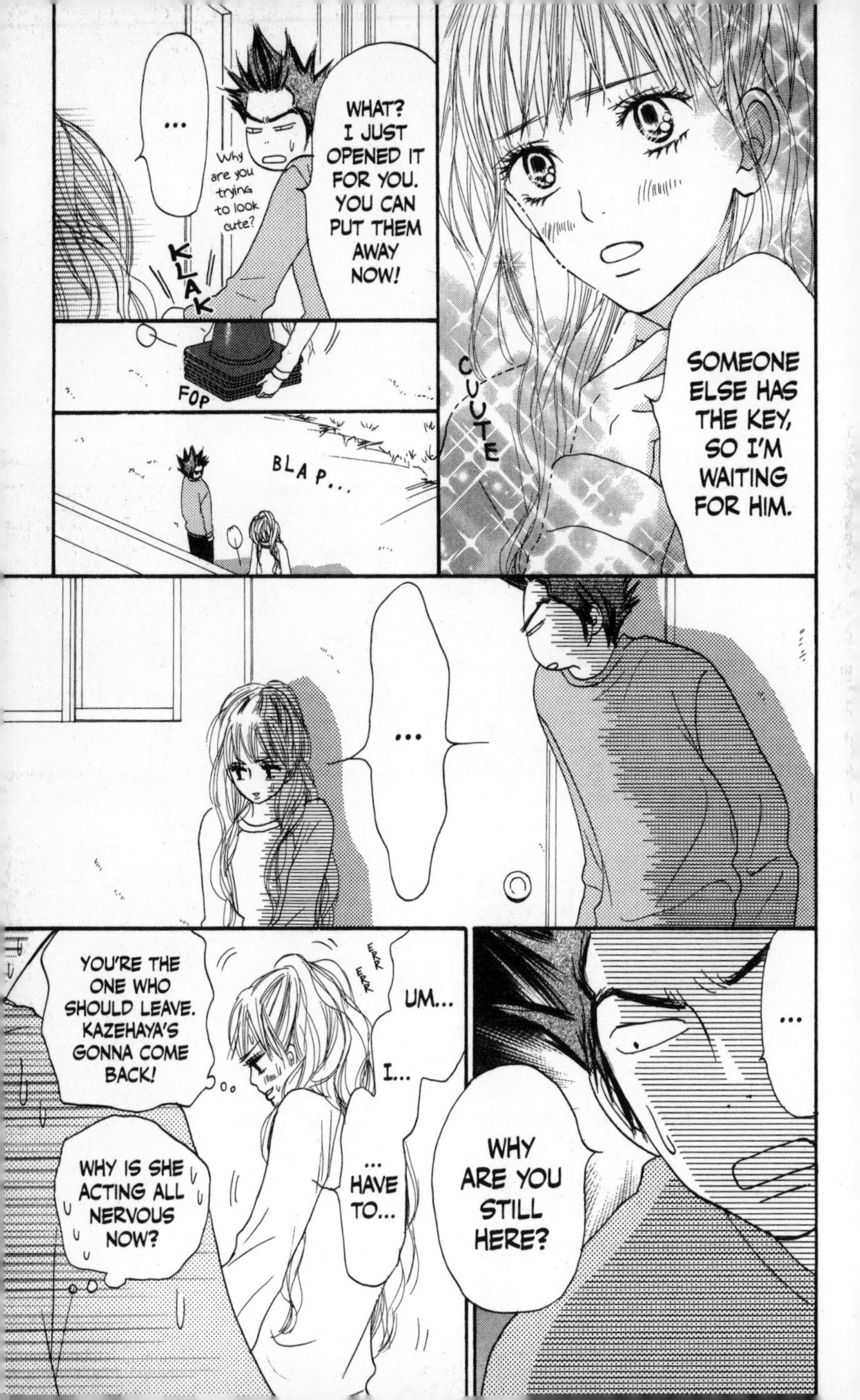
CUUTE
SOMEONE ELSE HAS THE KEY, SO I'M WAITING FOR HIM.
WHAT? I JUST OPENED IT FOR YOU. YOU CAN PUT THEM AWAY NOW!
Why are you trying to look cute?
...
KLAK
FOP
BLAP...
...
...
WHY ARE YOU STILL HERE?
UM...
I...
... HAVE TO...
YOU'RE THE ONE WHO SHOULD LEAVE. KAZEHAYA'S GONNA COME BACK!
WHY IS SHE ACTING ALL NERVOUS NOW?

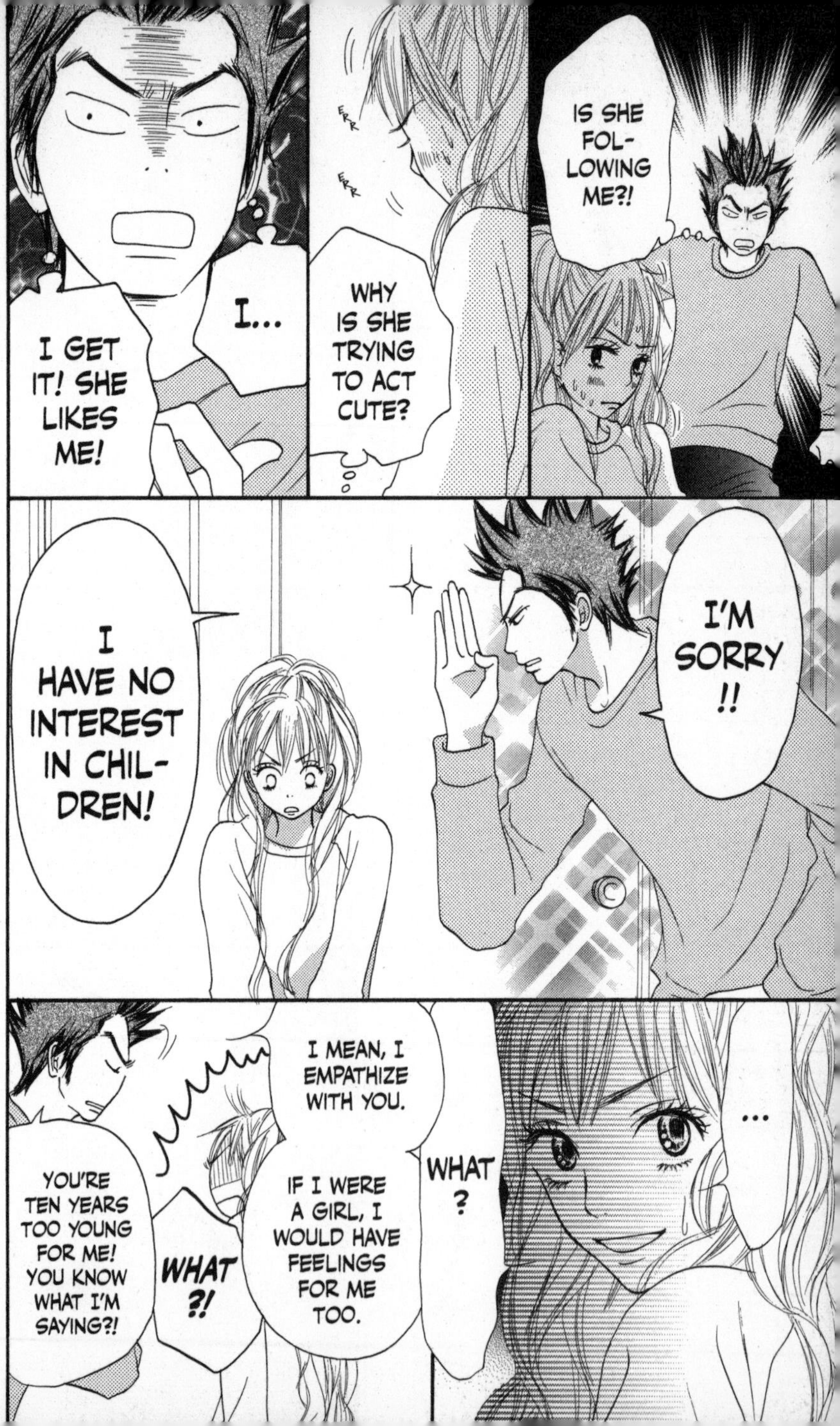
IS SHE FOL-LOWING ME?!
ERR
ERR
WHY IS SHE TRYING TO ACT CUTE?
I...
I GET IT! SHE LIKES ME!
I'M SORRY !!
I HAVE NO INTEREST IN CHIL-DREN!
...
I MEAN, I EMPATHIZE WITH YOU.
WHAT ?
IF I WERE A GIRL, I WOULD HAVE FEELINGS FOR ME TOO.
WHAT ?!
YOU'RE TEN YEARS TOO YOUNG FOR ME! YOU KNOW WHAT I'M SAYING?!

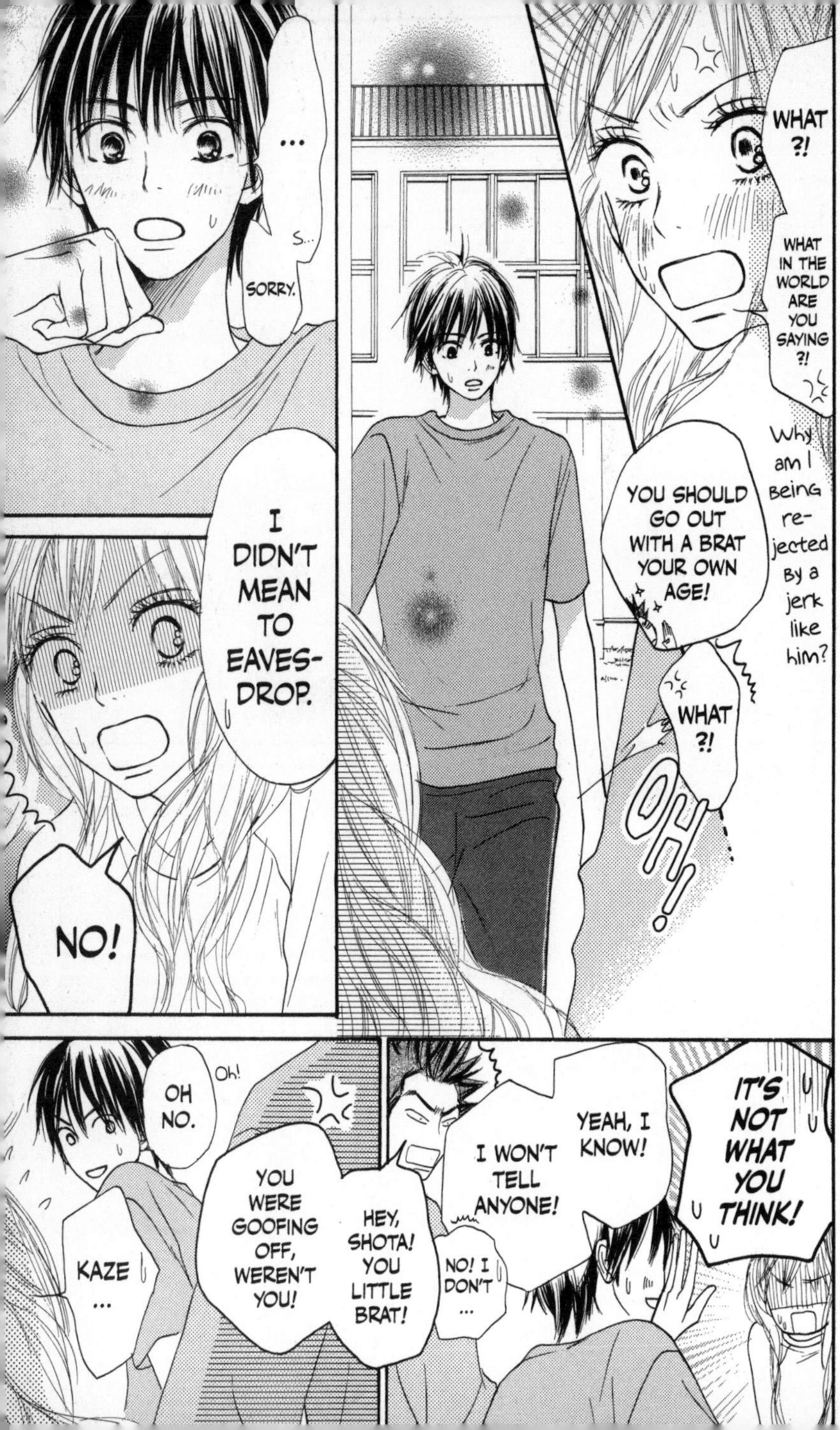
WHAT ?!
WHAT IN THE WORLD ARE YOU SAYING ?!
Why am I being re-jected by a jerk like him?
YOU SHOULD GO OUT WITH A BRAT YOUR OWN AGE!
WHAT ?!
OH!
...
S...
SORRY.
I DIDN'T MEAN TO EAVES-DROP.
NO!
IT'S NOT WHAT YOU THINK!
YEAH, I KNOW!
I WON'T TELL ANYONE!
NO! I DON'T ...
HEY, SHOTA! YOU LITTLE BRAT!
YOU WERE GOOFING OFF, WEREN'T YOU!
Oh!
OH NO.
KAZE ...

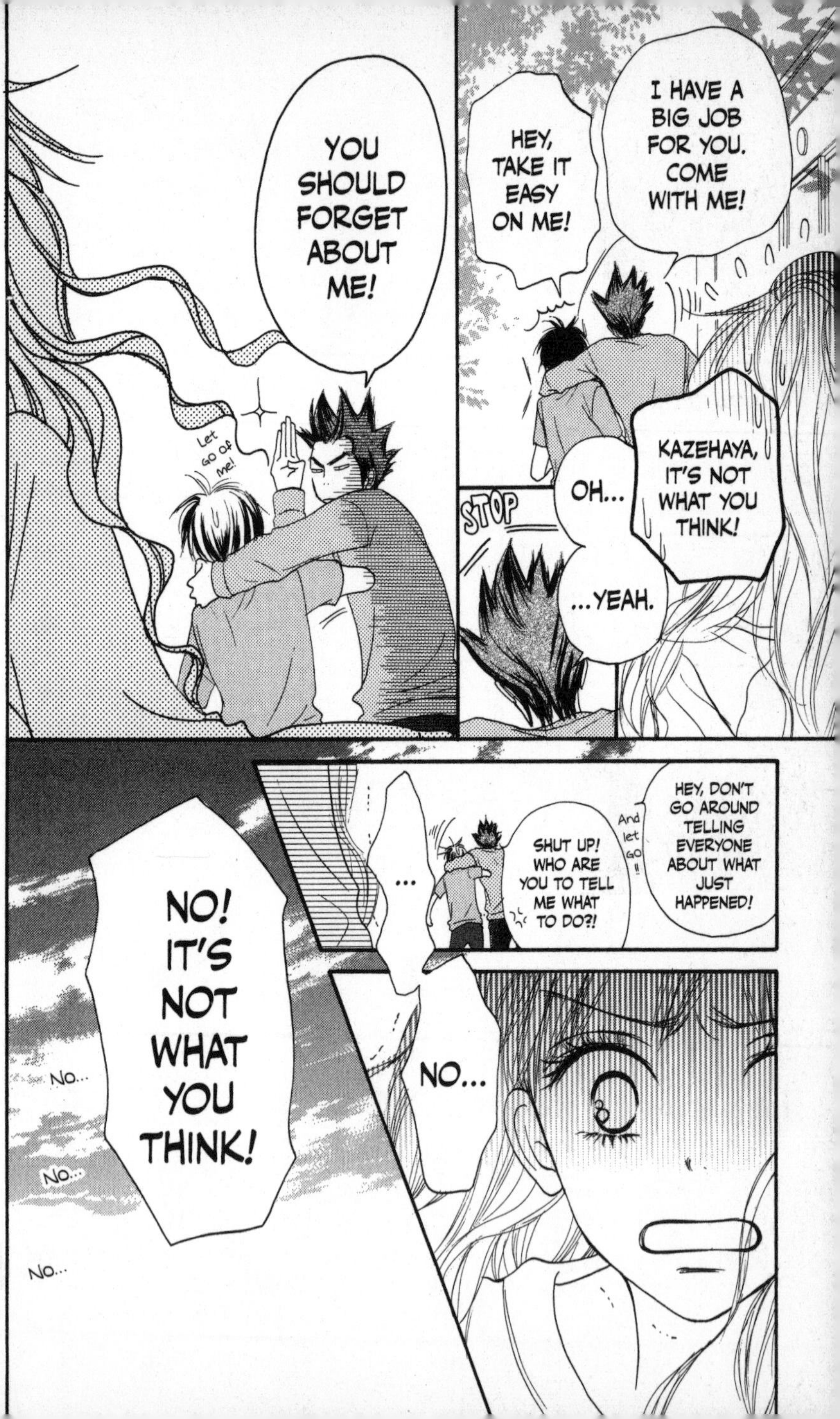
I HAVE A BIG JOB FOR YOU. COME WITH ME!
HEY, TAKE IT EASY ON ME!
KAZEHAYA, IT'S NOT WHAT YOU THINK!
STOP
OH...
...YEAH.
YOU SHOULD FORGET ABOUT ME!
Let go of me!
HEY, DON'T GO AROUND TELLING EVERYONE ABOUT WHAT JUST HAPPENED!
And let GO!!
SHUT UP! WHO ARE YOU TO TELL ME WHAT TO DO?!
...
NO...
NO! IT'S NOT WHAT YOU THINK!
No...
No...
No...

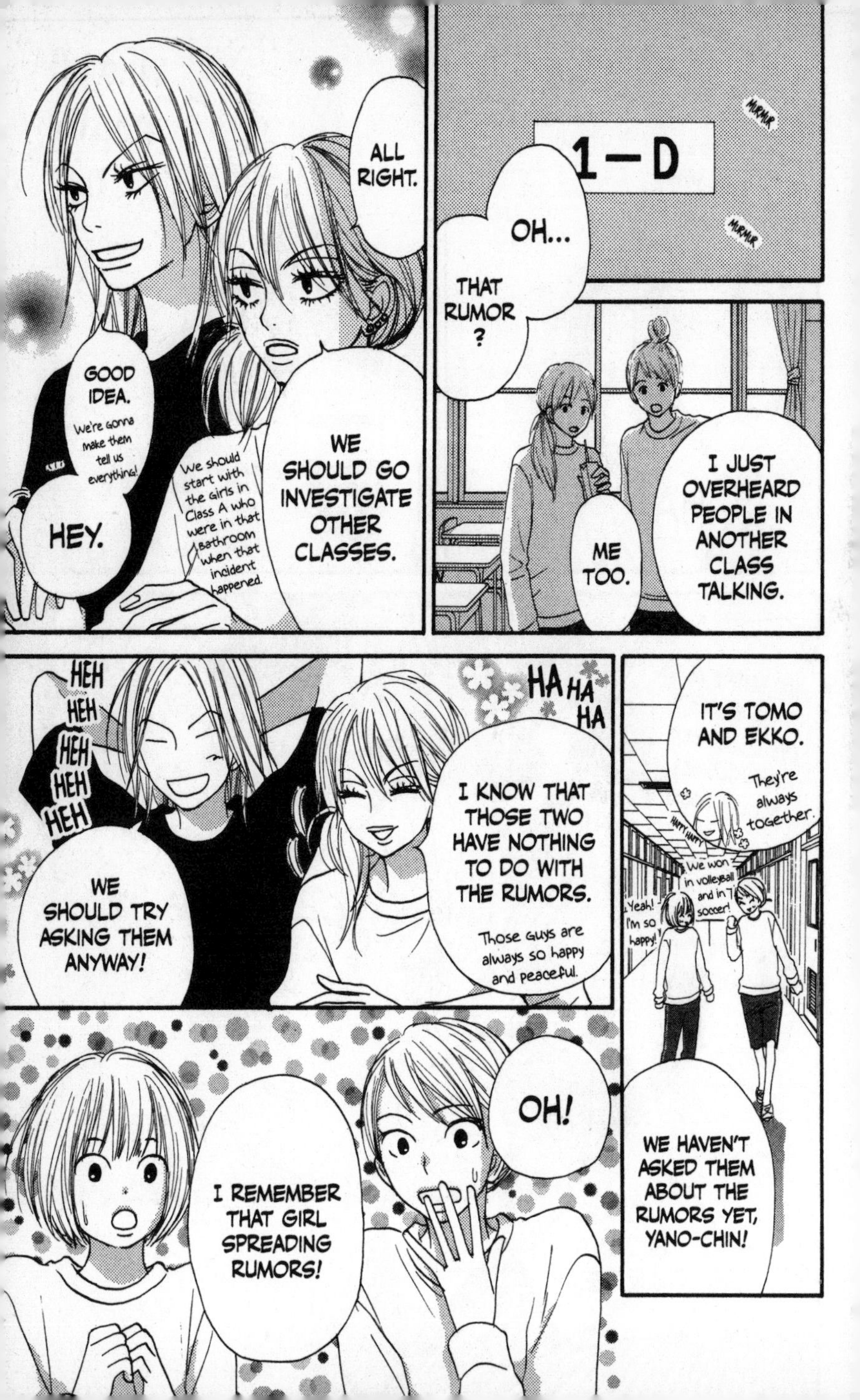
MURMUR
1-D
MURMUR
OH...
THAT RUMOR?
I JUST OVERHEARD PEOPLE IN ANOTHER CLASS TALKING.
ME TOO.
ALL RIGHT.
WE SHOULD GO INVESTIGATE OTHER CLASSES.
We should start with the Girls in Class A who were in that Bathroom when that incident happened.
GOOD IDEA.
We're gonna make them tell us everything!
HEY.
IT'S TOMO AND EKKO.
They're always together.
HAPPY HAPPY
We won in volleyball and in soccer!
Yeah! I'm so happy!
WE HAVEN'T ASKED THEM ABOUT THE RUMORS YET, YANO-CHIN!
HA HA HA
I KNOW THAT THOSE TWO HAVE NOTHING TO DO WITH THE RUMORS.
Those Guys are always so happy and peaceful.
HEH HEH HEH HEH HEH
WE SHOULD TRY ASKING THEM ANYWAY!
OH!
I REMEMBER THAT GIRL SPREADING RUMORS!

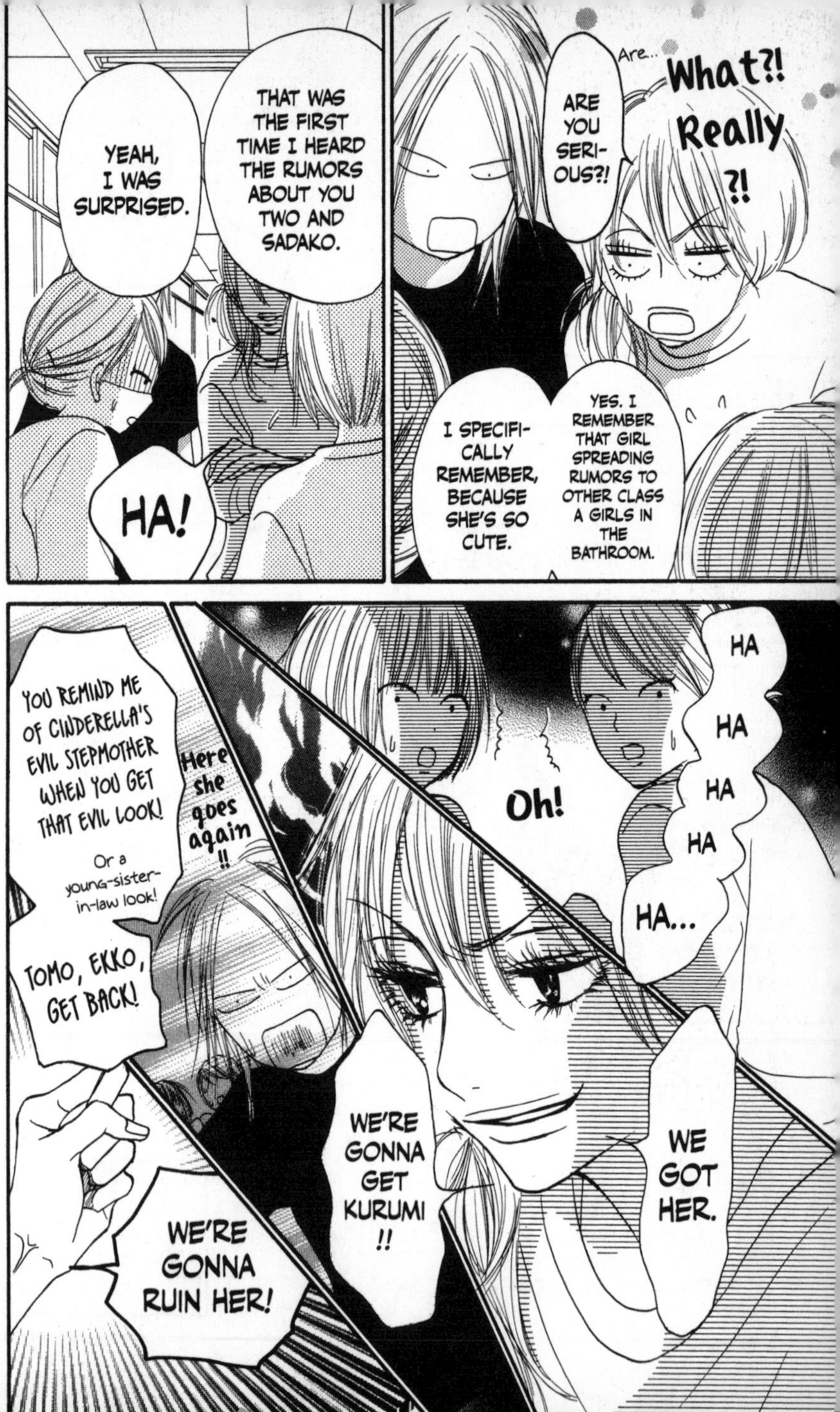
Are...
ARE YOU SERIOUS?!
What?! Really?!
YES. I REMEMBER THAT GIRL SPREADING RUMORS TO OTHER CLASS A GIRLS IN THE BATHROOM.
I SPECIFICALLY REMEMBER, BECAUSE SHE'S SO CUTE.
THAT WAS THE FIRST TIME I HEARD THE RUMORS ABOUT YOU TWO AND SADAKO.
YEAH, I WAS SURPRISED.
HA!
HA HA HA HA HA...
WE GOT HER.
WE'RE GONNA GET KURUMI!!
Oh!
Here she goes again!!
YOU REMIND ME OF CINDERELLA'S EVIL STEPMOTHER WHEN YOU GET THAT EVIL LOOK!
Or a young-sister-in-law look!
TOMO, EKKO, GET BACK!
WE'RE GONNA RUIN HER!

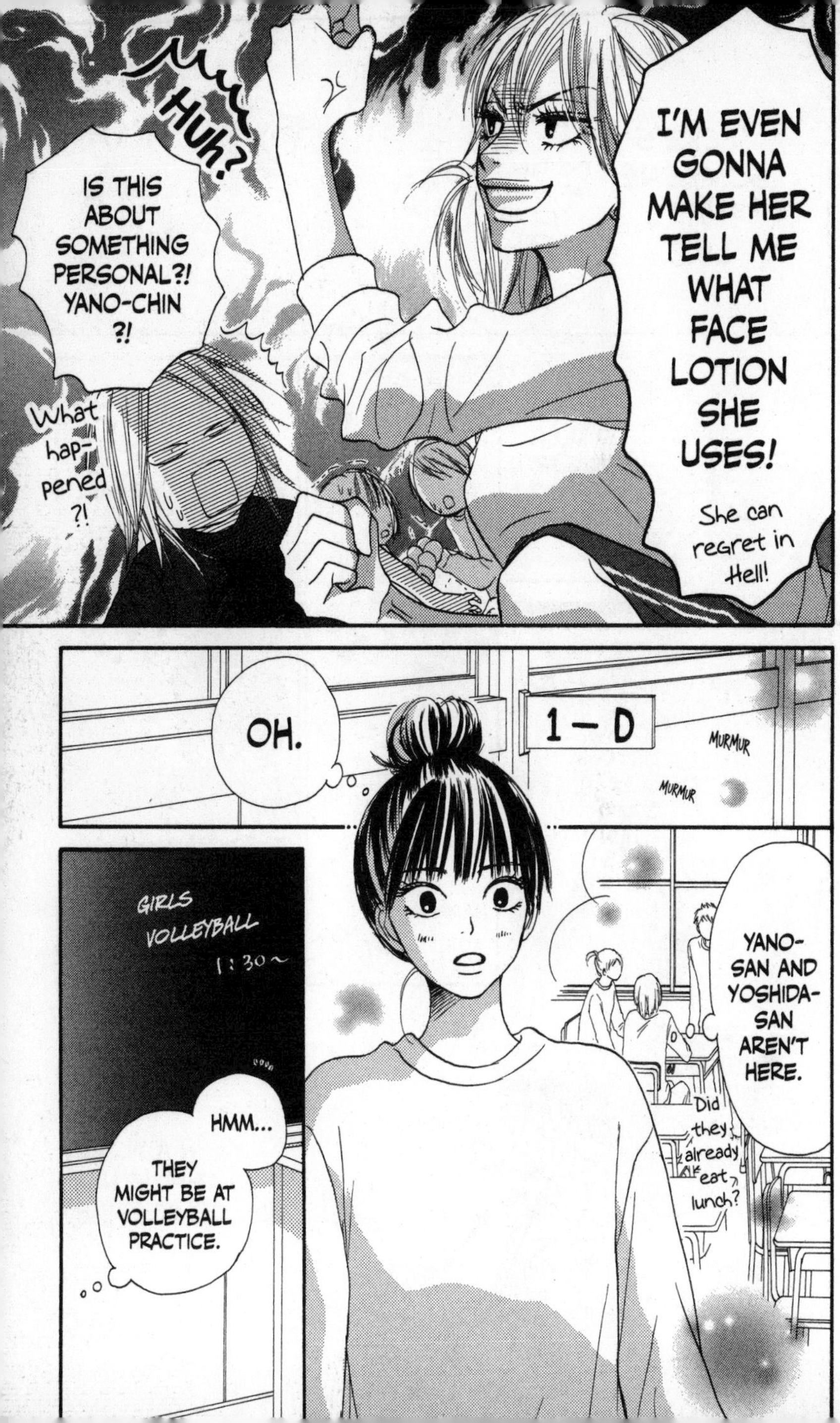
I'M EVEN GONNA MAKE HER TELL ME WHAT FACE LOTION SHE USES!
She can regret in Hell!
Huh?
IS THIS ABOUT SOMETHING PERSONAL?! YANO-CHIN?!
What hap-pened?!
1 — D
MURMUR
MURMUR
OH.
YANO-SAN AND YOSHIDA-SAN AREN'T HERE.
Did they already eat lunch?
GIRLS VOLLEYBALL 1:30~
HMM...
THEY MIGHT BE AT VOLLEYBALL PRACTICE.

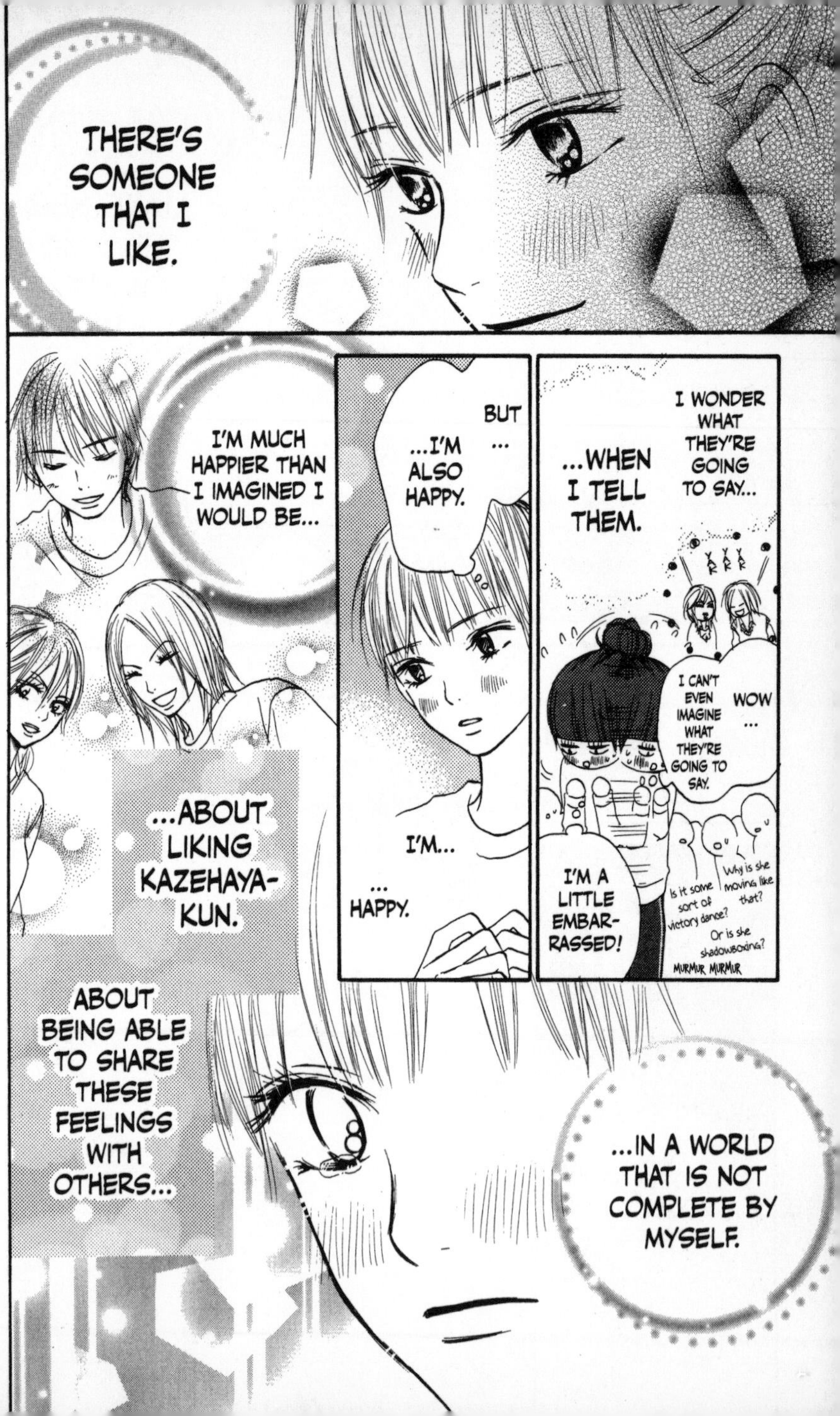
THERE'S SOMEONE THAT I LIKE.
I WONDER WHAT THEY'RE GOING TO SAY...
...WHEN I TELL THEM.
WOW ...
I CAN'T EVEN IMAGINE WHAT THEY'RE GOING TO SAY.
Why is she moving like that?
Is it some sort of victory dance?
Or is she shadowboxing?
MURMUR MURMUR
I'M A LITTLE EMBARRASSED!
BUT ...
...I'M ALSO HAPPY.
I'M...
... HAPPY.
I'M MUCH HAPPIER THAN I IMAGINED I WOULD BE...
...ABOUT LIKING KAZEHAYA-KUN.
ABOUT BEING ABLE TO SHARE THESE FEELINGS WITH OTHERS...
...IN A WORLD THAT IS NOT COMPLETE BY MYSELF.

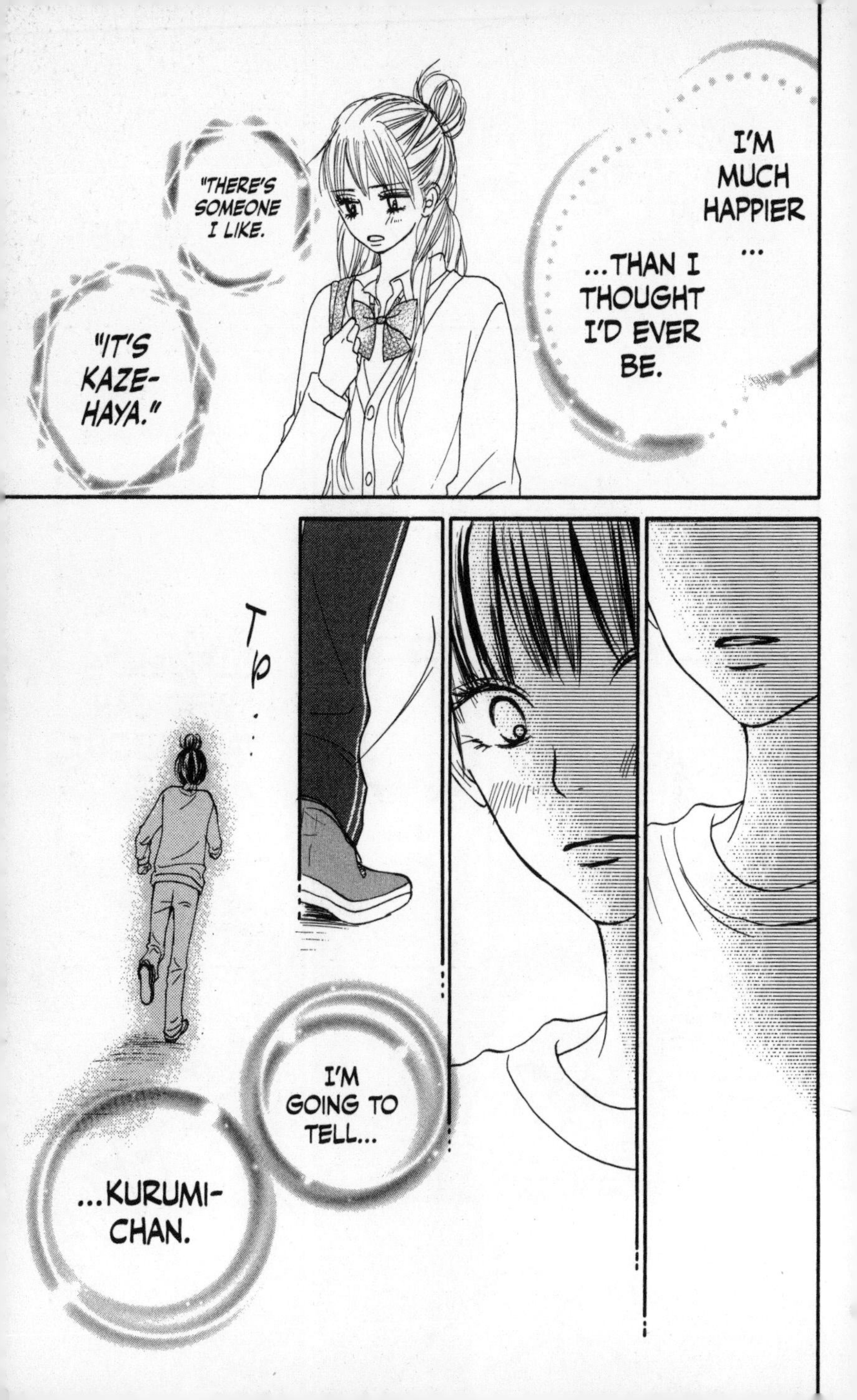
I'M MUCH HAPPIER...
...THAN I THOUGHT I'D EVER BE.
"THERE'S SOMEONE I LIKE.
"IT'S KAZE-HAYA."
Tp...
I'M GOING TO TELL...
...KURUMI-CHAN.

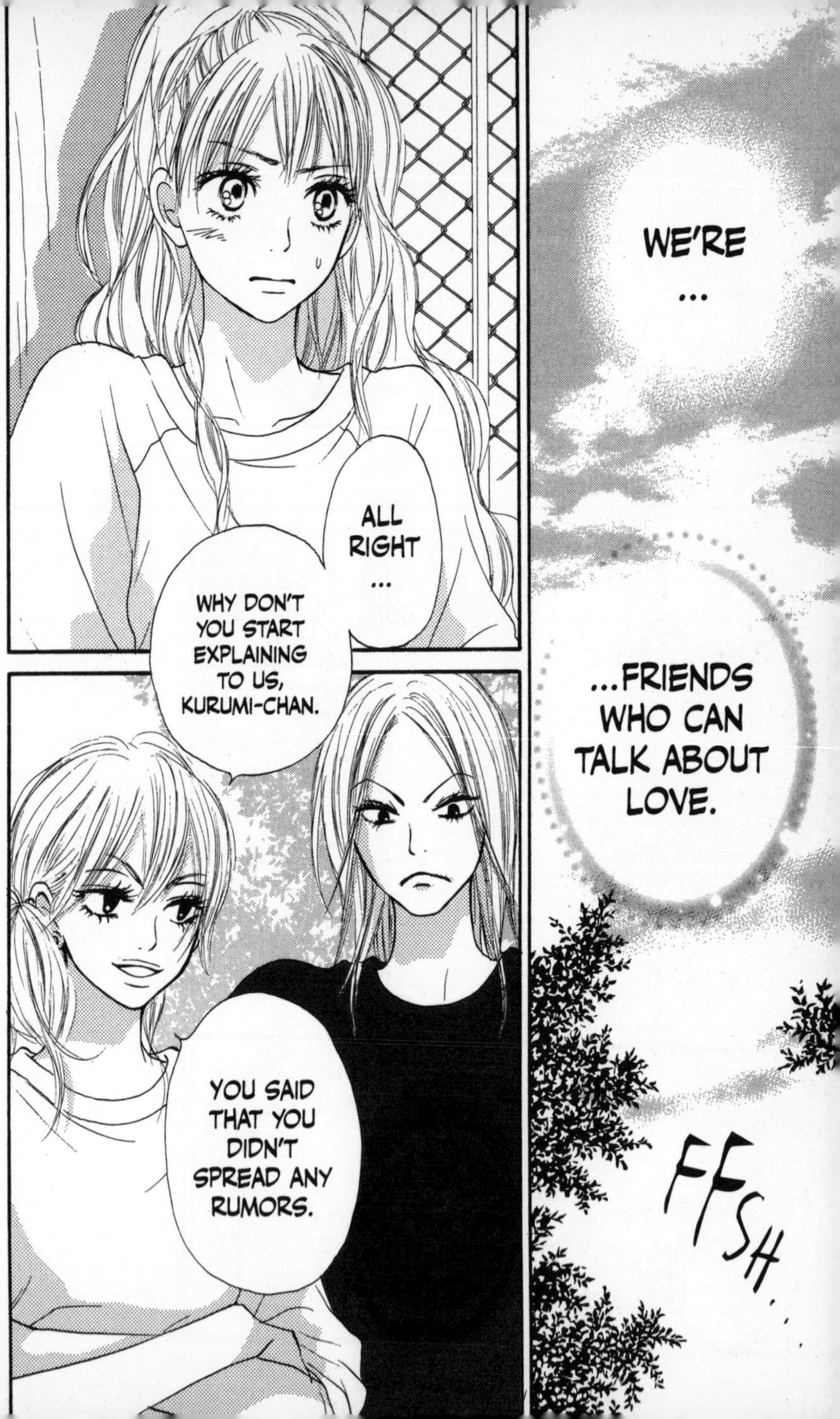
WE'RE ...
...FRIENDS WHO CAN TALK ABOUT LOVE.
FFSH...
ALL RIGHT ...
WHY DON'T YOU START EXPLAINING TO US, KURUMI-CHAN.
YOU SAID THAT YOU DIDN'T SPREAD ANY RUMORS.

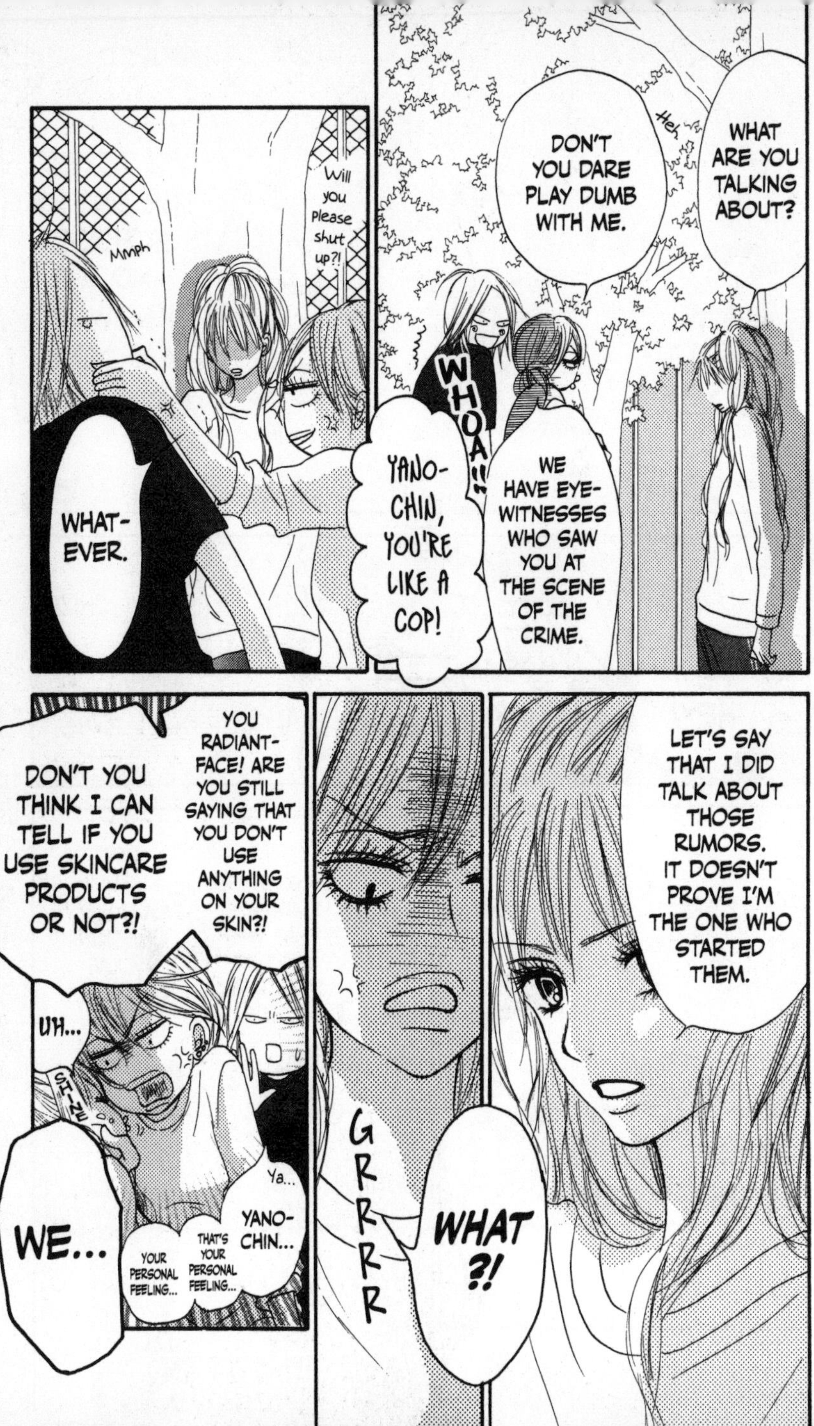
WHAT ARE YOU TALKING ABOUT?
Heh
DON'T YOU DARE PLAY DUMB WITH ME.
WHOA!!
WE HAVE EYE-WITNESSES WHO SAW YOU AT THE SCENE OF THE CRIME.
YANO-CHIN, YOU'RE LIKE A COP!
Will you please shut up?!
Mmph
WHAT-EVER.
LET'S SAY THAT I DID TALK ABOUT THOSE RUMORS. IT DOESN'T PROVE I'M THE ONE WHO STARTED THEM.
GRRRR
WHAT?!
YOU RADIANT-FACE! ARE YOU STILL SAYING THAT YOU DON'T USE ANYTHING ON YOUR SKIN?!
DON'T YOU THINK I CAN TELL IF YOU USE SKINCARE PRODUCTS OR NOT?!
Ya...
YANO-CHIN...
THAT'S YOUR PERSONAL FEELING...
YOUR PERSONAL FEELING...
UH...
SHINE
WE...

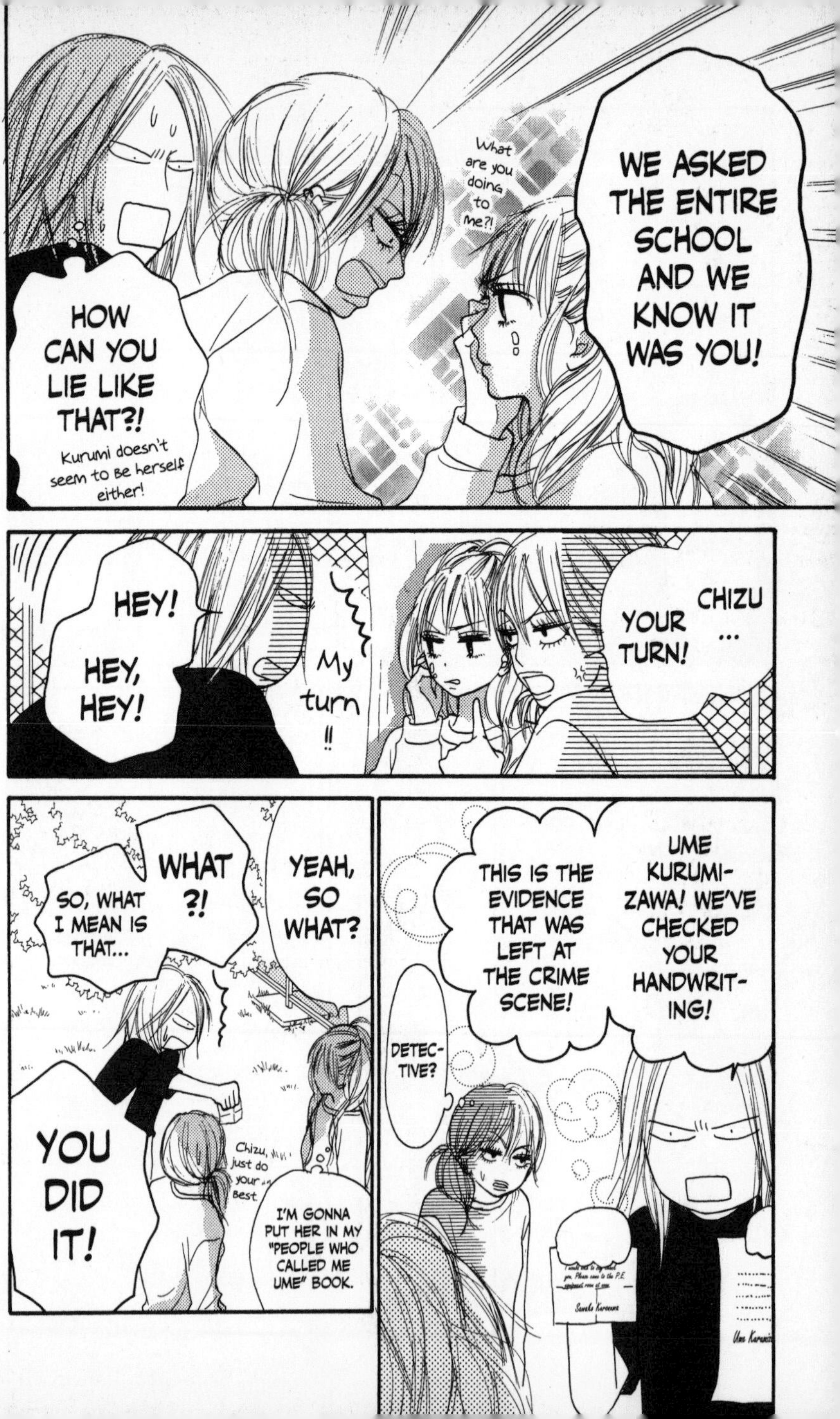
WE ASKED THE ENTIRE SCHOOL AND WE KNOW IT WAS YOU!
What are you doing to me?!
HOW CAN YOU LIE LIKE THAT?!
Kurumi doesn't seem to be herself either!
CHIZU... YOUR TURN!
My turn!!
HEY! HEY, HEY!
UME KURUMIZAWA! WE'VE CHECKED YOUR HANDWRITING!
THIS IS THE EVIDENCE THAT WAS LEFT AT THE CRIME SCENE!
DETECTIVE?
YEAH, SO WHAT?
WHAT?!
SO, WHAT I MEAN IS THAT...
I'M GONNA PUT HER IN MY "PEOPLE WHO CALLED ME UME" BOOK.
Chizu, just do your best.
YOU DID IT!

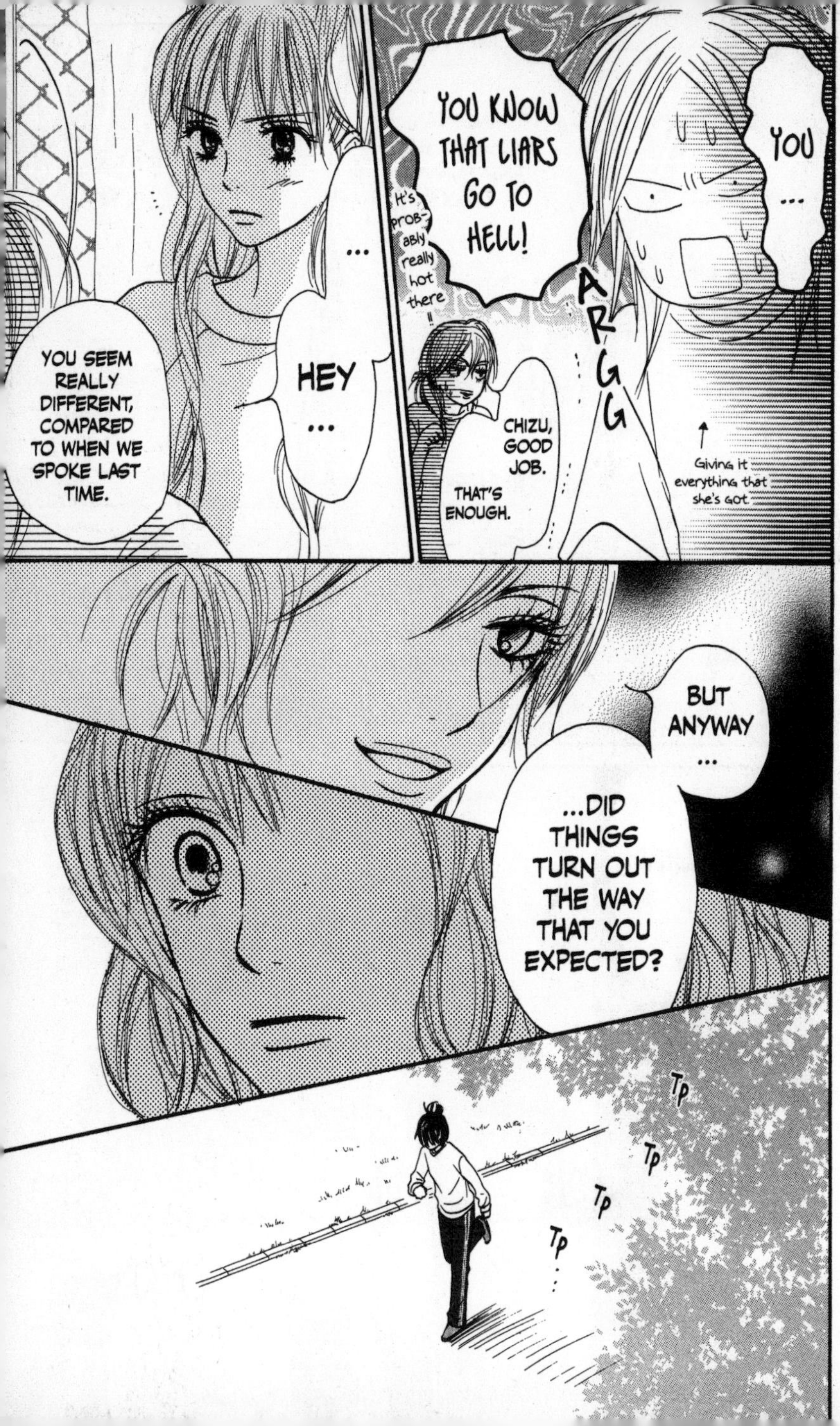
YOU ...
Giving it everything that she's got
ARGG
YOU KNOW THAT LIARS GO TO HELL!
It's probably really hot there!!
CHIZU, GOOD JOB.
THAT'S ENOUGH.
...
HEY ...
YOU SEEM REALLY DIFFERENT, COMPARED TO WHEN WE SPOKE LAST TIME.
BUT ANYWAY ...
...DID THINGS TURN OUT THE WAY THAT YOU EXPECTED?
Tp
Tp
Tp
Tp ...

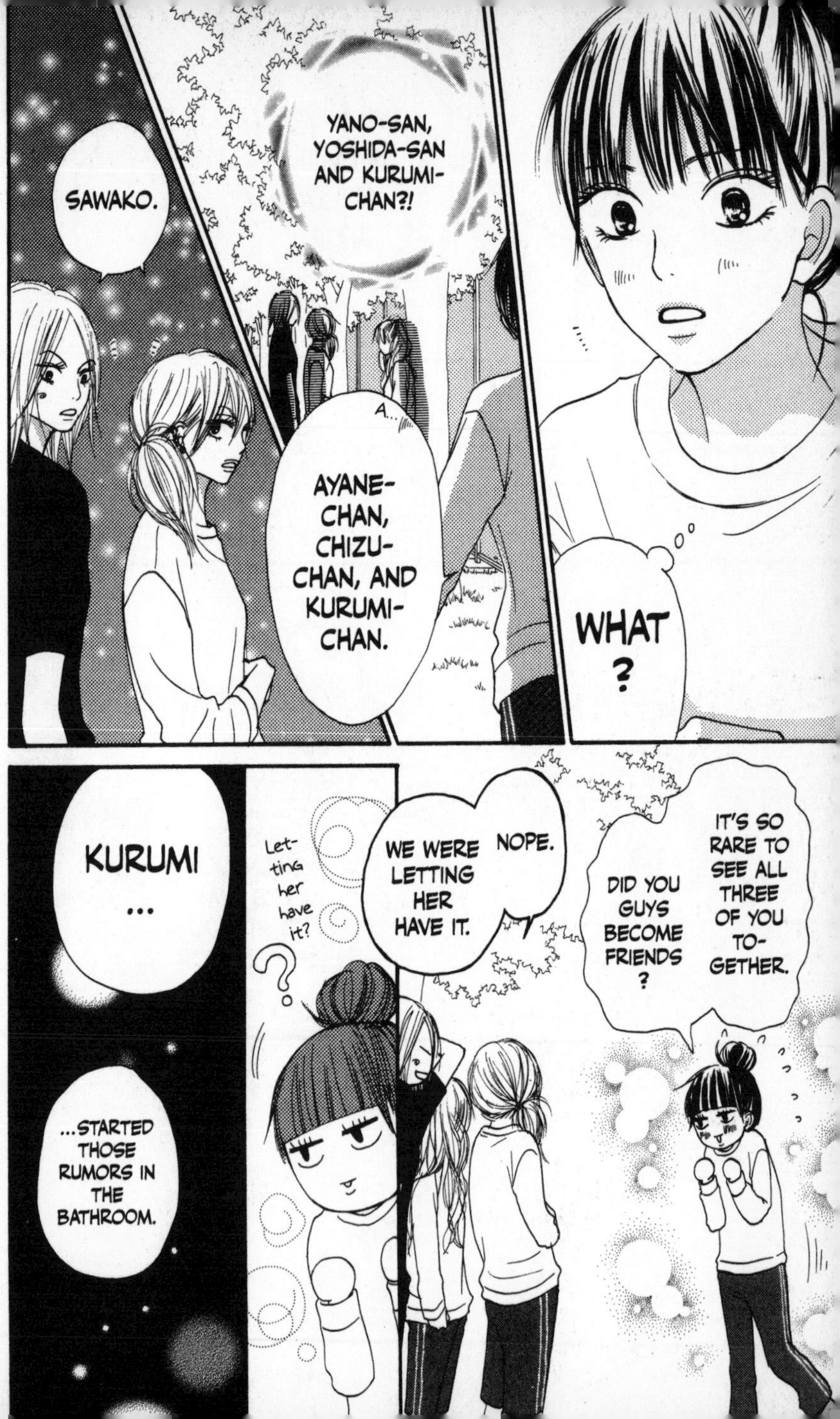
WHAT?
YANO-SAN, YOSHIDA-SAN AND KURUMI-CHAN?!
A...
AYANE-CHAN, CHIZU-CHAN, AND KURUMI-CHAN.
SAWAKO.
IT'S SO RARE TO SEE ALL THREE OF YOU TOGETHER.
DID YOU GUYS BECOME FRIENDS?
NOPE.
WE WERE LETTING HER HAVE IT.
Letting her have it?
KURUMI...
...STARTED THOSE RUMORS IN THE BATHROOM.

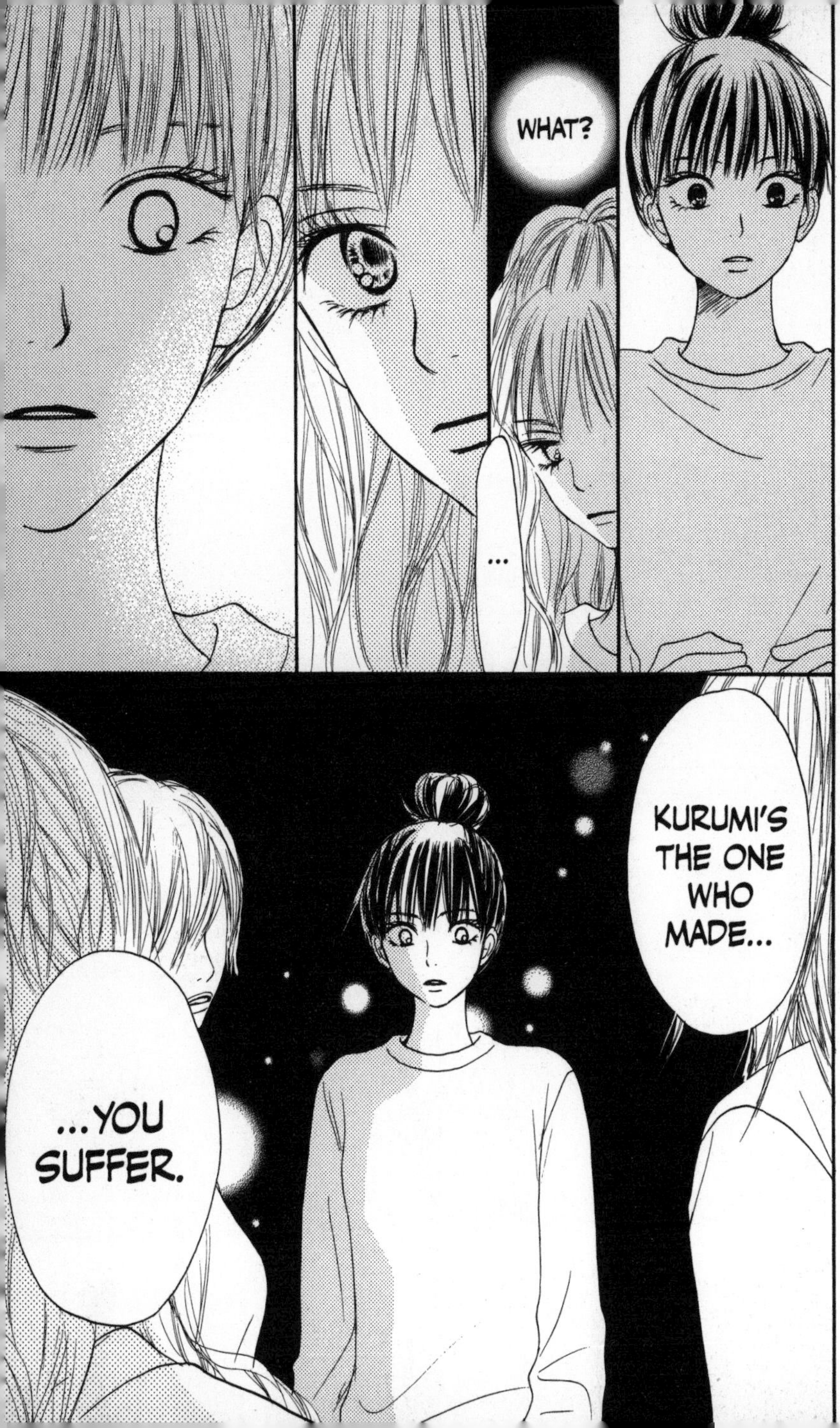
WHAT?
...
KURUMI'S THE ONE WHO MADE...
...YOU SUFFER.

Here you go.

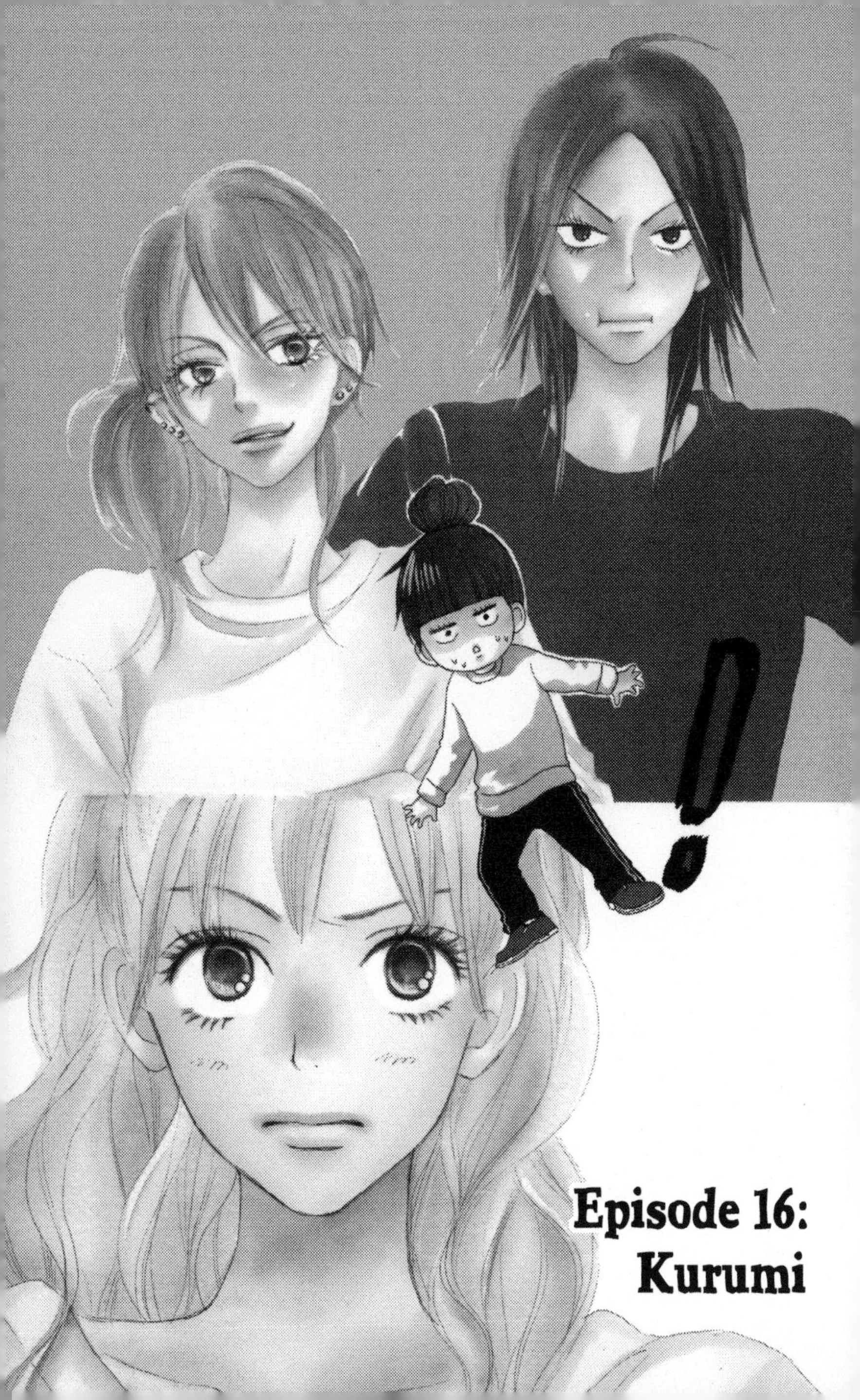
Episode 16:
Kurumi

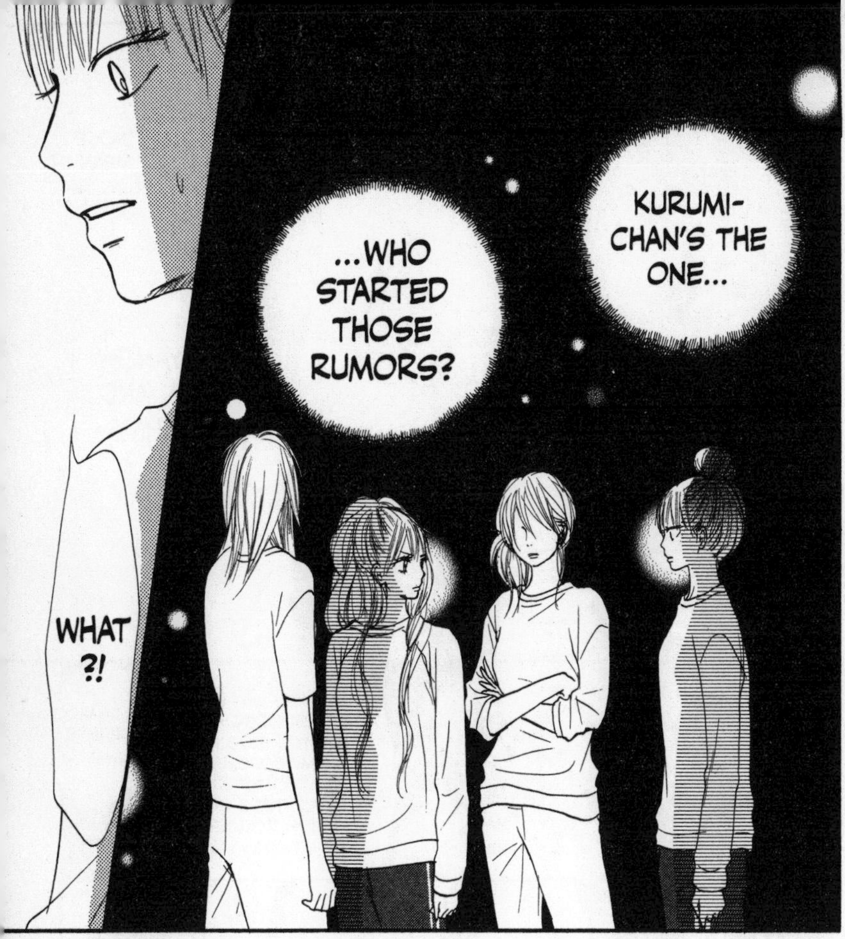
KURUMI-CHAN'S THE ONE...
...WHO STARTED THOSE RUMORS?
WHAT ?!

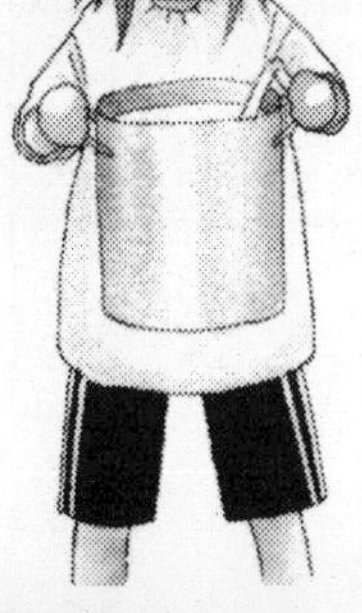
Lunch Monitor

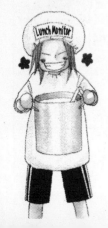

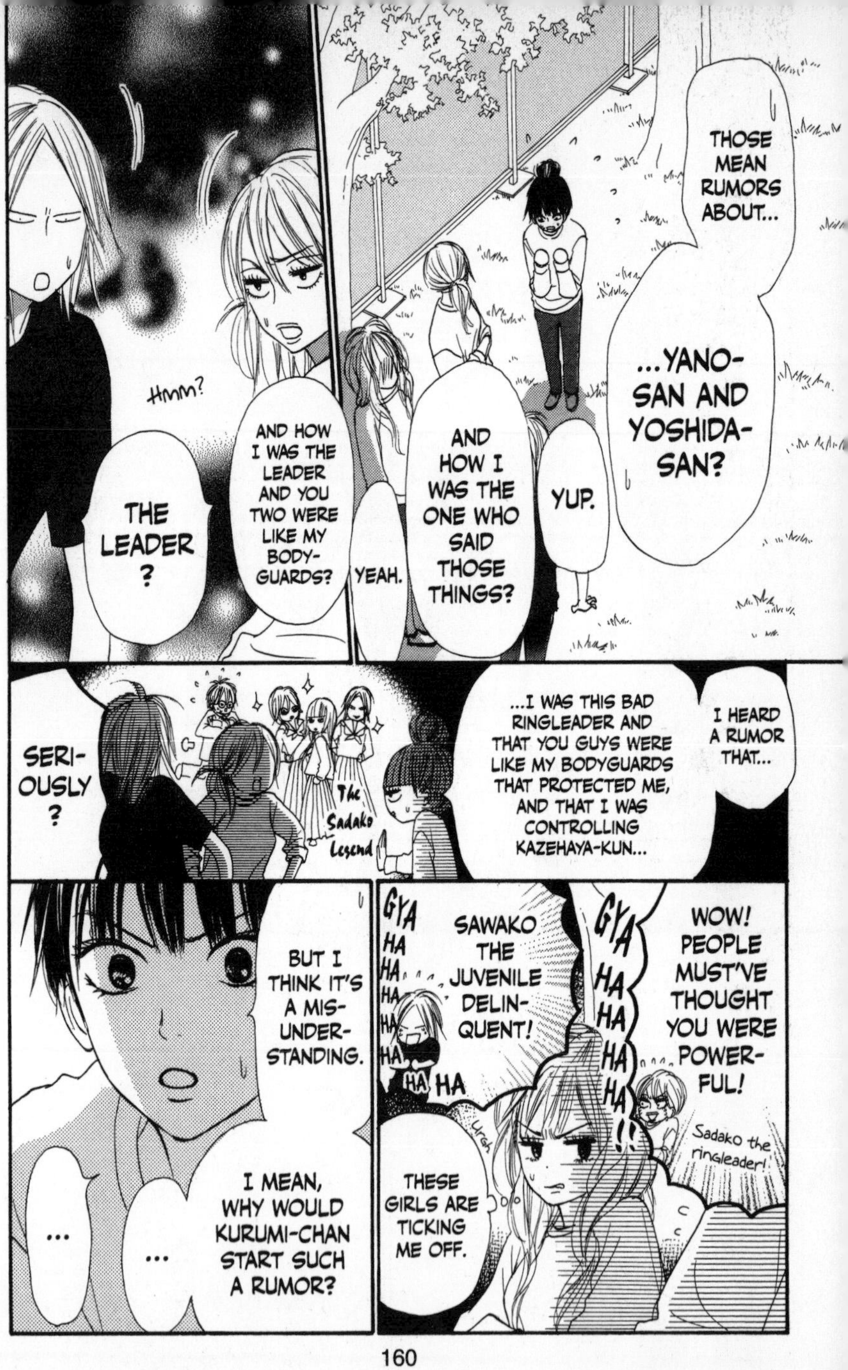
THOSE MEAN RUMORS ABOUT...
...YANO-SAN AND YOSHIDA-SAN?
YUP.
AND HOW I WAS THE ONE WHO SAID THOSE THINGS?
YEAH.
AND HOW I WAS THE LEADER AND YOU TWO WERE LIKE MY BODY-GUARDS?
Hmm?
THE LEADER?
I HEARD A RUMOR THAT...
...I WAS THIS BAD RINGLEADER AND THAT YOU GUYS WERE LIKE MY BODYGUARDS THAT PROTECTED ME, AND THAT I WAS CONTROLLING KAZEHAYA-KUN...
The Sadako Legend
SERIOUSLY?
WOW! PEOPLE MUST'VE THOUGHT YOU WERE POWER-FUL!
Sadako the ringleader!
GYA HA HA HA HA HA!!
SAWAKO THE JUVENILE DELIN-QUENT!
GYA HA HA HA HA HA HA HA
Urgh
THESE GIRLS ARE TICKING ME OFF.
BUT I THINK IT'S A MIS-UNDER-STANDING.
I MEAN, WHY WOULD KURUMI-CHAN START SUCH A RUMOR?
...
...

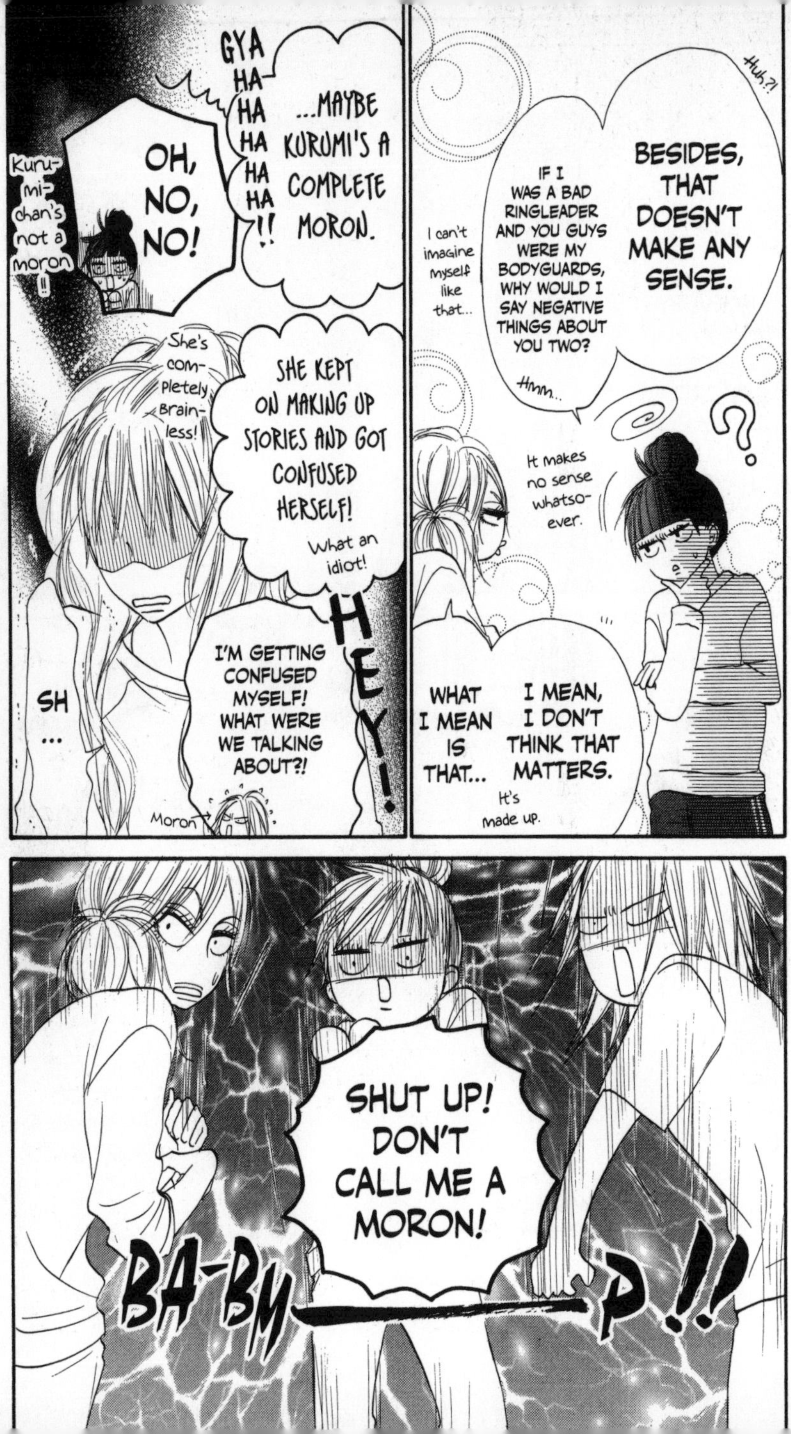
Huh?!
BESIDES, THAT DOESN'T MAKE ANY SENSE.
IF I WAS A BAD RINGLEADER AND YOU GUYS WERE MY BODYGUARDS, WHY WOULD I SAY NEGATIVE THINGS ABOUT YOU TWO?
I can't imagine myself like that...
Hmm...
It makes no sense whatsoever.
I MEAN, I DON'T THINK THAT MATTERS.
WHAT I MEAN IS THAT...
It's made up.
...MAYBE KURUMI'S A COMPLETE MORON.
GYA HA-HA HA HA HA HA!!
OH, NO, NO!
Kuru-mi-chan's not a moron!!
SHE KEPT ON MAKING UP STORIES AND GOT CONFUSED HERSELF!
What an idiot!
She's com-pletely Brain-less!
HEY!
I'M GETTING CONFUSED MYSELF! WHAT WERE WE TALKING ABOUT?!
SH...
Moron
SHUT UP! DON'T CALL ME A MORON!
BA-BM—P!!

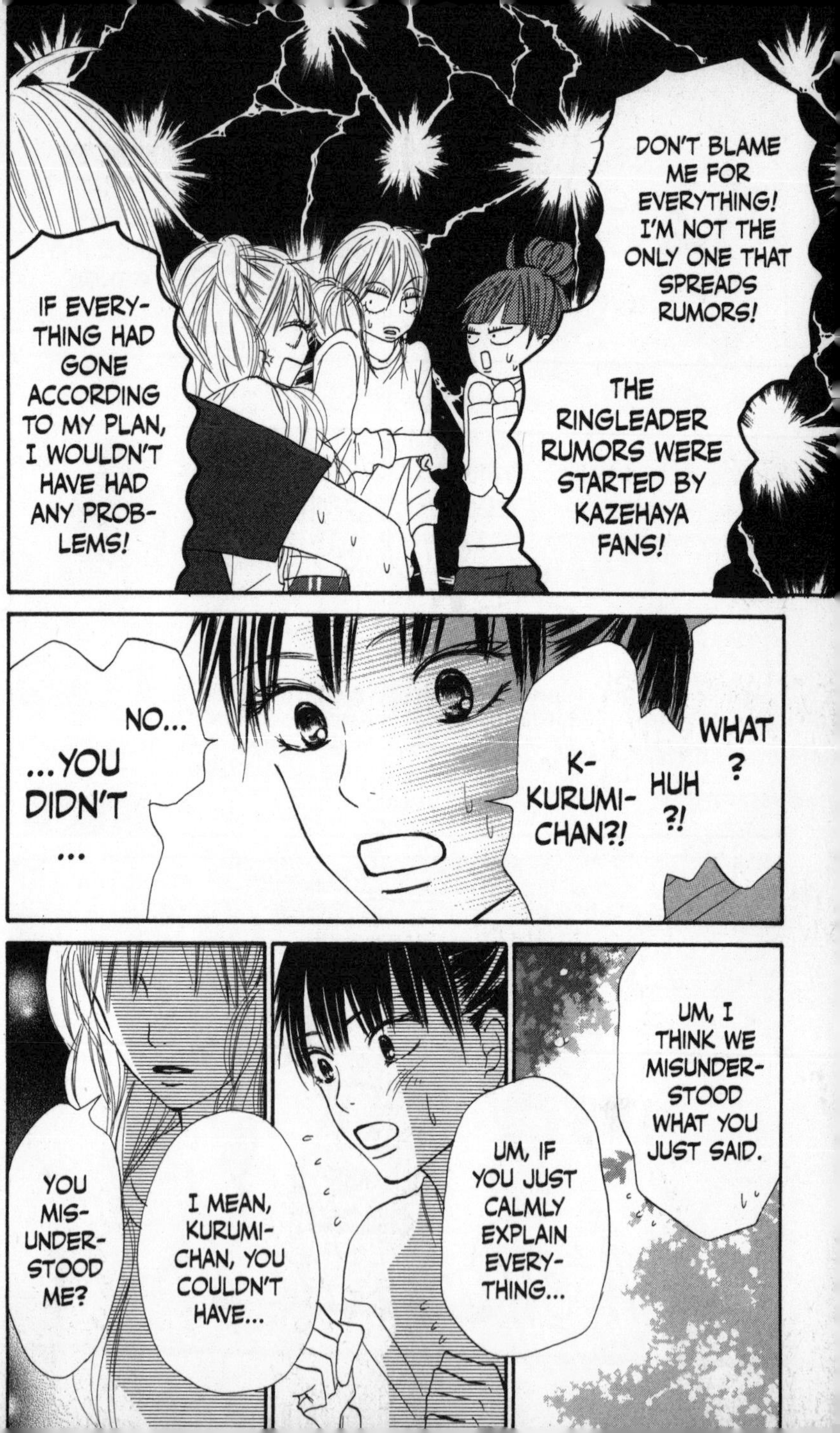
DON'T BLAME ME FOR EVERYTHING! I'M NOT THE ONLY ONE THAT SPREADS RUMORS!
THE RINGLEADER RUMORS WERE STARTED BY KAZEHAYA FANS!
IF EVERYTHING HAD GONE ACCORDING TO MY PLAN, I WOULDN'T HAVE HAD ANY PROBLEMS!
WHAT?
HUH?!
K-KURUMI-CHAN?!
NO...
...YOU DIDN'T...
UM, I THINK WE MISUNDERSTOOD WHAT YOU JUST SAID.
UM, IF YOU JUST CALMLY EXPLAIN EVERYTHING...
I MEAN, KURUMI-CHAN, YOU COULDN'T HAVE...
YOU MISUNDERSTOOD ME?

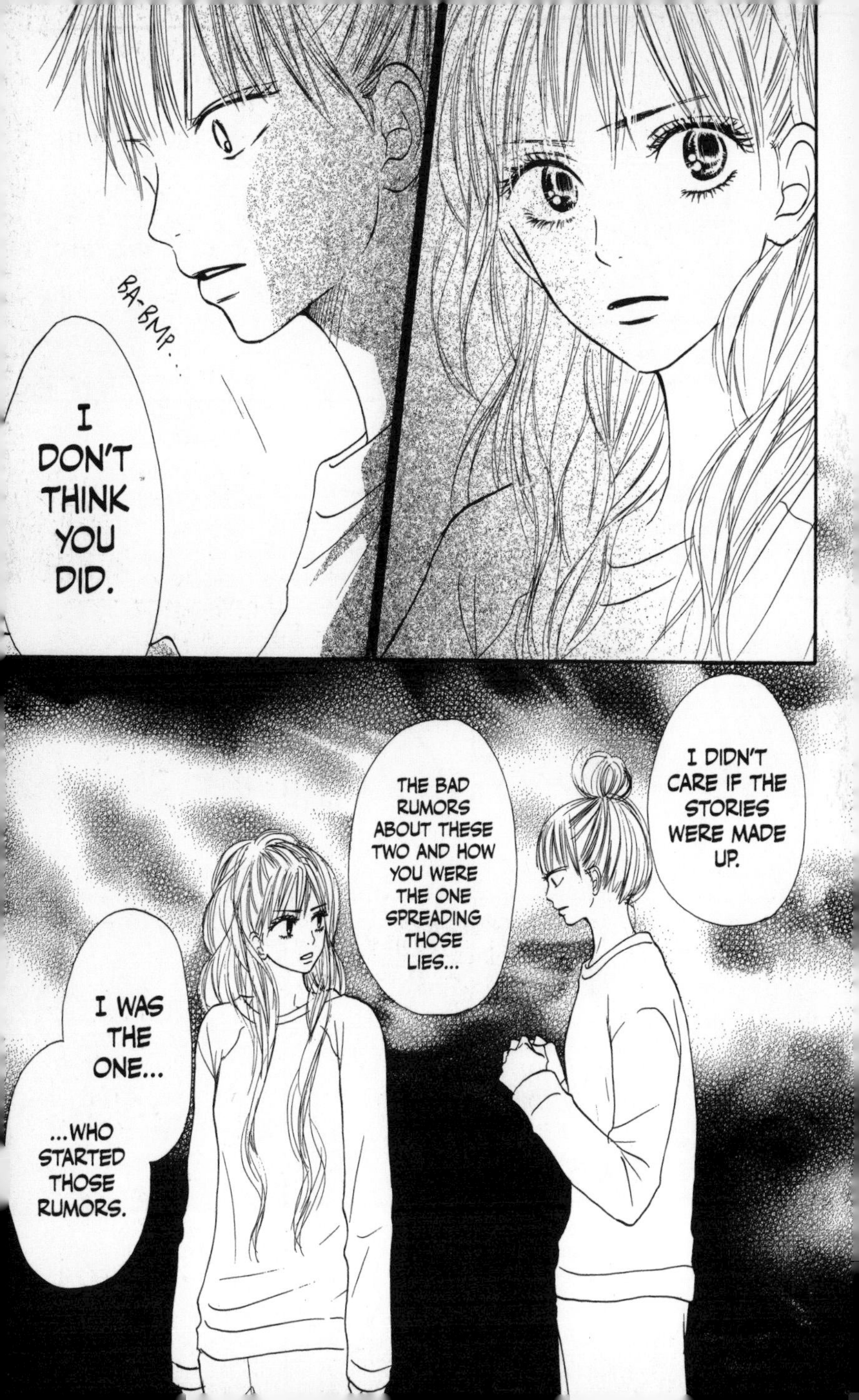
BA-BMP...
I DON'T THINK YOU DID.
I DIDN'T CARE IF THE STORIES WERE MADE UP.
THE BAD RUMORS ABOUT THESE TWO AND HOW YOU WERE THE ONE SPREADING THOSE LIES...
I WAS THE ONE...
...WHO STARTED THOSE RUMORS.

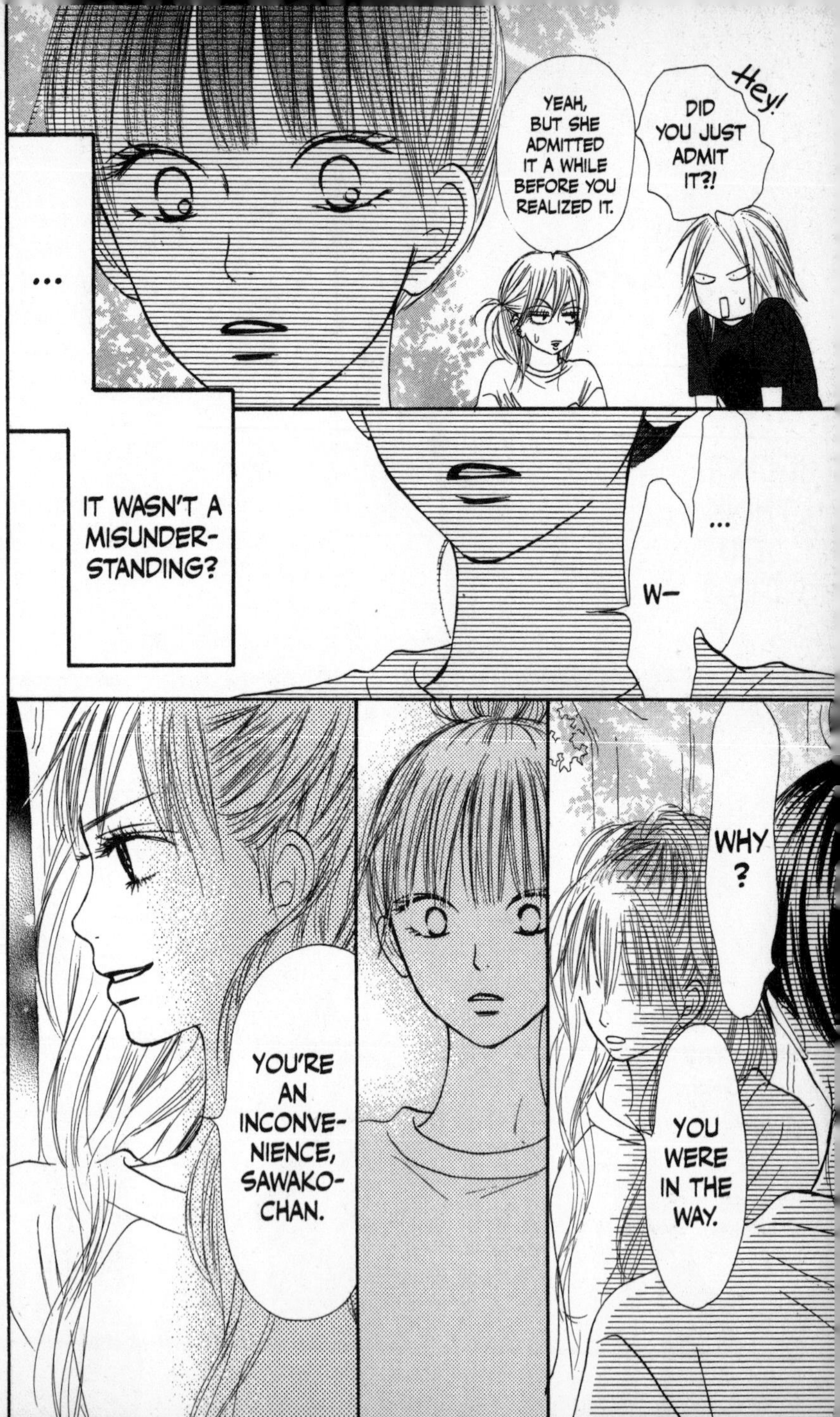
Hey!
DID YOU JUST ADMIT IT?!
YEAH, BUT SHE ADMITTED IT A WHILE BEFORE YOU REALIZED IT.
...
... W–
IT WASN'T A MISUNDER-STANDING?
WHY?
YOU WERE IN THE WAY.
YOU'RE AN INCONVE-NIENCE, SAWAKO-CHAN.

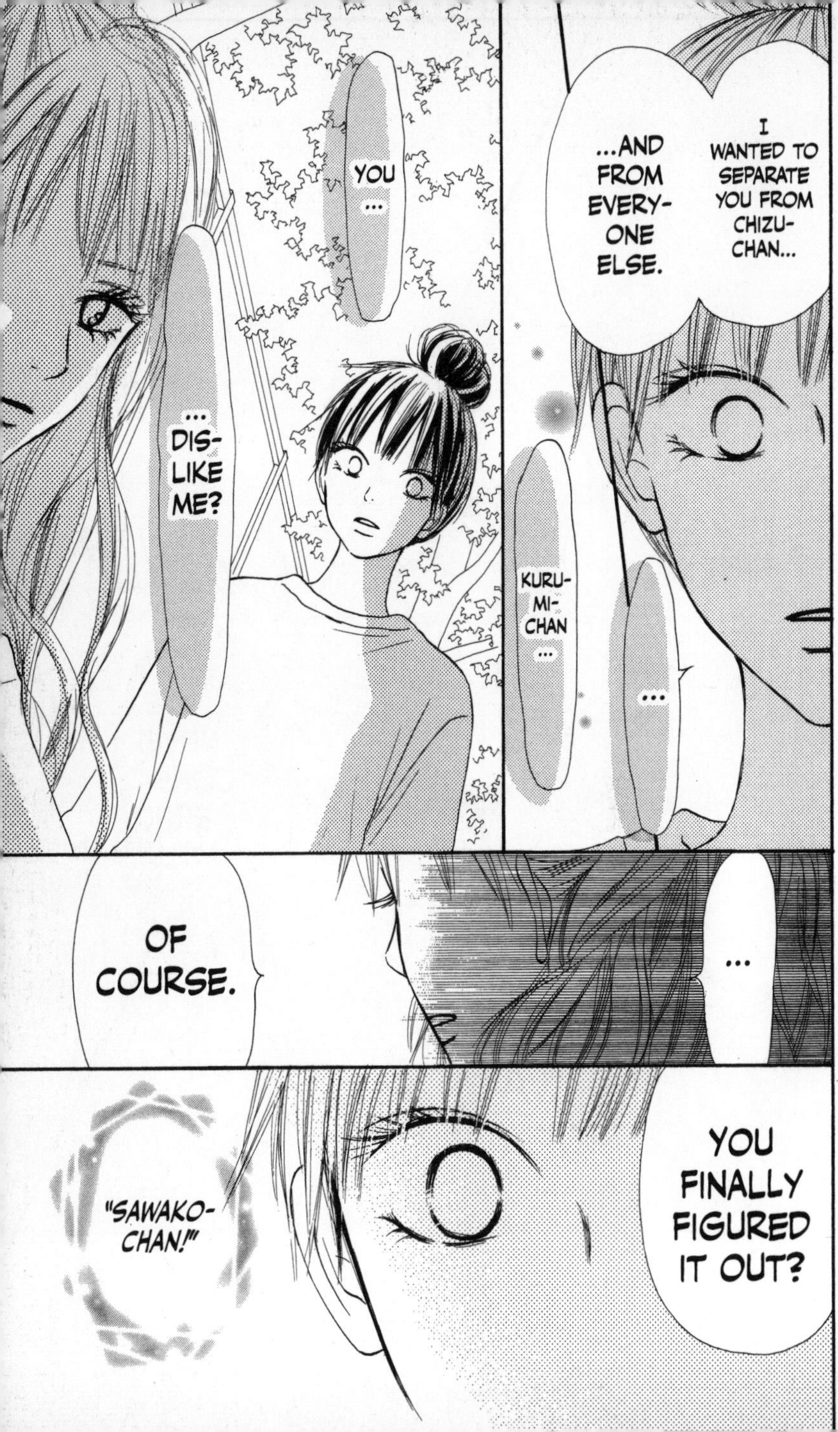
I WANTED TO SEPARATE YOU FROM CHIZU-CHAN...
...AND FROM EVERY-ONE ELSE.
KURU-MI-CHAN...
...
YOU...
...DIS-LIKE ME?
...
OF COURSE.
YOU FINALLY FIGURED IT OUT?
"SAWAKO-CHAN!"

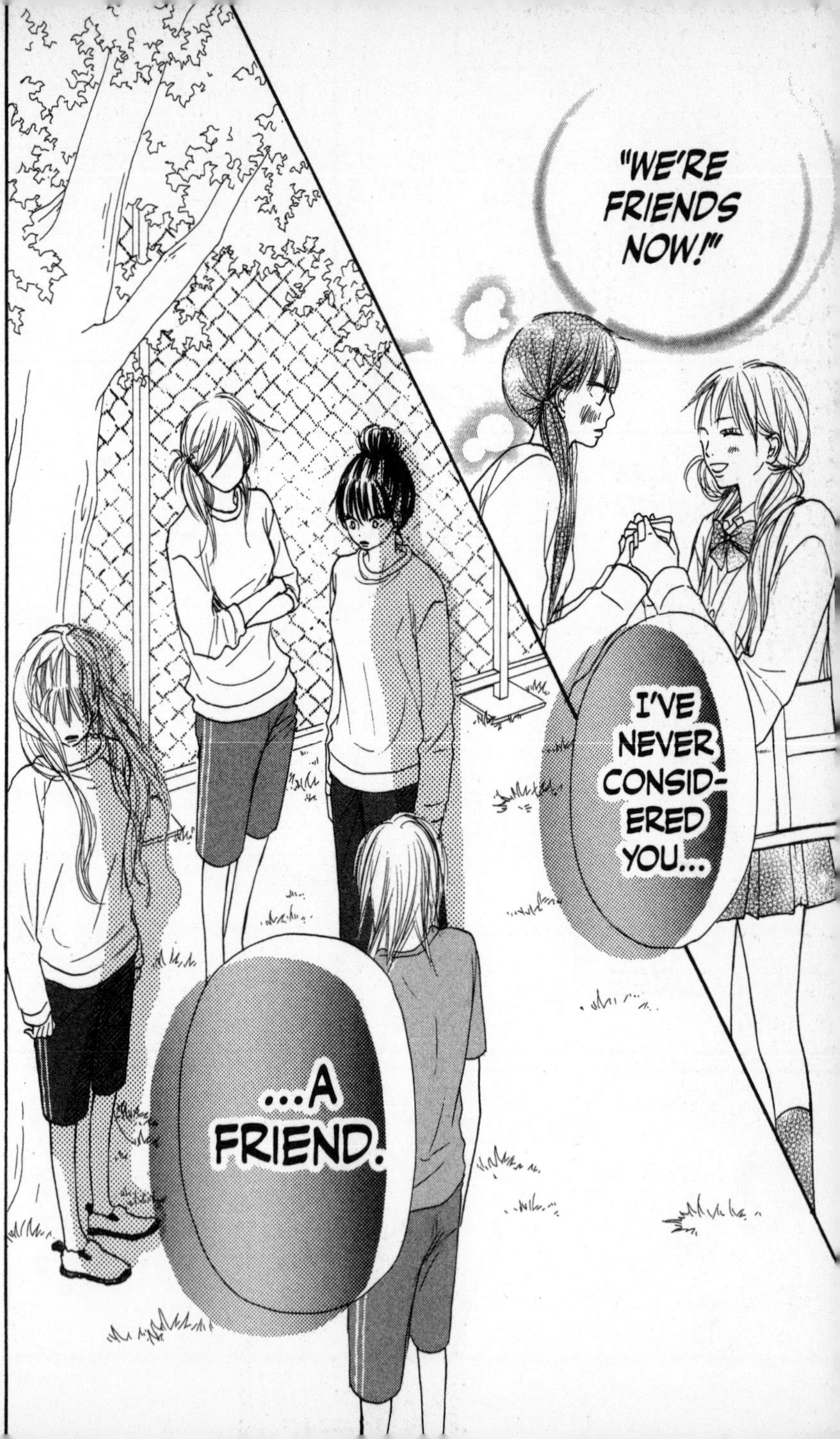
"WE'RE FRIENDS NOW!"
I'VE NEVER CONSID-ERED YOU...
...A FRIEND.

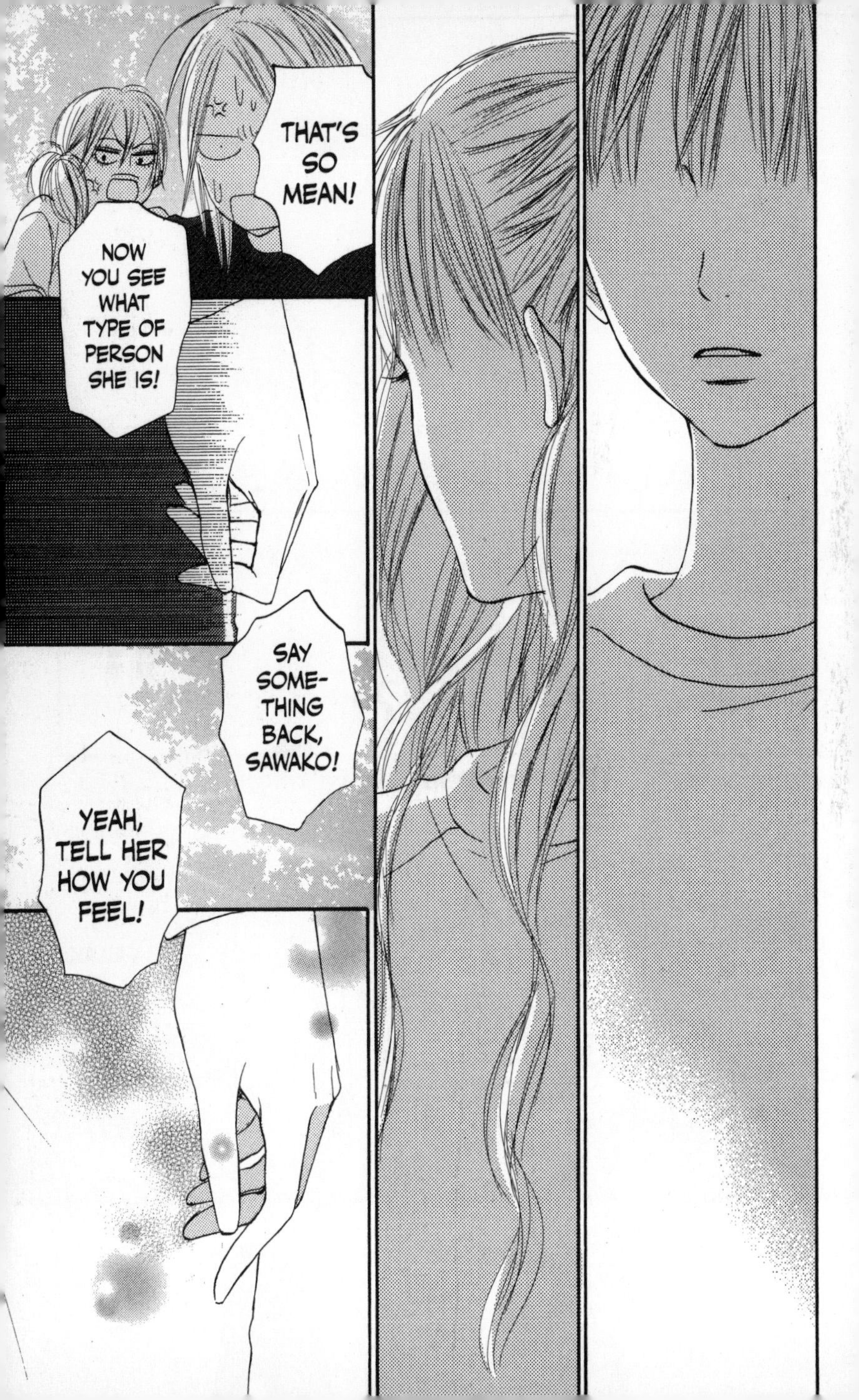
THAT'S SO MEAN!
NOW YOU SEE WHAT TYPE OF PERSON SHE IS!
SAY SOME-THING BACK, SAWAKO!
YEAH, TELL HER HOW YOU FEEL!

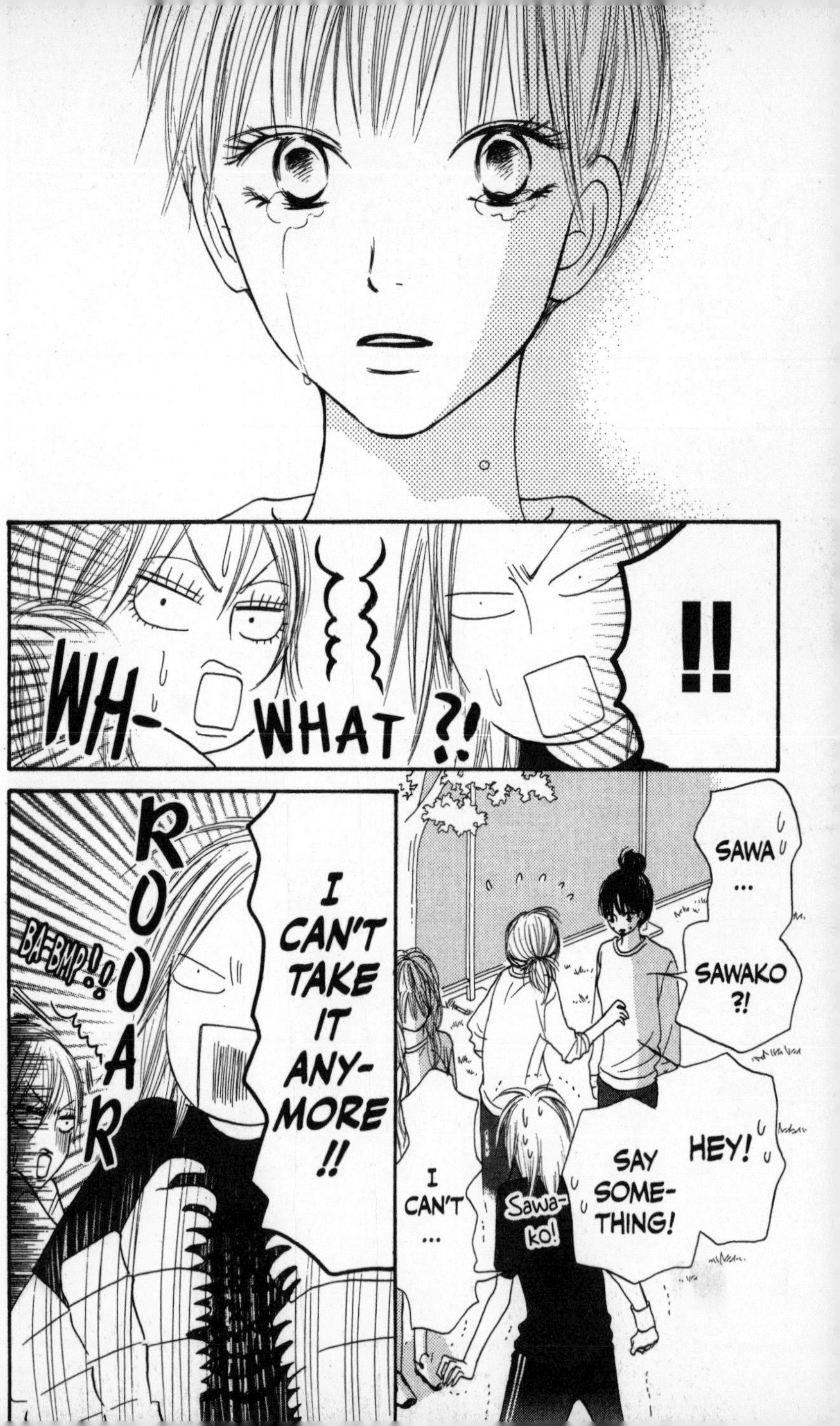
!!
WH- WHAT?!
SAWA ...
SAWAKO?!
HEY!
SAY SOMETHING!
Sawa-ko!
I CAN'T ...
I CAN'T TAKE IT ANYMORE!!
ROOOAR
BA-BMP!!

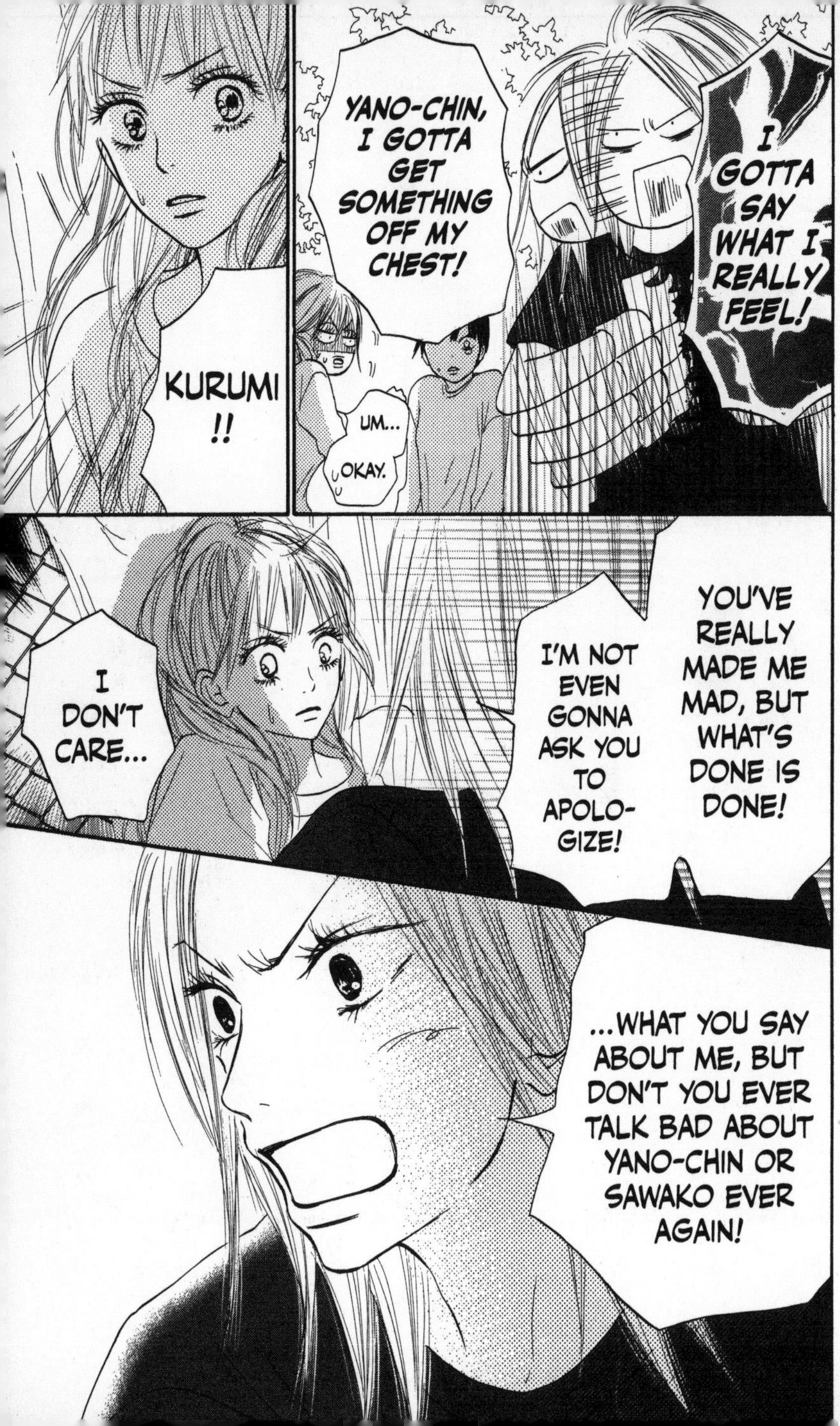
I GOTTA SAY WHAT I REALLY FEEL!
YANO-CHIN, I GOTTA GET SOMETHING OFF MY CHEST!
UM... OKAY.
KURUMI !!
YOU'VE REALLY MADE ME MAD, BUT WHAT'S DONE IS DONE!
I'M NOT EVEN GONNA ASK YOU TO APOLO-GIZE!
I DON'T CARE...
...WHAT YOU SAY ABOUT ME, BUT DON'T YOU EVER TALK BAD ABOUT YANO-CHIN OR SAWAKO EVER AGAIN!

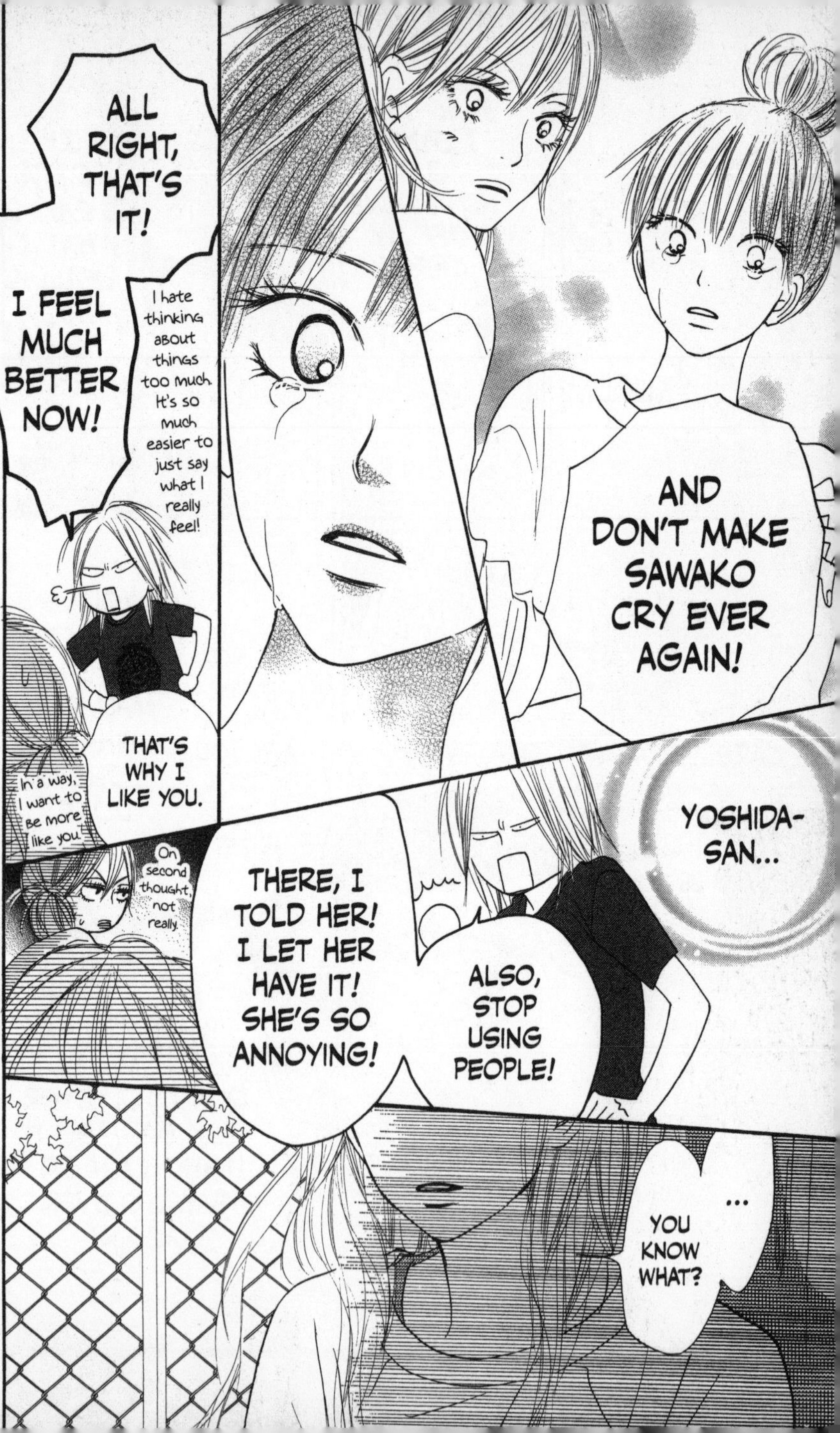
AND DON'T MAKE SAWAKO CRY EVER AGAIN!
ALL RIGHT, THAT'S IT!
I FEEL MUCH BETTER NOW!
I hate thinking about things too much. It's so much easier to just say what I really feel!
THAT'S WHY I LIKE YOU.
In a way, I want to be more like you.
YOSHIDA-SAN...
ALSO, STOP USING PEOPLE!
THERE, I TOLD HER! I LET HER HAVE IT! SHE'S SO ANNOYING!
On second thought, not really.
... YOU KNOW WHAT?

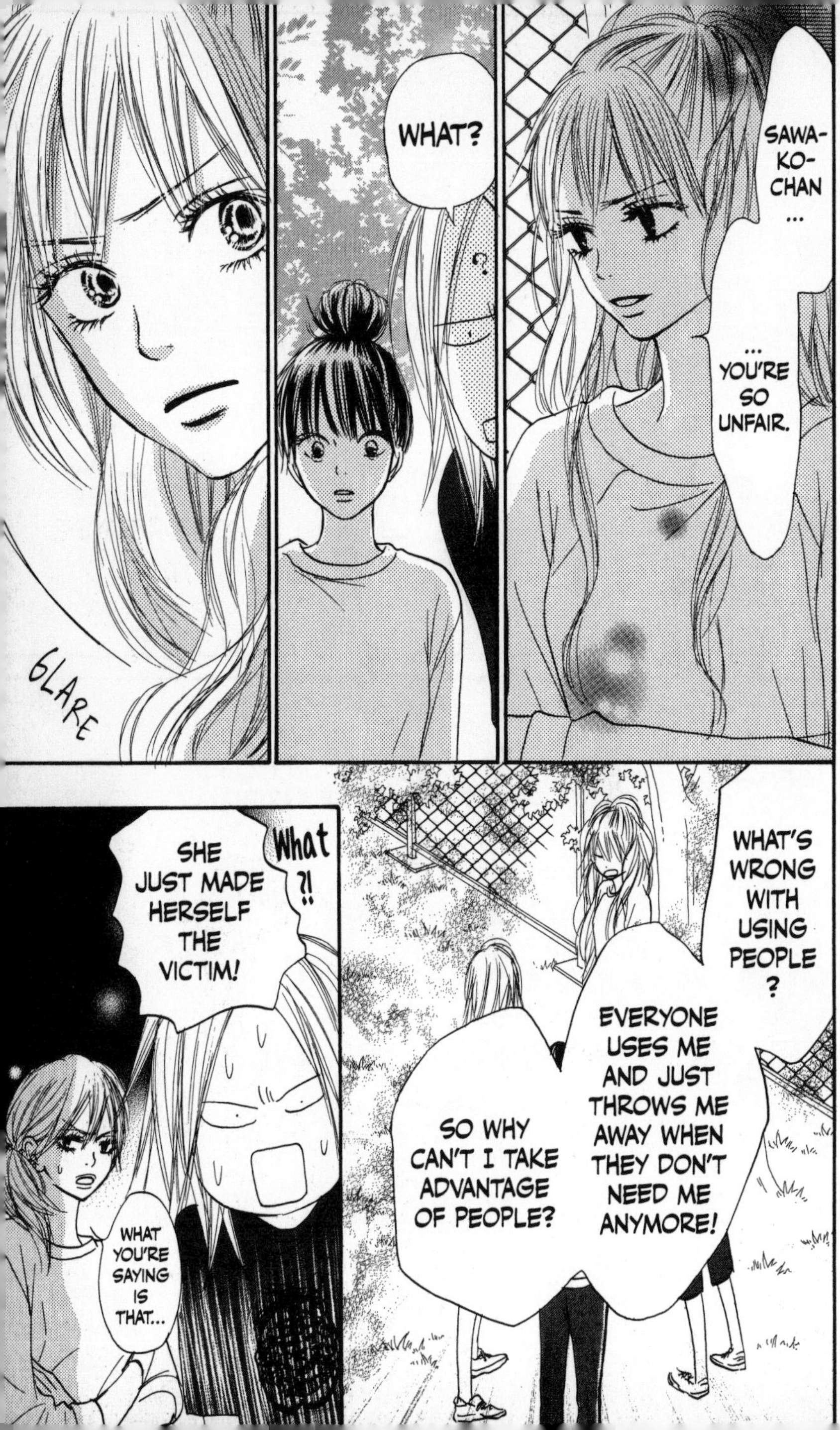
SAWAKO-CHAN...
...YOU'RE SO UNFAIR.
WHAT?
GLARE
WHAT'S WRONG WITH USING PEOPLE?
EVERYONE USES ME AND JUST THROWS ME AWAY WHEN THEY DON'T NEED ME ANYMORE!
SO WHY CAN'T I TAKE ADVANTAGE OF PEOPLE?
What?!
SHE JUST MADE HERSELF THE VICTIM!
WHAT YOU'RE SAYING IS THAT...

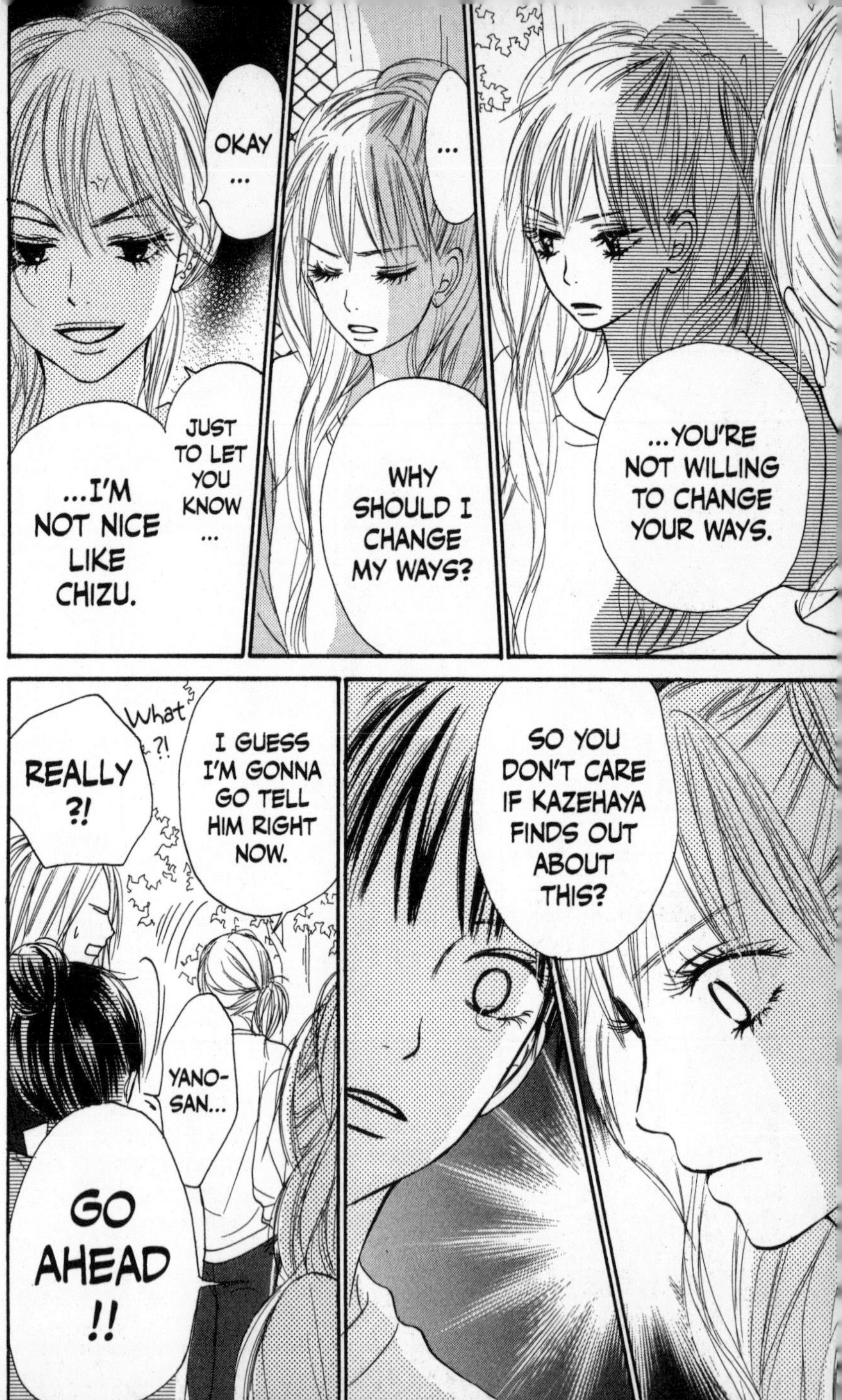
...YOU'RE NOT WILLING TO CHANGE YOUR WAYS.
...
WHY SHOULD I CHANGE MY WAYS?
OKAY ...
JUST TO LET YOU KNOW ...
...I'M NOT NICE LIKE CHIZU.
SO YOU DON'T CARE IF KAZEHAYA FINDS OUT ABOUT THIS?
I GUESS I'M GONNA GO TELL HIM RIGHT NOW.
What ?!
REALLY ?!
YANO-SAN...
GO AHEAD !!

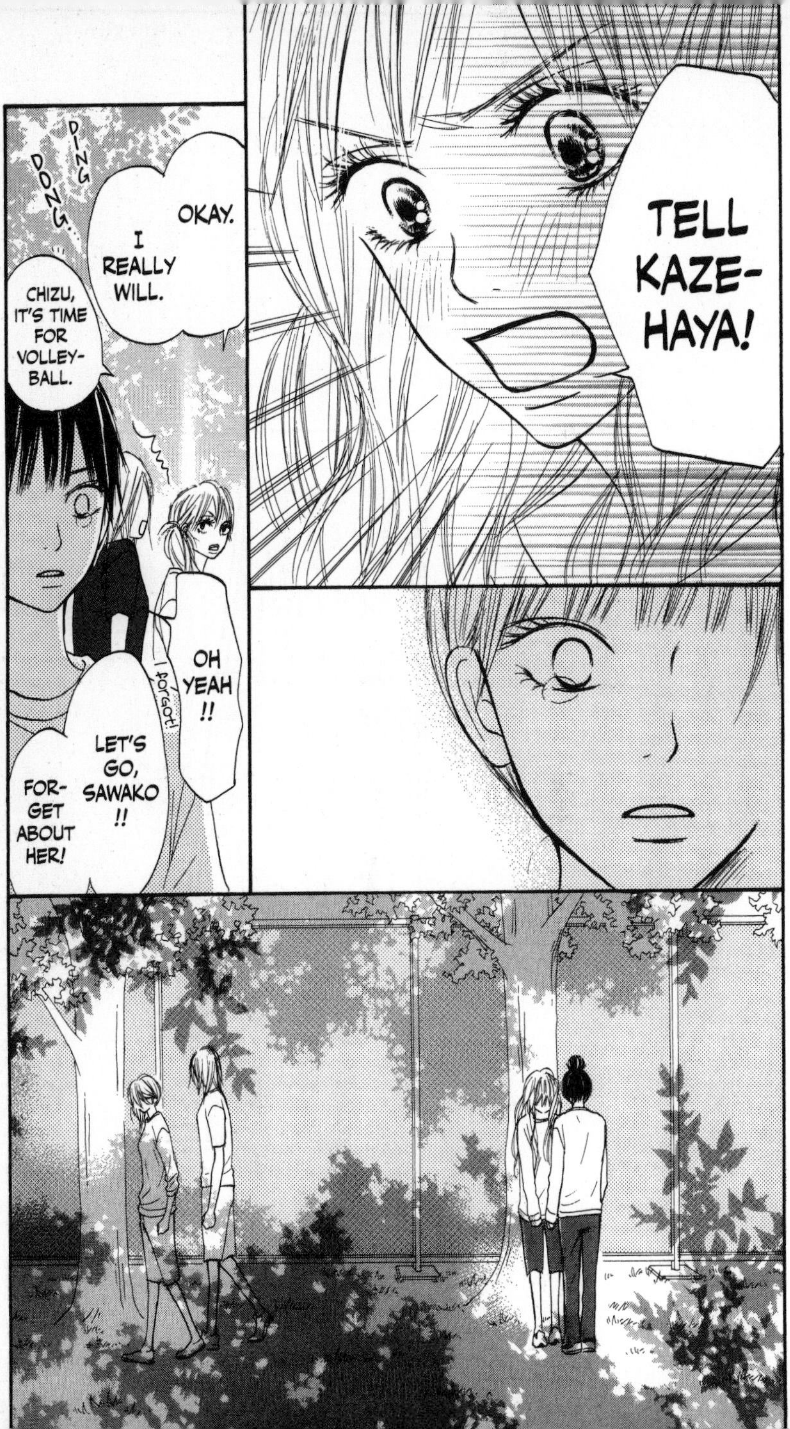
TELL KAZE-HAYA!
OKAY. I REALLY WILL.
DING DONG...
CHIZU, IT'S TIME FOR VOLLEY-BALL.
OH YEAH!!
I forgot!
LET'S GO, SAWAKO!!
FOR-GET ABOUT HER!

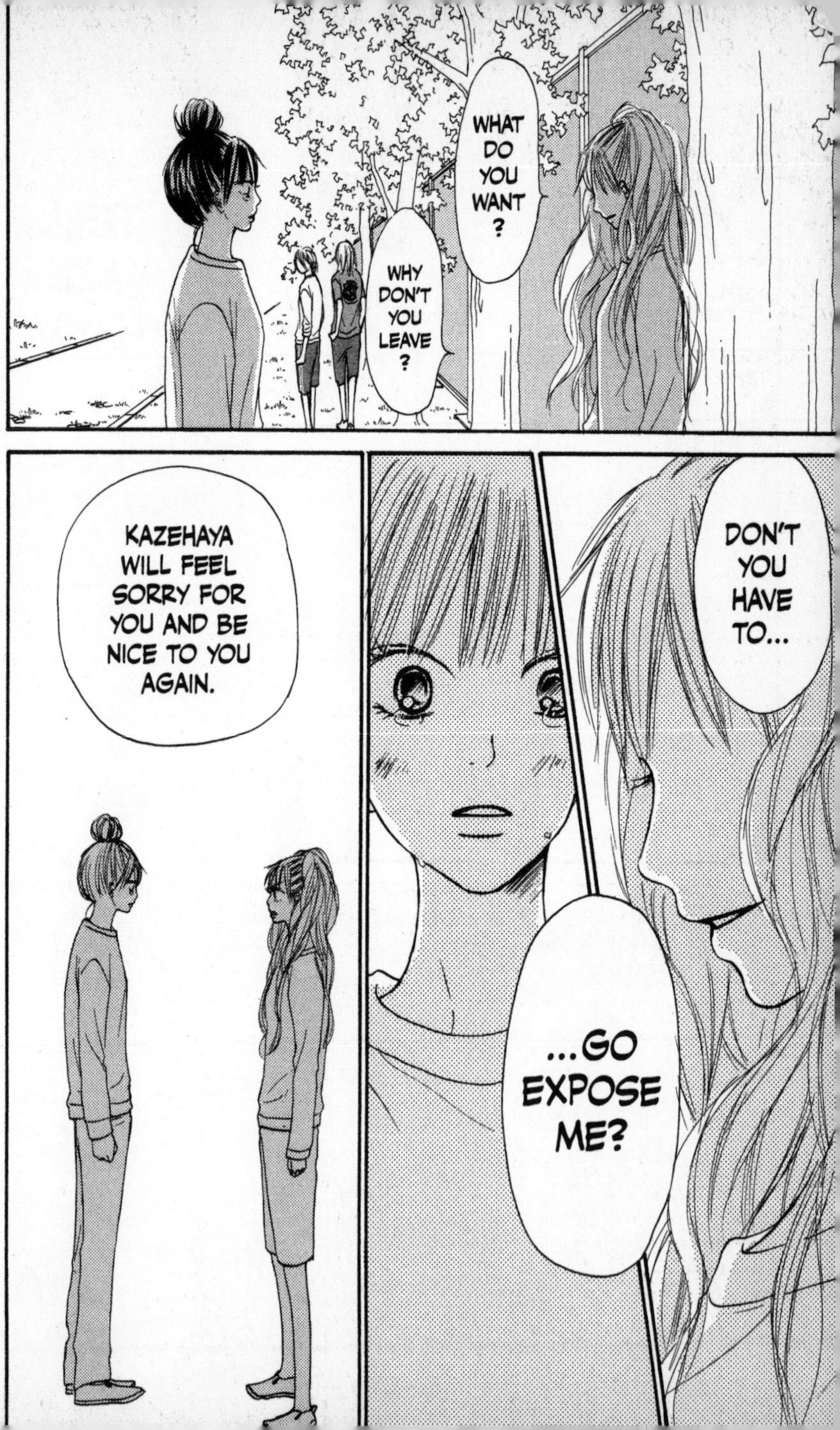
WHAT DO YOU WANT?
WHY DON'T YOU LEAVE?
DON'T YOU HAVE TO...
...GO EXPOSE ME?
KAZEHAYA WILL FEEL SORRY FOR YOU AND BE NICE TO YOU AGAIN.

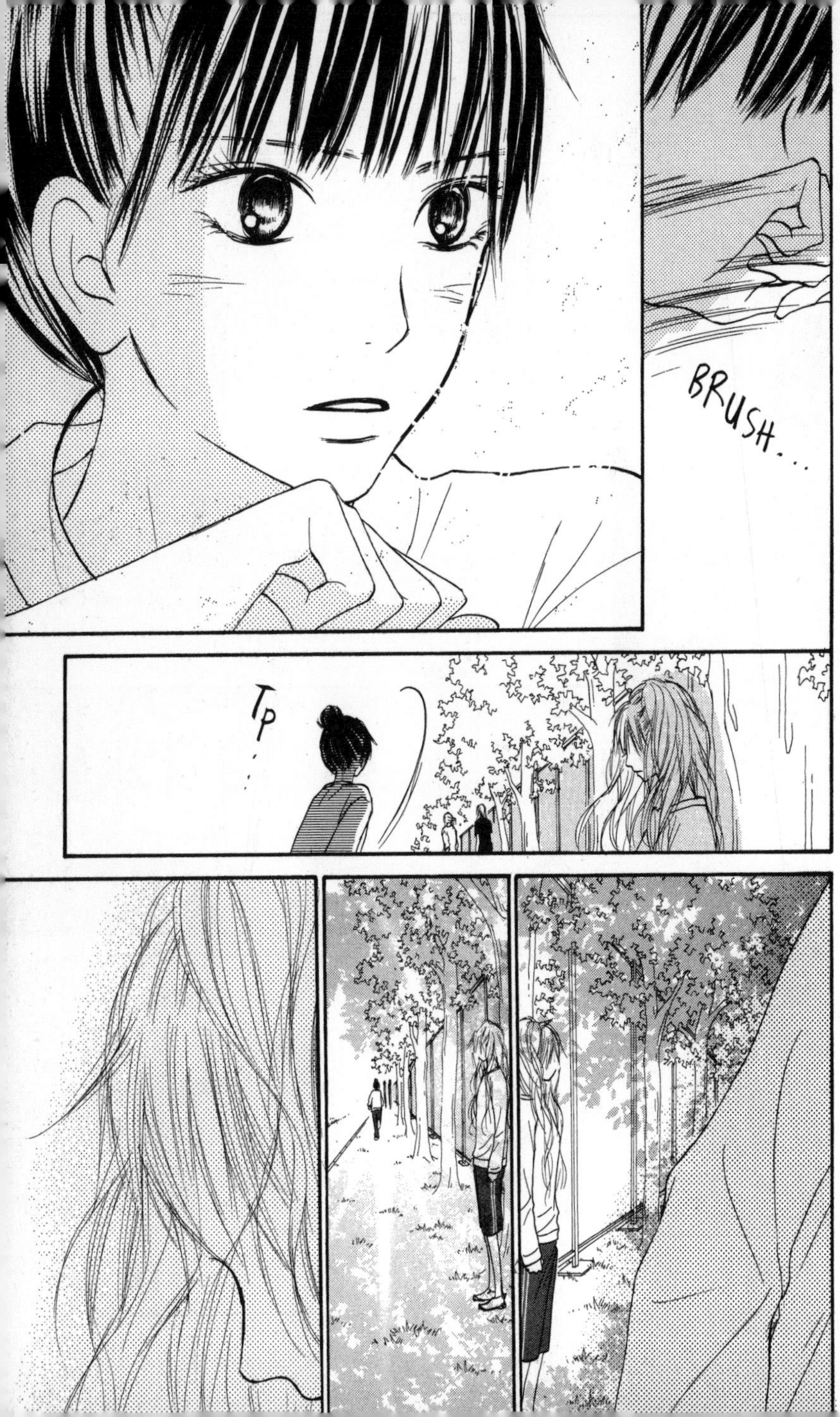
BRUSH...
TP...

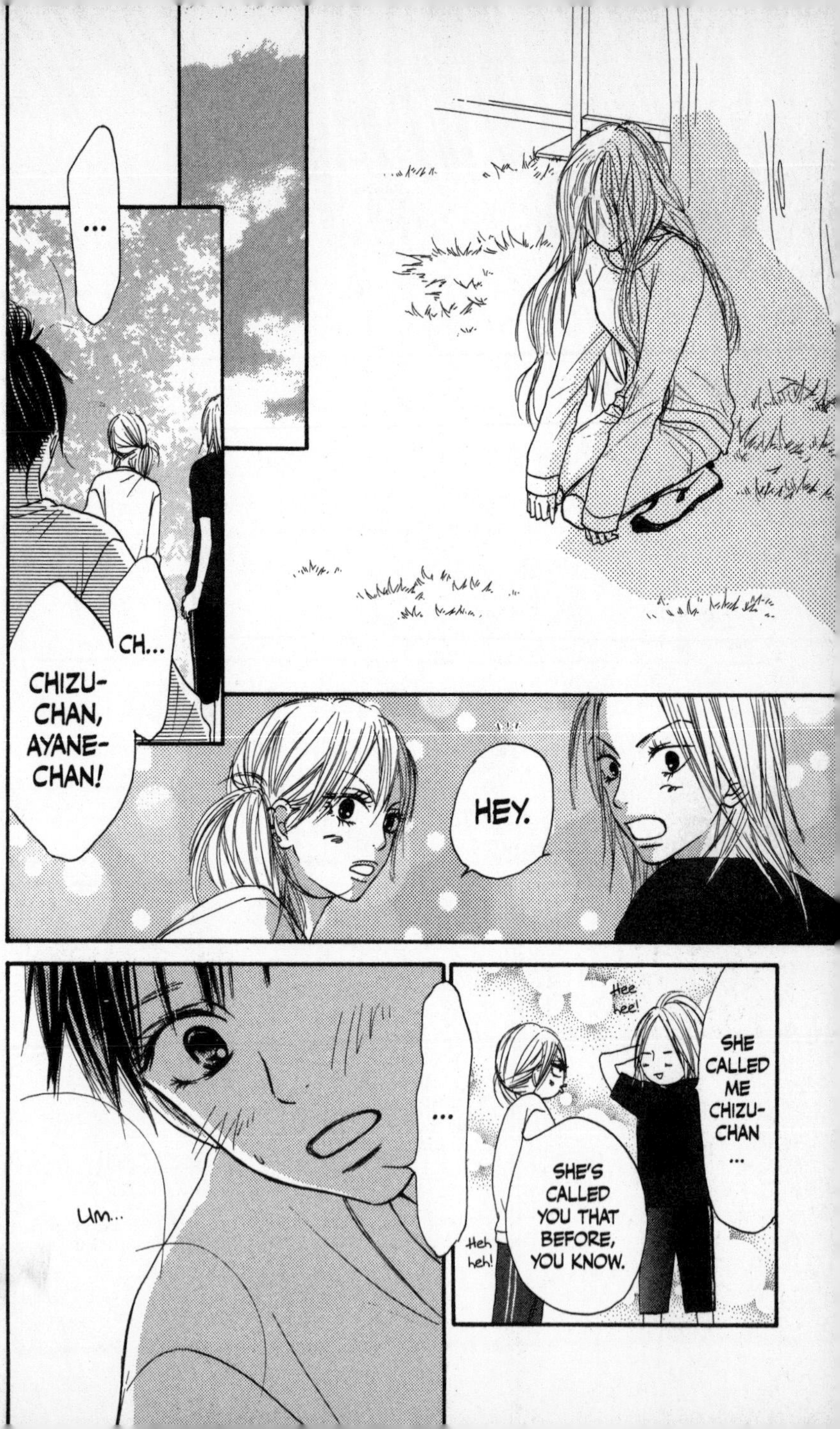
...
CH...
CHIZU-CHAN, AYANE-CHAN!
HEY.
Hee hee!
SHE CALLED ME CHIZU-CHAN ...
SHE'S CALLED YOU THAT BEFORE, YOU KNOW.
Heh heh!
...
Um...

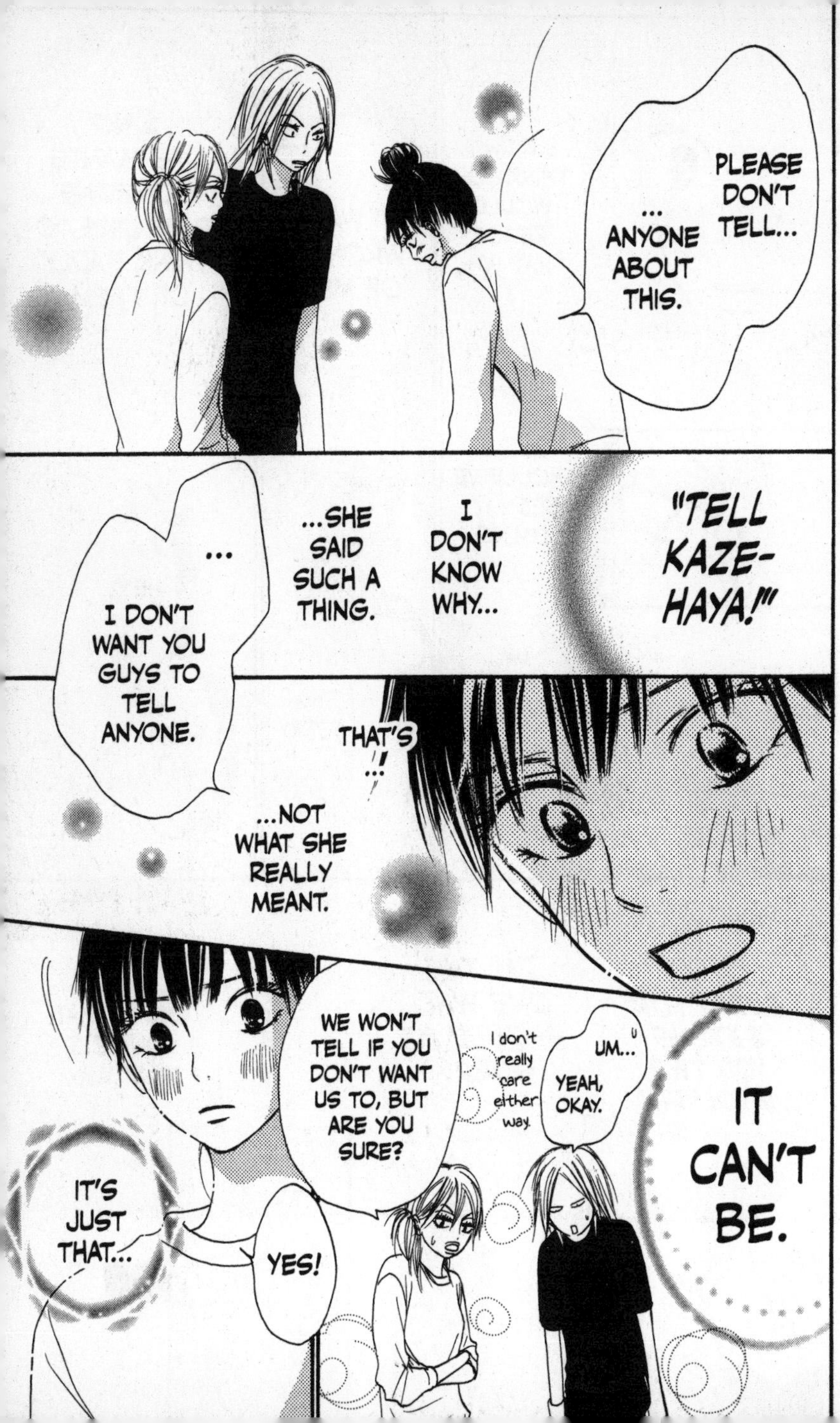
PLEASE DON'T TELL...
... ANYONE ABOUT THIS.
"TELL KAZE-HAYA!"
I DON'T KNOW WHY...
...SHE SAID SUCH A THING.
... I DON'T WANT YOU GUYS TO TELL ANYONE.
THAT'S ...!
...NOT WHAT SHE REALLY MEANT.
IT CAN'T BE.
UM... YEAH, OKAY.
I don't really care either way.
WE WON'T TELL IF YOU DON'T WANT US TO, BUT ARE YOU SURE?
YES!
IT'S JUST THAT...

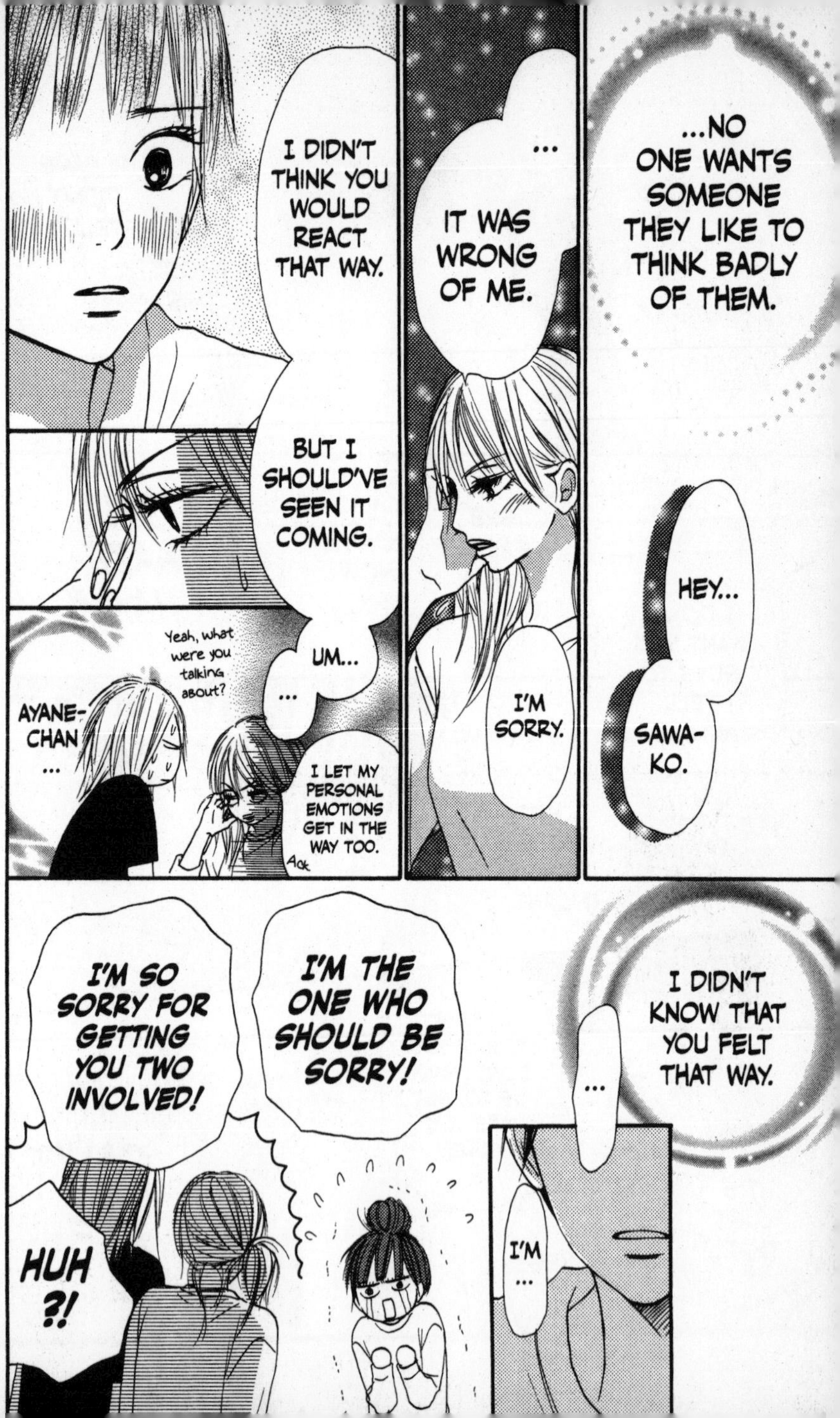

...NO ONE WANTS SOMEONE THEY LIKE TO THINK BADLY OF THEM.
HEY...
SAWA-KO.
...
IT WAS WRONG OF ME.
I'M SORRY.
I DIDN'T THINK YOU WOULD REACT THAT WAY.
BUT I SHOULD'VE SEEN IT COMING.
UM...
...
I LET MY PERSONAL EMOTIONS GET IN THE WAY TOO.
Ack
Yeah, what were you talking about?
AYANE-CHAN ...
I DIDN'T KNOW THAT YOU FELT THAT WAY.
...
I'M ...
I'M THE ONE WHO SHOULD BE SORRY!
I'M SO SORRY FOR GETTING YOU TWO INVOLVED!
HUH ?!

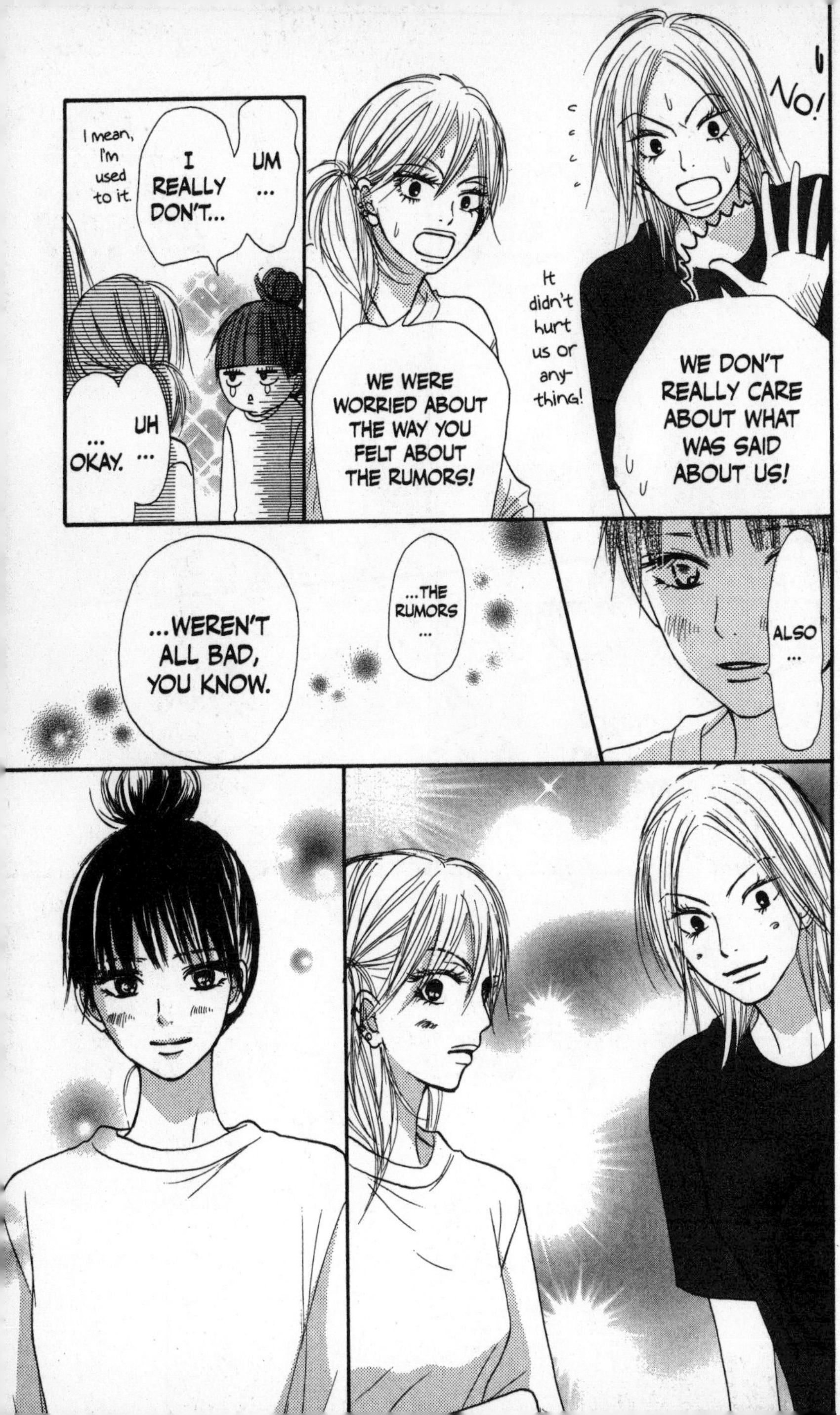
NO!
WE DON'T REALLY CARE ABOUT WHAT WAS SAID ABOUT US!
It didn't hurt us or any-thing!
WE WERE WORRIED ABOUT THE WAY YOU FELT ABOUT THE RUMORS!
UM ...
I REALLY DON'T...
I mean, I'm used to it.
UH ... OKAY.
ALSO ...
...THE RUMORS ...
...WEREN'T ALL BAD, YOU KNOW.

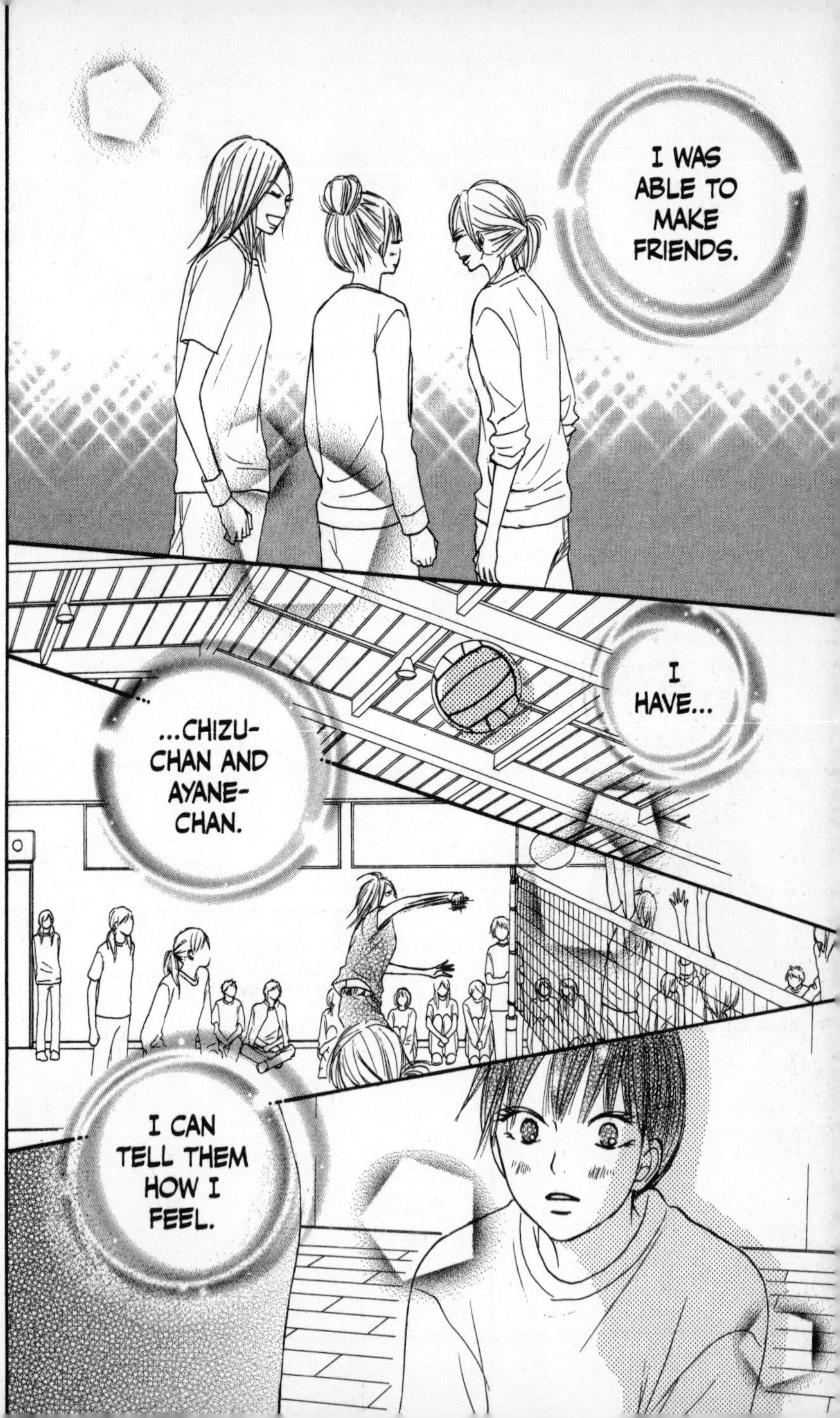
I WAS ABLE TO MAKE FRIENDS.
I HAVE...
...CHIZU-CHAN AND AYANE-CHAN.
I CAN TELL THEM HOW I FEEL.

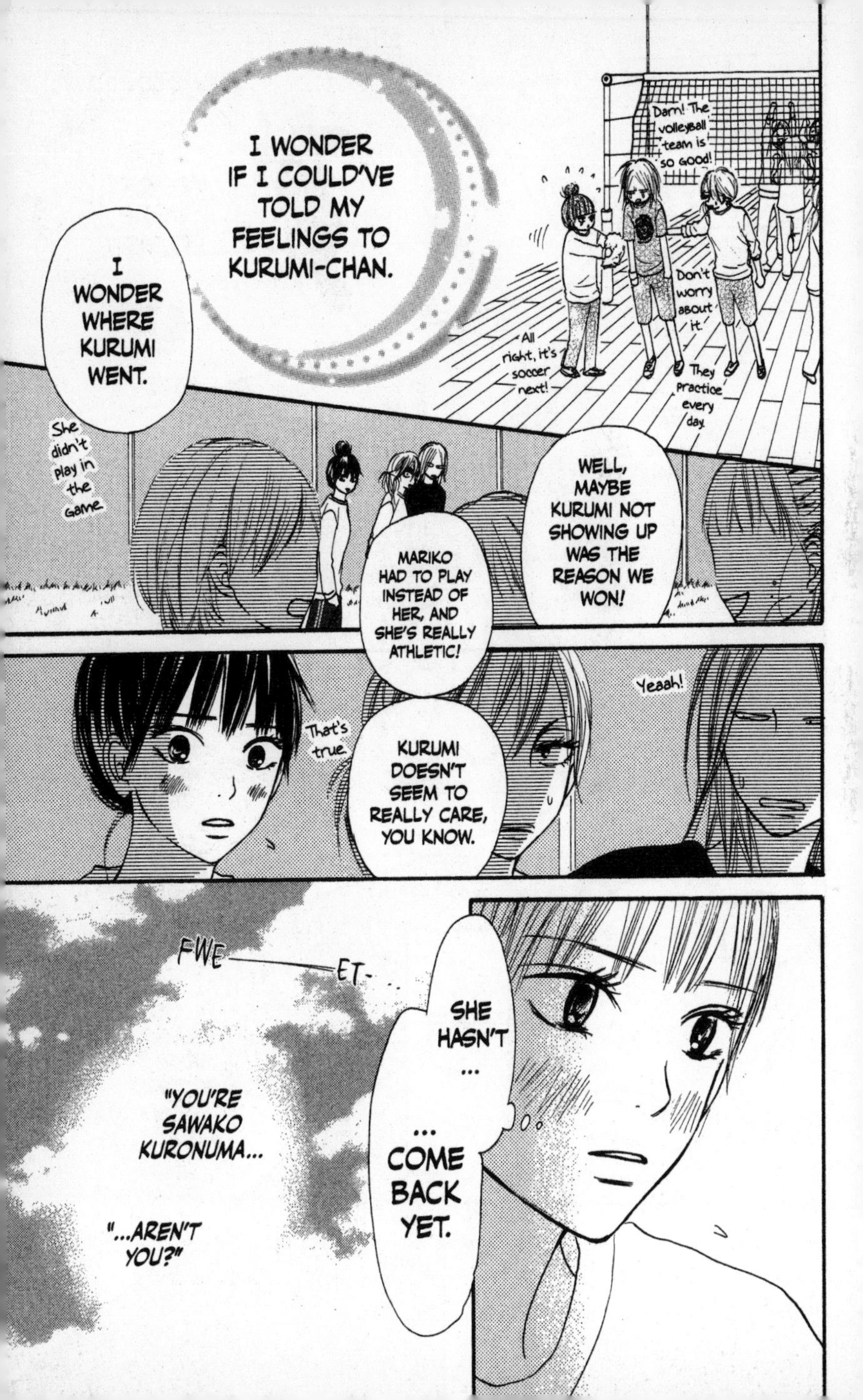
Darn! The volleyball team is so good!
Don't worry about it.
They practice every day.
All right, it's soccer next!
I WONDER IF I COULD'VE TOLD MY FEELINGS TO KURUMI-CHAN.
I WONDER WHERE KURUMI WENT.
She didn't play in the game.
WELL, MAYBE KURUMI NOT SHOWING UP WAS THE REASON WE WON!
MARIKO HAD TO PLAY INSTEAD OF HER, AND SHE'S REALLY ATHLETIC!
Yeaah!
KURUMI DOESN'T SEEM TO REALLY CARE, YOU KNOW.
That's true.
SHE HASN'T ... ... COME BACK YET.
FWE——ET-..
"YOU'RE SAWAKO KURONUMA...
"...AREN'T YOU?"

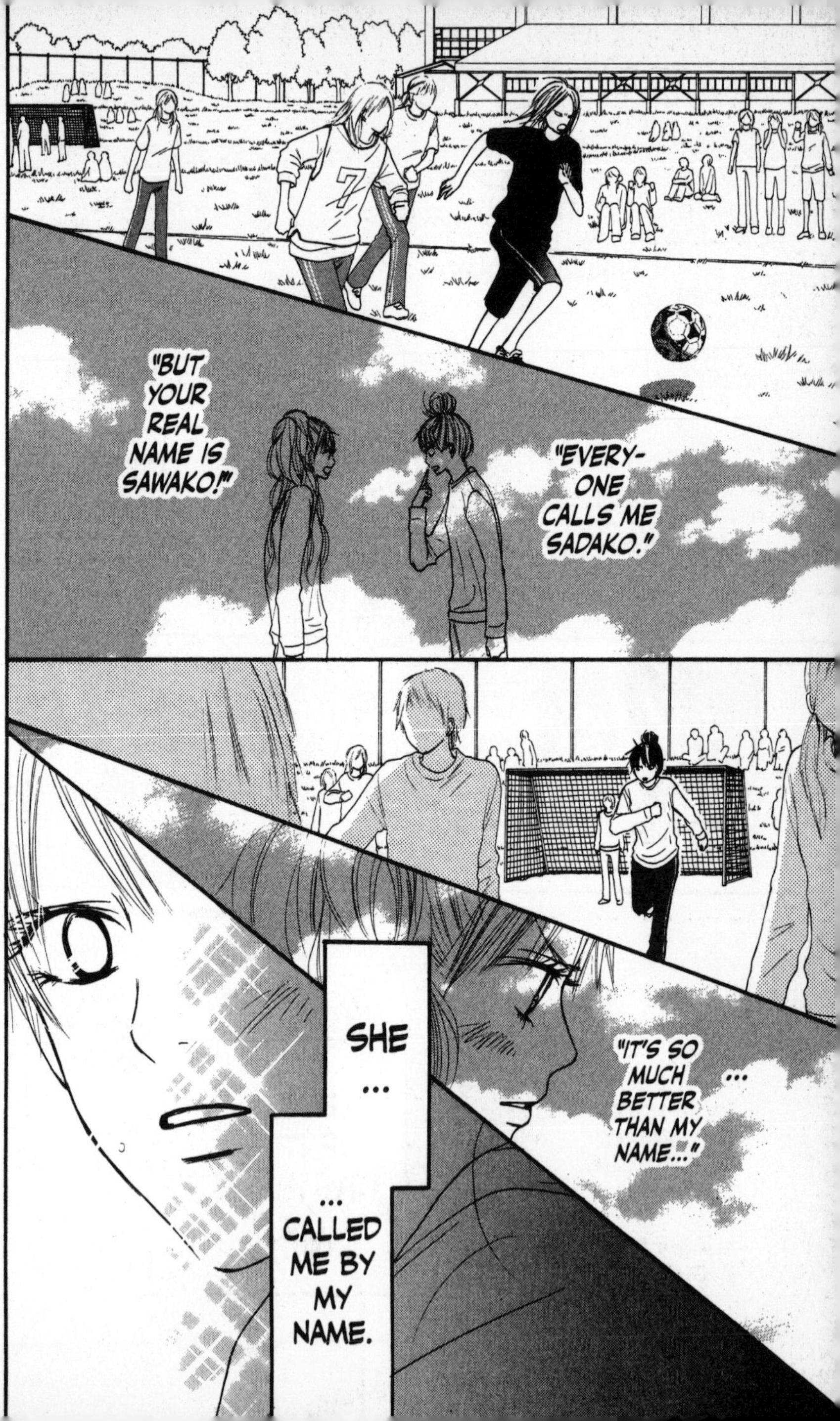
"EVERY-ONE CALLS ME SADAKO."
"BUT YOUR REAL NAME IS SAWAKO!"
"IT'S SO MUCH BETTER THAN MY NAME..."
...
SHE ...
... CALLED ME BY MY NAME.

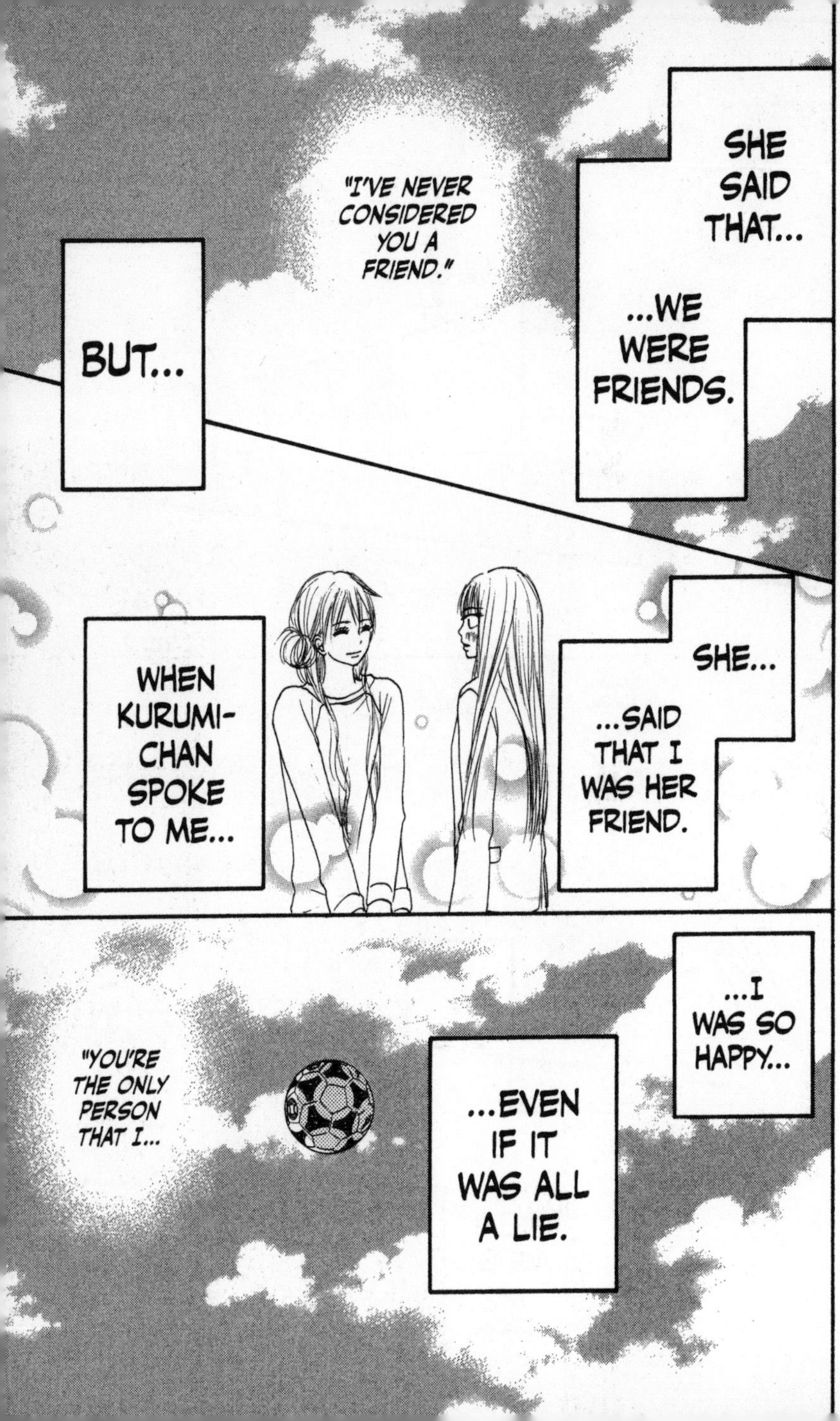
SHE SAID THAT...
...WE WERE FRIENDS.
"I'VE NEVER CONSIDERED YOU A FRIEND."
BUT...
SHE...
...SAID THAT I WAS HER FRIEND.
WHEN KURUMI-CHAN SPOKE TO ME...
...I WAS SO HAPPY...
...EVEN IF IT WAS ALL A LIE.
"YOU'RE THE ONLY PERSON THAT I...

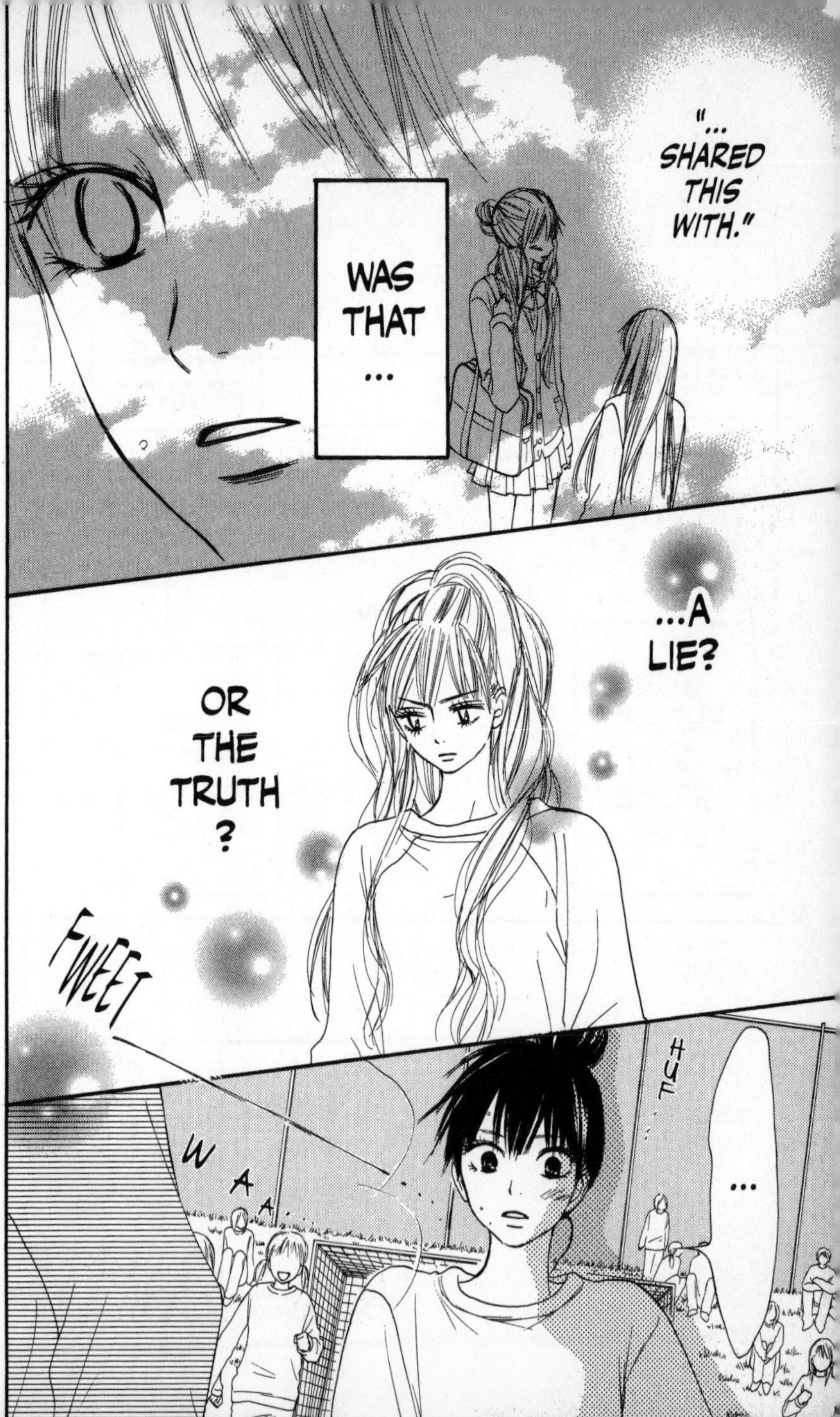
"... SHARED THIS WITH."
WAS THAT ...
...A LIE?
OR THE TRUTH ?
FWEET
HUF
...
WAA...

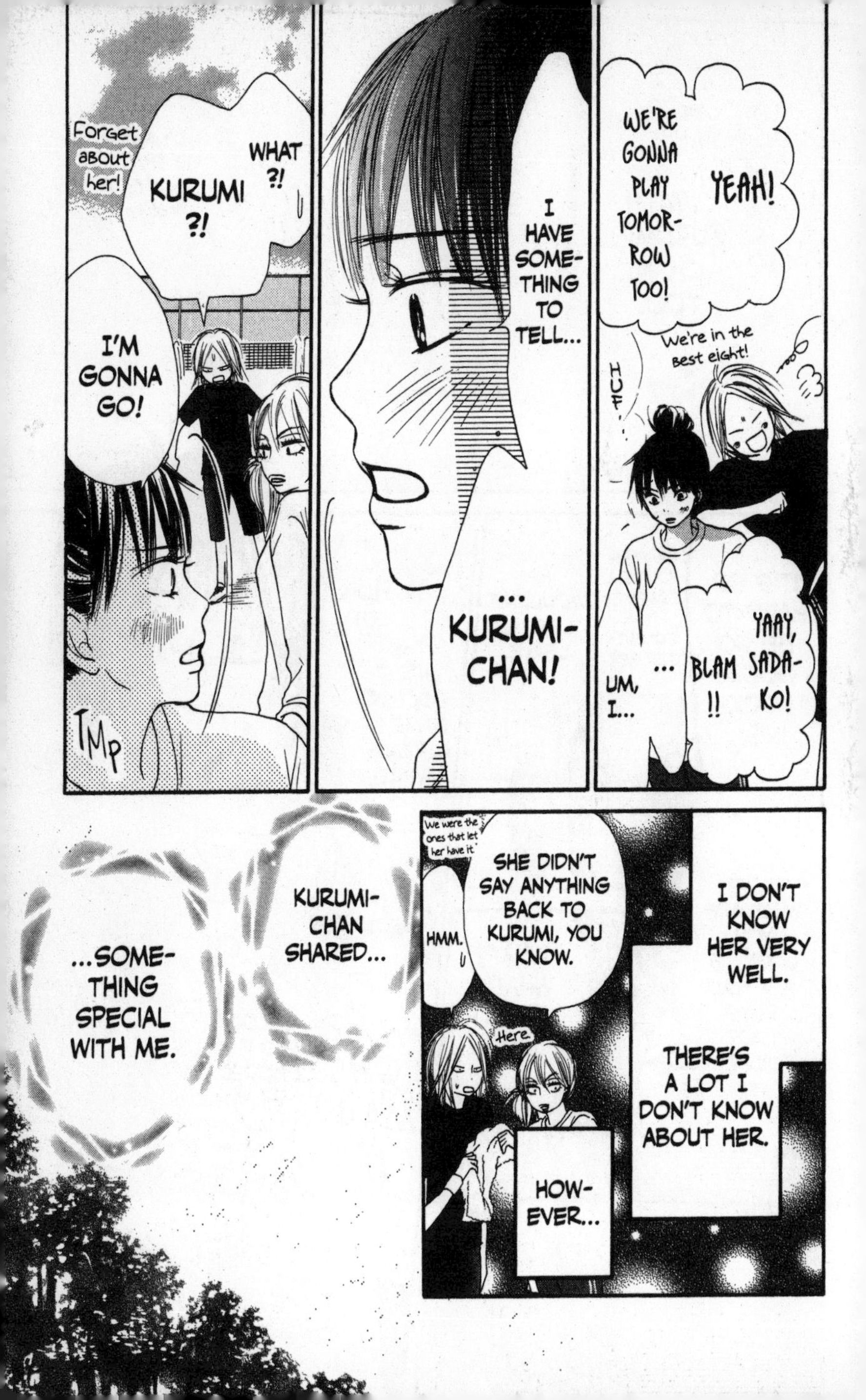

YEAH!
WE'RE GONNA PLAY TOMORROW TOO!
We're in the best eight!
HUF...
YAAY, SADAKO!
BLAM!!
...
UM, I...
I HAVE SOMETHING TO TELL...
...KURUMI-CHAN!
WHAT?!
KURUMI?!
Forget about her!
I'M GONNA GO!
TMP
I DON'T KNOW HER VERY WELL.
SHE DIDN'T SAY ANYTHING BACK TO KURUMI, YOU KNOW.
We were the ones that let her have it.
HMM.
Here.
THERE'S A LOT I DON'T KNOW ABOUT HER.
HOWEVER...
KURUMI-CHAN SHARED...
...SOMETHING SPECIAL WITH ME.

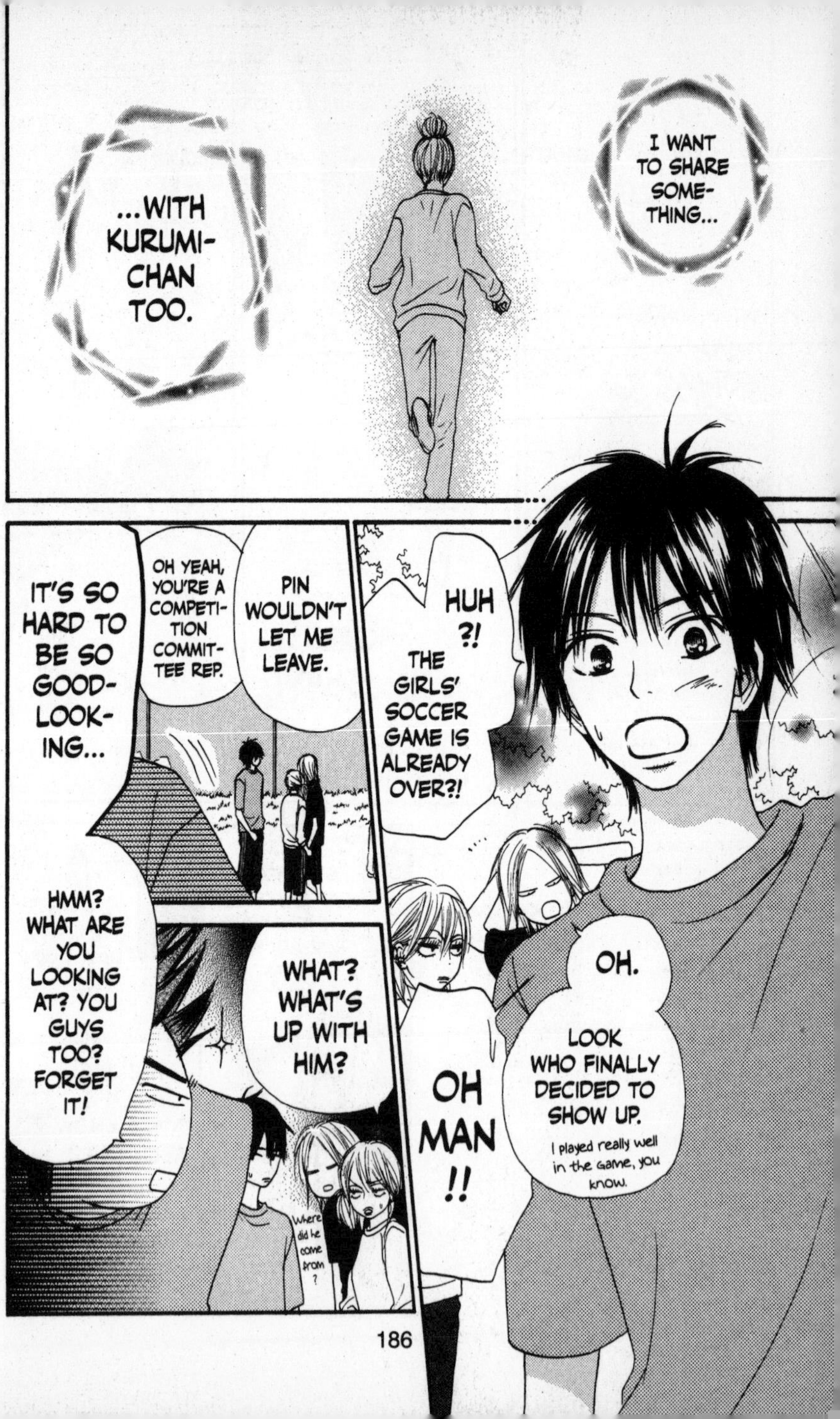
I WANT TO SHARE SOMETHING...
...WITH KURUMI-CHAN TOO.
HUH?!
THE GIRLS' SOCCER GAME IS ALREADY OVER?!
...
OH.
LOOK WHO FINALLY DECIDED TO SHOW UP.
I played really well in the game, you know.
OH MAN!!
PIN WOULDN'T LET ME LEAVE.
OH YEAH, YOU'RE A COMPETITION COMMITTEE REP.
IT'S SO HARD TO BE SO GOOD-LOOKING...
WHAT? WHAT'S UP WITH HIM?
Where did he come from?
HMM? WHAT ARE YOU LOOKING AT? YOU GUYS TOO? FORGET IT!

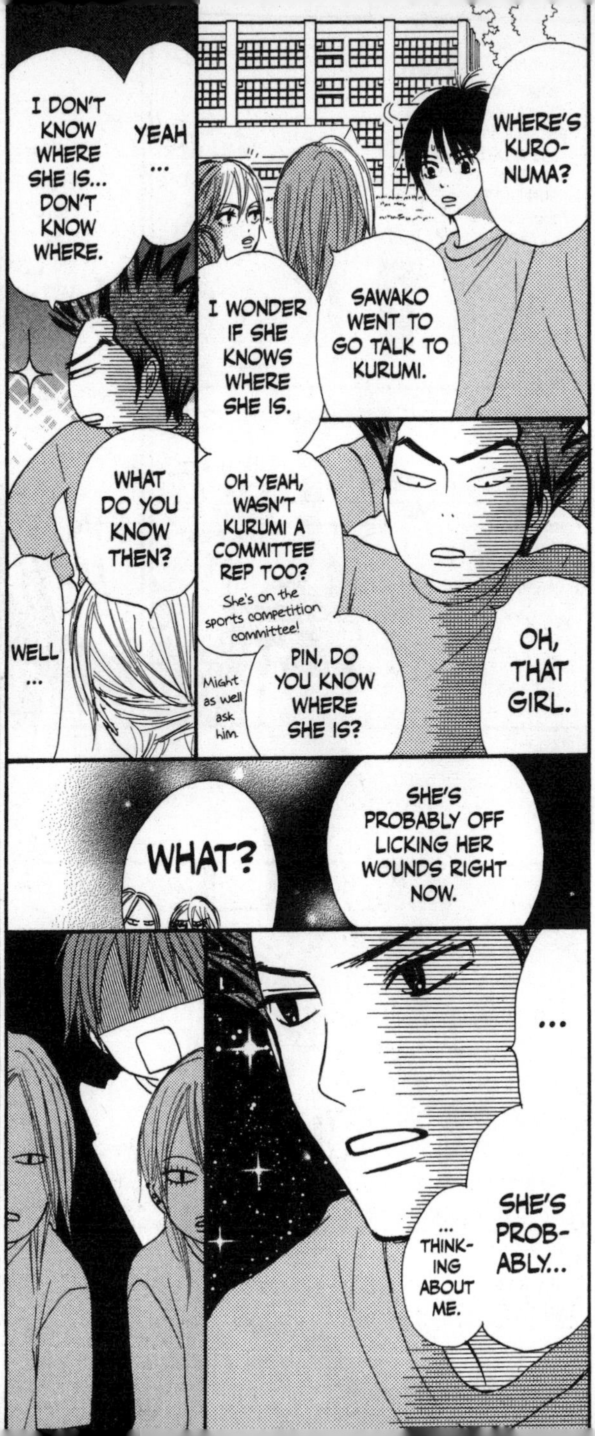
WHERE'S KURONUMA?
SAWAKO WENT TO GO TALK TO KURUMI.
I WONDER IF SHE KNOWS WHERE SHE IS.
OH, THAT GIRL.
OH YEAH, WASN'T KURUMI A COMMITTEE REP TOO?
She's on the sports competition committee!
PIN, DO YOU KNOW WHERE SHE IS?
Might as well ask him.
YEAH ...
I DON'T KNOW WHERE SHE IS... DON'T KNOW WHERE.
WHAT DO YOU KNOW THEN?
WELL ...
SHE'S PROBABLY OFF LICKING HER WOUNDS RIGHT NOW.
WHAT?
...
SHE'S PROBABLY...
... THINKING ABOUT ME.

KARUPIN on JAPAN 4

This is the last episode.

I haven't had enough pages for a bonus manga since the second volume, so if you were looking forward to them, I apologize!

Also, I haven't had an opportunity to explain this since the second volume, but when Chizu said, "Group hug!" she's actually using a phrase that my coworker, Ao-chan, used to say. I thought that the line was so funny, so I used it. This was a while back, but thank you for letting me use that line!

And I was just writing an email to Ao-chan, complaining about how I'm unable to speak comfortably.

She wrote back, "If you were able to speak your mind freely, that would make me feel weird."

"I've never heard you speak comfortably."

"You're fine the way you are, so don't change."

Seriously? Wow, that makes me feel a lot better. Ao-chan, thank you! You're the best! I'll live as an uncomfortable person!

Okay, I hope to see you again in volume 5.

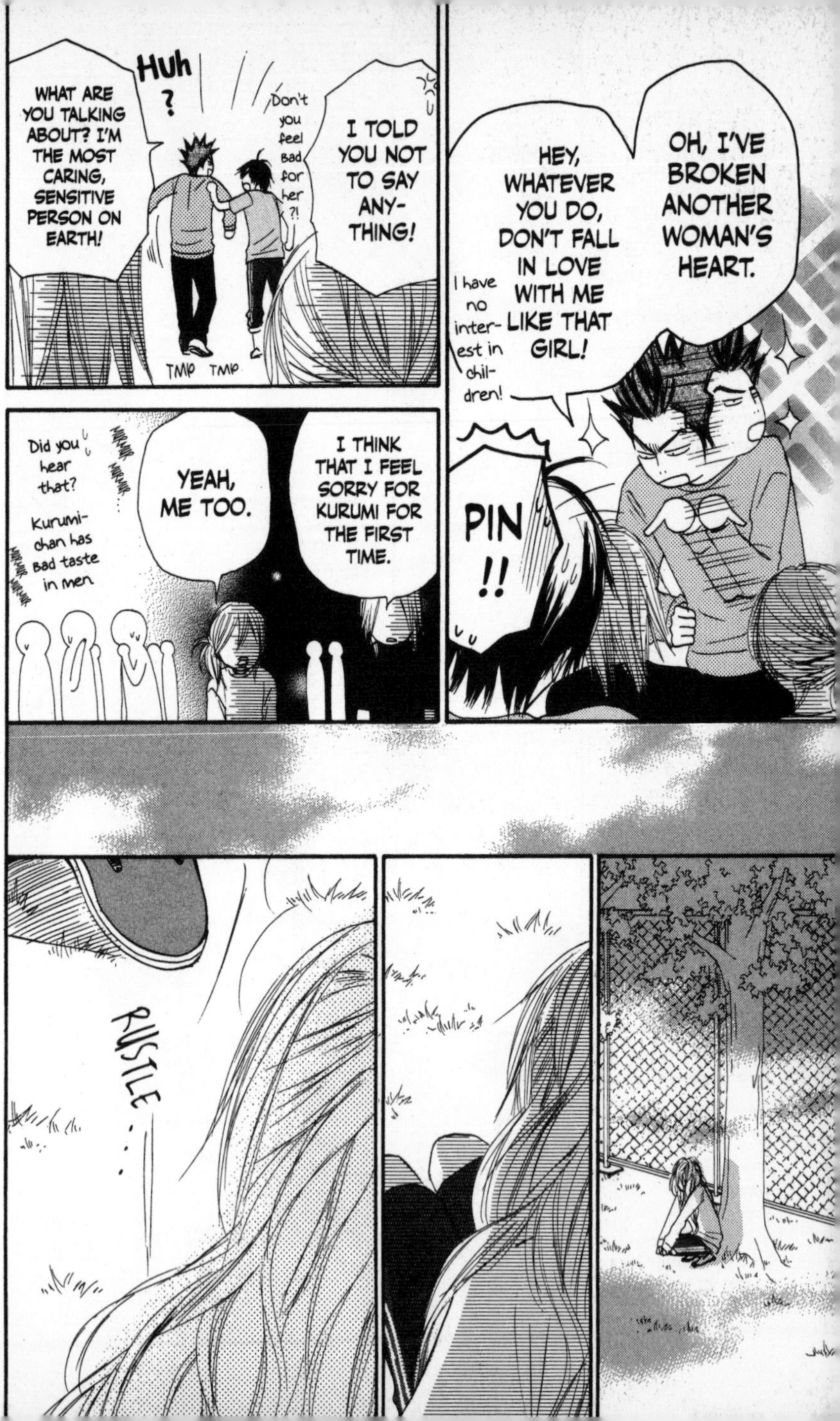
OH, I'VE BROKEN ANOTHER WOMAN'S HEART.
HEY, WHATEVER YOU DO, DON'T FALL IN LOVE WITH ME LIKE THAT GIRL!
I have no inter-est in chil-dren!
PIN !!
I TOLD YOU NOT TO SAY ANY-THING!
Don't you feel bad for her?!
Huh?
WHAT ARE YOU TALKING ABOUT? I'M THE MOST CARING, SENSITIVE PERSON ON EARTH!
TMP TMP
I THINK THAT I FEEL SORRY FOR KURUMI FOR THE FIRST TIME.
YEAH, ME TOO.
Did you hear that?
Kurumi-chan has bad taste in men
RUSTLE...

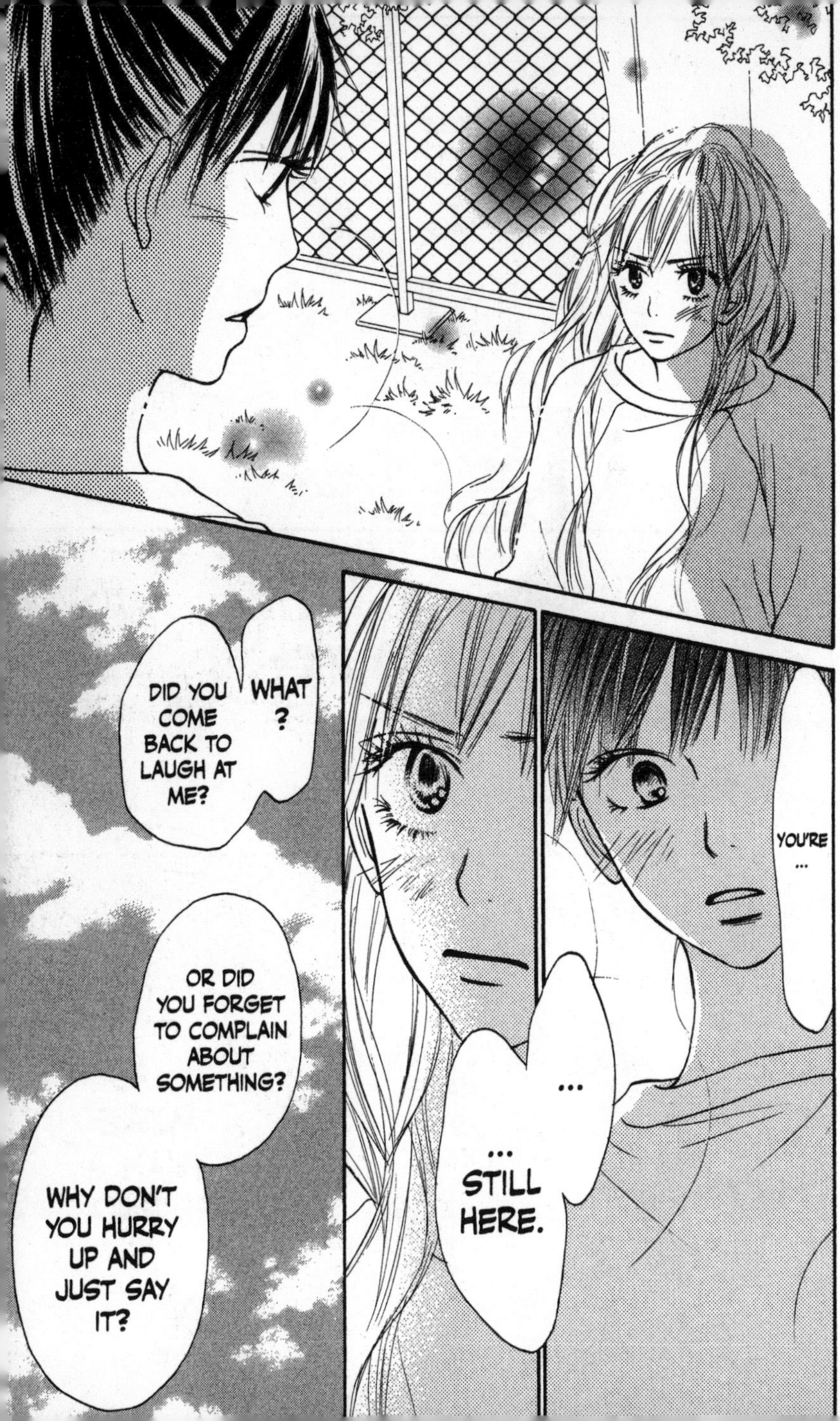
YOU'RE ...
...
... STILL HERE.
WHAT?
DID YOU COME BACK TO LAUGH AT ME?
OR DID YOU FORGET TO COMPLAIN ABOUT SOMETHING?
WHY DON'T YOU HURRY UP AND JUST SAY IT?

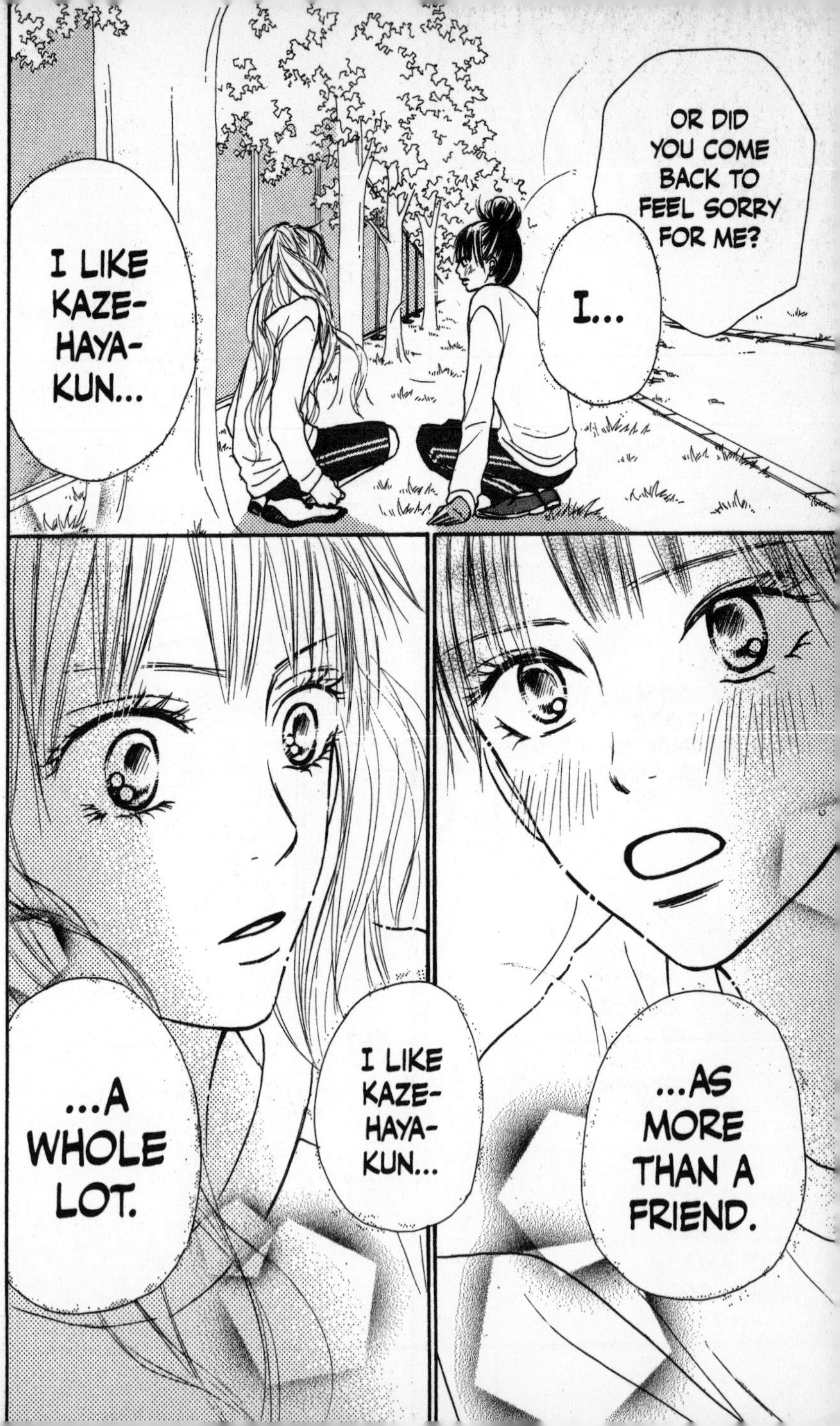
OR DID YOU COME BACK TO FEEL SORRY FOR ME?
I...
I LIKE KAZE-HAYA-KUN...
I LIKE KAZE-HAYA-KUN...
...AS MORE THAN A FRIEND.
...A WHOLE LOT.

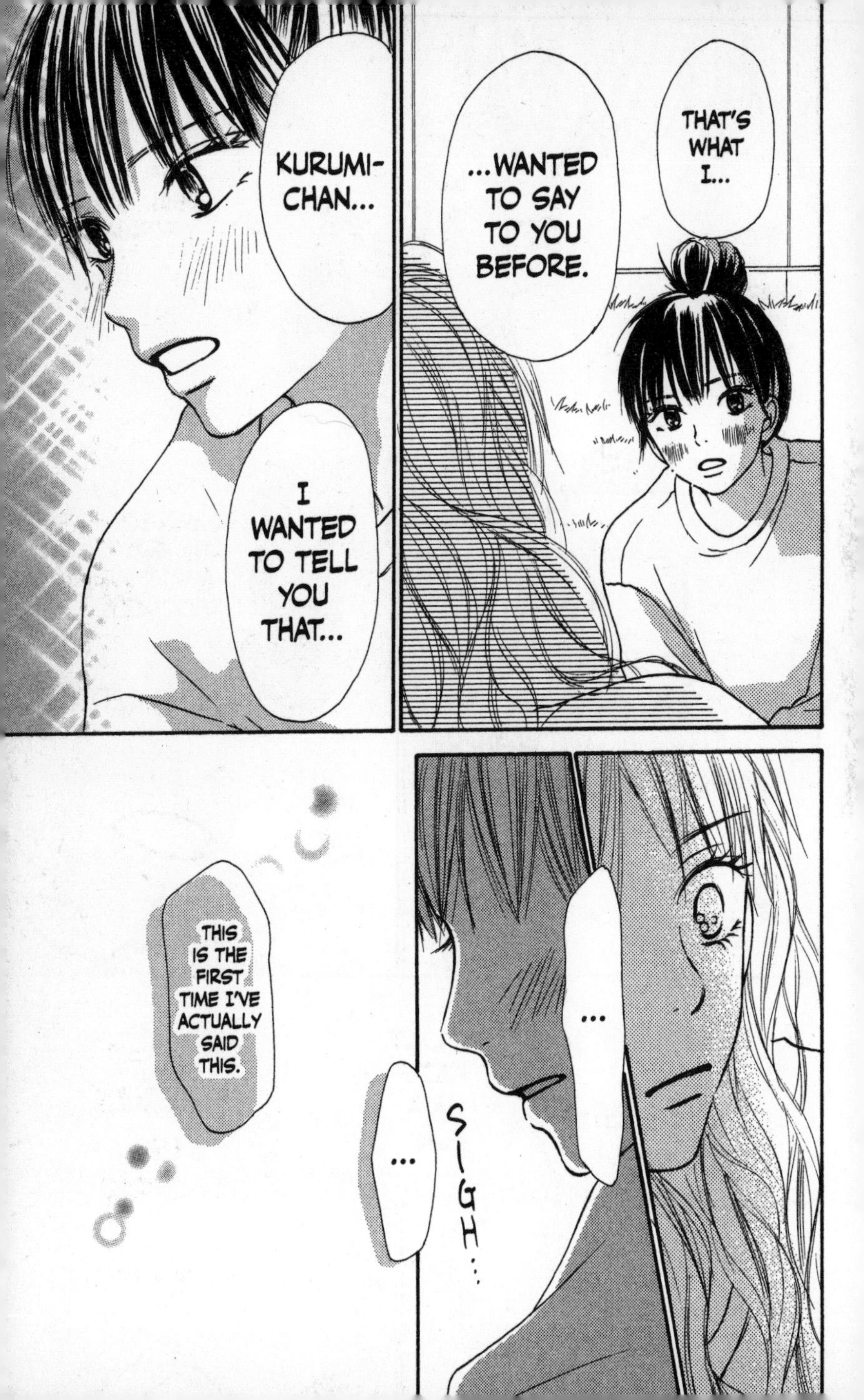
THAT'S WHAT I...
...WANTED TO SAY TO YOU BEFORE.
KURUMI-CHAN...
I WANTED TO TELL YOU THAT...
...
SIGH...
...
THIS IS THE FIRST TIME I'VE ACTUALLY SAID THIS.

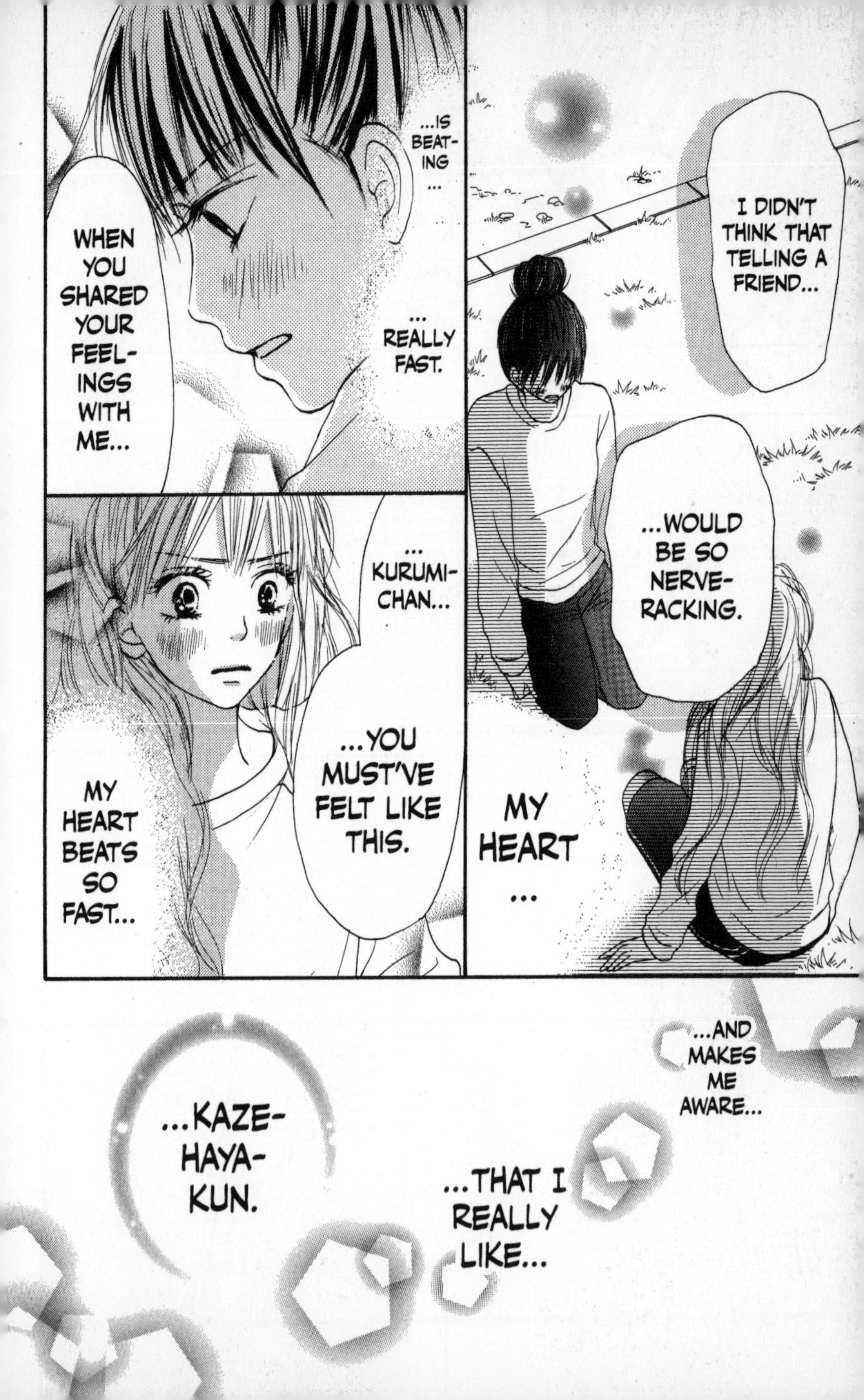
I DIDN'T THINK THAT TELLING A FRIEND...
...WOULD BE SO NERVE-RACKING.
MY HEART ...
...IS BEAT-ING ...
... REALLY FAST.
WHEN YOU SHARED YOUR FEEL-INGS WITH ME...
... KURUMI-CHAN...
...YOU MUST'VE FELT LIKE THIS.
MY HEART BEATS SO FAST...
...AND MAKES ME AWARE...
...THAT I REALLY LIKE...
...KAZE-HAYA-KUN.

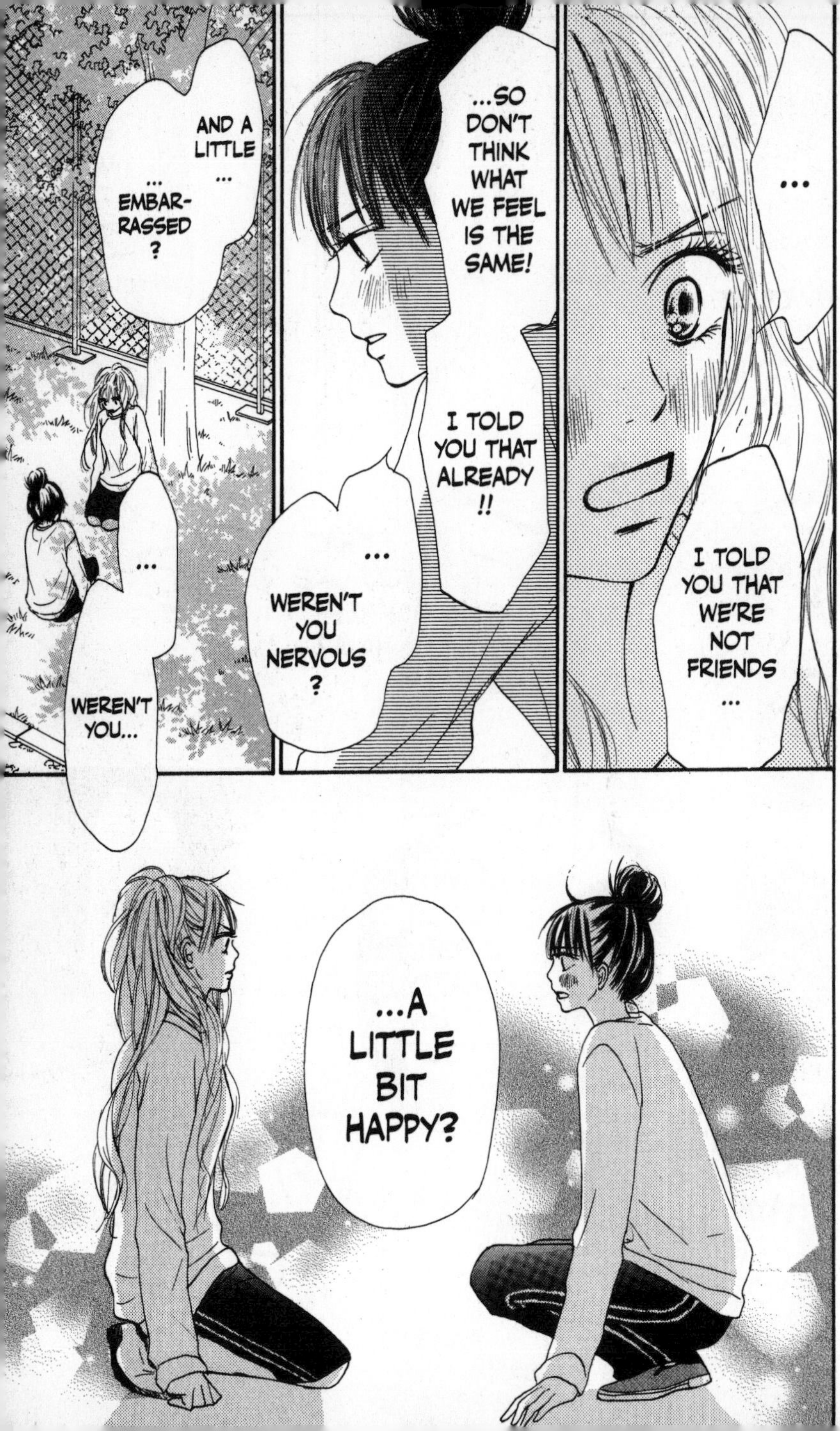
...
I TOLD YOU THAT WE'RE NOT FRIENDS ...
...SO DON'T THINK WHAT WE FEEL IS THE SAME!
I TOLD YOU THAT ALREADY !!
... WEREN'T YOU NERVOUS ?
AND A LITTLE ... EMBAR-RASSED ?
... WEREN'T YOU...
...A LITTLE BIT HAPPY?

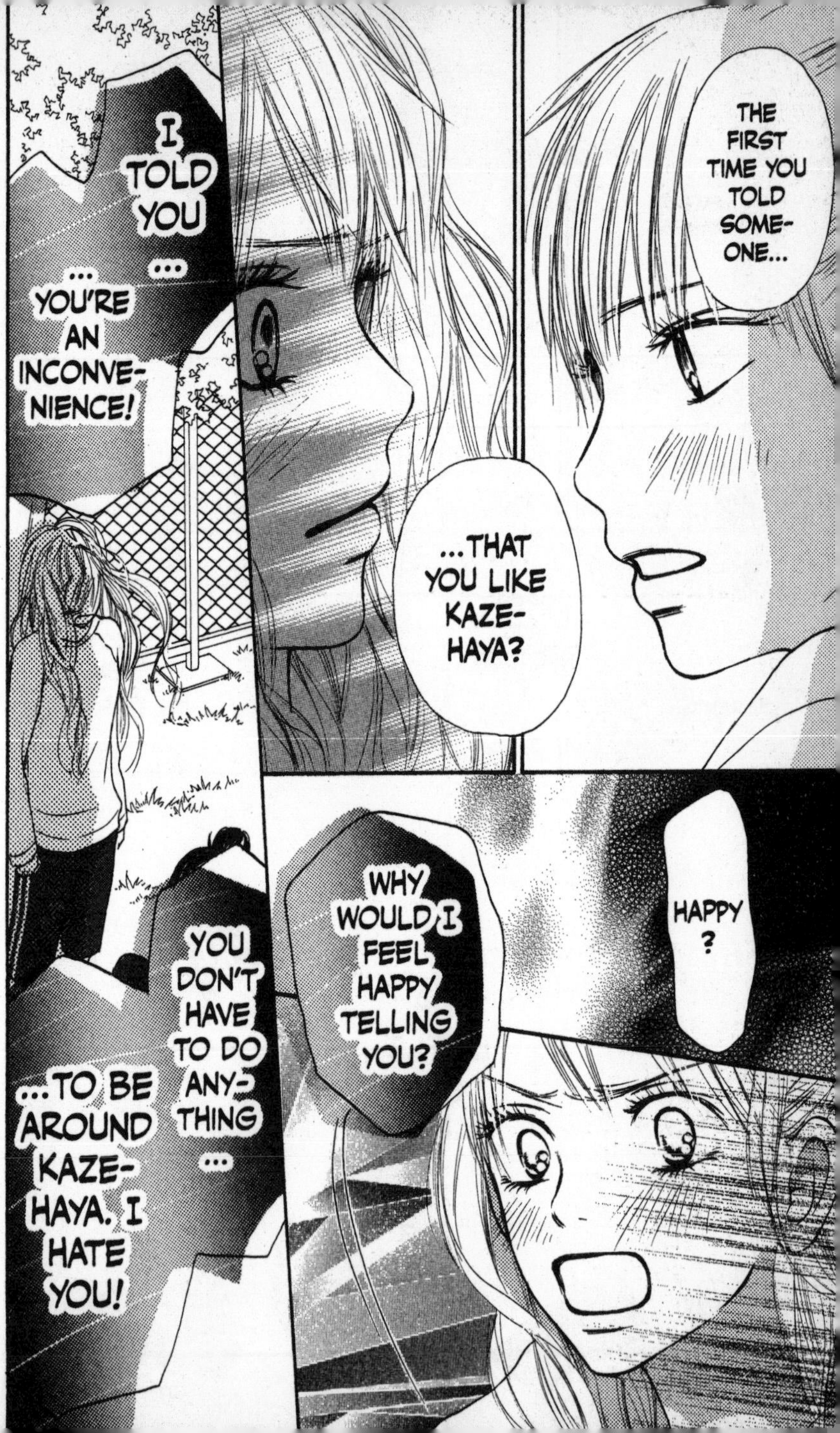
THE FIRST TIME YOU TOLD SOME-ONE...
...THAT YOU LIKE KAZE-HAYA?
HAPPY?
WHY WOULD I FEEL HAPPY TELLING YOU?
I TOLD YOU...
...YOU'RE AN INCONVE-NIENCE!
YOU DON'T HAVE TO DO ANY-THING...
...TO BE AROUND KAZE-HAYA. I HATE YOU!

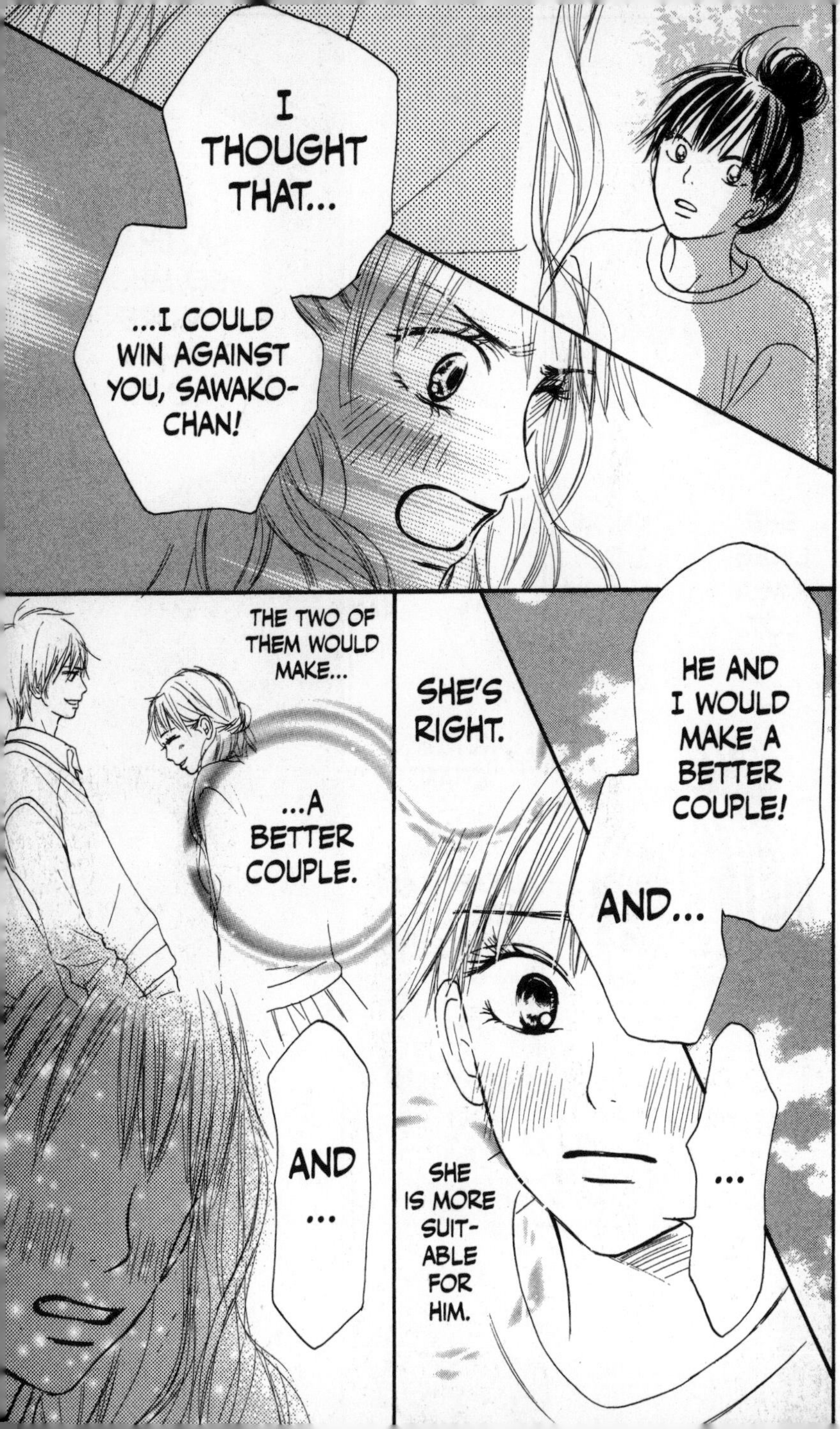
I THOUGHT THAT...
...I COULD WIN AGAINST YOU, SAWAKO-CHAN!
HE AND I WOULD MAKE A BETTER COUPLE!
SHE'S RIGHT.
AND...
...
SHE IS MORE SUITABLE FOR HIM.
THE TWO OF THEM WOULD MAKE...
...A BETTER COUPLE.
AND ...

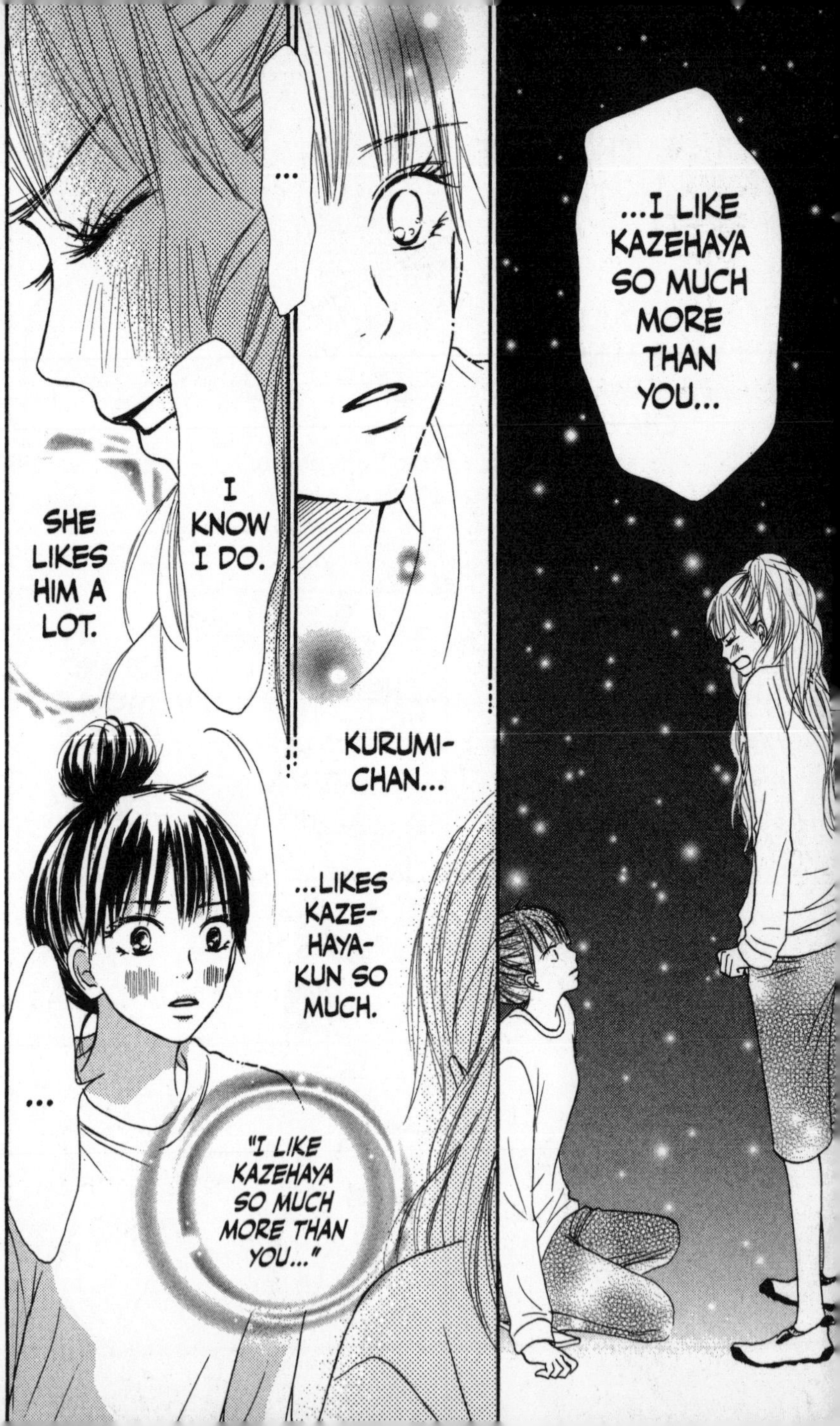

...I LIKE KAZEHAYA SO MUCH MORE THAN YOU...
...
I KNOW I DO.
SHE LIKES HIM A LOT.
KURUMI-CHAN...
...LIKES KAZE-HAYA-KUN SO MUCH.
"I LIKE KAZEHAYA SO MUCH MORE THAN YOU..."
...

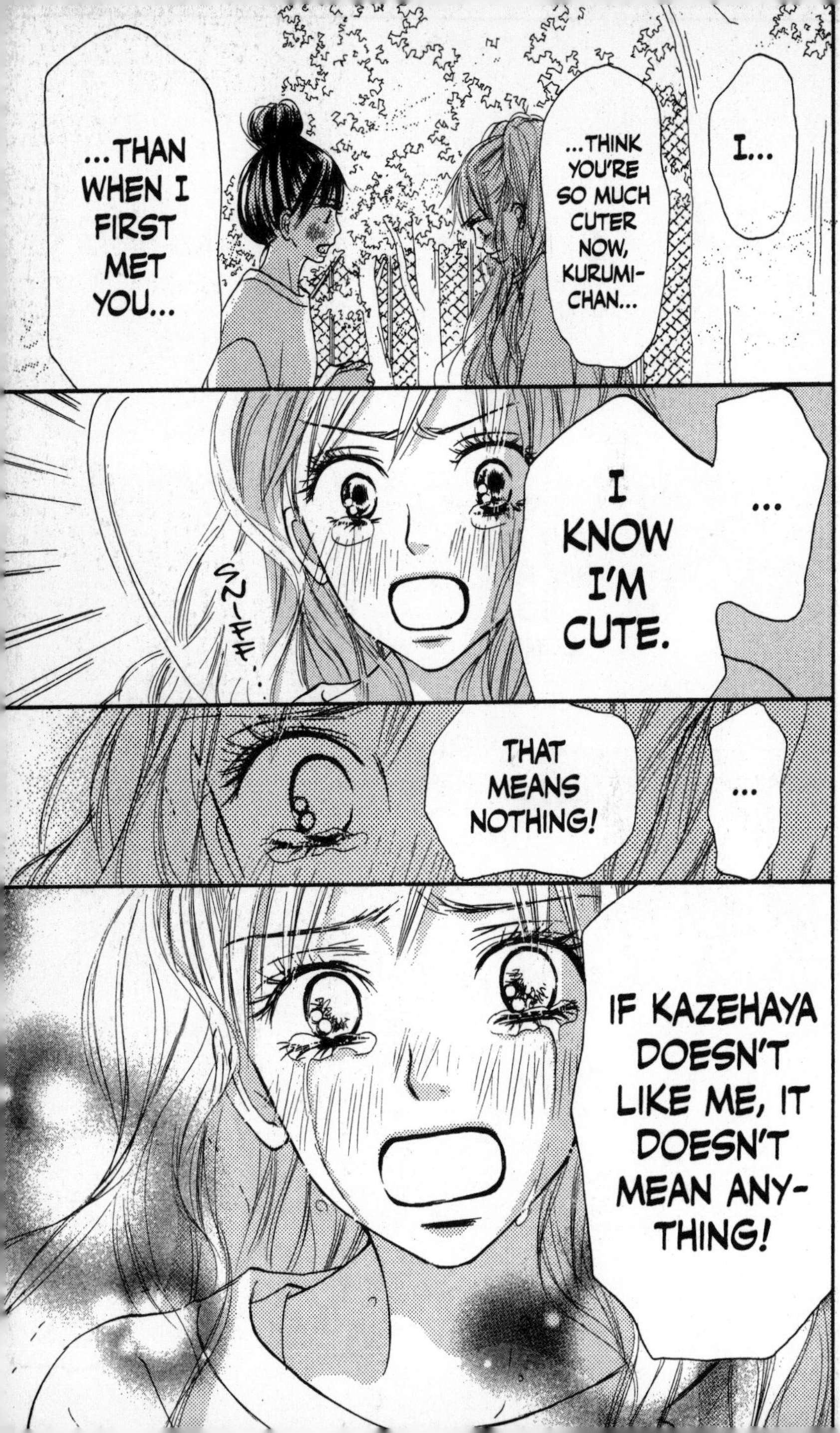
I...
...THINK YOU'RE SO MUCH CUTER NOW, KURUMI-CHAN...
...THAN WHEN I FIRST MET YOU...
...
I KNOW I'M CUTE.
SNIFF...
...
THAT MEANS NOTHING!
IF KAZEHAYA DOESN'T LIKE ME, IT DOESN'T MEAN ANY-THING!

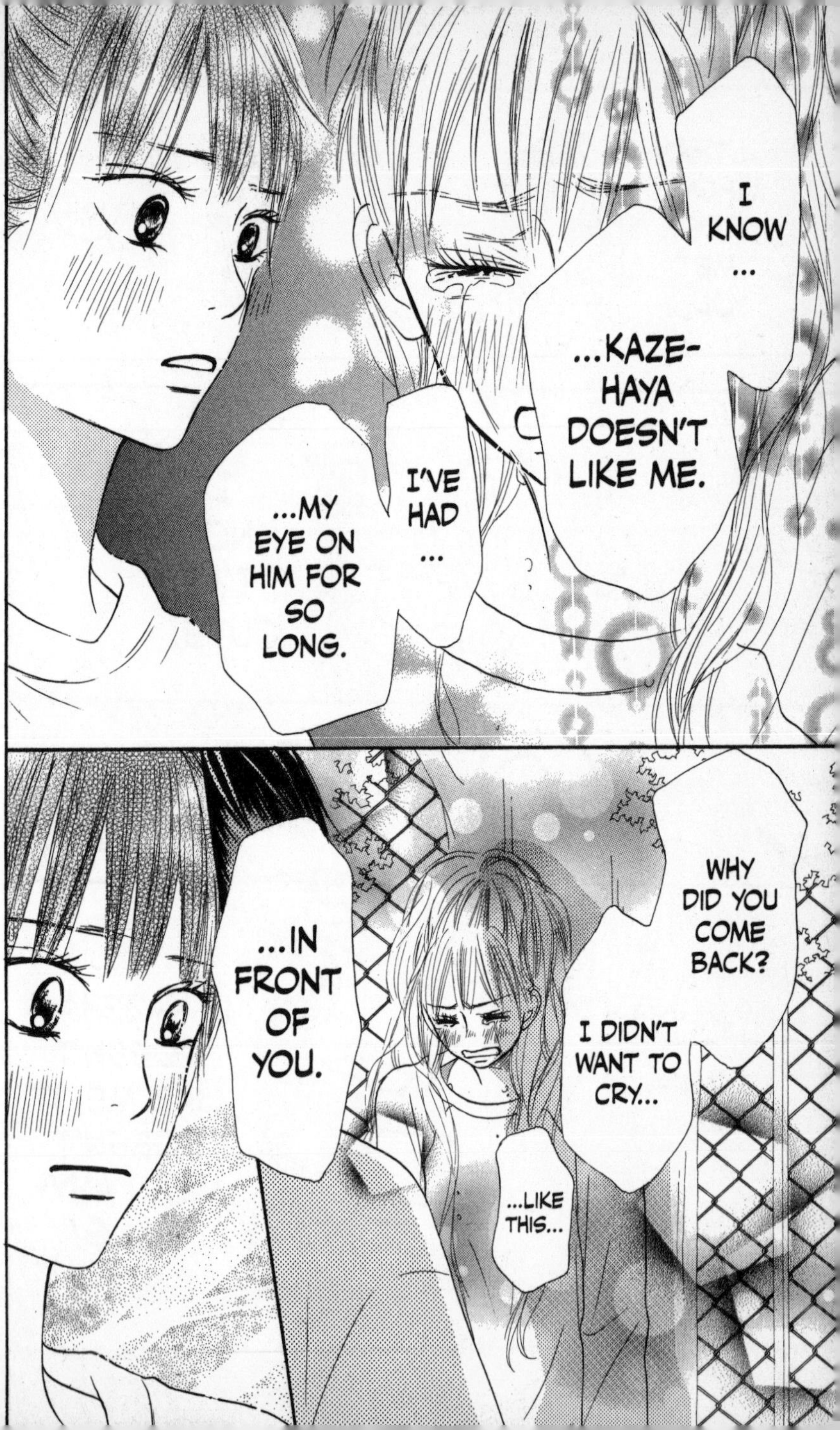
I KNOW...
...KAZE-HAYA DOESN'T LIKE ME.
I'VE HAD...
...MY EYE ON HIM FOR SO LONG.
WHY DID YOU COME BACK?
I DIDN'T WANT TO CRY...
...LIKE THIS...
...IN FRONT OF YOU.

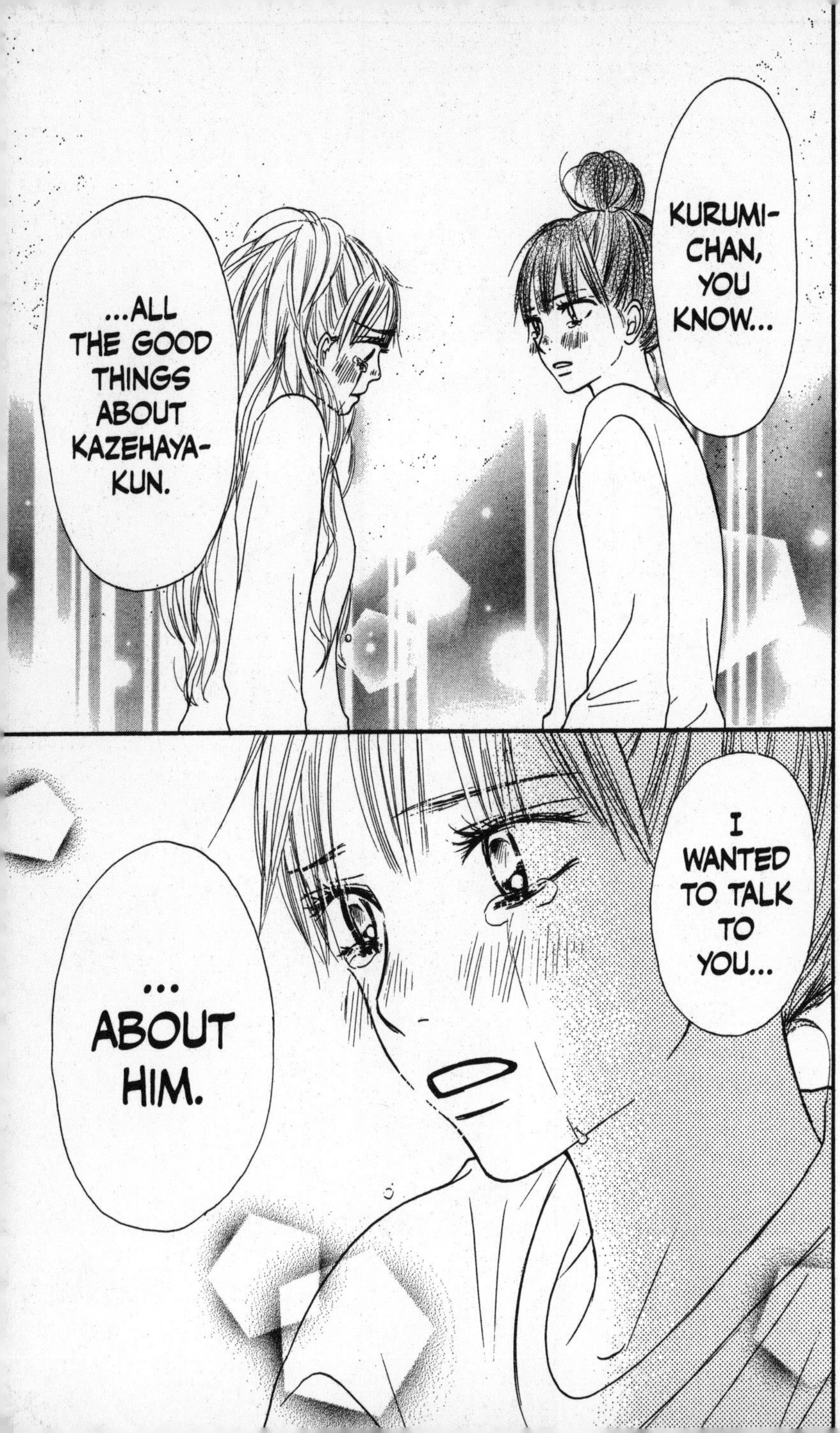
KURUMI-CHAN, YOU KNOW...
...ALL THE GOOD THINGS ABOUT KAZEHAYA-KUN.
I WANTED TO TALK TO YOU...
... ABOUT HIM.

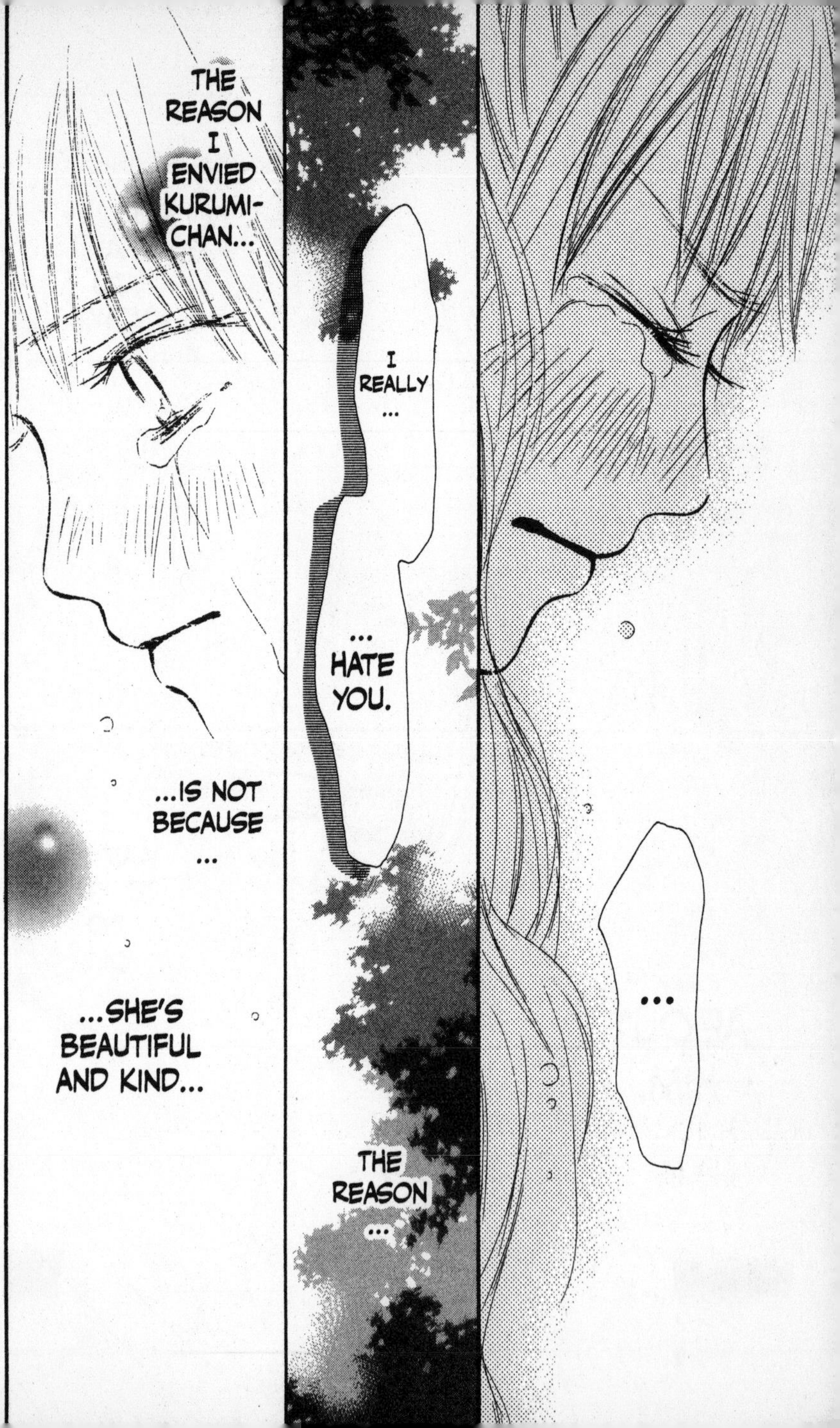
...
I REALLY ...
... HATE YOU.
THE REASON ...
THE REASON I ENVIED KURUMI-CHAN...
...IS NOT BECAUSE ...
...SHE'S BEAUTIFUL AND KIND...

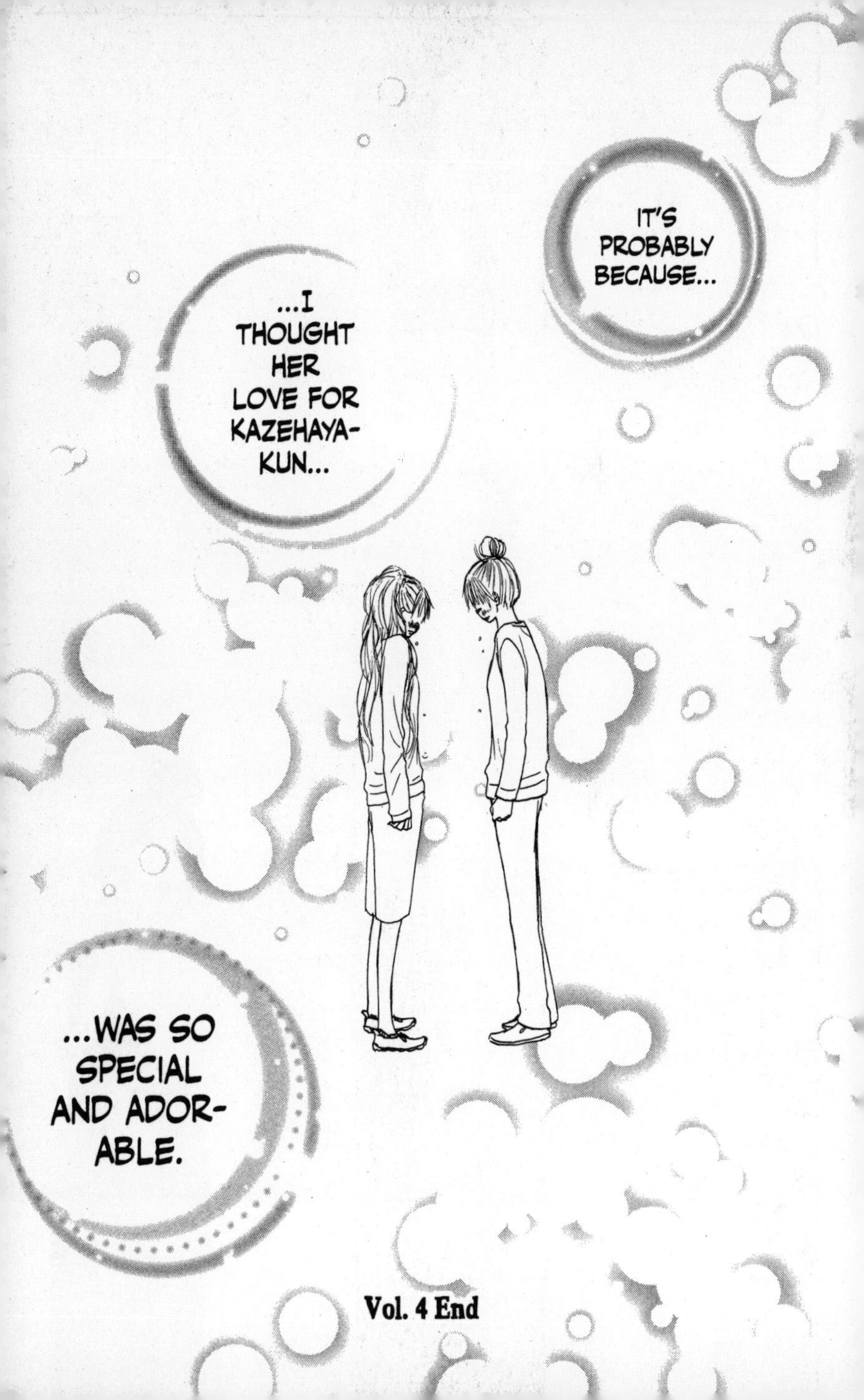
IT'S PROBABLY BECAUSE...
...I THOUGHT HER LOVE FOR KAZEHAYA-KUN...
...WAS SO SPECIAL AND ADOR-ABLE.
Vol. 4 End

From me (the editor) to you (the reader).

Here are some Japanese culture explanations that will help you better understand the references in the *Kimi ni Todoke* world.

Honorifics:
When saying someone's name in Japanese, a suffix is often attached to indicate how familiar the speaker is with the person. Some are more polite and respectful, while others are endearing. Calling someone by just their first name is the most informal.
-kun is used for young men or boys, usually someone you are familiar with.
-chan is used for young women, girls or young children and can be used as a term of endearment.
-san is used for someone you respect or are not close to, or to be polite.

Page 32, Ume:
Ume means "plum" or "plum blossom" in Japanese and can be a girl's name, though it's a bit old-fashioned. This is probably why Kurumi goes by her last name, Kurumizawa. *Kurumi* means "walnut" and *zawa* (or *sawa*) means "mountain stream."

Page 33, Sakura:
Sakura means "cherry blossom" in Japanese and can be a girl's name.

Page 39, Kuranuma:
Kura(i) means "dark" in Japanese. Ryu was pretty close since *kuro* means "black."

The picture is a mini Sawako doll that Ôtaki-san from Keibunsha bookstore's Banbio branch made. I was able to see it firsthand—it is so well made and super cute!

I also received an even smaller mini Sawako doll and have it displayed in my living room. This one's super cute too!

Ôtaki-san, thank you so much for the lovely dolls! And, Sawako, it's so great how you're beloved by your fans. (*sniff*)

--Karuho Shiina

Karuho Shiina was born and raised in Hokkaido, Japan. Though *Kimi ni Todoke* is only her second series following many one-shot stories, it has already racked up accolades from various "Best Manga of the Year" lists. Winner of the 2008 Kodansha Manga Award for the shojo category, *Kimi ni Todoke* also placed fifth in the first-ever Manga Taisho (Cartoon Grand Prize) contest in 2008. An animated TV series debuted in October 2009 in Japan.

Kimi ni Todoke
VOL. 4

Shojo Beat Edition

STORY AND ART BY
KARUHO SHIINA

Translation/Koichiro Kensho Nishimura, HC Language Solutions, Inc.
Touch-up Art & Lettering/Vanessa Satone
Design/Yukiko Whitley
Editors/Carrie Shepherd & Yuki Murashige

KIMI NI TODOKE © 2005 by Karuho Shiina
All rights reserved. First published in Japan in 2005 by SHUEISHA Inc.,
Tokyo. English translation rights arranged by SHUEISHA Inc.

Printed in the U.S.A.

Published by VIZ Media, LLC
P.O. Box 77010
San Francisco, CA 94107

10 9 8 7 6 5 4 3 2
First printing, May 2010
Second printing, April 2011

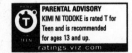

MP

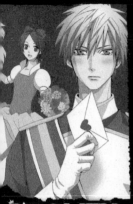

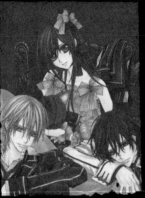

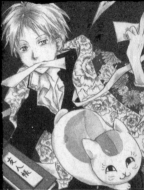